Women Who Kill

Library of Gender and Popular Culture

From *Mad Men* to gaming culture, performance art to steampunk fashion, the presentation and representation of gender continues to saturate popular media. This series seeks to explore the intersection of gender and popular culture, engaging with a variety of texts – drawn primarily from Art, Fashion, TV, Cinema, Cultural Studies and Media Studies – as a way of considering various models for understanding the complementary relationship between 'gender identities' and 'popular culture'. By considering race, ethnicity, class, and sexual identities across a range of cultural forms, each book in the series adopts a critical stance towards issues surrounding the development of gender identities and popular and mass cultural 'products'.

For further information or enquiries, please contact the library series editors:

Claire Nally: claire.nally@northumbria.ac.uk
Angela Smith: angela.smith@sunderland.ac.uk

Advisory Board:

Dr. Kate Ames, Central Queensland University, Australia

Prof. Leslie Heywood, Binghamton University, USA

Dr. Michael Higgins, Strathclyde University, UK

Prof. Åsa Kroon, Örebro University, Sweden

Dr. Niall Richardson, Sussex University, UK

Dr. Jacki Willson, Central St Martins, University of Arts London, UK

Library of Gender
& Popular Culture

Published and forthcoming titles:

Women Who Kill

*Gender and Sexuality in Film and
Series of the Post-feminist Era*

Edited by Cristelle Maury and David Roche

BLOOMSBURY ACADEMIC
LONDON • NEW YORK • OXFORD • NEW DELHI • SYDNEY

BLOOMSBURY ACADEMIC
Bloomsbury Publishing Plc
50 Bedford Square, London, WC1B 3DP, UK
1385 Broadway, New York, NY 10018, USA
29 Earlsfort Terrace, Dublin 2, Ireland

BLOOMSBURY, BLOOMSBURY ACADEMIC and the Diana logo are trademarks
of Bloomsbury Publishing Plc

First published in Great Britain 2020
This paperback edition published in 2021

Cover design: Charlotte Daniels
Cover image: Chloe Grace Moretz in *The 5th Wave* (2016)
Directed by J Blakeson (© Columbia Pictures / GK Films /
Collection Cristophel / ArenaPAL)

A catalogue record for this book is available from the British Library.

A catalog record for this book is available from the Library of Congress.

ISBN: HB: 978-1-3501-1559-0
PB: 978-1-3502-7245-3
ePDF: 978-1-35011560-6
eBook: 978-1-3501-1561-3

Typeset by Deanta Global Publishing Services, Chennai, India

To find out more about our authors and books, visit www.bloomsbury.com
and sign up for our newsletters

Contents

Series Editors' Foreword

In common with many other volumes in the Gender and Popular Culture Library Series, this edited collection highlights the discourses surrounding appropriate gender behavior and specifically, how far women who kill violate these social constructs. Indeed, as the editors of this book point out, the discourses surrounding women who kill are frequently used as a measurement of normative behavior to apply to women as a whole. In exploring these paradigms, the authors of each chapter in this volume consider various stereotypical figures from fiction, film, television, and history: the vigilante, the *femme fatale*, the madwoman, and the monstrous feminine.

Such analyses cross genre conventions as well as media: this book addresses the representation of women who kill in documentary, film noir, sci-fi, TV series, and horror, among many others, and whether such women can be viewed as patriarchal victims. In the context of the post-#MeToo movement, such questions remain at the forefront of any critical engagement with gender and popular culture.

Relatedly, our series is indebted to the development of postfeminist and, latterly, fourth-wave feminism, especially with reference to the visibility of theories such as intersectionality. This contemporary climate is especially apparent in the current volume, with chapters focusing on the special attention given to women of color, transwomen, and the effect of technology on constructions of gender. More familiar ideas of femininity are also apparent here, with discussions on domesticity and nurturing, and how women who kill complicate such representations.

In addressing films such as *Mad Max: Fury Road* (2015) and *Crimson Peak* (2015), this book finds common ground with many others in the Gender and Popular Culture Library Series, in prioritizing cultural products that are emphatically mainstream and have much to say about the contemporary moment. While it may be evident that women are becoming more visible in wider culture, it also remains important to question the nature of such representation. In the light of this, the current book explores the portrayal of women who kill, alongside their complicated and fraught relationship with different versions of feminism. Such an argument, drawing on a discussion of genre conventions, as well as popular media, evokes themes that are evident across the Library and clearly convey some of the most pressing concerns of today's society. In representing established scholars as well as emerging academics in the field, we are confident that this book, and our series, will provide an important intervention in gender and popular culture.

Angela Smith and Claire Nally

Acknowledgments

We would like to start by thanking the authors for their patience and for their willingness to set our standards so high, as well as the editorial team at I.B. Tauris and Bloomsbury (Rennie Alphonsa, Camilla Erskine, Lisa Goodrum, Angélique Neumann and Rebecca Richards) for supporting the project and seeing it through. This collected volume started out as a one-day symposium held in October 2016 at the Université Toulouse–Jean Jaurès, France, with funding from our research group CAS (EA 801) and the Film Studies society SERCIA; it is also part of a French research project on series called GUEST-Normandie. We'd like to thank Zachary Baqué for helping us organize the event and Aurélie Guillain and Emeline Jouve, who had previously worked on women who kill in literature, for their feedback. Thanks are also due to the friends and colleagues who helped us review the chapters: Mehdi Achouche, Donna Andréolle, Zachary Baqué, Nicole Cloarec, Florent Christol, Claire Cornillon, Anne Crémieux, Elizabeth De Cacqueray, Gaïd Girard, Christophe Gelly, Christopher Jon Sieving, Marianne Kac-Vergne, Delphine Letort, Gilles Ménégaldo, Monica Michlin, Yann Roblou, Janet Staiger, and Dennis Tredy.

Much love to our partners (Linda and Virginie), friends and families, and to our children (Iris, Lisa and Tim), who will have to keep the feminist flame alive and pursue the fight for equal rights.

Introduction

Cristelle Maury and David Roche

June 2, 2017 saw the release of a blockbuster featuring one of the most famous women who kill of American popular culture: Wonder Woman. The film was widely anticipated for a variety of reasons: *Batman v. Superman: Dawn of Justice* (Zack Snyder, 2016), though successful at the box office, had disappointed many viewers; *Wonder Woman* was the first major superheroine movie since the disastrous *Catwoman* (Pitof, 2004); and though it was entirely written by men, it was directed by a woman, Patty Jenkins, known for the critically acclaimed *Monster* (2003), a biopic of infamous serial killer Aileen Wuornos. The anxiety around the film was patent in the articles on test screenings. On February 22, 2017, Syfy.com published the following post:

The general consensus is that **the movie is . . . fine.**

Okay. Not terrible, and not all that great. **Some dug it, some didn't.**

Which, admittedly, is still better than **initial rumors** that the flick was a *Dawn of Justice*-sized train wreck.[1]

Wonder Woman was charged with two Herculean tasks: proving that superheroines could make money and that DC movies could finally rival with Marvel.

But superhero fans were not the only ones who wanted the film to succeed. In a highly charged political context, where many felt the election of the first woman president of the United States had been robbed by a racist misogynist with multiple harassment allegations, a man whose advice when it came to seducing women was to "grab them by the pussy," a superheroine putting down protofascist forces—although reset during the First World War—took on an added symbolic value. On January 21, 2017, in Washington, DC and all over the world, many protesters at the Women's March dressed as Wonder Woman and Supergirl.[2] Wonder Woman became one of the movements' spearheads. Some even compared Senator Elizabeth Warren's bravery to Wonder Woman's,[3] while the film's success was commended in similar terms as the real-life politician's persistence.[4]

Wonder Woman ultimately defied expectations. With $103,251,471, it broke the weekend box-office record of a film directed by a woman[5] and went on

to make $821,763,408 worldwide. The Alamo Drafthouse chain proposed
a few women-only screenings in Austin, Brooklyn, and Denver, drawing
controversy in the process, especially from men who complained of sexism
and misandry,[6] and ultimately ending with the chain apologizing for violating
anti-discrimination laws.[7] Women who attended these screenings said they
valued the sense of "sisterhood" in the audience and welcomed the opportunity
to enjoy the film without enduring lewd comments concerning the lead actress's
(Gal Gadot's) physique. Yet if its success has reinforced the heroine's symbolic
power, *Wonder Woman* itself is as politically ambivalent as any Hollywood
blockbuster. Critics have endeavored to untangle the feminist and postfeminist
strands. One critic noted the inconsistency that the heroine "remains slender and
feminine in her embodied strength" in contrast to the other more "masculine"
Amazons;[8] another argued that Wonder Woman's ignorance of ideology, due to
her sheltered upbringing, makes her resolutely postfeminist but that her actions
are "humane" and resonate with feminist resolve.[9] Nor does the movie question
the fact that its heroine must reap destruction to save the day, unlike *Batman
v. Superman* and *Captain America: Civil War* (Anthony and Joe Russo, 2016).
Wonder Woman is thus a prime example of a woman who kills who has been
fashioned[10] and negotiated by a wide variety of feminist discourses and who
has been upheld as a symbol, in this case not of female oppression but of female
wherewithal. And yet if she is undoubtedly exceptional, little is made of the fact
that she kills, even though killings committed by women, whether in fiction or
in real life, tend to draw a lot of attention.

Women do kill. But they kill far less than men; according to Laurie Nalepa
and Richard Pfefferman, the number in the United States had even dropped
from 16.2 percent of all murders in 1976 to 9.5 percent in 2005 (xi), and less
than 10 percent of all serial killers are women (120), while according to Helen
Birch, "in England and Wales, only about 14 per cent of suspects of homicides
recorded between 1983 and 1990 were women."[11] In *The Murder Mystique*
(2013), a nod to Betty Friedan's seminal *Feminine Mystique* (1963), Nalepa
and Pfefferman insist on the fascination these women hold in media and
popular culture, a fascination that occasionally contaminates their own case
studies with sensationalistic overtones. Women like Aileen Wuornos and Myra
Hindley have, indeed, become household names and the subject of books,
movies, shows, and songs[12]. And in 2004, Oxygen Network even launched a
TV show entitled *Snapped* exclusively devoted to female criminals. Nalepa and
Pfefferman list many of the questions these women and their actions raise:

> What was her motive? Was it in any way justifiable? How will she be
> portrayed in the media? How will society judge her? In what ways is this
> murder different from those committed by men? Does the explanation

fit our common notions about women? If not, how should our beliefs
about women change in light of this event? And if women *have* changed,
how has our culture contributed to those changes?[13]

If women who kill are an enigma to mainstream culture, Nalepa and
Pfefferman note that they are equally problematic for feminists.[14] And it
is these problems that are central both to Elizabeth Seal's *Women, Murder,
and Femininity* (2010), Annette Burfoot and Susan Lord's collected volume
Killing Women (2006) and Lisa Downing's *The Subject of Murder: Gender,
Exceptionality, and the Modern Killer* (2013).

Feminist research has tended to relate women who kill to domestic
violence, thus justifying the murder as self-defense, as in the case of "the
vengeful wronged woman and the maternal protector."[15] More troubling
cases—women who kill other women or children—are often ignored;[16]
Belinda Morrissey (2006) similarly claims that malaise would account for the
lack of interest in a "female sadist" such as Karla Homolka, who raped and
murdered several women with her husband Paul Bernado and was thus seen
as a traitor to her gender.[17] Yet, Seal contends, even these less sympathetic
cases shed light on the regimes of femininity that govern society: "a key aspect
of these feminist arguments about gender constructions of violent women
and women who kill is that the discourses of womanhood they reproduce
play a role in the wider social regulation of femininity."[18] Not all women who
kill may be recuperable as feminist figures of patriarchal oppression, but the
(legal, moral, political, sexual, etc.) discourses their actions set in motion beg
critical and political attention. For "by analysing gender representations of
women who have carried out acts considered antithetical to femininity, the
cultural construction of appropriate femininity becomes clearer, as do the
wider cultural meanings that circulate around it."[19] Seal concludes:

> The focus on unusual cases of women accused of murder allows
> themes of sexuality, pathology, duty/care and family life to be analysed
> in relation to women who occupied a variety of social positions, and
> provides access to a range of representations. [. . .] The value of these
> cases is in what they can reveal about representations of gender and the
> symbolic meanings attached to femininity.[20]

Regardless of whether they can be construed as victims of patriarchy, women
who kill set in motion a network of discourses that delimit the boundaries of
appropriate femininity:[21] in other words, their acts are framed and interpreted
by discourses on femininity and masculinity that reveal the predominance of
patriarchy and heteronormativity. In effect, all women who kill "violate [. . .]

norms of femininity, such as nurturance, gentleness and social conformity."[22] Women "involved in masculine crimes" have often been "identified with the masculine gender role,"[23] and "defeminising female defendants in capital cases" is "a key strategy in securing the capital conviction of a woman."[24] In her study of "the modern killer," Lisa Downing makes a similar assessment by showing that a sort of idealization of the murdering subject is effected which highlights the exceptionality of the individual and thereby silences "gender-aware, class-based analyses about murder," leading women to be relegated to the role of victim. This leads her to contend that female murderers "become doubly aberrant exceptions in this culture, unable to access the role of transcendental agency since, as Simone de Beauvoir made clear in 1949, only men are allowed to be transcendent, while women are immanent."[25]

The fall from femininity paves the way both for masculinization and "monsterization,"[26] while pardon may depend on the extent to which the murderer is prepared to repent and thereby reintegrate traditional norms (this is the case of Karla Faye Tucker in Kathleen O'Shea's 2006 analysis). The discourses that attempt to circumscribe women who kill are of interest to identity politics in general; in effect, class, ethnicity, and race also come into play, as women who kill are often "economically marginalised,"[27] and middle- and upper-middle-class women tend to benefit from the respectability attached to their social status.[28] Downing, Seal, Annette Burfoot, and Susan Lord[29] thus call for an intersectional approach to the study of women who kill because these individuals are "sites of contested meaning."[30]

As Seal notes, "cultural representations of women who kill tend to draw on stock stories,"[31] sometimes even on myths such as Medea, the mother who kills,[32] or Clytemnestra, the jealous wife.[33] While Nalepa and Pfefferman's case studies are organized according to a typology based on motive (women who kill in self-defense, for revenge, love, money, or because they are crazy), Seal's types are intimately connected to cultural types and mythical figures: the masculine woman; the muse/mastermind dichotomy; the damaged personality; the respectable woman; and the witch. By identifying discourses rather than actions, Seal's typology allows for more flexibility, since several discourses can be summoned up for a specific case. Furthermore, "the five discourses that constitute the typology are not solely relevant to women who kill, but construct women in relation to other situations,"[34] and thus reveal their role in the construction of femininity in general. Finally, these discourses make it possible to engage with works of fiction because they consider culture as a dialogue between various discourses and practices, fact and fiction, history and myth. In the context of fiction on film and television, women who kill are almost always incorporated into genre conventions, primarily those of crime fiction and *noir*, horror, melodrama, and more recently, action and adventure. No doubt, these generic figures—the female vigilante, the *femme fatale*, the jealous wife, the madwoman, the monstrous woman—which largely overlap with the more general cultural figures identified by Seal, work to simultaneously construct the sensational—and thus deviant—"nature" of the woman who kills, while containing her safely within the realm of genre fiction, in a sense, normalizing her uniqueness and making her comprehensible. Drawing on Angela Carter's "counterintuitive" reading of Sade's Marquis de as "protofeminist" ("Sade allows more fully for the possibility of female agency than other writers of his time. Women are not reduced to their biological functions of gestation and lactation in Sade, but are permitted to be sovereign murdering subjects, on a par with men, even if this murderousness will necessitate a form of monstrosity"[35]), Downing, on the other hand, stresses the emancipatory function of murder for women in fiction and contends that, in Sade's fantasy, killing is an act of destruction but also "is, or has proximity to, an act of creativity."[36]

Unlike literary studies[37] and perhaps because of the prevalence of film genre studies within the field, film studies have long been interested in women who kill. Feminist film studies in particular have, since the early 1980s, abundantly examined these figures in classical and contemporary cinema. Mary Ann Doane's *The Desire to Desire* (1987) identifies several strands of the woman's film, one of which—films of the medical discourse—regularly features women who kill or try to: in *The Letter* (William Wyler, 1940), a jealous wife, Leslie Crosbie, shoots her manservant dead; in *Possessed* (Curtis Bernhardt, 1947), a madwoman almost murders her stepdaughter; in *Johnny Belinda* (Jean Negulesco, 1948), Belinda kills her rapist; *Beyond the Forest* (King Vidor, 1949) opens with an inquest into the possible murder of a man by the female protagonist, Rosa Moline, who ends up committing suicide and killing her unborn child.[38] For Doane, these Warner Bros. productions either dramatize the threat of female desire and subjectivity[39] or safely frame the act within traditional views of femininity—for instance, "maternal instinct" rather than "narrative justice" in *Johnny Belinda*.[40]

The seminal *Women in Film Noir* (1978), edited by E. Ann Kaplan, was the first to re-examine the *femme fatale* of classical film noir as a malevolent woman through a feminist lens.[41] Authors Christine Gledhill, Sylvia Harvey, Janey Place, Pam Cook, E. Ann Kaplan, Richard Dyer, and Claire Johnston took the figure of the lethal *femme fatale* as a stepping-stone to denounce women's subjection to male dominance and challenge patriarchal order. The analysis of the venomous *femme fatale* using her charms to get her way, and of the typical plot in which a woman seduces a man into treading the wrong path, either stealing or killing, enabled them to foreground the oppressive or emancipatory values of the figure, on both the narrative and visual levels.

Famous examples of film noirs unfolding this archetypal plot include *Double Indemnity* (Paramount, Billy Wilder, 1944), *The Postman Always Rings Twice* (MGM, Tay Garnett, 1946), *The Killers* (Universal, Robert Siodmak 1946), and *Criss Cross* (Universal, Robert Siodmak 1949). For the BFI scholars, the representation of women who kill in classical film noir either shows the repression of women that is at work or conversely offers a progressive outlook for women, thus confirming Kaplan's contention that "there is no single position here on whether film noir as such is progressive or not."[42] Ten years later, in her monograph on *femmes fatales*, Mary Ann Doane gave an unequivocal answer to the question of the ideological orientation of film noir's *femme fatale*: "she is not the subject of feminism but a symptom of male fears about feminism."[43] This view is widely shared in more recent feminist scholarship on classical film noir.[44] Even if the critical consensus on the lethal *femme fatale* has since been broken,[45] there is little doubt that the women who kill studied in this book have been influenced by this scholarship.

In the early 1990s, Carol Clover and Barbara Creed published two books, *Men, Women, and Chain Saws* (1992) and *The Monstrous-Feminine* (1993), dealing with women, gender, and femininity in the horror genre. Clover's first chapter examines the rise of the Final Girl in 1970s and 1980s slashers, the heroine-victim who usually bests the psycho-killer; she argues that, in a genre believed to target teenage males,[46] the figure does not represent a "feminist development" so much as a "male surrogate in things oedipal, a homoerotic stand-in, the audience incorporate,"[47] and thus a site for potential "cross-gender identification."[48] Creed, on the other hand, endeavors to seek out the specifically feminine in the horror genre by demonstrating that many of the female figures of horror—the archaic mother, the possessed monster, the monstrous womb, the vampire, the witch, the *vagina dentata*, the *femme castratrice*, and the castrating mother—and the folk and mythical figures they descend from, display a monstrosity that is not a mere usurpation of masculinity and "speak to us more about male fears [regarding the feminine] than about female desire or subjectivity."[49] Beyond the shared psychoanalytic framework, Clover, Creed, and Doane have in common the postulate that the wide variety of women who kill all point to a specific view of femininity as constructed by patriarchal discourses, with some films (John Carpenter's TV movie *Someone's Watching Me* [NBC, 1978], for instance) responding to feminism quite directly.

Birch claims that "the rampaging female has become a new cliché of Hollywood cinema."[50] It is the emergence of "action women" in 1980s and 1990s movies that Yvonne Tasker studies in *Working Girls*. She shows that they are "constructed in narrative terms as macho/masculine, as mothers or as Others"; if "the maternal recurs as a motivating factor" in films like

Fatal Beauty (Tom Holland, 1987), while heroines like Clarice Starling in *The Silence of the Lambs* (Jonathan Demme, 1991) "are identified with the father" and thus aligned with the figure of the tomboy,[51] the female action hero challenges, in effect, gendered binaries by combining feminine and masculine features.

Women Who Kill: Gender and Sexuality in Film and Series of the Post-feminist Era is indebted to the abundant literature on women who kill in 1930s–1980s cinema but proposes to consider the figure exclusively from the 1990s to today. The book thus aims to gauge the impact the ideas of Clover, Creed, Doane, Tasker, and others (Pam Cook, bell hooks, Annette Kuhn, Laura Mulvey, Teresa de Lauretis, Kaja Silverman, Linda Williams, to name a few) may have had on contemporary productions. Indeed, these writings have been highly influential in both feminist film studies and film genre studies, so much so that producers, directors, and screenwriters who attended film school or studied film in college inevitably came across them at some point or another. Directors and screenwriters have openly described their films as responses to film criticism and theory. Todd Haynes, who directed the readaptation of *Mildred Pierce* (HBO, 2011), the story of a mother who almost kills her daughter, studied with Doane.[52] Diablo Cody, who wrote the screenplay for *Jennifer's Body* (Karyn Kusama, 2009), stated in interviews that she wrote it with Barbara Creed's study of the *vagina dentata* in mind, while writer-director Mitchell Lichtenstein stated that *Teeth* (2007) aimed to "take a misogynist myth and turn it around."[53] And Quentin Tarantino, who did not attend film school, declared that Clover's book was his favorite work of film criticism and used her term "Final Girl" in his screenplay; the opening credits of *Death Proof* (2007), with its close-up of anonymous female feet on a dashboard, which crosscuts with a semi-POV shot of the road from the male killer's perspective, "announce how self-conscious the film is about the generic and theoretical framework [. . .] the devices it exploits are grounded in, to the point of parody."[54] The influence of feminist film theory on the horror genre has become especially salient, as Donato Totaro has noted.[55]

But the circulation of such theories is not restricted to the film and television industry; the issues raised by feminist, gender, queer, and race studies and intersectional theories are now very much part of the mainstream, in Great Britain and the United States notably, though, granted, sometimes in bastardized forms. The focus on contemporary film and television is also a means of interrogating a context. The scholars of the 1980s and 1990s were firmly inscribed within second-wave feminism. Our book proposes to examine a wide variety of women who kill in a context rife with tensions between a variety of feminist discourses, often referred to as third-wave feminism and postfeminism, focusing to what extent contemporary women are symptomatic of postfeminism or to what extent they exemplify the tensions between different feminist discourses.

The relationship between second-wave feminism and postfeminism is complex. There is no clear-cut chronological progression from one to the other, in which postfeminism would simply repudiate a now obsolete movement. Many of the core principles of second-wave feminism have been retained in third-wave feminism, a movement that emerged in the 1990s among a younger generation of women who wanted to establish a continuity with second-wave feminism while renewing feminist commitments by taking into account economic and racial inequalities and embracing the contradictions of postmodernity. They also wanted to differentiate themselves from postfeminism; that's why third-wave feminism and postfeminism are often presented as antithetical.[56] However, as Genz and Brabon have observed, there are many "rifts and overlaps between the third wave and postfeminism."[57] Indeed, postfeminism is not a pure and simple rejection of second-wave feminism. In fact, the postfeminist era is marked by numerous debates, schisms, and differing viewpoints, and is in this respect entirely in keeping with the history of feminism. Like second-wave feminism, postfeminism "has never had a universally accepted agenda and meaning."[58] If, as Sarah Gamble puts it, "feminism has always been a dynamic and multifaceted movement," then "the postfeminist debate merely dramatizes a situation which has always, in fact, held true for feminism, a movement which thrives on diversity."[59] Circumscribing postfeminism is particularly difficult given that the term "itself originated from within the media in the early 1980s"; as a "market-led phenomenon" with no clear spearheads, the term does not refer to a movement.[60] There is no critical agreement over the definition of postfeminism, but, rather, a host of sometimes contradictory definitions so that "the attempt to fix *the* meaning of postfeminism looks futile and even misguided."[61] According to Gamble, "even the most cursory reading of texts tagged with the 'postfeminist' label reveals that there is little agreement among those with whom it is popularly associated as to a central canon or agenda."[62]

The definition of postfeminism as backlash against second-wave feminism, which was put forward by Susan Faludi in her best-selling book *Backlash: The Undeclared War against the American Woman* (1991), has often been the starting point of one of the ways in which postfeminism has been and is still understood. The notion was taken up and expanded by Imelda Whelehan, who called it "retrosexism,"[63] "premised on real fears about the collapse of masculine hegemony."[64] Angela McRobbie similarly proposed a "complexification of the backlash thesis,"[65] which would take into account the gains of second-wave feminism. As an "aftermath of feminism,"[66] postfeminism "positively draws on and evokes feminism as that which can be taken into account, to suggest that equality is achieved, in order to install a whole repertoire of new meanings which emphasize that it is no longer needed, it is a spent force."[67] This "complexification of backlash" led McRobbie to propose the notion of "double entanglement" to describe the "co-existence of neo-conservative values in relation to gender, sexuality and family life [. . .] with processes of liberalisation in regard to choice and diversity in domestic, sexual and kinship relations."[68] From this emerged the contradictory nature of postfeminism, which Rosalind Gill pinned down as an "entanglement of feminist and antifeminist ideas."[69] In this sense, postfeminism is not so much a backlash as a site of tensions and contradictions in which "feminist ideas are both articulated and repudiated, expressed and disavowed."[70] This is what Gill has called a "postfeminist sensibility."[71]

The meaning of postfeminism is not just contradictory; it is also controversial. It has often been presented in a positive light ("a healthy rewriting of feminism,"[72] "an epistemological break within feminism,"[73] a way of articulating changes in the evolution of feminist thinking,[74] "a political shift in feminism's conceptual and theoretical agenda,"[75] "a dynamic movement capable of challenging modernist, patriarchal and imperialist frameworks"[76]). For self-proclaimed postfeminist critics such as Rene Denfeld, Naomi Wolf, and Katie Roiphe, postfeminism is a constructive alternative to the project of feminism, which they view as outdated. For them, "the notion of backlash [. . .] operates in the opposite direction."[77] They attack second-wave feminism as "self-defeating"[78] (Roiphe), as fostering "an inappropriate image of female victimisation"[79] (Denfeld), or as "victim feminism" (Wolf). They are distinct from third-wave feminists and the Riot Grrrl movement who accommodate contradiction and diversity without rejecting second-wave feminism.[80]

Conversely, such views have triggered many reactions on the part of "anti-postfeminist critics," especially on the part of Angela McRobbie, Rosalind Gill, and Christine Scharff, who have denounced postfeminism as a powerful way to subject women and enforce oppression. McRobbie contends that "through an array of machinations, elements of contemporary popular culture are perniciously effective in regard to this undoing of feminism, while simultaneously appearing to be engaging in a well-informed and even well-intended response to feminism."[81] Gill's outline of the elements of a "postfeminist sensibility" ultimately aims to castigate postfeminism. In her 2007 article "Postfeminist Media Culture," she suggested that there were stable features that comprise or constitute a postfeminist discourse and outlined the elements of a "postfeminist sensibility":

> the notion that femininity is a bodily property; the shift from objectification to subjectification; the emphasis upon self-surveillance, monitoring and discipline; a focus upon individualism, choice and empowerment; the dominance of a makeover paradigm; a resurgence in

ideas of natural sexual difference; a marked sexualisation of culture; and an emphasis upon consumerism and the commodification of difference. These themes coexist with and are structured by stark and continuing inequalities and exclusions that relate to 'race' and ethnicity, class, age, sexuality and disability—as well as gender.[82]

Gill and Scharff also noted "a powerful resonance between post-feminism and neoliberalism"[83]: the postfeminist sensibility fits perfectly with neoliberal ideas as both are structured by a current of individualism and both focus on self-regulating individuals.[84] Recently, Gill has noted that postfeminism had both "spread out and intensified" so as to "instantiate [. . .] a common sense that operates as a kind of gendered neoliberalism."[85]

As Jessie Butler has shown, postfeminism does not take multiple oppressions into account;[86] the subject of postfeminism being youthful white middle-class heterosexual women, it does not take intersectional (age, class, ethnicity, race, sexuality, etc.) stakes into account. The necessity to reverse this tendency and "think intersectionally"[87] has been highlighted by several postfeminist scholars. In Diane Negra and Yvonne Tasker's words, "such a limited vision of gender equality as both achieved and yet still unsatisfactory underlines the class, age, and racial exclusions that define postfeminism."[88] Gill has thus stressed the need to think of postfeminism as structured by stark and continuing inequalities[89] and to open up postfeminism to intersectional interrogations.[90] This is what Kimberly Springer has done, with her focus on black women.[91] Similar criticisms have repeatedly been voiced by black feminist scholars who saw second-wave feminism as dominated by white middle-class women and resulted, for example, in Alice Walker creating the notion of "womanism";[92] more recently, the term "post-womanism" has been used to oppose the considerations of white, middle-class, Western postfeminism.[93]

Most of the scholarship devoted to postfeminist questions until now has been founded on analyses of media representations. Such works mainly explore theoretical questions through examples and case studies taken from contemporary media and popular culture, including reality TV shows and makeover shows, women's magazines, teen television programs, social networking sites, advertising, chick lit.[94] The goal is not to identify a "post-feminist sensibility" within particular genres, show types, or media, but to address how it informs popular and local cultural texts in order to better understand systems of media and representation.[95]

As Melanie Waters has remarked, "perhaps the most salient, and least controversial, feature of post-feminism is its inextricability from popular, and particularly visual, culture."[96] In this context, film and series are just two forms among many others, and studies tend to favor genres such as romcoms and chick flicks.[97] This is what Tasker and Negra noted in 2005: "existing scholarship on postfeminist media culture tilts heavily toward analysis of the romantic comedies and female-centred sitcoms and dramas that have been strongly associated with female audiences since the 1990s."[98] This is only partially true today. Since then, Samantha Lindop's *Postfeminism and the Fatale Figure in Neo-Noir Cinema* has filled in the gap for the *noir* genre; her study of postmillennial incarnations of the *femme fatale*—the lesbian killers of *Mulholland Drive* (David Lynch, 2001) and *Chloe* (Atom Egoyan, 2009), the deadly prostitutes of *Sin City* (Frank Miller and Robert Rodriguez, 2005), the postfeminist *fille fatale* of postfeminist culture in *Hard Candy* (David Slade, 2005), *Brick* (Rian Johnson, 2005), and *Stoker* (Chan-wook Park, 2013)—demonstrates how the "dominant postfeminist discourse weaves its own agendas into established conventions of *noir* and how this in turn shapes the construction of the postmillennial spider woman."[99]

Women Who Kill: Gender and Sexuality in Film and Series of the Post-feminist Era pursues the important work of Gill, Lindop, McRobbie, and others but focuses the attention exclusively on the various avatars of women who kill. The questions about real women who kill listed by Nalepa and Pfefferman remain relevant to the study of fiction and documentary, but studying representations means taking into account not just narrative and characterization but also costume, staging, camerawork, editing, and sound. The book takes stock of the increasing presence of women who kill in genre productions—from horror (*Hereditary* [Ari Aster, 2018]) and rape-revenge (*Revenge* [Coralie Fargeat, 2018]) to superhero productions (Black Widow in the Avengers franchise [2010–], Jessica Jones [Netflix, 2015–], Wonder Woman) to political thrillers (*The Americans* [FX, 2013–18], *House of Cards* [Netflix, 2013–18]) or fantasy (*Game of Thrones* [HBO, 2011–19])—but seeks to determine whether this increase in quantity is matched by a significant change in the cultural constructions we are being presented. The aim of the book is thus twofold: first, to study the evolution of women who kill in films and series and, more generally, to interrogate them as sites of various, sometimes conflicting, discourses on feminism in order to determine what they can tell us about contemporary feminist concerns in the broadest sense. Are contemporary women who kill systematically victims? Are the killings depicted differently because of the killer's gender, or is it merely that the act is framed differently in terms of motivation? To what extent do films and series, including more independent productions, rely on genre conventions? Do they attempt to subvert them, and if so, is it a sign of increasing familiarity with feminist film theory? Finally, to what extent are these figures fashioned by postfeminist discourses circulating in the media, and are they also engaging with feminist, gender, queer, and intersectional discussions in general?

Motives are, no doubt logically, almost always gendered: men kill because they're men, women don't because they're women, but when they do, they do it as women. The values traditionally associated with male and female, and masculinity and femininity, are often preserved and even essentialized, but they can also be called into question as cultural constructs. If film and television representations of women who kill have increased in number, female violence continues to be justified according to two primary characteristics: motherhood or victimization. Women have regularly been shown as capable of violence out of self-defense (Clover's Final Girl, Louise in *Thelma and Louise* [Ridley Scott, 1991], Clarice Starling in *The Silence of the Lambs* [Jonathan Demme, 1991], Miriam in *Butterfly Kiss* [Michael Winterbottom, 1995], Marge Gunderson in *Fargo* [Joel and Ethan Coen, 1996], Kate in *LOST* [ABC, 2004–10]) and/or to protect children (Sarah Connor's transformation into an action heroine from *Terminator 2* [James Cameron, 1991] on). Even Sethe's infanticide in *Beloved* (Jonathan Demme, 1998), an adaptation of Toni Morrison's 1987 novel, is framed as the desperate act of a mother who refuses to bring a child into a life of slavery—the infanticide committed by Alison Garrs in episode S2E5 of *Happy Valley* (BBC, 2014–) is, likewise, framed as a mercy killing. The rape-revenge narrative of 1970s exploitation movies such as *I Spit on Your Grave* (Meir Zarchi, 1978) and *Ms. 45* (Abel Ferrara, 1981) was quickly integrated into mainstream fare like *Sudden Impact* (Clint Eastwood, 1983) and lives on as an embedded structure in movies like *Kill Bill* (Quentin Tarantino, 2003), *Death Proof* (Tarantino, 2007), and *Mad Max: Fury Road* (George Miller, 2015). The two justifications are often combined, in *Kill Bill*, for instance, where the Bride's righteousness is also fueled by the loss of her child, more symbolically in Marcus Nispel's 2003 remake of *The Texas Chain Saw Massacre* where the Final Girl's valor is ultimately confirmed by her ability to best the killer family and save a child.[100] Even sociopaths like Mrs. Mott in *The Hand That Rocks the Cradle* (Curtis Hanson, 1992), Aileen Wuornos in *Monster*, Snoop in *The Wire* (HBO, 2002–08), Alice Morgan in *Luther* (BBC, 2010–), Amy Dunne in *Gone Girl* (David Fincher, 2014), and Daisy Domergue in *The Hateful Eight* (Tarantino, 2015) are portrayed as victims of circumstances, of a patriarchal and/or capitalist society that has subjected them to physical and/or psychological abuse at an early age. Purely sadistic female killers, such as Catherine Tramell in *Basic Instinct* (Paul Verhoeven, 1992), Bridget Gregory in *The Last Seduction* (John Dahl, 1994), the eponymous heroine of *All the Boys Love Mandy Lane* (Jonathan Levine, 2006), and Mrs. Bathory in *Hostel 2* (Eli Roth, 2007) remain fairly rare. In them, the articulation between gender and genre begs to be explored because female killers often resemble excuses for neat narrative twists—a famous example is *Friday the 13th* (Sean S. Cunningham, 1980). In other words, the reversal of gender roles may often serve a dramatic play on expectations more than a political intent, though they are unquestionably intertwined.

The final revelation of *All the Boys Love Mandy Lane*, for instance, that the Final Girl is actually a diabolical mastermind, enables the film to further the instability of point of view that is so typical of the slasher subgenre[101] [70:45–73:35]. When Mandy exits the cabin with a weapon, something draws her attention, and she pauses on the steps in a frontal close-up (Figure I.1). A reverse shot tracks up her right leg to reveal her right hand steadying her grip on a knife; rack focusing then reveals one of her friends, Chloe, running down a lane (a staple horror movie scene) pursued by a car in the right background, followed by a zoom-in on the potential victim that fails to keep her in focus (Figure I.2). As Mandy beckons to her, Chloe runs right into her friend's arms, impaling herself on the knife in a back shot that prevents us from anticipating such an outcome by observing the protagonist's features or position (Figure I.3). Everything—camerawork, editing, Amber Heard's acting—is orchestrated in the interest of this narrative twist; the back shot conceals Mandy's motives, and her disgust at the bloody rag in the cabin is not in keeping with her subsequently goring Chloe in her arms—the emotion could only be feigned, meaning that she was acting solely for our (the real audience's) benefit. There is no justification for Mandy's sadism—other than that she herself represents the stand-in of the spectator, as the play on gazes, the zoom-in on the pursuit, and the blurry image (which calls attention to the image as image) suggest. The twist is merely a millennial update of the ending of *Friday the 13th* (1980), with two significant differences: Mandy's sadism warrants no justification, and as the film's Final Girl, she is also the audience's stand-in. It is in these respects that Mandy Lynn is symptomatic of postfeminist discourses in the Girl Power version. She is as vicious as her male counterparts in other films and derives her strength from her capacity to master traditional feminine attributes. As the audience surrogate, she is also indicative of the evolution of the horror movie audience or, at least, of our awareness of it: that is, that fans of the genre are equally female and male. But Mandy is also typical of some of the perceived limitations of postfeminism. By donning the mask of the sweet horror heroine, she certainly displays the constructedness both of gender and of the Final Girl as a genre convention, but her empowerment is exclusively in the service of her own personal gratification. Like the classical heroines Doane discusses, Mandy's desire is reduced to pathology and denied any political effectiveness beyond the statement that women like horror, too. The same can be said of the character of Raiman in *Black Mirror* S3E5, a female soldier gone berserk who reflexively points to the number of women gamers.

The introduction of women in the action movie genre can be just as problematic. They are often masculinized. This is the case of Sarah Connor in *Terminator 2: Judgment Day* (James Cameron, 1991), of Starbuck in *Battlestar*

Figure I.1 *All the Boys Love Mandy Lane* (Levine, 2006): close-up as Mandy emerges from the shed.

Figure I.2 *All the Boys Love Mandy Lane* (Levine, 2006): camera tracks up her body as Mandy watches Chloe running away from the killer.

Figure I.3 *All the Boys Love Mandy Lane* (Levine, 2006): Mandy welcomes Chloe with a deadly embrace.

Galactica (SyFy, 2004–09), of Imperator Furiosa in *Mad Max: Fury Road*, and to a lesser extent perhaps, of Rey in the new Star Wars trilogy (2015–19). The masculinization of women who kill is typical of culture's struggle to safeguard its values. First, it can work to safeguard femininity by implying that the transgression of gender lines makes the woman who kills deviant and exceptional, as in the case of the discourses surrounding real women who kill discussed by Seal; this would be the case in classical cinema, according to Doane. But the contemporary examples listed earlier, which recognize the fluidity of femininity and masculinity, raise another question: do such heroines ultimately serve to value femininity or salvage and maybe even redeem masculinity? The effect is reinforced by the pairing up of such heroines with masculine heroes. Mad Max may be momentarily neutralized, but in *Battlestar Galactica* (SyFy, 2004–09), Starbuck's flyboy attitude is entirely consistent with her male model in the original series (ABC, 1978–79)—she is brave, cocky, and proud, making her the best fighter pilot in the fleet—but her edginess in the final season makes way for a behavior verging on hysteria, making her at least temporarily inefficient and ultimately linking her to two traditional tropes— the madwoman and the motherly savior—that return with a vengeance. In the age of constructivism, the fundamental binary would, then, be displaced from male/female to masculine/feminine, with the feminine retaining its subordinate position and, historically, its essential connection to the female. The pairing of such heroines with hypermasculine males (the Terminator, Mad Max, Luke Cage in *Jessica Jones*, the Machete films [Ethan Maniquis and Robert Rodriguez, 2010–13] featuring the female character Luz) tends to tip the balance in favor of a masculine, if not male, ideal.

This is also the case in more naturalistic works such as *Monster* or the HBO series *The Wire* (2002–08). In S3E7 of *The Wire*, Snoop, a young female soldier in Marlo Stanfield's drug-dealing organization who actively and devotedly participates in the turf war over the sale of drugs, is assigned a drive-by shooting in which she kills Rico, a member of the Barksdale gang, in retaliation for taking one of Poot Carr's corners [51:20–51:38]. The camera movements and rapid editing (lateral tracking shots and wipe-bys) convey the extremely quick and surprising outburst of violence, as well as the killer's expert gestures. The fact that Snoop is the first and only female killer in the series is signaled by her physical appearance and her movements, which foreground her femininity. She is clad in a pink jacket and capri pants, and sitting at the back of the motorbike, she holds a gun and shoots at Rico in a graceful movement (Figure I.4). The motorbike rides off, revealing the colorful and very girly ribbons in Snoop's braided hair. This sequence is the only one in which the sartorial codes foreground her gender, while the action presents her as an extremely skilled shooter. In all the other contract killings

Figure I.4 *The Wire* (HBO, 2002-8): Marlowe's assassin, Snoop.

she carries out, she is represented exactly like the male shooters: she wears dark hoods and large T-shirts, adopts the "gangster" walk with an exaggerated bounce added to the step, and fires in a standing position, holding her gun in two hands for more stability. For example, in another drive-by shooting in S5E2 (this time to assault Webster Franklin's drug-dealing crew), she starts by overwhelming her target with a sudden massive amount of firepower and then she gets off the car and shoots at point-blank range, killing one of Webster's men [41:35–42:40]. Clearly, Snoop's transformation into a professional killer has led her to shed her feminine attributes.

And yet another moot point concerning contemporary representations of women who kill has to do with the hypersexualization of the body. This discourse enables films like *The Texas Chainsaw Massacre* (Marcus Nispel, 2003), *Sin City* (Robert Rodriguez and Frank Miller, 2005 and 2014), *Planet Terror* (Robert Rodriguez, 2007), and *Wonder Woman* (2017) to simultaneously present powerful women and even matriarchs while excessively fetishizing their heroines to the point of parody. Granted, this may be tempered in works where male and female bodies are equally fetishized, as in *The Texas Chainsaw Massacre* (2003) and *LOST* (heartthrobs Jack, Sawyer, and Sayid in particular), but feminist viewers may be left with the impression that straight male audiences are being allowed to have their cake and eat it, too—a policy that would be entirely in keeping with Hollywood and the entertainment industry's talent for catering to all audiences. The problem with the equalizing of fetishization is that it ultimately denies the history of patriarchal fashioning of women's images and its continuing power today (why a simple visit to the clothing or toy aisle of any store is not enough to convince people of the power of consumer society to construct gender in blue and pink is beyond us).

With the threat of hypersexualization on the one side, and that of being constructed as masculine on the other, women who kill are problematic and thus relevant for feminist inquiry because they are sites where traditional notions of femininity and masculinity are combined, sometimes questioned, always questionable, and ultimately difficult to resolve. This is further complicated, of course, by the recourse to violence and, sometimes, the pleasure with which it is exacted. If motivation has always been a central concern in the portrayal of female violence, it seems to us that the act itself begs for in-depth analysis. Is female violence represented differently than male violence? In *Happy Valley*, a cut to an establishing shot of the Garrs house occurs before Alison Garrs's mercy killing and subsequent suicide, so that the act, rife with melodramatic excess, is viewed from a distance and reduced to a synecdoche: the rifleshot and the splash of blood on the window (Figure I.5) [S2E5 48:20][102]. Mandy Lane's goring of Chloe is made particularly perverse because of the gentleness with which it is effected and is thus contrasted with her male accomplice's murders. Snoop, on the other hand, does her job without batting an eyelid and, unlike Cutty and Michael, never questions her missions (both male characters are shown hesitating to shoot in episodes S3E6 and S5E2). Clearly, the act itself is inevitably framed in traditional views of feminine and masculine behaviors.

Figure I.5 *Happy Valley* (BBC, 2014–): cut to an establishing shot of the house as a mother kills her serial killer son.

Women who kill prove how difficult it is to do without stereotypes or archetypes, an awareness that leads some works to use them as reference points for deconstruction. In film and television, even less mainstream fare tends to invoke genre conventions and past traditions; the title of Jenkins's 2003 Aileen Wuornos biopic is a deliberate nod both to the horror movie and to the "monsterization" female killers undergo, while the road movie/crime thriller *Butterfly Kiss* resembles both a nihilistic *Thelma and Louise* and a female version of the more specifically British Angry Young Man narrative. Thus, *Women Who Kill: Gender and Sexuality in Film and Series of the Post-Feminist Era* is divided into three sections according to the three generic archetypes that seem the most prevalent today: the *femme fatale* of noir, the action movie heroine, and the monstrous-feminine of horror. Each part is organized chronologically in order to emphasize the evolution of the representations of women who kill across time and media. With the exception of an independent short film, a documentary, and an exploitation film, the majority of the works under study are mainstream fare, ranging from Hollywood blockbusters like *The Hunger Games* franchise to successful series like *American Horror Story* to the art cinema tradition of *The Neon Demon*.

In the first chapter, Delphine Letort analyzes the *femmes fatales* of some of the major mainstream neo-noirs of the 1990s including *Basic Instinct*, *Body of Evidence* (Uli Edel, 1993), *The Last Seduction*, and *Bound* (The Wachowskis, 1996) as postfeminist killers, while in Chapter 2, Emilie Herbert studies the character of the African *femme fatale* in a short film by British-Nigerian filmmaker Ngozi Onwurah *White Men Are Cracking Up* (1994). In Chapter 3, Isabelle Schmitt-Pitiot focuses on British television series *Hit & Miss* (2012) about a transgender contract killer. In Chapter 4, Christophe Gelly looks at the female characters of *Sin City: A Dame to Kill For* (Frank Miller and Robert Rodriguez, 2014), a film that recreates the comic book aesthetic universe of Frank Miller in a noir fashion. In the last chapter, Cristelle Maury foregrounds the deconstruction of both the noir and neo-noir *femmes fatales* in David Fincher's 2014 thriller, *Gone Girl*.

Relying on the definition of the archetypal *femme fatale* as a deadly seductress, all the authors show how contemporary films reframe the *femme fatale* imagery in a postfeminist discourse. They all note the contradiction of the archetypal character who is both represented as a sexual object and offers an empowering model of femininity; as Letort puts it, "her agency is concomitant with her sexual commodification." As such, the films and series are the site where "feminist ideas are both articulated and repudiated, expressed and disavowed."[103]

More specifically, Letort reads the *femmes fatales* of 1990s neo-noir as the products of neoliberal values that entrap them in what Rosalind Gill called "subjectification," an allegedly freely chosen decision to represent themselves as objects of the male gaze. Herbert associates the African *femme fatale* of *White Men Are Cracking Up* with Blaxploitation heroines, but proposes the apt term of "post-womanism" to describe the African *femme fatale* in order to take into account the racial dimension and to acknowledge the exclusion of black women from white middle-class postfeminist discourses. Schmitt-Pitiot puts the case of a transwoman who kills in the postfeminist context of "resexualisation of women's bodies in the media,"[104] in which material success has, according to a neoliberal logic, become a sign of individual freedom; emphasis is put on physical appearance, femininity, and material success, which are intrinsically linked as the protagonist needs money to become a beautiful woman. Gelly analyzes the representation of femininity as a form of postfeminist parody based on the stereotypes of female submissiveness and domination. Maury similarly shows that the female protagonist of *Gone Girl* goes beyond this contradiction as she undergoes a process of de-eroticization and becomes an ironic product of postfeminism.

The authors diverge, however, on the interpretation of the politics of the films they analyze. For Letort, the erotic thrillers of the 1990s are definitely conservative because, in "neo-noir, murder is no longer a route to the woman's social liberation; it clearly appears as a consequence." For Herbert, *White Men Are Cracking Up* is a site of contestation. For Gelly, the representation of the *femme fatale* is self-consciously stereotypical and thus "calls attention to the prevalence of stereotypes to which females are reduced," but he warns against exaggerating the metacritical dimension of the film. For Maury, *Gone Girl* distances itself from feminist theories altogether through irony. One way in which the contradictions of postfeminism come to the surface is via the blurring of noir with other genres: *White Men Are Cracking Up* also resorts to the magical realism of the post-womanist narrative and the fantasy world of Nollywood; *Hit & Miss* "wavers between the urban thriller and the rural melodrama"; *Sin City* taps into the comics aesthetics of the source text; and *Gone Girl* borrows from horror and comedy.

In the second part of the book on action heroines, Marianne Kac-Vergne and Adrienne Boutang analyze the interactions between two generations of action heroines and show that they embody the different waves of feminist thought. Kac-Vergne shows that, in the *Terminator* franchise, young women reject "second Wave feminism as outdated and ineffective and celebrate the possibilities offered to young women by post-feminism." Boutang compares the teenage heroines and the older women of young adult dystopias *The*

Hunger Games (Gary Ross 2012, Francis Lawrence 2013, 2014, 2016), *The Divergent Series* (Neil Burger 2014, Robert Schwentke 2015 and 2016), and *The Fifth Wave* (Jonathan Blakeson, 2016), foregrounding the generational gap between two waves of feminism, with the young heroines who evince nurturing abilities and true heroism, and older women who are particularly negative caricatures of second-wave feminism. For both, the second-wave feminists are masculinized, have repudiated any trace of femininity (they are either bad mothers or childless), lack emotions, and ultimately appear as outmoded compared to the younger heroines. The latter retain their femininity and embody, for Kac-Vergne, Girl Power feminism, while, for Boutang, they "illustrate the ambiguities of post-feminist girl culture." In her chapter on *The Walking Dead*, Marta F. Suarez seeks to unravel the different strands of feminism evident in the three women who kill, including first- and second-wave feminism, postfeminism, and womanism. Each character initially embodies one stereotype of femininity (passivity and weakness, the postfeminist babe, the angry black woman) but evolves to problematize various strands of feminism, by fighting either for voting rights, equality, and/or their own empowerment, and by combining masculine and feminine traits that allow them to be become resourceful, rich, and complex action heroines evincing both nurturing traits and fighting skills.

Concerning the ideological orientation of the works under study, Kac-Vergne and Boutang stress the adhesion to patriarchal structures of power through the negation of second-wave feminism in typical postfeminist fashion. The conservative implications of postfeminist representations emerge very clearly from Kac-Vergne and Boutang's chapters. For Kac-Vergne, girlishness allows killer women to be appealing without challenging patriarchy. For Boutang, the films "endorse an essentialist stance and punish the overt transgressions of its powerful females." For Suarez, *The Walking Dead* provides a more nuanced representation of gender politics; she concludes her chapter on the transformation of the female protagonists into real action heroines and on the evolution of the politics of the series, with the stereotypical representations of femininity involving racial stereotyping, tokenism, and sexism of the first seasons replaced by more challenging patriarchal notions of femininity.

The last two chapters of this section adopt a reception studies approach to look at how viewers are affected by the films instead of focusing on the films as sites of meaning. They show that the reception of the films very much depends on the status of the audience (whether they are fans or mainstream critics) and on their gender. Connor Winterton analyzes the diverging reactions to Quentin Tarantino's *Kill Bill* and *Death Proof* both in academic discourses and on fan sites. While some feminist critics have criticized Tarantino's version of violent femininity, most fans seem to find it justified, probably because the motives are in keeping with the category of murders Lizzie Seal considers natural[105]: that is to say, murders that fit mainstream constructs of behaviors deemed instinctive in women, such as the protection of their children and family. Remarking that critics and fans either denounce the treatment of female violence or, on the contrary, find it perfectly acceptable—often failing to see that the metadiscourses of Tarantino's films target the racism and sexism at the heart of American popular cinema[106]—Winterton concludes that the reception of the killer women in *Kill Bill* and *Death Proof* is "a site of interpretative conflict" that relates to tensions between feminism and postfeminism and that results in women's paradoxical representation, at once as sexualized and objectified, and as powerful and empowering.

Elizabeth Mullen compares the reception of two films featuring strong female protagonists, *Mad Max: Fury Road* and *Spy* (Paul Feig, 2015), in mainstream criticism and in online criticism by men's rights activists. Her analysis sheds light on gender dynamics in the postfeminist era. She especially documents the outrage created by Furiosa (Charlize Theron) in the men's rights groups, while noting that Paul Feig's parody of James Bond films staging a trained female killer "provoked barely a blip." After establishing *Mad Max: Fury Road* as a feminist film, Mullen goes on to show that it ignited the most virulent antifeminist discourses. The reception of *Fury Road* illustrates the tensions of the postfeminist era with the concomitant expression of feminist and anti-feminist views. She sees it as symptomatic of our current extremely polarized times with the advent of truly positive feminist characters on screen and the extreme reactions of what she calls "toxic masculinity" that they trigger. Mullen relates her findings directly to the current political context, with Trump "unleashing waves of pent-up toxic nostalgia," and the violent demonstrations by white supremacist groups.

The third section aims to reassess the female figures of horror films, as described by Carol Clover, Barbara Creed, and Linda Williams in the light of postfeminist theories. Creed's notion of the "monstrous-feminine" is aptly used in several texts to uncover the postfeminist implications of the films and series under study. In her chapter on the medical thriller *Contagion* (Steven Soderbergh, 2011), Julia Echeverría uses Creed's category of *femme castratrice* and Linda Williams's point about the likeness between the monster and the female victim in classical horror films[107] to explain how the female Patient Zero, who is supposed to be a victim, is criminalized and thus transformed into a woman who kills. Mikaël Toulza's chapter on the "monstrous feminists" of the FX anthology series *American Horror Story: Coven* concentrates on another female figure of horror identified by Creed: the witch. Samantha Lindop and Hélène Charlery read their female killers as

"monstrous" versions of Clover's Final Girl. Charlery applies Robin Means
Coleman's notion of the "Enduring Woman"—the Blaxploitation version
of Clover's Final Girl whose killing impulse is geared toward the survival
of her racial community—to the character of Ganja in her analysis of the
"contemporization" of the feminist discourse of Spike Lee on black female
sexuality in *Da Sweet Blood of Jesus*, a remake of the faux exploitation horror
film *Ganja & Hess* (Bill Gunn, 1973). Charlery also uses Creed's theory on the
female vampire and *vagina dentata* to show that Ganja is "a monstrous figure
who survives without having to be tamed or killed to express male power."
Lindop shows how British science-fiction thriller *Ex Machina* (Alex Garland,
2015) activates the figure of the Final Girl of rape-revenge films through the
figure of the robotic female avenger Ava, who is "an avenger with a justified
desire for retribution." Horror is conveyed through the enmeshment between
woman and machine, which contributes to fashioning artificial women into
monstrous embodiments of otherness. In their analysis of two contemporary
filmic revisitations of early and Victorian Gothic tropes, *Byzantium* (Neil
Jordan, 2012) and *Crimson Peak* (Guillermo del Toro, 2015), Carolina Abello
and Christophe Chambost argue that the heroines' status as vampires and
murderesses renders them "monstrous" in that they cross the borders of
gender roles and threaten the stability of patriarchal institutions. They also
call upon the figure of the Final Girl to foreground the feminist stamina of
these heroines. Finally, Janice Loreck's chapter focuses on figures of horror
that go beyond both Creed's and Clover's typologies through her exploration
of how "fashion-slasher" *The Neon Demon* (Nicolas Winding Refn, 2016)
establishes both the pleasure and destructiveness of beauty. Cosmetic surgery
and the invitation to take pleasure in beauty are both marked by horror.
Loreck uses the notion of aestheticized gore to show that beauty is both erotic
and horrifying.

The films and the series analyzed in this section all point to the fact that the
horror genre expresses male fears of the feminine. Thus, the chapters all draw
attention to the political dimension of the films and series. The criminalization
of the female Patient Zero enables Echeverría to show how the character of
the "post-feminist super spreader" (Sarah Poltrow) is representative of a
postfeminist sensibility in its connections with neoliberalism in the wake of
Gill and Scharff's work[108]. Echeverría contends that the female protagonist,
as an embodiment of otherness, "stands for a new emancipated femininity
in tune with neo-liberal discourses of individualism, empowerment and an
ethos of success associated with agency and global mobility." While Echeverría
exposes the postfeminist critique at work in *Contagion*, Charlery hints at the
postfeminist dimension of Lee's film through a comparative analysis with
Ganja & Hess. The absence of discourse on the abject constructs Ganja as a
victim with only temporary empowerment; intersectionality is downplayed,

in keeping with the postfeminist tendency to reject second-wave feminist ideas, and the female protagonist "shifts from sexual objectification to sexual subjectification" in that she willingly participates in her sexual objectification, offering an image of a "sexual autonomous heterosexual young woman who plays with her sexual power and is forever 'up for it,'" as Gill has shown[109]. Toulza, Abello and Chambost focus on the feminist potential at a more subtextual level. Toulza's reading of the interactions of a coven of witches in New Orleans as allegories of the successive feminist movements in their embodiment of figures of power menacing the patriarchal order aims at showing that the battles between the witches can be read as illustrations of the rivalries between the different generations of feminists and the different forms and facets of feminism. The second-wave feminist is in conflict with the "postfeminist babe," which results in murder; racial tensions between black feminism and second-wave feminism are implicit in the conflict between the white witches and the black voodoo practitioner. Toulza contends that the series' subtext is critical of postfeminist individualism and advocates Naomi Sack's theory of inclusive feminism. Carolina Abello Onofre and Christophe Chambost argue that *Byzantium* and *Crimsom Peak* subvert the female Gothic tradition to "convey a topical and timely vision of female empowerment" by establishing a parallel between murder and feminist thinking. Like Toulza, they see the heroines-murderesses as embodiments of different strands of feminism: the New Woman of first-wave feminism; the Victorian antifeminist; the second-wave feminist who fights for her right to write and criticizes the beauty-pleasure culture; the neoliberal postfeminist focused on individual identity, pleasure, and desire. The absence of a supporter of third-wave feminism is thus particularly conspicuous. Both Lindop and Loreck foreground the contradictions of postfeminism. Lindop's contention that the female robots waver between retrograde a portrayal of hypersexualized femininity and pro-feminist representation leads her to pinpoint the postfeminist contradictions around women and technology. Feminist discourses and activism resurface, while new and old misogynies remain prevalent in this "masochistic articulation of techno-terror." Loreck highlights the contradictions inherent in the simultaneous expression of beauty and violence. She shows how *The Neon Demon* "incorporates some feminists' condemnation of beauty as a mutilating imperative, while also adhering to postfeminist understandings of beauty as pleasurable affect." Ultimately, these films and series also address contemporary feminist preoccupations, such as the excesses of neoliberalism (Echeverría), the failure to take into account intersectionality (Charlery), the resolution of the contradictions of postfeminism thanks to inclusive feminism (Toulza), female empowerment (Abello Onofre and Chambost), techno-sexism (Lindop), and practices of body discipline, self-surveillance, and beautification (Loreck).

Finally, Rosie White sets out to consider the case of Aileen Wuornos as dealt with by British documentary filmmaker Nick Broomfield in his second documentary devoted to the serial killer, *Aileen: Life and Death of a Serial Killer* (2003). The film presents her crimes in relation to her class and social background in an endeavor to construct her as a deviant, victimized figure, and thus to demonstrate the inequity of the judicial system and condemn the death penalty in the United States. White criticizes Broomfield's "populist representations of Aileen Wuornos" and argues instead that her case exposes postfeminist media representations as fantasies, drawing attention to "how they can damage or destroy the nonconforming subject." She uses Laura Berlant's notion of the "cruel optimism" of the American Dream to show that Wuornos pursues neoliberal dreams of perfection embedded in popular media culture and reads her story as an example of the "toxicity of such neoliberal optimism." White describes Wuornos's apparently incoherent fits of madness and mental instability before her execution as a coherent attempt to control her own narrative in an "assertion of selfhood," in which she assumes "the role of agent within her own drama." Ultimately, the real serial killer is by no means a postfeminist genre icon, but a manifestation of the cruel optimism of the American Dream that endows her life with meaning and makes her death more bearable.

Notes

1 https://www.syfy.com/syfywire/wonder-woman-test-screening-reactions (accessed September 25, 2018).
2 Jessica Valenti, "The Women's march reminded us: We are not alone," *The Guardian,* January 22, 2017. Available at https://www.theguardian.com/commentisfree/2017/jan/21/womens-march-worldwide-voters-not-alone (accessed November 1, 2018).
3 Taylor M. Riley, "Some heroes don't wear capes: Elizabeth Warren could get an action figure," *The Courier-Journal,* June 8, 2017. Available at https://eu .courier-journal.com/story/entertainment/2017/06/08/elizabeth-warren-wonder-woman-figurine/380010001/ (accessed September 25, 2018).
4 Scott Mendelson, "*Wonder Woman* Box Office: Nevertheless, she persisted," *forbes.com,* July 10, 2017. Available at https://www.forbes.com/sites/scottm endelson/2017/07/10/wonder-woman-box-office-nevertheless-she-pers isted/ (accessed September 25, 2018).
5 Cara Buckley, "Solidarity at an all-female screening of wonder woman," *nytimes.com,* June 5, 2017. Available at https://www.nytimes.com/2 017/06/05/movies/wonder-woman-all-female-screening.html (accessed September 25, 2018).
6 Ibid.

7 Alessandra Maldonado, "Dang—looks like those women-only Wonder Woman screenings were illegal," *salon.com*, August 8, 2017. Available at https://www.salon.com/2017/08/08/woman-woman-women-only-scre enings-lawsuit/ (accessed September 25, 2018).

8 Janell Hobson, "The feminist promise of *Wonder Woman*," *MS. Magazineblog*, June 8, 2017. Available at http://msmagazine.com/blog/201 7/06/08/feminist-promise-wonder-woman/ (accessed September 25, 2018).

9 Kshitij Rawat, "Wonder woman: The significance of this post-feminist heroine," *indianexpress.com*, June 2, 2018. Available at https://indianexpres s.com/article/entertainment/hollywood/wonder-woman-post-feminist-heroine-5201170/ (accessed September 25, 2018).

10 William Moulton Marston deliberately created Wonder Woman as a model of strength for girls.

11 Helen Birch, "Introduction," in H. Birch (ed.), *Moving Targets Women, Murder and Representation* (Berkeley, Los Angeles: University of California Press, 1993), p. 1.

12 Lizzie Seal, *Women, Murder and Femininity: Gender Representations of Women Who Kill* (Houndmills, Basingstoke: Palgrave Macmillan, 2010), pp. 33, 41.

13 Laurie Nalepa and Richard Pfefferman, *The Murder Mystique: Female Killers and Popular Culture* (Santa Barbara, CA, Denver, CO, Oxford: Praeger, 2013), p. x.

14 Nalepa and Pfefferman, *The Murder Mystique,* pp. 9, 135.

15 Annette Burfoot and Susan Lord, "Introduction," in A. Burfoot and S. Lord (eds.), *Killing Women: The Visual Culture of Gender and Violence* (Waterloo, ON: Wilfrid Laurier University Press, 2006), p. xiii.

16 Seal, *Women, Murder and Femininity*, pp. 2–3.

17 Belinda Morrissey, "'Dealing with the devil' Karla Homolka and the absence of feminist criticism," in A. Burfoot and S. Lord (eds.), *Killing Women: The Visual Culture of Gender and Violence* (Waterloo, ON: Wilfrid Laurier University Press, 2006), pp. 84, 89.

18 Seal, *Women, Murder and Femininity*, p. 7.

19 Ibid., p. 18.

20 Ibid., pp. 164–65.

21 Ibid., p. 6.

22 Ibid., p. 1. See also Lisa Downing, *The Subject of Murder: Gender, Exceptionality, and the Modern Killer.* Chicago: University of Chicago Press, 2013, p. 16.

23 Ibid., p. 26.

24 Ibid., pp. 31–32.

25 Downing, *Subject of Murder*, p. 10.

26 Seal., p. 8.

27 Ibid., p. 7.

28 Ibid., p. 85.

29 Burfoot and Lord, "Introduction," p. xii.

30 Seal, *Women, Murder and Femininity,* p. 164.
31 Ibid., p. 4.
32 Ibid., p. 2.
33 Ibid., p. 40.
34 Ibid., p. 84.
35 Downing, *Subject of Murder,* p.14.
36 Ibid., p. 18.
37 The 2016 collected volume, *Unspeakable Acts: Murder by Women* was meant to make up for this lack (*L'Acte inqualifiable ou le meurtre au féminin/Unspeakable Acts: Murder by Women,* E. Jouve, A. Guillain and L. Talairach-Delmas (eds.) (Bruxelles, Bern, Berlin, Frankfurt am Main, New York, Oxford, Wien: Peter Lang, 2016).
38 See Mary Ann Doane, *The Desire to Desire: The Woman's Film of the 1940s* (Bloomington and Indianapolis: Indiana University Press, 1987), pp. 56–57, 65, 110.
39 Ibid., p. 122.
40 Ibid., p. 56.
41 The *femme fatale* had been consistently described as a manipulative malevolent woman since film noir had become the object of critical attention in 1946. See Jean-Pierre Chartier, "Les Américains aussi font des films 'noirs,'" La Revue du cinema 2ᵉ série 2 (novembre 1946), pp. 67–70; Raymond Borde and Etienne Chaumeton, *A Panorama of American Film Noir 1941–1953,* translated from the French by Paul Hammond (San Francisco: CityLight Books, 2002 1955), p. 9; Paul Schrader, "Notes on film noir" 1972, Charles Higham and Joel Greenberg, "Noir cinema" 1968, James Damico, "Film noir: A modest proposal" 1978, Janey Place, and Lowell Peterson, "Some visual motifs of *film noir*" 1974, Robert Porfirio, "No way out: Existential motifs in film noir" 1976 in A. Silver and J. Ursini (eds.), *Film Noir Reader* (New York: Limelight, 1996); See also Foster Hirsch, *The Dark Side of the Screen: Film Noir* (San Diego: A.S. Barnes, 1981) and Thomas Schatz, *Hollywood Genres: Formulas, Filmmaking, and the Studio System* (Boston: McGraw-Hill, 1981) Alain Silver and Elizabeth Ward, *Film Noir: An Encyclopedic Reference to the American Style* (Woodstock: The Overlook Press, 1979).
42 E. Ann Kaplan, "Introduction," in E. A. Kaplan (ed.), *Women in Film Noir* (London: British Film Institute, 1978), p. 4.
43 Doane, *Femmes Fatales: Feminism, Film Theory, Psychoanalysis* (New York: Routledge, 1991), pp. 2–3.
44 I. Cameron (ed.), *The Movie Book of Film Noir* (London: Studio Vista, 1992); Joan Copjec (ed.), *Shades of Noir* (London and New York: Verso, 1993); Helen Hanson "The big seduction: Feminist film criticism and the *Femme Fatale*," in H. Hanson and C. Rawe (eds.), *The Femme Fatale, Images, Histories, Contexts* (Houndmills Basingstoke: Palgrave Macmillan, 2010); Frank Krutnik, *In a Lonely Street: Film Noir, Genre Masculinity* (London and New York: Routledge, 1991); Yvonne Tasker, "Women in

film noir," in A. Spicer and H. Hanson (eds.), *A Companion to Film Noir* (Chichester, West Sussex: Wiley-Blackwell, 2013), pp. 353–68.

45 See Julie Grossman, "'Well, Aren't We Ambitious,' or 'You've Made Up Your Mind I'm Guilty': Reading women as wicked in American *Film Noir*," in H. Hanson and C. Rowe (eds.), *The Femme Fatale*, pp. 199–213 and Angela Martin, "'Gilda Didn't Do Any of Those Things You've Been Losing Sleep Over!': The central women of 40s films noirs," in E A. Kaplan (ed.), *Women in Film Noir*, expanded edition (London: British Film Institute, 1998), pp. 202–28.

46 Carol Clover, *Men, Women, and Chainsaws: Gender in the Modern Horror Film* (Princeton: Princeton University Press, 1992), p. 7.

47 Ibid., p. 53.

48 Ibid., p. 43.

49 Barbara Creed, *The Monstrous-Feminine: Film, Feminism, Psychoanalysis* (London and New York: Routledge, 1993), p. 7.

50 Ibid.

51 Yvonne Tasker, *Working Girls: Gender and Sexuality in Popular Cinema* (London and New York: Routledge, 1998), p. 69.

52 Clayton Dillard, "Hearth of darkness: Rob White's *Todd Haynes*," *slantmagazine.com*, April 3, 2003. Available at https://www.slantmagazine. com/house/tags/5513-superstar-the-karen-carpenter-story (accessed on November 1, 2018).

53 Melanie Haupt, "This Kitty's got claws," *austinchronicle.com*, January 25, 2008. Available at https://www.austinchronicle.com/screens/2008-01-25 /584326/ (accessed October 31, 2018).

54 David Roche, *Quentin Tarantino: Poetics and Politics of Cinematic Metafiction* (Jackson: University Press of Mississippi, 2018), p. 120.

55 See Donato Totaro, "When women kill: Recent North American horror films," *offscreen.com* 18/8, August 2014. Available at https://offscreen.com/ view/when-women-kill (accessed September 24, 2018).

56 Stéphanie Genz and Benjamin Brabon give examples of third-wave feminists who present their movement as antithetical to postfeminism: *Listen Up: Voices From the Next Feminist Generation* (1995, ed. Barbara Findlen), *To Be Real: Telling the Truth and Changing the Face of Feminism* (1995, ed. Rebecca Walker) and *Manifesta: Young Women, Feminism, and the Future* (2000, Jennifer Baumgardner and Amy Richards) in Stéphanie Genz and Benjamin Brabon, *Postfeminism: Cultural Texts and Theories* (Edinburgh: Edinburgh University Press, 2009), p. 157.

57 Genz and Brabon, *Postfeminism*, p. 156.

58 Ibid., p. 4.

59 Sarah Gamble, "Editor's Introduction: The controversies of feminism," in S. Gamble (ed.), *The Routledge Companion to Feminism and Postfeminism* (London and New York: Routledge, 2001), p. viii.

60 Sarah Gamble, "Postfeminism," in Gamble (ed.), *The Routledge Companion to Feminism and Postfeminism* (London and New York: Routledge, 2001), pp. 36–37.

61 Genz and Brabon, *Postfeminism*, p. 4.
62 Gamble, "Postfeminism," p. 36.
63 Whelehan, Imelda, *Overloaded: Feminism and Popular Culture* (London: Women's Press, 2000).
64 Rosalind Gill and Christine Scharff, "Introduction," in R. Gill and C. Scharff (eds.), *New Femininities, Postfeminism, Neoliberalism and Subjectivity* (Houndmills Basingstoke: Palgrave Macmillan, 2011), p. 3.
65 Angela McRobbie, "Post-feminism and popular culture," *Feminist Media Studies*, 4/3 (2004), p. 255.
66 Angela McRobbie, *The Aftermath of Feminism: Gender, Culture and Social Change* (London and New York: Sage, 2012), p. 12.
67 Angela McRobbie, "Post-feminism and popular culture," p. 255.
68 Ibid., pp. 255–56.
69 Rosalind Gill, "Postfeminist media culture: Elements of a sensibility," *European Journal of Cultural Studies*, 10/2 (2007), p. 161.
70 Gill, "Postfeminist media culture," p. 163.
71 Ibid.
72 Genz and Brabon, *Postfeminism*, p. 11.
73 Gill and Scharff, "Introduction," p. 3.
74 Ann Braithwaite, "The personal, the political, third-wave and postfeminisms," *Feminist Theory*, 3/3 (2002), p. 340.
75 Ann Brooks, *Postfeminisms, Feminism, Cultural Theory and Cultural Forms* (London and New York: Routledge, 1997), p. 4.
76 Ibid.
77 Gamble, "Postfeminism," p. 38.
78 Ibid.
79 Ibid.
80 Genz and Brabon, *Postfeminism*, p. 15.
81 McRobbie, "Post-feminism and popular culture," p. 255.
82 Gill, "Postfeminist media culture," pp. 147–48.
83 Gill and Scharff, "Introduction," p. 7.
84 Ibid.
85 Rosalind Gill, "The affective, cultural and psychic life of postfeminism: A postfeminist sensibility 10 years on," *European Journal of Cultural Studies*, 20/6 (2017), p. 606.
86 Jess Butler, "For white girls only? Postfeminism and the politics of inclusion," *Feminist Formations*, 25/1 (2013), pp. 35–58.
87 Gill, "The affective, cultural and psychic life of postfeminism," p. 613.
88 Yvonne Tasker and Diane Negra, "Introduction: Feminist politics and postfeminist culture," in Y. Tasker and D. Negra (eds.), *Interrogating Postfeminism: Gender and the Politics of Popular Culture* (Durham: Duke University Press, 2007), p. 2.
89 Gill, "Postfeminist media culture."
90 Gill, "The affective, cultural and psychic life of postfeminism," pp. 612–15.

91 Kimberly Springer, "Divas, evil black bitches and bitter black women: African American women," in Y. Tasker and D. Negra (eds.), *Interrogating Postfeminism: Gender and the Politics of Popular Culture* (Durham: Duke University Press, 2007), pp. 249–76.

92 Alice Walker, *In Search of Our Mothers' Gardens, Womanist Prose* (London: Phoenix, 2011 [1984]).

93 See Emilie Herbert's chapter in this collection.

94 See Rosalind Gill and Christine Scharff (eds.), *New Femininities* for examples of studies based on makeover shows, advertising, social networking sites, and film; see also Angela McRobbie's reading of Bridget Jones in the first chapter of her book "Post-feminism and popular culture: Bridget Jones and the new gender regime," in *The Aftermath of Feminism*, pp. 11–23; see Anthea Taylor, *Single Women in Popular Culture: The Limits of Postfeminism* (Houndmills Basingstoke: Palgrave Macmillan, 2012), for an example of a comprehensive study of popular culture based on series, sitcoms, chick flicks, romantic comedies, neo-noir movies, women's magazines, reality television, makeover shows, and blogs. Melanie Waters's monograph *Women on Screen Feminism and Femininity in Visual Culture* (Houndmills Basingstoke: Palgrave Macmillan, 2011) also offers a study based on chick flicks, series, makeover shows, James Bond franchise, action films, television films, chick flicks, series, noir, teenage films, romance; the collection edited by Joel Gwynne and Nadine Muller, *Postfeminism and Contemporary Hollywood Cinema* (Houndmills Basingstoke: Palgrave Macmillan, 2013) contains texts based on contemporary romantic comedies and teen comedy, with one chapter on crime film *Heat*, one foray into the horror genre, and one on sports film; Hilary Radner and Rebecca Stringer (eds.), *Feminism at the Movies: Understanding Gender in Contemporary Popular Culture* (London and New York: Routledge, 2011), which deals with chick flicks, teen pics, hommecoms, horror, action adventure, indie flicks, and women lawyer films. See also Sarah Projansky, *Watching Rape Film and Television in Postfeminist Culture* (New York: New York University Press, 2001).

95 This is what Sarah Projansky argues about rape: "my goal is not to identify the specificity of rape within particular genres (e.g., melodrama, comedy, horror), show types (e.g., soap opera, cop show, advertisement, talk show), or media (e.g., film, television, print). Because representations of rape appear indiscriminately in nearly all genres, show types, and media, a genre- or media-specific approach would not allow me to address how rape and feminism *cross* popular and local cultural texts and how they can help us understand *systems* of media and representation." (*Watching Rape*, p. 17).

96 Waters, *Women on Screen Feminism and Femininity in Visual Culture*.

97 Radner and Stringer (eds.), *Feminism at the Movies*; Waters's monograph *Women on Screen*; Gwynne and Muller (eds.), *Postfeminism and Contemporary Hollywood Cinema*.

98   Yvonne Tasker and Diane Negra, "Introduction: In focus: Postfeminism and contemporary media studies," *Cinema Journal*, 44/2 (2005), p. 107.

99   Samantha Lindop, *Postfeminism and the Fatale Figure in Neo-Noir Cinema* (Houndmills Basingstoke, 2015), p. 76.

100 David Roche, *Making and Remaking Horror in the 1970s and 2000s: Why Don't They Do It Like They Used To?* (Jackson: University Press of Mississippi, 2014), pp. 108–9, 114.

101 See David Roche, "'(In)stability of point of view' in when a stranger calls and eyes of a stranger," in Wickham Clayton (ed.), *Style and Form in the Hollywood Slasher* (Houndmills Basingstoke: Palgrave Macmillan, 2015), pp. 17–36.

102 Timing from Netflix.

103 Gill, "Postfeminist media culture," p. 163.

104 Gill, "From Sexual Objectification to Sexual Subjectification: The Resexualisation of Women's Bodies in the Media," *Feminist Media Studies*, 3/1 (2003), pp. 100–6.

105 Seal, *Women, Murder and Femininity*.

106 See chapter 3 of Roche, *Quentin Tarantino*.

107 Linda Williams, "When the woman looks," in M. A. Doane, P. Mellencamp and L. Williams (eds.), *Re-Vision: Essays in Feminist Film Criticism* (Los Angeles: University Publications of America, 1984), p. 87.

108 Gill and Scharff, "Introduction."

109 Rosalind Gill, "From sexual objectification to sexual subjectification: The resexualisation of women's bodies in the media," *Feminist Media Studies*, 3/1 (January 2003), p. 101.

Filmography

All the Boys Love Mandy Lane, directed by Jonathan Levine, written by Jacob Forman, performances by Amber Heard (Mandy Lane), Whitney Able (Chloe), and Michael Welch (Emmet), music by Mark Schulz, cinematography by Darren Genet, edited by Josh Noyes, Occupant Entertainment, 2006. DVD. Wild Side Video, 2006.

Happy Valley, created, written, and directed by Sally Wainwright, produced by Karen Lewis (series 1) and Juliet Wharlesworth (series 2), performances by Sarah Lancashire (Catherine Cawood), Siobhan Finneran (Clare Cartwright), Charlie Murphy (Ann Gallagher), and James Norton (Tommy Lee Royce), music by Ben Foster, Red Production Company, BBC, 2014–. Netflix.

The Wire, created by David Simon, performances by Dominic West (James McNulty), Wendell Pierce (Bunk Moreland), Deirdre Lovejoy (Rhonda Pearlman), Lance Reddick (Cedric Daniels), and Felicia Pearson (Snoop), music by Tom Waits, HBO, 2002–08. DVD. Warner Bros., 2010.

Part One

Neo-*Femmes Fatales*

1

The *Femme Fatale* of the 1990s Erotic Thriller

A Postfeminist Killer?

Delphine Letort

The *femme fatale* is an iconic figure of film noir, arousing both fear and fascination in the shady world of crime fiction. Drawing power from her deadly eroticism and sexuality, and often symbolized by an idealized female beauty captured in chiaroscuro, she is first and foremost a manipulative and calculative killer. However, the noir *femme fatale* is rarely depicted as violent, for she is never filmed in the act of killing. The screen goes black when Cora is about to hit her husband in *The Postman Always Rings Twice* (Tay Garnett, 1946), while Ellen watches her young brother-in-law Danny drown without intervening in *Leave Her to Heaven* (John M. Stahl, 1945) and voluntarily falls down the stairs to end the pregnancy that makes her housebound.[1] Murder is most often a veiled topic of discussion in film noir, a dangerous threat surrounding the *femme fatale*, which translates into symbolic lighting. Richard Dyer observes that film noir exploits the contrast between light and shadow to express the femininity of evil: "There is a frightening, disfiguring darkness to the sexuality that, moth to a flame, yearns towards the pure light of desirability."[2] The *femme fatale*'s deathly power resides in her mastery over her own sexuality outside patriarchal control; the knowledge of her sexuality endows her with power over the men who fall for her. This knowledge can only be alluded to in classical Hollywood cinema—through suggestive clothes such as *Gilda*'s (Charles Vidor, 1946) black satin split-skirt dress and gloves, metaphorical conversations between lovers in *The Big Sleep* (Howard Hawks, 1946), shots of closed doors behind which intimacy is preserved in *Double Indemnity* (Billy Wilder, 1946). However, sexuality is nothing but a means to an economic end for the noir *femme fatale*, and murder the path to her liberation from patriarchal authority. Chris Straayer remarks that "her sexuality *per se* was passive, limited to its allure. Although narratively she maneuvered the male protagonist with her sexuality, the specifically sexual desire and pleasure it served belonged to the male."[3] The focus on the *femme fatale*'s sexuality deviates attention away from her power to kill. Although Molly Haskell celebrates the untamed character of a "woman who begins as a victim of discriminatory circumstances and rises, through pain, obsessions, or defiance, to become mistress of her fate,"[4] her inability to kill by herself entrenches rigid gender roles. The *femme fatale* rarely kills with her own hands—Brigid O'Shaughnessy in *The Maltese Falcon* (Roy Del Ruth, 1931; John Huston, 1941) and Ellen Berent in *Leave Her to Heaven* are notable exceptions; rather, she conceives plots that she would have others (often subjugated males) carry out for her. Instead of acting on her own, she is the passive spectator of an act committed by another. The fetishistic spectacularization of the female body, spotlighting Barbara Stanwyck's braceleted ankle in *Double Indemnity* or Lana Turner's naked legs in *The Postman Always Rings Twice*, and its objectification for voyeuristic consumption undermine the subversive power of the *femme fatale*. The conspicuous spectacle of her body downplays her desire to break the interdictions of the Hays Code ("technique of committing murder by whatever method") and the taboos of female sexuality, for she has to conform to cinematic codes of representation that limit her power to effects of mise-en-scène. The *femme fatale* is subjected to barriers that lay bare the ideological crisis triggered by a woman who will not restrain her ambition to the domestic sphere; her marriage, often her only route to economic comfort, is a source of frustration that breeds and fuels her desire for murder. The *femme fatale* does not aim for domestic bliss but for power in a society where she is a second-class citizen; her shenanigans, however, are bound to fail in the noir narrative. Although she does unsettle the male narrator's position of authority by seducing him into crime, her final death or imprisonment serves to reinforce the morality of the tale and respect for the patriarchal order.

A wave of erotic thrillers emerged in the 1980s and 1990s that imposed a new figure of the *femme fatale*, which many scholars associated with a postmodern revision of noir conventions they described as neo-noir.[5] French critic Michel Cieutat berated these films, which he accused of exploiting women's sexual liberation for the spectator's voyeuristic gaze through carefully constructed narratives. The new *femme fatale* asserted her sexuality in films that displayed more than her tantalizing figure; no longer restricted by the moral concerns underlying the Hays Code, neo-noir directors were more than willing to depict the spectacle of the *femme fatale*'s sexual audacity and murderous impulses. Cieutat observed that Hollywood producers introduced an erotic touch in all kinds of film genres, making sex a depoliticized act for women whose liberated sexuality translated into a sense of bodily empowerment.[6] Geoffrey Nowell-Smith also noticed that a new film rhetoric emerged from the deployment of exciting sex and violence on screen, which eventually became normalized through repetition:

> Nor does this apparently transgressive rhetoric any longer have the power to shock, since what seems like excess has become a routine selling element to which regular audiences have become inured. Often, too, behind the sex-and-violence rhetoric and the occasional grotesquerie, the new Hollywood films turn out to be quite conventional in their narrative forms and even in their moral values.[7]

The erotic thriller epitomized the new trend; it displayed the woman's body as a source of entertainment, using provocative sex scene adverts to entice viewers into indulging in soft-porn features. Nowell-Smith also underlined the exhibition of violence that undergirds the representation of sexuality in the genre. The erotic thriller shows women whose sexual drives have lethal consequences. While film noir made the link between sex and death an object of repression, the erotic thriller foregrounds the *femme fatale*'s deadly sexual power. Paradoxically, it is the essence of woman's evil that is revived in these films, which portray the financially independent woman as an "orgasmic *femme fatale*,"[8] who draws pleasure from the act of murderous penetration. In neo-noir, murder is no longer a route to the woman's social liberation; it clearly appears as its consequence in the conservative 1990s, a decade during which the AIDS epidemic was on the rise. *Basic Instinct* (Paul Verhoeven, 1992) epitomized the new threat of the *femme fatale*, using Catherine Trammel's book as a reflexive device that describes in details the killing scene that is investigated in the film. The suspected killer sardonically states: "I'd have to be pretty stupid to write a book about a killer . . . and then kill somebody the way I described it in my book" [26:00]. This ambiguous confession suggests the tortuous mind of a killer who has made a literary career out of writing about real murders that she treats on the fictional mode.

In her recent investigation into the contemporary *femme fatale*, film scholar Katherine Farrimond observes that the *femme fatale* remains a complex figure, a site of tension where contradictory desires are projected, for "the *femme fatale* can be read both in terms of conservative anxiety and feminist empowerment."[9] Indeed, it is striking to note that the figure of the *femme fatale* returned in the 1980s and 1990s cinema, when feminism was experiencing an ideological backlash and postfeminism was beginning to surface.[10] The contradictory interpretations of the neo-noir *femme fatale* as either a hypersexualized figure of empowerment or an objectified sexual fantasy illustrates the fraught debates associated with postfeminism.

This chapter examines how postfeminist theories may allow for a new understanding of the killer instinct of the neo-noir *femme fatale*, with special attention to *Basic Instinct, Body of Evidence* (Uli Edel, 1993), *The Last Seduction* (John Dahl, 1994), and *Bound* (The Wachowskis, 1996).

Sex, Money, Murder

The formula of the erotic thriller relies on three key terms: sex, money, and murder. Kate Stables identifies *Basic Instinct* as "the mother of all 90s *fatale movies*,"[11] suggesting that the film provides a matrix for all subsequent productions. Author of the seminal book *The Erotic Thriller in Contemporary Cinema*, Linda Ruth Williams scathingly critiques the erotic thrillers as "basic stories of sexual intrigue that use some form of criminality or duplicity as the flimsy framework to support on-screen sex which is as explicit as possible."[12] The opening sequence of *Basic Instinct* illustrates the merging of sex and death, Eros and Thanatos, when a naked woman violently and energetically stabs an ice pick into a man's neck during a sex scene [4:00]. She is straddling the man who is lying on his back, with his hands tied to the bed bars, like a sacrificial victim. A close-up of his head shows blood splashing out, merging the orgasmic climax with the act of killing. The murder is represented in an illustration to the book Catherine Trammel has authored (Figure 1.1), offering a *mise en abyme* of the opening sequence: the male victim lies in a bath of blood with his arms stretched backward as though on a cross, whereas the figure of a blond sexy half-naked woman occupies the middle ground contemplating the scene. The ice pick stands out in the foreground with a

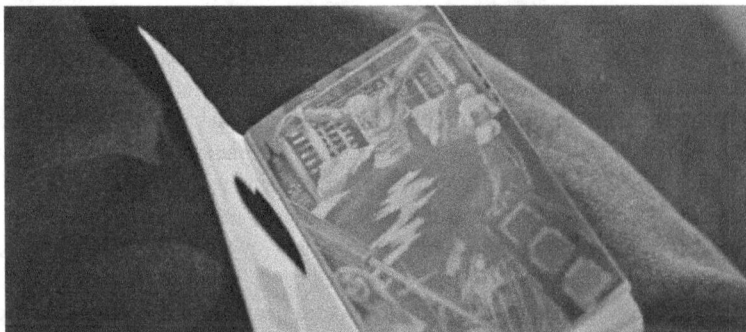

Figure 1.1 *Basic Instinct* (Verhoeven, 1992) : the cover of Catherine Trammel's novel provides a model for the real killings.

shining blade as a piece of evidence. The drawing conveys the self-satisfaction of an all-powerful woman killer who gazes at the scene of a murder she has committed in defiance of the phallic buildings looming in the background. The focus on the weapon in the illustration echoes the final shot of the film and evokes the deadly penetration that turns a sex scene into murder, thereby pathologizing and containing the sexual quest of a woman who does not content herself with submitting to male desire. Catherine Trammel leaves scratch marks on Nick Curran's back when she has sex with him as evidence of the orgasmic violence, her fingers digging into his flesh being another sign of penetration and deadly desire [71:30]. *Basic Instinct* characterizes the sexually emancipated woman as a bloodthirsty serial killer, whose pleasure is tied to the objectification of the man she physically dominates. Julianne Pidduck expressed some satisfaction as a female viewer, enthused by the sense of self-confidence conveyed by the neo-noir *femme fatale*, a powerful figure who steals narrative agency from the male protagonist:

> Where in our everyday lives as women we are bombarded by the evidence of our increasing vulnerability, poverty, and limited social power, the fatal femme's embodied social, sexual, and physical powers offer an imagined point of contact, if not simply identification—an imagined momentum or venting of rage and revenge fantasies—the importance of which cannot be underestimated.[13]

This reversal of power between male and female has ambiguous connotations in the neo-noir crime narrative. Although the neo-noir *femme fatale* reverses gender roles by taking action as she carries out her deadly plot on her own, her agency is concomitant with her sexual commodification.

While the portrayal of women who actively seek to satisfy their own pleasure by assuming authority over their own body and their partner's may offer an empowering model for female viewers who claim their sexuality, the connection between female sexuality and murder creates a pathological framework for the understanding of female sexual emancipation. Linda Williams further disapproves of the "gross display of the human body"[14] in films that center on the "sexually saturated female body,"[15] which dominates the screen. The woman's "sexy body" is associated with the "power to kill" in the erotic thriller, two notions that are key to female empowerment in a postfeminist context. Commenting on female sexual agency in advertising, Rosalind Gill argues that women can achieve subjecthood and transcend sexual objectification in the contemporary media context: "Where once sexualized representations of women in the media presented them as passive, mute objects of an assumed male gaze, today women are presented as active, desiring sexual subjects who choose to present themselves in a seemingly objectified manner because it suits their (implicitly 'liberated') interests to do so."[16] Although the act of killing may be considered as an expression of agency in the erotic thriller, Gill opposes the woman's search for sexual satisfaction as postfeminist empowerment and the revenge narrative as "powerlessness." She refers to *Fatal Attraction* (Adrian Lyne, 1987) as a case in point, a film that exploits the Manichean opposition between the cheated-upon housewife and the *femme fatale* to ultimately champion domesticity.[17] The visual references to film-noir aesthetics speak to the nostalgia characteristic of the 1980s, a conservative decade that prized family values, individuality, and national strength.[18] In *Fatal Attraction*, the recourse to violence appears to be a sign of weakness on the part of the single woman who has failed to secure a husband. The film dwells on Alex Forrest's desperate acts of violence, as she first attempts to kill herself before she turns her desire for revenge on Dan Gallagher's family in response to his rejection of her after being his one-night stand.

Rather than promote sexual pleasure as a source of female emancipation and personal growth, the erotic thriller interweaves sex and crime in a pathological fashion. The *femme fatale*'s excessive sexuality is a metaphor for her killing instinct; she is a figure of violence that calls for some form of punishment. Catherine Trammel, a blonde woman with a Spyker C8 Laviolette sports car, exudes self-confidence and power by driving dangerously at high speed along a coastline road [39:00]. Luxury props underpin the woman's identity within a neoliberal context where consumption is "a tool to achieve power and pleasure, an alternative route for self-esteem; women construct their identity and receive societal appreciation by means of consuming."[19] The ice pick she uses is not only a weapon but also a signifier of class and power in the film; her breaking ice for a drink allows her to display the strength of a woman who will not be dominated [61:55–62:25]. As a white, upper-class character whose lifestyle exhibits her wealth as a successful crime fiction author, Catherine Trammel embodies the postfeminist ethos of the 1990s. Her independence of mind and her uncompromised and unbound freedom are materialized in the luxury mansion that she owns and where she lives without relying on a male breadwinner to entertain her. The neo-noir *femme fatale* derives power from her consumer status, and her materialistic desire underlies her plot to gain wealth and power. In the neo-narrative, the *femme fatale* manages to "have it all"—Catherine Trammel is never arrested, although the final shot of the ice pick clearly indicates that she is the suspected serial killer [46:15]. While the title of *Basic Instinct* refers to her breaking all social and moral norms as regards sexuality, it also serves to signify her killing impulse—a desire to overthrow the patriarchal order.

Watching a Soft-Porn Kill

Redefining the neo-noir *femme fatale* through her performance of Rebecca Carlson in *Body of Evidence*, Madonna turns her sexualized body into a weapon and uses sadomasochistic practices to murder her wealthy lover with heart problems in the opening sequence. She literally embodies the *femme fatale*'s killer instinct, using her body and her sexuality to assassinate her lovers. Her venality translates into a sexual appetite that leads her to explore the physical limits of her male partner's body. Georges-Claude Guilbert analyzes Madonna's performance of femininity as a "bad girl" construct, for she is "an exhibitionist stripper" who "pretends to denude herself, but uses props that 'mask' her nudity or get attention away from it, while valorizing it."[20] *Body of Evidence* explores the *femme fatale*'s sexual masquerade to draw attention onto the male body of the attorney Madonna's character has sex with, as she pours candle wax on his chest to sexually tease him with pain, making him the object of her fantasies. The film essentializes the *femme fatale* by reducing her body to a sexual and lethal weapon; the woman is endowed with no interiority and expresses no feeling. She is reduced to an image, a figure, a spectacle. Her desire to kill is thus depoliticized, resulting from a sense of sexual frustration that she transcends through murder. Killing becomes part of the spectacle—just like the sex act.

Carolyn Blyth contends that, "for the neo-noir *femme fatale*, sex is currency—sometimes their only currency—that they can use to control events, exert their agency, and get exactly what they need and want in life."[21] While postfeminists put forth sexualization as empowerment, the erotic thriller uses soft-porn spectacle to downplay the socially subversive concerns of the *femme fatale*. By talking her male partner into committing a crime in film noir, the woman expressed the frustration of a condition she aimed to change. Murder was her only path to freedom from a life of subservience. The neo-noir *femme fatale*, on the other hand, enjoys material bliss, and her killing act materializes her desire for patriarchal power. Killing the male during the sex act becomes an act of female empowerment, which *Basic Instinct* exploits by building on the porn spectacle of Catherine Trammel's liberated sexuality. Her provocative clothing style and body language denote the self-confidence of a woman who stages her own body for the concupiscent male gaze. Sexual and verbal provocation is a tool that she uses to resist moral taboos and challenge the patriarchal order when being interviewed by male police officers after the murder of Johnny Boz [24:00]. She subverts the politically correct through her body language, inspiring embarrassment when uncrossing her legs to invite them to glance at her sex. By observing the reactions of uneasiness among the sexually aroused audience of men, she reverses the male/female hierarchy and the policeman/suspect relationship.

She thus overturns the power relationship between the active male onlookers and the passive looked-at female by assuming a new subjecthood. By answering questions before they are even asked and deceiving the lie detector, she dominates the police interview. The sequence further deconstructs the male gaze by including surveillance screens, which capture the voyeuristic desire of male spectators staring at the video recordings of the woman sitting in front of them and showing her sex in a self-conscious performance.

Rosalind Gill argues that female empowerment means "the capacity to embody or performatively affect a sense of power and confidence, [that] has itself become a normatively demanded feature of young women's sexual subjectivity, such that they are called on routinely to perform confident, knowing hetero-sexiness."[22] Erotic thrillers such as *Basic Instinct* marketed a hypersexualized image of woman and, in the United States at least, brought soft porn into the mainstream. The film contributed to the promotion of a self-conscious performance of a sexualized femininity, which female viewers absorbed as a new definition of female subjectivity. Going even further, Gill noted "a cynical rhetoric, wrapping sexual objectification in a shiny, feisty, post-feminist packaging that obscures the continued underlying sexism."[23] The merging of sex and suspense in the erotic thriller made it easier to depoliticize the negative impact of its soft-porn crime narrative, dismissing its inherent sexism transformed into bodily sexiness and suspense.

The development of a neoliberal, postfeminist consumer culture impacted the representation of the female body, and traces of its influence can be grasped through neo-noir. Although the *femme fatale* revels in her own sexuality as signified by the close attention paid to her bare white skin,[24] she is also trapped by a consumer culture that limits her power to her sexuality. The portrayal of the female orgasm may appear as a challenge to dominant media representations of sexuality; however, it also relies on two porn elements—"maximum visibility" of the bodies and a variety of "sexual numbers,"[25] which Linda Williams associates with a "quintessential male genre":[26] pornography. The fact that the woman's orgasm is equated to the murder of the male in the erotic thriller turns the woman's body into a threat to be contained and even destroyed—this is the fate that Alex Forrest expects at the end of *Fatal Attraction*.

The Lesbian Killer

Mary Anne Doane framed the *femme fatale*'s moral and sexual transgressions in psychoanalytic terms: "The power accorded to the *femme fatale* is a function of fears linked to the notions of uncontrollable drives, the fading of subjectivity, and the loss of conscious agencies—all themes of the emergent theories of psychoanalysis."[27] In neo-noir, these uncontrollable drives are associated with the *femme fatale*'s daring, "polymorphous sexuality," which the erotic thriller assimilates to suspense and danger.[28] While Catherine Trammel is a castrating figure wielding an ice pick in *Basic Instinct*, she is also a bisexual *femme fatale*. Her impulse to kill straight men caused an outcry among the lesbian audience, who both contested the film's pathological representation of homoerotic desire and celebrated its "revolutionary" impact because the film "pushed a porn style and language into Middle America";[29] these comments by Camille Paglia convey the postfeminist look at a film that broke new ground by giving visibility to same-sex desire. However, in *Basic Instinct*, the spectacle of two women kissing each other is clearly staged as a teaser for Nick Curran's male gaze. As Susan Driver explains, queer girls provide "glamorous erotic spectacles and marketable hip signs of transgression" on screen.[30] Paul Verhoeven films the women kissing each other from a distance, with the camera aligned to Nick Curran's subjective look at what could be an erotic fantasy. The narration translates an uneven attention at homoerotic desire; the sex act between Catherine and Roxy is not shown, unlike sex between Catherine and Nick, which is a physical performance, and which the latter describes as "the fuck of the century" [74:06]. Catherine Trammel manipulates both men and women, and her bisexuality becomes a sign of her duplicitous and murderous character. Rather than highlight same-sex desire, Katherine Farrimond points out that "the addition of bisexual activity into the repertoire of *femme fatale* figures functions as an effective way of affirming the sense of their treacherous untrustworthiness, menace, excessive sexual appetites and lack of sexual responsibility."[31]

The neo-noir *femme fatale* must be punished for daring to challenge heteronormative gender roles, which leads violence to be directed against women in these films. Violent sex is also characteristic of the erotic thriller; *Basic Instinct* and *The Last Seduction* include rape scenes that are incorporated into their plotlines and have drawn little critical attention. In *Basic Instinct*, the sequence when detective Nick Curran aggressively forces his date Elisabeth Garner into having sex is ambiguously treated, for her resistance weakens into sexual orgasm by the end of the act [37:00].[32] In *The Last Seduction*, Bridget manipulates Mike into raping her in order to have him arrested [87:00]. Both films, as Linda Williams noted, actually convey "the notion that rape can be both pleasurable and consensual for its victim."[33] The rape loses its significance from the victim's point of view when it is depicted as a device to release one's frustration. Remarking a shift in the representations of rape on screen, Sarah Projansky observes that the line between rape and sexuality is particularly blurry in postfeminist culture: "For example, thrillers or horror films that incorporate rape or the threat of rape specifically in order to produce spectatorial anxiety often resolve that anxiety through an independent woman character who triumphs in the end."[34] In other words, these films praise the woman's capacity to overcome victimization. In *The Last Seduction*, it even represents the female protagonist's moment of emancipation, which the ending sequence aptly conveys by showing Bridget leave in a luxury car [89:30]; rape is even key to her empowerment into an independent social agent.

Although the *femme fatale* appears to be a strong character, her body is subjected to repeated abuse in neo-noir and reduced to abjection. Barbara Creed has famously contended that "all human societies have a conception of the monstrous-feminine, of what it is about woman that is shocking, terrifying, horrific, abject."[35] The abject is rooted in the woman's body constructed as "a fearful and threatening form of sexuality."[36] In *Bound*, it is abjection that inspires violence. Although the film includes scenes of lesbian sex and female intimacy that are not exploited as a source of visual pleasure for the male gaze, it also displays a high level of violence that turns bodies into corpses, these figures of abjection thereby haunting the film visually. Corky discovers the gangsters' violence through the cries and thumps coming from the toilet of her bathroom, connecting her to the man whose body is being viciously beaten up elsewhere and whose blood soon covers the toilet of another bathroom [26:13]. Lying on the floor where he receives a series of kicks, the man's shape is reduced to abject matter. The scene foretells the violence Caesar lashes out on both Violet and Corky when he realizes he has been betrayed by Violet, the woman whose body he claims ownership over [77:00]. Violet, however, chooses to partner with Roxy and shoots Caesar point blank. The close shot of her face as she is about to pull the trigger on Caesar conveys the power of the decision she has made to put an end to their affair (Figure 1.2); she gains her freedom from an unequal relationship where she is subjected to physical and verbal abuse by killing him. The women of *Bound*, B. Ruby Rich argues, "make the link between lesbian desire and crime utterly explicit, restore the male as sole target of violence, escape punishment, and get to drive off into the sunset."[37] *Bound* portrays lesbian love in a distinct light as Violet and Corky team up to trap and rob the money stolen by Caesar, an Italian gangster who believes in the essential superiority of men. Violet explains to Roxy that sex with men is just "work," but she is a lesbian who loves women. The two women pair up to achieve independence from the gangster Violet sells herself to. Their success counters the ideological slant of classical film noir, for "*Bound* suggests that, in contrast to the heterosexual failing of classic film noir, women can trust one another. Because they are same sexed, lesbians make better partners in crime than heterosexual pairings."[38]

Figure 1.2 *Bound* (Wachowskis, 1996): Corky, the lesbian *femme fatale*.

Conclusion

Chris Straayer extolls the neo-noir *femmes fatales'* choice of independence and underlines a shift of allegiance that might impact the viewer's perception of gender:

> *The Last Seduction* offers a prime example of neo-noir's implied author switching his sympathy from the male protagonist to the *femme fatale*, or, to put it another way, allowing his superego to lighten up. With resolute style, *The Last Seduction's femme fatale* rejects romance, claims abundant sexual satisfaction, and walks away free with the money.[39]

The neo-noir *femme fatale* mirrors a postfeminist vision of society in which women combat patriarchal structures on their own terms. She performs a self-reflexive femininity, replicating the classic noir *femme fatale* style with a *différance* that evokes the empowering project of postfeminism. In effect, the neo-noir *femme fatale* models her style on the noir figure, using the male vision of her body as an object to be possessed, in order to overturn the patriarchal order. While the classic *femme fatale* was a subversive character that challenged the patriarchal order by avoiding family constraints and motherhood,[40] the neo-noir *femme fatale* embodies the transgression of moral, social, and sexual norms. By killing the male, she achieves liberation from masculine domination and heteronormative conventions, which society uses to reify her sex. The murder of the male can be understood in terms of empowerment and subjectification from a postfeminist perspective. Confidently baring her body to feel empowered and using it as a weapon to achieve her liberation, the neo-noir *femme fatale* performs a self-conscious role in the erotic thriller; this is aptly signified by the reference to the crime story that allows Catherine Trammel to be known as a popular best-selling writer in *Basic Instinct*. In a postfeminist context, she is a powerful figure that can only be contained by violence, like the single woman who threatens to destroy the family unit in *Fatal Attraction*. The shift from feminism to postfeminism obviously affects the meaning of the figure, drawing attention away from structural gender inequalities to put forth her individual fight against the men that fail to dominate her. The erotic thriller has introduced the lesbian or bisexual *femme fatale* as a new figure of the killer, thereby pathologizing a sexual orientation through the representation of the monstrous woman. A film like *Bound*, however, celebrates female bonding as a counter-narrative to hegemonic sexual models by allowing its lesbian characters to best the gangsters.

Notes

1 Delphine Letort, "*Femme fatale*/femme assassine dans le film noir : dévier le stéréotype," *Cycnos,* 23/2 (2006). Available at http://revel.unice.fr/cycnos/index.html?id=705 (accessed October 8, 2018).
2 Richard Dyer, *White* (London: Routledge, 1997), p. 134.
3 Chris Straayer, "*Femme fatale* or lesbian femme: *Bound* in sexual différance," in E. A. Kaplan (ed.), *Women in Film Noir*, expanded edition (London: British Film Institute, 2001), p. 153.
4 Molly Haskell, *From Reverence to Rape* (Chicago: University of Chicago Press, 1974), p. 160.
5 Kate Stables, "The Postmodern always rings twice: Constructing the *femme fatale* in 90s cinema," in Kaplan (ed.), *Women in Film Noir*, expanded edition (London: British Film Institute, 2001), pp. 164–82.
6 Michel Cieutat, "Chronique d'une imposture," *Positif* 422 (avril 1996), pp. 99–100.
7 Geoffrey Nowell-Smith, "The resurgence of cinema," in G. Nowell-Smith (ed.), *The Oxford History of World Cinema* (Oxford: Oxford University Press, 1996), p. 765.
8 Straayer refers to as *Black Widow* (1986), *Fatal Attraction* (1987), *After Dark, My Sweet* (1990), *Basic Instinct* (1992), *Body of Evidence* (1992), *Romeo is Bleeding* (1994), *The Last Seduction* (1994), *Diabolique* (1996) and *Lost Highway* (1997) (Straayer, "*Femme fatale* or lesbian femme," p. 153).
9 Katherine Farrimond, *The Contemporary Femme Fatale: Gender, Genre and American Cinema* (New York: Routledge, 2018), p. 1.
10 Susan Faludi, *Backlash: The Undeclared War Against American Women* (New York: Anchor Books, 1991).

11 Stables, "The postmodern always rings twice," p. 165.
12 Linda Ruth Williams, "Erotic thrillers and rude women," *Sight & Sound*, July 1993, p. 12.
13 Julianne Pidduck, "The 1990s Hollywood fatal femme: (Dis)figuring feminism, family, irony, violence," *Cineaction*, 38 (1995), p. 69.
14 Linda Williams, "Film bodies: Gender, genre, and excess," *Film Quarterly*, 44/4 (Summer 1991), p. 2.
15 Ibid., p. 6.
16 Rosalind Gill, "Empowerment/sexism: Figuring female sexual agency in contemporary advertising," *Feminism and Psychology*, 18/1 (2008), pp. 35–60.
17 Leighton Grist ironically explains: "The opposition of good woman and *femme fatale* works to naturalise a misogynistic denial of 'transgressive' female (sexual) independence before a championing of woman's 'traditional' subordinate domesticity. [. . .] What could be a potentially complex analysis of the repressions and tensions of patriarchal marriage swiftly degenerates into an unequivocal, pernicious attack on the single, 'liberated' working woman" (Leighton Grist, "Moving targets and black widows," in I. Cameron (ed.), *The Book of Film Noir* (London: Studio Vista, 1994), p. 276).
18 Graham Thompson, *American Culture in the 1980s* (Edinburgh: Edinburgh University Press, 2007).
19 Fien Adriaens, "Postfeminism in popular culture: A potential for critical resistance?" *Politics and Culture*, 4 (2009). Available at https://politicsandc ulture.org/2009/11/09/post-feminism-in-popular-culture-a-potential-for -critical-resistance/ (accessed on September 7, 2018).
20 Georges-Claude Guilbert, *Madonna as Postmodern Myth: How One Star's Self-Construction Rewrites Sex, Gender, Hollywood, and the American Myth* (Jefferson, NC: MacFarland, 2002), pp. 99–100.
21 Caroline Blyth, *Reimagining Delilah's Afterlives as Femme Fatale: The Lost Seduction* (London: Bloomsbury, 2017), p. 44.
22 Rosalind Gill, "Media, empowerment and the 'sexualization of culture' debates," *Sex Roles*, 66/11–12 (2012), p. 737.
23 Ibid.
24 Sara Ahmed and Jackey Stacey, *Thinking Through the Skin* (London and New York: Routledge, 2001).
25 Linda Williams, *Hard Core: Power, Pleasure, and the "Frenzy of the Visible"* (Berkeley and Los Angeles: University of California Press, 1989), p. 5.
26 Ibid., p. 49.
27 Mary Anne Doane, *Femme Fatales: Feminism, Film Theory, Psychoanalysis* (New York: Routledge, 1991), p. 2.
28 Stables, "The Postmodern always rings twice," p. 179.
29 Camilla Paglia cited in Luca Prono, *Encyclopedia of Gay and Lesbian Popular Culture* (Westport, CT: Greenwood Press, 2008), p. 26.
30 Susan Driver, *Queer Girls and Popular Culture, Reading, Resisting, and Creating Media* (New York: Peter Lang, 2007), p. 8.

31 Farrimond, *The Contemporary Femme Fatale*, p. 97.
32 For Camille Paglia, the brutality of the scene is "in keeping with the theme" of the film. Stevie Simkin comments that "Paglia *is* prepared to frame the scene [of Nick forcing sex on Beth from behind] as a rape, but suggests that to complain about the film's representation of a date rape is simple-minded, over-sensitive and overly politically correct" (Stevie Simkin, *Basic Instinct* (Basingstoke: Palgrave Macmillan, 2013), p. 63). The postfeminist scholar Camille Paglia argues: "'Rape culture' is a ridiculous term—mere gassy propaganda, too rankly bloated to critique. Anyone who sees sex so simplistically has very little sense of world history, anthropology, or basic psychology. I feel very sorry for women who have been seduced by this hyper-politicized, victim-centered rhetoric, because in clinging to such superficial, inflammatory phrases, they have renounced their own power and agency" (Camille Paglia, *Free Women, Free Men: Sex, Gender, Feminism* (New York: Pantheon, 2017), p. 273).
33 Linda Ruth Williams, *The Erotic Thriller in Contemporary Cinema* (Bloomington and Indianapolis: Indiana University Press, 2005), p. 386.
34 Sarah Projansky, *Watching Rape: Film and Television in Postfeminist Culture* (New York and London: New York University Press, 2001), p. 97.
35 Barbara Creed, "Horror and the monstrous-feminine," in Mark Jancovich (ed.), *Horror, the Film Reader* (London: Routledge, 2001), p. 67.
36 Ibid., p. 6.
37 B. Ruby Rich, *New Queer Cinema: The Director's Cut* (Durham and London: Duke University Press, 2013), p. 113.
38 Straayer, "*Femme fatale*," p. 160.
39 Ibid., pp. 154–55.
40 Sylvia Harvey, "Woman's place: The absent family of film noir," in Kaplan (ed.), *Women in Film Noir*, expanded edition (London: British Film Institute, 2001), pp. 35–68.

Filmography

Basic Instinct, directed by Paul Verhoeven, produced by Alan Marshall, written by Joe Eszterhas, with Michael Douglas, Sharon Stone, George Dzundza, Jeanne Tripplehorn, music by Jerry Goldsmith, cinematography by Jan de Bont, edited by Frank J. Urioste, Carolco/Le Studio Canal+, 1992. DVD Studiocanal, 2000.

Body of Evidence, directed by Uli Edel, produced by Dino De Laurentiis, written by Brad Mirman, performances by Madonna, Willem Dafoe, Joe Mantegna, Anne Archer, Julianne Moore, Jürgen Prochnow, music by Graeme Revell, cinematography by Douglas Milsome, edited by Thom Noble, Dino De Laurentiis Communications, 1993.

Bound, directed by The Wachowskis, produced by Stuart Boros and Andrew Lazar, written by The Wachowskis, performances by Jennifer Tilly, Gina Gershon, Joe Pantoliano, John Ryan, music by Don Davis, cinematography by Bill Pope, edited by Zach Staenberg, Dino De Laurentiis Company/Spelling Group, 1996. UGC DVD 2007.

The Last Seduction, directed by John Dahl, produced by Jonathan Shestack, written by Steve Barancik, performances by Linda Fiorentino, Peter Berg, Bill Pullman, music by Joseph Vitarelli, cinematography by Jeff Jur, edited by Eric L. Beason, ITC Entertainment, 1994.

2

The African *Femme Fatale*

Reappropriation of a Mythical Figure in *White Men Are Cracking Up* (Ngozi Onwurah, 1994)

Emilie Herbert

The *femme fatale* is certainly one of the most captivating figures in film history and is generally racially coded as Western and white;[1] the black *femme fatale* is largely absent from cultural production. Inspired by her African heritage and an early career as an "exotic" model in the fashion industry,[2] British-Nigerian filmmaker Ngozi Onwurah creates her own version of the African *femme fatale* in *White Men Are Cracking Up*,[3] through the character of a beautiful and mysterious black woman named Maisie Blue. By reappropriating the figure of the *femme fatale*, the filmmaker brings two cultures together—Western and African—and questions the power of stereotypes. The short film experiments with the film-noir genre in order to reflect on the fetishization of black female bodies in contemporary Britain and echoes black feminist criticism on the representations of black women within postcolonial society.[4] Often portrayed as erotic and exotic figures, passive victims, or bad mothers within mainstream media, black women frequently end up being the "object, not the subject of [their] story."[5]

Although attacked by Paul Gilroy for its "vicious antifeminism,"[6] I argue that Onwurah's work is, on the contrary, very much informed by feminist theory. The filmmaker readily admits that she has a "different concept and agenda for film-making"[7] and draws attention to the fact that her films feature strong female characters and "Black women with guns."[8] *White Men Are Cracking Up* follows the investigation of a morose white detective named Margrave, who suspects a black *femme fatale* of being the murderer of important members of the British ruling class. In the opening scene [0:12–3:48], we witness the bloody encounter between an old white British colonialist and Maisie Blue, who performs a "tribal" dance that seems to sexually tantalize him, before driving him to suicide. The detective watches helplessly as one man after another calls upon the venomous Maisie Blue, until he himself falls for her charms and decides to end his life. Here, sexuality and violence—traditionally male-dominated territories—actually turn out to be empowering and liberating tools for the *femme fatale*, described by the detective as a "black angel" who "eases [men] into the next world" [3:30]. If the status of the 1940s Hollywood *femme fatale* as a feminist icon has been contested by second-wave feminists such as Mary Ann Doane,[9] her 1990s alter ego has recently received more lenient readings,[10] associating her with postfeminist ideas of female empowerment and agency. I will examine how, with *White Men Are Cracking Up*, Onwurah interrogates the archetype of the black *femme fatale* in the postfeminist era, using the noir genre as an aesthetic framework to portray Maisie Blue's revenge against white men.

The Black *Femme Fatale* as a (Post)feminist Icon?

As the *femme fatale* is mainly a male creation and because film noir and neo-noir are perceived as a predominantly male-centered genre,[11] most analyses of the archetype have focused on gender rather than other aspects of identity politics such as race.[12] Yet while she embodies "the glamour and the horror of otherness,"[13] the non-Caucasian—and particularly black—*femme fatale* is not depicted in similar ways as her white counterpart, as "the 'to-be-looked-at-ness' embodied in erotic pleasure functions differently with regard to the racial dynamics of the gaze."[14] In American cinema, the portrayal of glamorous and venomous black heroines has been a key feature of blaxploitation.[15] The eponymous heroines of *Cleopatra Jones* (Jack Starrett, 1973) and *Foxy Brown* (Jack Hill, 1974) can, indeed, be associated with the figure of the *femme fatale*. Characterized by her "independence, toughness, violence and intelligence,"[16] the blaxploitation heroine uses "her beauty to get what she wants or to get closer to what she is looking for."[17] But if the traditional *femme fatale* is said to embody male anxieties about shifting gender roles,[18] the "Bad Black Woman"[19] of blaxploitation reflects both second-wave feminism and the political heritage of the Civil Rights movement that took shape within 1970s American society.[20] In Brazilian films such as *Xica da Silva* (Carlos Diegues, 1976), the black *femme fatale* expresses "colonial anxieties as she is presented as a threat that is not easy to control."[21] Like the blaxploitation heroine, who is presented as an erotic fantasy who fuels white male desire, the otherness and exoticism of the Brazilian *femme fatale* in *Xica da Silva* are shown to be irresistible for the European male colonizer.

Through traditionally masculine attributes (ambition, independence, and sexual appetite), these black heroines challenge prescribed gender and social roles, which often constrain women into passivity and subservience to men. However, by disrupting power relations that have historically resulted in the double oppression of black women because of their gender and their racial identity, they can be perceived as emblems of both a feminist and an antiracist agenda. And although their portrayal has been accused of being often stereotypical,[22] these black heroines broaden common understandings of *what* defines a feminist fictional character. Film scholar Julie Grossman pointedly reminds us that "a female character may not in herself be feminist, but her story may be."[23] Xica da Silva, Cleopatra Jones, and Foxy Brown are partly represented through an objectifying perspective, yet these black heroines paradoxically embody a feminist ideal of female empowerment and agency. Patricia Hilliard-Nunn exemplifies this seeming contradiction with the case of Robin Given's character in the blaxploitation-inspired film *A Rage in Harlem* (Bill Duke, 1991): although "the first image viewers get of Givens's character is of her rear end as she struts through a train station,"[24] Hilliard-Nunn recognizes that the heroine was also "socially significant because she was a woman in control and simply used her body to get what she wanted."[25]

This paradox is, in fact, at the core of postfeminist thought, which, according to British cultural theorist Angela McRobbie, works in a process of "double entanglement,"[26] disavowing *and* celebrating feminism at the same time. In several respects, Maisie Blue could be described as a postfeminist emblem, as she certainly displays a sense of independence, agency, and sexual freedom. Furthermore, through her use of wigs, costumes, jewelry—she wears no less than six different outfits in the film (Figure 2.1)—and long ritualized bubble baths, Maisie Blue demonstrates a preoccupation with her body, involving self-celebration, maintenance, and surveillance, which British cultural theorist Rosalind Gill also identifies as a feature of postfeminism.[27] Last but not least, her sexual objectification for the white male gaze through her exotic/erotic dances is actually reclaimed as a form of liberation, as she seems to be financially and emotionally independent from anyone and most importantly because men *need* her—and not the contrary.

According to sociologist Jess Butler, "women of color are largely excluded from post-feminist discourses and representations; or, to put it another way, the idealized post-feminist subject is a white, Western, heterosexual woman."[28] Several black feminists, such as Patricia Hill Collins and bell hooks, have, indeed, asserted that postfeminism has actually nothing to do with black women.[29] A few contemporary black female popular icons have nonetheless been situated within the context of postfeminism.[30] Pop stars Nicki Minaj and Beyonce, or athletes Venus and Serena Williams, have openly discussed

Figure 2.1 *White Men Are Cracking Up* (BBC, Onwurah, 1994): the post-womanist Maisie Blue with wig and jewelry.

the need for gender equality, "girl power,"[31] and the celebration of black womanhood; they are living proof that black (in their case, North-American) women can have a thriving professional career, financial independence, sexual freedom, and a family life. However, as Kimberley Springer has argued, this postfeminist discourse of "having it all" plays out in racially distinct ways: juggling between a career and a family has been a reality for black and working-class women long before feminist struggles opened up the middle-class workplace.[32] And if some of these women have distanced themselves from the term feminism[33] (a common attribute of postfeminism), I wish to argue that, for black women, this ambiguous discourse is indicative of the historical distrust they have had toward dominant white feminism. Black feminists have consistently pointed at what Adrienne Rich names the "white solipsism"[34] of dominant feminism—or the belief that white women's experiences are universal and, therefore, enable them to speak in the name of *all* women. For the late 1970s British Organisation of Women of Asian and African Descent (OWAAD), feminism was associated not only with whiteness but also with a clear anti-men discourse: "We're not feminists—we reject that label because we feel that it represents a white ideology. In our culture the term is associated with an ideology and practice which is anti-men. Our group is not anti-men at all."[35] Various terms have been suggested over the years to replace the word feminism; *Stiwanism* and *Misovirism* have been used by Nigerian feminists,[36] while in the United States, Freida High W. Tesfagiorgis has used the word *Afrofemcentrism*,[37] and perhaps more successfully, Alice Walker has introduced the term *Womanism*.[38] For the African American author and poet who coined the term in 1983, a womanist is "a black feminist

or feminist of color"[39] who is "responsible. In charge. Serious,"[40] "a woman
who loves other women, sexually and/or nonsexually"[41] and "is to feminist as
purple is to lavender."[42] Through this concept, Walker takes a critical stance
toward white feminist scholars and holds mainstream feminism accountable
for its historical erasure of the experiences of black women. This perspective
on womanism has further been enriched by scholars Chikwenye Okonjo
Ogunyemi's and Clenora Hudson-Weem's coining the terms African and
Africana womanism, and whose writings ground womanism within the
context of African culture and history.[43] Ngozi Onwurah herself stated in
a recent interview that she, in fact, identified more as a womanist than as
a feminist,[44] adding that "feminism is a movement built for and by middle
class white women. [. . .] I find the history of the feminist movement very
dishonourable in terms of their positioning around issues to do with race."[45]

If the trivialization of the term "post-womanism" might threaten to erase the
work of previous generations of womanists,[46] as conceptualized by Chikwenye
Okonjo Ogunyemi, post-womanism turns out to be a cultural tool that can help
to better understand contemporary representations of black womanhood. In
a critical reading of Bessie Head's novel *Maru* (1971), Ogunyemi once again
opposes the considerations of white, middle-class, Western postfeminism to
those of African post-womanism.[47] She praises black women writers' use of
magical realism as a way to transcend the boundaries of gender and race but also
class. For her, the fictional post-womanist heroine is an "astute woman,"[48] who
seduces men through both physical and intellectual exchange, and actively works
to shatter patriarchy. Through *Maru*, Ogunyemi analyzes the description of the
West African practice of "juju" witchcraft as part of a post-womanist discourse.
As an ambiguous practice "where women are both insignificant yet powerful
witches,"[49] African *jujuism* enables *Maru's* main character to "mesmerize the
rulers, gain access to them, and [. . .] surreptitiously and magically revolutionize
the kingdom."[50] In *White Men Are Cracking Up*, Maisie Blue also creates,
through her mysterious rituals, an intimate relationship with white men whose
colonial "kingdom" comes to an end with her. By rejecting the "white solipsism"
of dominant feminism and by presenting her character as a powerful sorceress,
White Men Are Cracking Up is grounded in a post-womanist discourse that
redefines its *femme fatale* through her blackness and African cultural heritage.

Maisie Blue as a Fantasy Figure

Through the character of the African *femme fatale*, Onwurah questions the
representation and "consumption" of black female bodies in Western society.
Maisie Blue's performance certainly reminds us of a young Josephine Baker's

exotic dancing in a banana skirt in the 1920s. Even though Baker was born in the United States, she was always thought of as African and was always staged as a "savage." She lamented: "People think I come from the jungle. The primitive instinct, isn't it? The madness of the flesh, the tumult of the senses, the delirious animality. . . . What people didn't write! White imagination is quite something when it comes to Black people."⁵¹ Maisie's dance confirms that the white men's idea of black womanhood is, in effect, a construct; her performance displaces the conventions of racial and gender hegemony in the same way that drags' performances are, for Judith Butler, "subversive to the extent that [they] reflect on the imitative structure by which hegemonic gender is itself produced."⁵² Maisie's Africanness, as she displays it in front of Carl and other men, is nothing but an illusion: this is further emphasized at the end of the film when she slowly removes a wig of afro hair from her head [17:38–18:06]. This type of hairdo, synonym of "authentic Black womanhood,"⁵³ appears as a mere accessory in her performance of blackness. Onwurah's short film *And Still I Rise* (1992) already criticized this fetishization of the black female body by introducing the film with these words: "Sultry, savage, dirty, hard, exotic, erotic. . . . Many people have trouble seeing Black women as they are because of an eagerness to impose an identity on us." Incidentally, the woman who delivers this monologue in *And Still I Rise* and Maisie Blue look very much alike; wearing a similar *simbi* hairstyle (where hair is curled up with the help of threads), traditional jewelry, and attire, they embody this constructed image of black womanhood. African women have been, as British sociologist Shirley Tate reminds us, historically described as "promiscuous, able to cope with the pain of childbirth, bestial, savages, anti-motherhood, naked, without shame,"⁵⁴ assumptions that are still disseminated in more current representations of black women—one well-known example of such a portrayal is French photographer Jean-Paul Goude's famous 1982 photograph of Grace Jones locked up in a cage with raw meat at her feet, in front of a white audience warned to "not feed the animal." In a way, Maisie Blue shares Grace Jones's desire to "scare as well as attract, to be a source of endless fascination."⁵⁵ From the first line of the film [0:12–0:48], Maisie is reduced to a mere fetish when Carl, a British settler in former Rhodesia, admits that, as a little boy, he was fascinated by Maisie Blue, her skin, and how "the light caught [her] flesh," even though "it was naughty to watch." Carl's living room, decorated with African artifacts, panther and zebra pelts, and gazelle heads, is a re-creation of the "porno-tropics"⁵⁶ associated with the African colonies: "a fantastic magic lantern of the mind onto which Europe projected its forbidden sexual desires and fears."⁵⁷

Maisie Blue's revenge can be seen as confronting the imperial nostalgia instilled in the collective consciousness, a salient feature of 1990s Britain.⁵⁸

The character operates as a "postcolonial ghost,"⁵⁹ reminding us that the colonial past is neither over nor done but lives on in the postcolonial present. Physical contact is rarely shown between Maisie Blue and her victims, emphasizing her ghostly presence and making it more difficult for the detective to prove her involvement in the murders: "Just like an angel, she leaves nothing behind: no prints, nothing" [3:49–4:15]. When Carl reminds Maisie Blue that he used to secretly watch her bathing as a child (even though he is actually much older than her), he shows how "to be haunted by a ghost is to be haunted by the past. Ghosts can, in some cases, manifest the weight of the past, disturbing the complacency of the present in the unsettling manner of a dark or guilty secret: a shameful past."⁶⁰ If Maisie Blue is not a ghost, she certainly belongs to the sphere of magic and mystery.

The film portrays the African *femme fatale* as a possible embodiment of the Nigerian goddess "Mami Wata," a figure of female empowerment who personifies "unattainable, exquisite beauty, vanity, jealousy, sexuality, romantic not maternal love."⁶¹ Celebrated across Africa and the African diaspora, she is more than a divinity and manifests important aspects of womanhood from precolonial African culture, when women were autonomous subjects and held high positions in society.⁶² The description of Mami Wata in African literature and art as a figure of female empowerment helps reshape negative assumptions about black womanhood. The goddess, who celebrates afrocentric codes of beauty, can be seen as an African version of the *femme fatale*, "instrumentalizing masculine discourses through her seduction of men and their subsequent devotion to her."⁶³ She is often represented surrounded by various objects and artifacts associated with self-care ("cosmetics and products for female grooming"⁶⁴) and beauty ("watches, sunglasses, etc."⁶⁵). The mirror is also an object commonly found in Mami Wata's iconography.⁶⁶ *White Men Are Cracking Up*'s main character shares with the goddess this interest for fashion accessories (hats, jewelry, and clothes that she displays in an open wardrobe), refined products (perfume bottles and bubble baths), and the mirror in which she admires herself [5:18–5:52].

Witch, phantom, angel, or goddess, Maisie Blue has an intangible character, a fact that is established from the outset, as the camera pans over an assemblage of newspaper clippings with one headline standing out: "The getaway girl" [3:49–4:15]. Her skills at escaping authorities will later be demonstrated in a car chase scene, as the detective loses track of the *femme fatale* while she fiercely looks back through the rear window [7:45–8:33]. Yet when her ghostly presence is invoked, Maisie Blue never seems too difficult to reach. She does not run away when the detective later confronts her as she exits one of her client's house. Wrapped in a long shawl, which evokes the white sheet of traditional ghost imagery, she quietly answers his questions before escaping again and blending into the night [11:43–12:55].

The film thematically borrows from two forms of filmmaking traditions: a Western genre (film noir) and Nollywood.[67] The crime drama, in which the supernatural plays a decisive role, is, indeed, a dominant component of Nollywood cinema, with its obsession with "the occult world (juju, black magic, sorcery, ritual murder, witchcraft etc . . .)."[68] Nollywood audiences seem fond of these types of stories and the mysterious female figures they are usually associated with. Sharon Stone even contended that her film *Basic Instinct* had become so popular in Southern Nigeria that her name could easily serve as shorthand for *femme fatale*.[69] It is common that women in Nollywood narratives use witchcraft in order to build a relationship with the men they desire; witchcraft is, therefore, highly gendered, and Mami Wata appears in various guises in Nollywood films.[70] As a female filmmaker, Onwurah subverts the traditional patriarchy at the heart of both noir and Nollywood, and shows Maisie Blue's use of sorcery as the symbol of a greater historical and political critique. It is through her mystical rituals that Maisie Blue can access one of the most intimate moments in these men's lives: their deaths. The "monstrous intimacies"[71] that usually characterized the relationships between white men and black women during the colonial era, and which involved "violence and forced submission in interpersonal spheres usually or ideally marked by affection, romance, or warmth,"[72] are, here, inverted, as Maisie Blue is the one who exercises violence on her clients through her macabre dance ritual. As an African *femme fatale* and a resurgence of the goddess Mami Wata, Maisie Blue reclaims her body and sexuality from the white male's control and overturns the dynamic between colonizer and colonized.

The Aesthetics of Revenge

The main characteristics of the noir genre are present in *White Men Are Cracking Up*: the figure of the private detective, the element of criminality, and various identifiable characteristics such as the use of strange camera angles, night-time settings, urban landscapes, and, of course, the archetype of the *femme fatale*.[73] The film alludes to film noir, combining "quotations, the memorialization of past genres, the reworking of past genres, *homages*, and the recreation of 'classic' scenes, shots, plot motifs, lines of dialogue, themes, gesture, and so forth from film history."[74] It plays with the color coding and uses neutral tones (whites, blacks, grays, browns) commonly found in neo-noir films,[75] as well as motifs like smoke—cigarette smoke and clouds of dust floating in Margrave's office [11:03–11:43], or fog slowly raising behind him and Maisie during their last encounter on a bridge [14:05–17:37]. The smoke, in conjunction with the dramatic musical score, creates an aura of mystery and secrecy, a (literally and metaphorically) dense atmosphere where death never seems too far away. In fact, the filmmaker disseminates other elements that symbolize and prefigure death: the presence of a man with a placard announcing the end of the world outside the police station [4:48–5:18], items of a typical *nature morte* on Carl's living-room table (an open melon, an empty glass, and the knife with which he will kill himself) [2:46–3:03], or the blaring ambulance that can be seen driving in the distance in the bridge scene [14:30–14:35]. Neo-noir films tend to emphasize early conventions of film noir through psychologically disturbed characters. This is clearly the case of the detective in *White Men Are Cracking Up*, with his family problems, his disappointment in his job as a "copper," and his obvious suicidal tendencies. Margrave portrays the typical antihero, the perfect neo-noir "loser," who seeks to conform to an idealized view of social success and recognition. When the detective summarizes his life, he complains: "What have we got now? Nothing. No homes, no kids, no wives, no futures, nothing. . . . Except Maisie Blue" [9:52–11:02]. In the film, as in the noir genre in general, this "moral, existential darkness"[76] is aesthetically symbolized through stark lighting and jarring angles, which evoke the character's "existential angst."[77] Margrave sees his confrontation with Maisie Blue as a "private little game," which soon "will be over. Winner takes all" [4:20–4:47]. Unsurprisingly, at the end of the film, Maisie Blue turns out to be the "winner." The black woman who kills remains unpunished, and in the last scene of the film [17:38–18:42], the message left by another desperate man on her answering machine makes us understand that the African *femme fatale*'s revenge is not over yet.

The avenging heroine is a popular character of the neo-noir film;[78] not only does the neo-*femme fatale* seek revenge, but she escapes forms of punishment that often awaited her 1940s counterpart. In *White Men Are Cracking Up*, the African *femme fatale*'s revenge is calmly calculated, organized, and professional. Onwurah personalizes the female revenge thread of neo-noir by engaging in a larger debate about postcolonial legacy. The film echoes Aimé Césaire's equation of "colonization = 'thingification,'"[79] the dehumanization of the colonized who actually becomes an object rather than a subject. In the film's final scenes, Maisie Blue's jaded attitude and "sexy" self-control eventually reveal a robotic, one-dimensional character. When the detective finally confronts her and arrests her on suspicion of murder, she is quiet and does not display any emotions. Torn between his duty and his irrepressible attraction for Maisie, the detective loses his temper: "Well don't you feel anything?!" "No," she answers, before adding with a touch of impatience: "Are you ready now?" [14:35–16:46]. The film repositions Maisie Blue as a killing machine, rather than as a friend or lover. In a low-angle shot, her lone silhouette is shown melting into an industrial landscape, as she watches the detective leave the scene. Here, Maisie Blue does not perform her usual tribal dance, but in her trench coat and sophisticated makeup, she reflects some of the detective's own fantasies: while she pretends that this is what she "really looks like," her interlocutor knows that it simply isn't true.

Maisie Blue is, until the very end, an indecipherable figure, thus embodying the "oneiric, strange, erotic, ambivalent, and cruel"[80] *femme fatale* to perfection. In the film, her elusiveness is symbolized by a constant barrier between Maisie and the voyeur (whether the male protagonist or the audience): she's always hidden behind a curtain, a veil, a window, inside a heavy fog, or behind her answering machine. Clothes, wigs, and makeup are also used as screens to hide her real nature; it is only in the very last shot that she appears as she really is, which is confirmed by the fact that the viewer is now admitted inside the veil that surrounds her bathtub. In an analysis of Onwurah's two earlier films (*The Body Beautiful* and *Coffee Colored Children*), Gwendolyn Audrey Foster argues that "the veil is dialogized as a signifier of the shroud that silences Black women's sexuality, and yet it can also represent a liberating force, a reclamation of Black female space, the female gaze, the scars of the body, and a new skin of self-ownership."[81] In *White Men Are Cracking Up*, it is in the bathwater, Mami Wata's natural element and an indication of "the suspect's overwhelming desire to come clean" according to the male detective, that Maisie Blue's identity is "unveiled." In the film's final shot [18:25–18:42], we discover a large clay statue behind Maisie's bathtub (Figure 2.2). Naked, with its head high and fist closed as a sign of

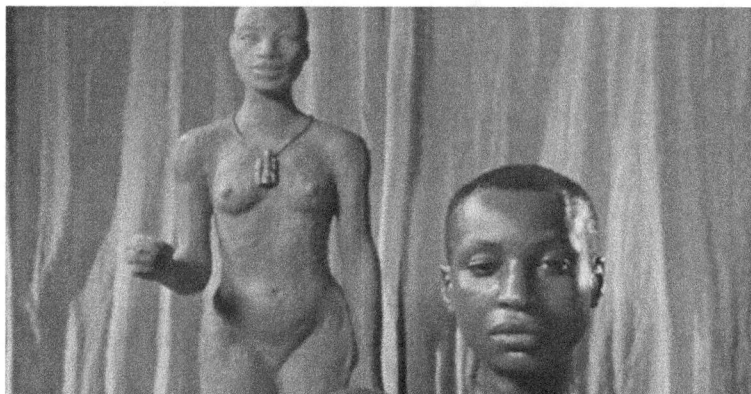

Figure 2.2 *White Men Are Cracking Up* (BBC, Onwurah, 1994): Maise Blue next to a ritual figurine representing precolonial black womanhood.

assertiveness, it stands behind Maisie Blue's face, highlighting their uncanny resemblance. It is only in this very last scene that the viewer finally sees the African *femme fatale* not performing: the figurine displays a precolonial representation of black womanhood associated with strength and power. Bearing in mind that in Africa, women are known to have dominated the production of pottery,[82] the nudity of the figurine can be interpreted as a figure of empowerment produced by a female hand rather than as a synonym of eroticism destined for the male gaze. This final image shows how, as a black female filmmaker, Onwurah reclaims the figure of the *femme fatale*, subverting hegemonic dynamics of the white male cinematic gaze.

Conclusion

White Men Are Cracking Up brings different cultural trends together: the aesthetic codes of noir and the magical realism of the post-womanist narrative collide with the occult world of Nollywood cinema. Through her mastery of the vocabulary and techniques of the film noir, Onwurah offers a convincing tribute to the genre. But her film is more than a simple homage: it subverts the typically male-run narratives of film noir in order to reappropriate the mythical figure of the *femme fatale* and highlight often minimized or overlooked ideas regarding the exoticization of the black female body. In keeping with the rest of her filmography, Onwurah takes control of the way black women like herself are represented. Just like the Western white *femme fatale* that we are more accustomed to, the African *femme fatale* of *White Men Are Cracking Up* is mysterious, unattainable, and erotic. She shares common features with postfeminist heroines: she is independent, in control of her sexuality, and is obsessed with her body and its adornment. However, the film interrogates the possibilities for black women to be situated within the context of a postfeminist culture that produces women of color's bodies in different ways than those of white women. black women have long taken a critical stance toward the dominance of white feminism. As a theoretical framework rooted in the experiences of black women, womanist thought seeks to counter dominant feminism's "white solipsism" and challenge common assumptions about black womanhood. Because the black female body—especially within the colonial context recalled in the film through Maisie Blue's exotic "tribal" dances—has historically been taken as a symbol of deviant sexuality and savage behaviors, the African *femme fatale* embodies, in Onwurah's short film, a critique of an equally racist and patriarchal system of representations. The black woman who kills thus reclaims her body as a site of contestation and resistance to hegemonic discourses on gender and race.

As a post-womanist figure, she uses her intellect as much as her body to obtain what she desires. Tapping into her African roots, she makes use of traditional witchcraft and magic to effect political changes. *White Men Are Cracking Up* calls upon African culture and history in various ways: the film borrows some of Nollywood's most popular themes (black magic, the ritual murders, the alluring black witch), and Maisie Blue recalls Mami Wata, the powerful and irresistibly beautiful African goddess. Black angel, postcolonial ghost, African Goddess, or mere product of the white imagination, Maisie Blue's intangibility evokes the enigmatic nature of the *femme fatale*, but she also demonstrates the impossibility to exorcise the colonial past and its current ramifications. She is a revenging heroine of a new kind, one who overturns century-old power relations. White men are cracking up, but the black woman carries on with her work, impassive, uncompromising, and unstoppable.

Notes

1 Katherine Farrimond, *The Contemporary Femme Fatale: Gender, Genre and American Cinema* (London and New York: Routledge, 2018).
2 A work experience she criticized in her short film *The Body Beautiful* (1991).
3 Ngozi Onwurah's White Men Are Cracking Up was produced by Leda Serene Films—a production company founded by fellow Black British female director Frances-Anne Solomon—and sponsored by the BBC as well as the BFI. The film was part of a television program called Siren Spirit, featuring four short dramas directed by women of color (Ngozi Onwurah, Frances-Anne Solomon, Pratibha Parmar and Dani Williamson). It was released on BBC2 on December 1994.
4 See the work of black British feminists such as Beverley Bryan, Stella Dadzie, and Suzanne Scafe; Heidi S. Mirza; Denise Noble; Sheila Sandapen; Julia Sudbury; Shirley Tate and Lola Young and the work of African American feminists such as Jacqueline Bobo; Maxine Craig; Patricia Hill Collins; bell hooks; Gloria Hull, Patricia Bell-Scott, and Barbara Smith; Barbara Thompson or Michele Wallace, among others.
5 Heidi S. Mirza (ed.), *Black British Feminism: A Reader* (London and New York: Routledge, 1997), p. 6.
6 Paul Gilroy, "Unwelcome," *Sight and Sound*, 5/2 (1995), pp. 18–19. Gilroy was here specifically referring to Onwurah's first long-feature film *Welcome II The Terrordome* (1995).
7 Gwendolyn A. Foster, *Women Filmmakers of the African & Asian Diaspora: Decolonizing the Gaze, Locating Subjectivity* (Carbondale, Edwardsville: Southern Illinois University Press, 1997), p. 38.
8 Ibid.

9   Mary Ann Doane, *Femmes Fatales: Feminism, Film Theory, Psychoanalysis*
     (London and New York: Routledge, 1991).
10 See Farrimond, *The Contemporary Femme Fatale*; Helen Hanson and
     Catherine O'Rawe, *The Femme Fatale: Images, Histories, Contexts* (London and
     New York: Palgrave Macmillan, 2010); Maysaa Jaber, *Criminal Femmes Fatales
     in American Hardboiled Crime Fiction* (London and New York: Palgrave
     Macmillan, 2016); Samantha Lindop, *Postfeminism and the Fatale Figure in
     Neo-Noir Cinema* (London and New York: Palgrave Macmillan, 2015).
11 Hanson and O'Rawe, *The Femme Fatale*.
12 Antonio Da Silva, *The "Femme" Fatale in Brazilian Cinema: Challenging
     Hollywood Norms* (London and New York: Palgrave Macmillan, 2014).
13 Ibid., p. 31.
14 Janell Hobson, "Viewing in the dark: Toward a black feminist approach to
     film," *Women's Studies Quarterly*, 30/1/2 (2002), pp. 45–59.
15 The blaxploitation genre emerged in the United States in the early 1970s
     and refers to black action films originally aimed at an African American
     audience. The main characteristics of blaxploitation films are the use of
     primarily black casts and funk and soul music in the soundtrack, the
     presence of violence, sex, and drug trade in the narratives and glamorous
     black action heroines.
16 Hilary Neroni, *The Violent Woman: Femininity, Narrative, and Violence in
     Contemporary American Cinema* (New York: State University of New York
     Press, 2005), p. 29.
17 Ibid.
18 Lindop, *Postfeminism and the Fatale Figure*; Helen Hanson, *Hollywood
     Heroines: Women in Film Noir and the Female Gothic Film* (London and
     New York: I.B. Tauris, 2007).
19 Cédric Robinson, "Blaxploitation and the misrepresentation of liberation,"
     Race and Class, 40/1 (1998), pp. 1–12.
20 Neroni, *The Violent Woman*.
21 Da Silva, *The "Femme" Fatale in Brazilian Cinema*, p. 32.
22 Yvonne Sims, *Women of Blaxploitation: How the Black Action Film Heroine
     Changed American Popular Culture* (Jefferson and London: McFarland &
     Company, Inc., 2012).
23 Julie Grossman, *Rethinking the Femme Fatale in Film Noir* (London and
     New York: Palgrave Macmillan, 2009), p. 6.
24 Patricia Hilliard-Nunn, "Representing African American Women in
     Hollywood movies: An African-conscious analysis," in J. Hamlet (ed.),
     Afrocentric Visions: Studies in Culture and Communication (London:
     McFarland & Company, Inc., 1998), p. 187.
25 Ibid.
26 Angela McRobbie, *The Aftermath of Feminism: Gender, Culture and Social
     Change* (London: Sage, 2009), p. 12.
27 Rosalind Gill, "Postfeminist media culture: Elements of a sensibility,"
     European Journal of Cultural Studies, 10/2 (2005), pp. 147–66.

28 Jess Butler, "For white girls only? Postfeminism and the politics of inclusion," *Feminist Formations*, 25/1 (2013), pp. 35–58.

29 Dayna Chatman, "Pregnancy, then it's 'back to business,'" *Feminist Media Studies*, 15/6 (2015), pp. 926–41.

30 See Laura Martinez-Jimenez, Lina Glavez-Munoz and Angela Solano-Caballero, "Neoliberalism goes pop and purple: Postfeminist empowerment from Beyoncé to Mad Max," *Journal of Popular Culture*, 51/2 (2018), pp. 399–420; Kristin Rodier and Michelle Meagher, "In her own time: Rihanna, post-feminism, and domestic violence," *Women: A Cultural Review*, 25/2 (2014), pp. 176–93; Kim Toffoletti, Holly Thorpe, and Jessica Francombe-Webb (eds.), *New Sporting Femininities: Embodied Politics in Postfeminist Times* (London and New York: Palgrave Macmillan, 2018).

31 Butler, "For white girls only?" pp. 35–58.

32 Kimberley Springer, "Divas, evil black bitches, and bitter black women: African American women in postfeminist and post-civil-rights popular culture," in Y. Tasker and D. Negra (eds.), *Interrogating Postfeminism: Gender and the Politics of Popular Culture* (Durham and London: Duke University Press, 2007).

33 Butler, "For white girls only?" pp. 35–58; Olivia Petter, "Venus Williams says she doesn't identify as a feminist 'I don't like labels,'" *The Independent*, May 10, 2018. Available at www.independent.co.uk/life-style/venus-williams-fe minist-labels-identify-elle-uk-interview-us-tennis-player-a8344411.html (accessed September 12, 2018).

34 Adrienne Rich, "'Disloyal to civilization': feminism, racism, and gynephobia," *Chrysalis*, 7/9 (1979) pp. 9–27.

35 Beverley Bryan, Stella Dadzie, and Suzanne Scafe, *The Heart of the Race: Black Women's Lives in Britain* (London: Virago Press Ltd, 1985), p. 173.

36 Béatrice Gallimore Rangira, "Écriture féministe ? Écriture féminine?: les écrivaines francophones de l'Afrique subsaharienne face au regard du lecteur/critique," *Études françaises*, 37/2 (2001), pp. 79–98.

37 Freida High W. Tesfagiorgis, "Afrofemcentrism, Black women artists, Black female perspective," *Sage: A Scholarly Journal on Black Women*, 4/1 (1987), pp. 25–29.

38 Alice Walker, *In Search of Our Mothers' Gardens, Womanist Prose* (London: Phoenix, 2011 [1984]).

39 Ibid., p. 1.

40 Ibid.

41 Ibid.

42 Ibid.

43 Monica Coleman, *Ain't I a Womanist Too? Third Wave Womanist Religious Thought* (Minneapolis: Fortress Press, 2013).

44 Dan Haze, "Interview with Ngozi Onwurah," *Don't Panic*, January 25, 2018. Available at www.dontpaniconline.com/magazine/arts/interview-with-ng ozi-onwurah (Accessed September 12, 2018).

45 Ibid.

46 Gary Dorrien, *Economy, Difference, Empire: Social Ethics for Social Justice* (New York: Columbia University Press, 2010).

47 Chikwenye Okonjo Ogunyemi, "Tête-à-tête with the chief: Post-womanist discourse in Bessie Head's," in F. Veit-Wild and D. Naguschewski (eds.), *Body, Sexuality, and Gender: Versions and Subversions in African Literatures* (Amsterdam and New York: Rodopi, 2005).

48 Ibid., p. 7.

49 Ibid., p. 10.

50 Ibid., p. 11.

51 Jean-François Staszak, "Performing race and gender: The exoticization of Josephine Baker and Anna May Wong," *Gender, Place & Culture*, 22/5 (2015), pp. 626–43.

52 Judith Butler, *Bodies That Matter: On the Discursive Limits of "Sex"* (London and New York: Routledge, 2014).

53 Shirley Tate, *Black Skins, Black Masks: Hybridity, Dialogism, Performativity* (Farnham: Ashgate Publishing, 2005).

54 Shirley Tate, *Black Women's Bodies and the Nation: Race, Gender and Culture* (London and New York: Palgrave Macmillan, 2015), pp. 1–2.

55 Ibid., p. 35.

56 Ginette Curry, *Toubab La! Literary Representations of Mixed-Race Characters in the African Diaspora* (Newcastle: Cambridge Scholars Publishing, 2007), p. 331.

57 Ibid.

58 Seumas Milne, "Britain: Imperial nostalgia," *Le Monde Diplomatique*, May 2005.

59 Mélanie Joseph-Vilain and Judith Misrahi-Barak, *Postcolonial Ghosts: Fantômes Post-coloniaux* (Montpellier: Presses Universitaires de la Méditerranée, 2009).

60 John Potts, "Rough justice and buried country: Australian ghosts," in Joseph-Vilain and Misrahi-Barak (eds.), *Postcolonial Ghosts: Fantômes Post-coloniaux* (Montpellier: Presses Universitaires de la Méditerranée, 2009), p. 114.

61 Barbara Thompson, *Black Womanhood: Images, Icons, and Ideologies of the African Body* (Seattle: University of Washington Press, 2008), p. 65.

62 Sabine Jell-Bahlsen, "The concept of mammywater in Flora Nwapa's novels," *Research in African Literatures*, 26/2 (1995), pp. 30–41.

63 Madhu Krishnan, "Mami Wata and the occluded feminine in Anglophone Nigerian-Igbo literature," *Research in African Literatures*, 43/1 (2012), pp. 1–18.

64 Chiara Bortolotto, "La Sirène Mami Wata: un cas de réemploi transculturel," *L'Autre*, 10/1 (2009), pp. 37–45.

65 Ibid.

66 Ibid.

67 Nollywood is a fusion of the words Nigeria and Hollywood and is the second-biggest film industry in the world according to a 2009 UNESCO's survey. Nollywood cinema is characterized by its handcrafted output: largely

filmed in video rather than film, projections are organized in informal settings and rarely in film theaters. Lack of proper budget can render the films amateurish and narratively weak, yet Nollywood made it possible for Nigerian filmmakers to tell their own stories and to cultivate a massive audience across Africa.

68 Patrick Ebewo, "The Emerging film industry in Nigeria: Challenges and prospects," *Journal of Film and Video,* 59/3 (2007), pp. 46–57.

69 Amanda Ann Klein and Robert Barton Palmer, *Cycles, Sequels, Spin-offs, Remakes, and Reboots: Multiplicities in Film and Television* (Austin: University of Texas Press, 2016).

70 Jonathan Haynes, *Nollywood: The Creation of Nigerian Film Genres* (Chicago and London: University of Chicago Press, 2016).

71 Paul Taylor, *Black Is Beautiful: A Philosophy of Black Aesthetics* (Malden and Oxford: Wiley Blackwell, 2016), p. 116.

72 Ibid.

73 See Raymond Borde and Etienne Chaumeton, *A Panorama of American Film Noir (1941–1953),* Translated by Paul Hammond (San Francisco: City Lights Books, 2002 [1955]).

74 Noël Carroll, "The Future of allusion: Hollywood and the seventies (and beyond)," *October,* 20 (1982), pp. 51–81.

75 Lindop, *Postfeminism and the Fatale Figure,* p. 10.

76 Delphine Letort, *Du Film Noir au Néo-Noir: Mythes et Stéréotypes de l'Amérique (1941–2008)* (Paris: L'Harmattan, 2010), p. 7. [My translation].

77 Carroll, "The Future of allusion," pp. 51–81.

78 Linda Williams, "A woman scorned: The neo-noir erotic thriller as revenge drama," in M. Bould, K. Glitre, and G. Tuck (eds.), *Neo-Noir* (London and New York: Wallflower Press, 2009).

79 Aimé Césaire, *Discourse on Colonialism,* Translated by Joan Pinkham (New York: Monthly Review Press, 2001), p. 42.

80 Borde and Chaumeton, *A Panorama of American Film Noir,* p. 2.

81 Thompson, *Black Womanhood,* p. 32.

82 Maria Berns, "Art, history, and gender: Women and clay in West Africa," *The African Archaelogical Review,* 11 (1993), pp. 129–48.

Filmography

White Men Are Cracking Up, directed by Ngozi Onwurah, produced by Ingrid Lewis, screenplay by Bonnie Greer, performances by Jon Finch, Theo Omambala, Daniel Thorndike, Tom Geoghegan, Nick Simons, Bernard Lawrence, John Rafferty, Howard Davis, cinematography by Alwin Küchler, Leda Serene Films, 1994.
Available at Distrify (https://distrify.com/videos/beXMSm-white-men-are-cracking-up).

3

Transwoman Who Kills

Hit & Miss (Sky Atlantic, 2012)

Isabelle Schmitt-Pitiot

When on May 22, 2012, British audiences discovered Sky Atlantic's first original drama commission, many, no doubt, found the first shots familiar: an urban setting of jaundiced lights and sharp angular lines, a deserted parking lot at night, a German luxury car, a silent hooded silhouette shooting a man [E1, 0:02–3:35]. In short, all the motifs we are used to seeing in crime films and series. The same can be said of devices such as the alternation between distance and proximity, and the soundtrack, in which the distant hum of the city is broken by diegetic sounds of keys and footsteps on cue with close-ups. The opening images of this new series seem to abide quite faithfully by noir conventions involving cold-blooded, dispassionate, and probably professional murder. However, a first surprise shatters conventional comfort after a moment, when the killer one may have assumed was a man, and a *hit*man based on the title, takes off her hood to reveal very feminine features (Figure 3.1) [E1, 1:10]. After a short, albeit slow-paced anthology of predictable signs, the unpredictable emerges. From then on, the whole opening sequence will juxtapose supposedly feminine and masculine attributes and moves—gun and lipstick, makeup and screwdriver, arabesques and push-ups—before the contradictions culminate in a second revelation: that of the assassin's hermaphrodite body [E1, 2:20]. To counter the slightly low angles of the first shots, the introduction scene closes on vertical high-angle shots that show a womanly figure walking some empty streets among Christmas illuminations and sporting the traditional film-noir trench coat in a very feminine way [E1, 03:37–04:05]. We are thus introduced to Mia, who used to be Ryan, transforming into a woman by shedding her male attributes and killing on contract to make enough money and reach her ideal: a woman's body.

The series' rich formula provides a twisted, some might say quirky, angle to examine the issue of female killers, the protagonist's many contradictions

Figure 3.1 *Hit & Miss* (Sky Atlantic, 2012): Mia, the hooded killer.

throwing into relief how biased our assumptions can be about women, especially when they kill. For Mia qualifies as a valid and, indeed, valuable example of the figure. If some may object that her being born male precludes her inclusion in that category, even before the final operation, Mia's transformation seems completed, if only in terms of her character. The fact that the part is played by an actress whose body is highlighted, in many scenes, by low-cut, clingy dresses and, above all, the character's choice of a name and, in effect, gender, emphasize her definite female identity. The "Miss" of the title clearly confirms that Mia has endeavored to construct herself as a woman, however difficult it might be, even if the negative meaning of the homographic verb qualifies the degree to which she has succeeded. Her decision to transform the body she feels trapped in into a female one, and of killing in order to achieve her goal, specially qualifies her for a study of women who kill in popular television fiction of the postfeminist era. For should postfeminism or going beyond feminism imply something more complex and genuinely new than a mere backlash or reaction to "the excesses of feminism,"[1] the case of a transwoman, that is one who deliberately redefines herself as a woman, who resorts to assassination to earn the necessary money, begs consideration.

Mia as a character embodies issues at the heart of the contemporary redefinitions of gender(s) and addresses these issues on individual as well as collective and artistic levels. As she challenges gender stereotypes through the means used in her construction, such as sexy clothes and makeup on the one hand, and guns and physical violence on the other, her quest may be assimilated to a queer construct, since the association of conventionally gendered attributes and behaviors unsettles these binary assumptions.[2] In order to measure how far Mia succeeds or fails as a feminist or queer heroine, the question that will be addressed in this chapter is that of the possible or impossible balance the show strikes in its characterization of Mia as she attempts to conform to her feminine ideal through such disruptive and supposedly masculine means as murder for money. That is why, after examining some of the incongruities and ambiguities building up the transwoman/killer character, I shall assess the possible evolution and maybe solution of the contradiction or blurring of lines between male and female roles in a criminal context and shall consider whether the series challenges or reinforces gender biases when choosing a transgender killer as its protagonist.

An Extreme Proposal

Mia was a hybrid creature from the start, as British creator Paul Abbott, well-known for such series as *State of Play* (BBC1, 2003), *Shameless* (Channel 4, 2004–13), or more recently *No Offence* (Channel 4, 2015–), had originally worked on two different characters, a transgender protagonist on the one hand and a hit man on the other, to feature in two different television dramas or series. In the DVD bonuses,[3] he explains how he merged the two figures into a transwoman, as he was interested in the character's complexity. A highly professional contract killer, Mia gets involved in the care and later guardianship of four children, including her own son. Abbott chose the improbable "hit" and "miss" formula, as well as the clashing concepts of contract killing and childcare, and he meant for the well-nigh impossible solution of the tensions and paradoxes to give the series its dynamics.

Mia's "impossible body"[4] visually incarnates the contradiction and doubles the impossible premise of a woman working as a professional killer. In the diegesis, be it from her/his own son and the two teenagers her/his deceased lover had from different fathers, from the young man she has a complicated affair with, or from her/his own brother, the spontaneous first reaction to the revelation of her conversion from man into woman or her being, to quote one of the characters, "a chick with a dick," is, the diegesis suggests, one of revulsion. The word "freak" immediately emerges as a reminder of the character's origins. The plot associates her with fairgrounds and the marginal, interloper world implied in Gram Rabbit's song "In the Devil's Playground" (2004) [E3, 00:33].[5] We learn about Mia's origin in the funfair sequence of the last episode where she is recognized, beaten up, and has her hair cut off by her violent brother, who forces her to say: "I'm a real boy" [E6, 07:10–08:13]. To punish her for betraying his worldview, he disfigures her in a savage act reminiscent of the conclusion to Tod Browning's *Freaks* (1932). However, while Browning's freaks punish the "normal" woman who had provoked them and mutilate her in order to turn her into another freak in the show, Mia's brother batters her for not sticking to the gender she was biologically born into. His running a shooting gallery adds yet another parodic twist to the question of who is a freak and who is not, as well as to the question of normality and conformity. When it comes to wielding firearms, Mia the hit person seems much closer to the "real thing" than her brother, a "real" man in his own eyes but a dealer in funfair guns.

Speaking of "real things," and contrary to the characters who never actually see Mia's vestigial penis, we are regularly reminded of it thanks to explicit full-frontal nudity shots, at least once in each episode, lest we should forget the transgender nature of a character played by a woman [E1, 02:20; E2, 11:48; E3, 07:08; E4, 05:29; E5, 11:40; E6, 17:07]. The disclosures appear matter-of-fact rather than provocative, since they occur in banal desexualized contexts, for instance, when she changes clothes or takes a shower. Though the nudity is not ellipticized, the shots do not linger indulgently nor show any furtiveness, embarrassment, or shame on Mia's part. The surprise effect of the first revelation soon wears off. Mia performs her hygiene routine in such a quiet, uninterested way that the viewer comes to consider her penis as an ineffectual appendix that fails to create the shock or revulsion expressed by most characters. In the end, the display of Mia as a hermaphrodite seems to make her impossible body more possible, that is, less freakish or threatening than when her nudity is left to the imagination.

In fact, these glimpses of Mia's hybrid anatomy are given less importance than the scenes in which she performs her duties as an assassin, her gun being far more threatening than her penis. Her boss Eddie, who works for organized crime and manages her contracts, seems to be the only adult character who is not shocked by her transitioning, and seems much more impressed by her skills as a highly professional and cold-blooded killer. Comparing her to a "bloody machine," it is even possible that Mia's employer regards her future operation as a way to transform her into an even more effective bloodletting weapon that looks like a woman but will never bleed like one. In other words, what the series dramatizes as shocking is not so much Mia's having a penis as her wielding a gun, a major disruption not only of stereotypical views of women and women who kill (who often do so out of revenge), but also to the sad fact that transsexual women run a higher risk of being killed by men.[6]

As the plot unfolds, Mia strives to balance her several parts: the assassin, the would-be woman, and the guardian. The last quarter of episode 1, which depicts her second contract, stages the major tensions shaping the character and driving the narrative, taking up and developing the contrasts of the opening

[E1, 30:55–44:20]. Although the narrative is linear, it resorts to brusque time and space ellipses, with no transition shots except for three very long shots of the wild and very open landscape the farm is set in [33:15; 36:11; 40:42]. Like the often low-angle long shots of the farmhouse, these views display very low or very high horizon lines, with characters or objects silhouetted against a landscape that seems on the verge of engulfing them. These long shots offer rare openings on a wider world and introduce outsider characters who risk harming the children, like their vagrant uncle or the owner of the farm. Most scenes cut to the next one despite drastic shifts in space; for example, the first scene of the sequence, which takes place in the village and ends on a long shot of Mia hurrying across the street, is immediately followed by an over-the-shoulder shot of her entering the restaurant backroom where she meets her employer [E1, 31:45]. A straightforward analysis would be that the clash between Mia's two worlds is emphasized by the extreme contrast between the bright sunlight of the street scene and the reddish gloom of Eddie's den, yet the schism also points to the plight of a character lost among conflicting aspirations. When Eddie remarks that the kids have a funny effect on her and asks whether she is sure she wants to keep on doing the assassination contracts, Mia answers, "No, I'm not," but nonetheless does the job four scenes later. Again, the night scene where the electricity of the farmhouse is cut off is immediately followed by the performing of the contract on the next morning, the viewer supplying the implicit causal link [E1, 34:59–35:14].

The abrupt cuts between scenes, in terms of timeline as well as localization, visualize Mia's contradictory setup and rocky evolution toward her new identity. Accordingly, the narration refuses dissolves but relies instead on a disruptive and sometimes unsettling concatenation of some fifteen scenes. The ninth and central scene [E1, 37:18], for instance, shows Mia in the shower and inserts close-ups of her hermaphrodite body, including a swift glimpse of her penis, between scene 8 when the girl Riley finds a wad of banknotes in the kitchen of the farm and realizes the envelope containing the guardianship order has disappeared, and scene 10 in which Mia reads the same order before a mirror. Reconstructing the narrative, we realize that Mia drove back to the farm to leave the money, then back again to her city loft. Though it seems rather illogical, what is essential here is the hurried juxtaposition of interwoven scenes illustrating Mia's difficult transition and contradictory plight. However, some clues work to link the scenes together, such as the farm owner's black dog sniffing between Mia's legs as she stands before a butcher's hanging carcasses in the first scene of the sequence. The dangerous-looking animal could be the twin of her victim's watchdog that Mia neutralizes with a piece of meat in the assassination scene, where the rich fat contract actually resembles the owner of the farm. The sequence of scenes and clues associates jarring contrasts and echoing signs, a system also reproduced in Mia's clothes when a flowing scarlet blouse tops denim shorts.

We have seen how the opening juxtaposes manly and womanly attributes and attitudes once the androgynous killer's costume has been shed. At the beginning, Mia's lifestyle seems quite ordered and almost acceptable despite the disreputable way she makes a living. After all, assassins dressing up as women are not unheard of in fiction, and Mia's transitioning could just be some screenwriter's original idea. However, the penultimate scene of the first episode shows Mia beating up the farm owner and displays the kind of violence usually associated with men, notably the striking image of her women's cowboy boot crushing the bully's hand [E1, 42:23]. This scene encapsulates the paradoxes of a character who tries to redefine herself as a woman by using means usually associated with male figures, then destroys her own construction when resorting to a more spontaneous form of violence as she fights for the children's farm. She goes so far as to force her son Ryan to hit the owner's son, who has been bullying the child. As with the boxing lesson that precedes the owner's arrival [E1, 39:31], Mia's adopting stereotypical male parenting attitudes helps solve some of the issues she and the children are faced with, and the enemy seems defeated. Then the pace slows down and the episode ends with Ryan, who had been sleeping outside ever since his mother's death, accepting to sleep inside again. In the last shot, the camera shows the sleeping boy, then tilts up to Mia, clad in the boy's mother's pink satin robe, looking down with a tender smile on her face. The peaceful moment may trigger some hopes for her metamorphosis into a new, complete being, a parenting figure challenging traditional divides. However, the respite will be short.

Improbable Syntheses

The family whose guardianship Mia assumes is conceived as the paradoxical cocoon in which metamorphosis is made possible, and the improbable premise of the would-be woman who kills as a job is made acceptable. "A lethal killer at the heart of a troubled family in the middle of nowhere": the dualism in the lead on the DVD sleeve fails to do the series justice because it misses the lethal killer's extremely complex gender construction. Nevertheless, it includes Mia's new responsibilities as a possible guardian: the plot revolves around the urgent matter of paying the rent of the impoverished smallholding to its ruthless, blackmailing owner after the children's mother has died. The representation of the place associates graphic depictions of the dire realities of farm life with breathtaking views of the Yorkshire countryside and poetic moments involving the children.

Mia's very special mix of extreme vulnerability, toughness, and resilience first contrasts, then merges with her image in the process of transitioning. Her metamorphosis provides the series with its central thrust, notably thanks to the obvious metaphor of the caterpillar becoming a butterfly embodied by Little Leoni's song, dance, and ragged princess or fairy or butterfly dresses. When Ryan tells Mia that he doesn't "want anything to change," she answers: "If things did not change, there wouldn't be any butterflies" [E1, 39:13]. Leoni is the youngest child and the only one who accepts Mia as she is. She embodies the different worlds that mingle in the diegesis; the derelict Yorkshire farm turns into a fairy tale or ghost story setting when the little girl dialogues with her dead mother whose physical presence the child conjures up. The crucial party scene at the end of episode 2 brings together Eddie and the children, the morbid urban underworld of Mia's job, and the tough but warm life of the family and farm. The little girl's absurd magic wand seems to work for a short while when Leoni has Mia singing and dancing "The Caterpillar Song" with her, from "There's a tiny caterpillar on a leaf (wiggle, wiggle)" to "Then he'll be a butterfly and fly away (flap, flap)"[7] in a moving metaphor for Mia's situation, with Eddie obviously enjoying the moment [E2, 41:00]. However fragile, Leoni's magic may prove to be the most effective or at least the most positive of the various narrative, symbolic, and visual means the series makes use of to narrate Mia's painstaking transition into a new identity.

Mirrors and doubling effects are, in addition to the butterfly analogy, another central motif used to depict the evolution. Mirrors abound, one appearing as early as the opening scene when Mia's naked body is first revealed [E1, 02:14]. In psychoanalysis, the mirror stage is crucial in the identification process of the child who realizes he is distinct from his mother when looking at his reflection. He, not she or they. As Mary Ann Doane highlights at the beginning of her article on "Film and the masquerade: Theorizing the female spectator,"[8] Freud admits that his theory does not apply to women. Moreover, the Lacanian theory of the mirror stage describes one specific stage in the evolution process of children, not adults. However, the series deliberately counters the theory and applies it to a transgender adult in her transition process. Contrary to the child for whom the mirror stage is an unconscious step in its development, Mia deliberately makes use of mirrors as she constructs herself as a woman. Her son Ryan, on the verge of becoming a teenager, also refers to the mirror when doubting his gender after the revelation of his father's metamorphosis. He then sits at his dead mother's dressing table to look at himself in dress and makeup [E2, 27:56]— the scene got the series some negative critical appraisal for being too heavy-handed and predictable.[9] Yet the transgender premise can also be viewed as a form of ironical commentary, a parody of Freudian theories focusing on boys and men when it comes to becoming an independent being and relegating women to their penis envy in one globalizing phallocentric theory. Mia, who hides her penis and kills to be able to afford the operation that will make it disappear, is both a literal and an ironic challenge to the notion of penis envy.

The deconstruction and reconstruction processes reach a more complex stage as some mirror scenes adopt a "behind-the-mirror" perspective and more precisely that of the children's dead mother, whose mirror it used to be. Mia has adopted, much to the children's dismay, her ex-lover's room as her own. The deceased woman explicitly haunts the series and acts as a benign guide comforting both her daughters and Mia on her way to becoming, not a mother, but a guardian and new parental figure that blurs gender lines. Nevertheless, one may wonder whether there is any irony in the fact that the ideal mother and woman can only be dead and was apparently a social outcast when alive, as she would not conform to the monogamous norm, with four children from four different fathers. Mia, twice marginalized as a transwoman and an assassin, seems set on taking the marginalization one step further in her attempt to become the children's guardian. This is illustrated metaphorically by her donning the dead woman's flamboyant Chinese silk robes and her sessions at the latter's dressing table as if to check whether she can compete with her as a motherly figure. One of the last stages of Mia's metamorphosis has her wearing the same kind of turban to hide her shorn hair, as the dead woman used to wear to hide the effects of chemotherapy, thereby establishing an analogy between her biological sex and a lethal disease: Mia must die to be born anew [E6, 28:24].

The double also represents a central motif with implications in terms of characterization and symbolism. Mia herself can be regarded as a variation on the Roman god Janus, one face or rather part of her body turned toward her past as a man and the rest facing her future as a woman. For that matter, a further stage toward Mia's definition or rather identification to different gender and genre models is effected when she becomes an accomplice in a murder that has nothing to do with her job but everything to do with her new parental role. Young Riley, initially most vocal in her rejection of Mia as a possible substitute for her dead mother, turns out to be a strong double and a foil in motherhood as well as murder. She also becomes a woman who kills when she shoots the farm owner who sexually abuses her in exchange for the rent. As pregnant Riley refuses to abort, he tries to strangle her on her dead mother's and now Mia's bed. The teenager then kills him with Mia's own gun that the latter had hidden in her deceased lover's bed, in a symbolic paroxysm that strikes as a baroque catalogue of sexual abuse [E4, 41:57]. Again, this ostensible accumulation of metaphors and symbols may read as implicit irony because the parallel between Mia and Riley is fraught with ambiguity. In fact, the teenager appears as a more conventional woman who kills, since she kills to save her life as well as the life she carries, fending off her abusive lover's vicious attempt at putting an end to a socially embarrassing liaison. Riley's killing enters the category of murders Lizzie Seal defines as "natural,"[10] that is, murders fitting mainstream constructs of behaviors deemed instinctive in women.

On the contrary, Mia's killings as an assassin would belong to the category of murders Seal labels as "unusual," such as infanticide or other "monstrous" deeds. Such murders do not fit a traditional image of women that may include the possibility of murder, but only when they are severely abused, victimized or when their children's or their own lives are in danger, as in Riley's case. In Seal's studies, killing for money, for instance, women murdering their employers, does not inspire the same indulgence among juries and in the media; forgiveness is possible only when the woman who kills can be pitied, as her act remains within the limits of what is accepted as "natural" on a woman's part. In the series, the two women have sharply different attitudes when they kill, depending on the way each one's killing will be regarded in the frame of traditional expectations of womanly behavior. Riley "naturally" wants to give herself up, which she will eventually do, to clear her conscience of an act many will consider justified, as she fits the part of the abused woman so well. On the contrary, Mia's association with the world of organized crime forbids both disclosure and possible indulgence. Although Riley's act brings the two women together in their shared concern for the safety of an expectant mother and her future child, when it comes to clearing up the mess, each is assigned a very different task and traditional gender divisions return. While a submissive Riley gets down on her knees to scrub the floor, a bossy Mia takes care of the body as a professional killer is supposed to. Each woman's killings clearly belong to different spheres. This gap is represented visually in the shots concluding the murders, between Riley's messy traces on a cheap wooden wardrobe and Mia's striking blood patterns on slick, transparent surfaces against a stylish urban background, as if they did not belong to the same generic world—Mia the hit person of noir or gangster films, Riley the abused woman of naturalist cinema.

Though mirrors and doubles multiply images in Mia's quest for a trans-identity, the question of an actual metamorphosis remains pending as roles still seem to obey traditional norms, especially when it comes to killing and then dealing with the consequences. Here, the series seems to waver between genres, the urban thriller or neo-noir for the assassination scenes and the rural melodrama when it comes to Riley's story. Although Riley does not evolve from the quite conventional character of the victim, the merger works when Mia's OC connections help her get rid of the body. And later on, the final crises may point to the possibility of Mia's departing from the convention and becoming a new kind of parenting figure, as the pregnant teenager asking for her expertise seems to get reconciled with the idea of recomposing a family under her guardianship.

Interruption and Conclusion

At this stage, we may ask ourselves to what extent the series resolves its contradictory premises and its attempt to deconstruct the stereotypes of gender division. The fact that a mainstream production depicts an individual recreating herself by transforming her anatomy seems to suggest that it has become more acceptable. However, would this have been the case if the part had been played by a transgender person? In a press conference, Paul Abbott hardly addresses the issue when he answers coyly that Chloe Sevigny was his one and only choice; according to him, she was the best actress for the part and he never looked any further.[11] While admiring the undeniable acting skills the actress displays throughout the series, we may regret such an "obvious" choice that ultimately seems to imply that a transgender character can be accepted only if they are impersonated by a woman wearing a prosthesis. Maybe one of the reasons the glimpses we get of Mia's full-frontal nudity fail to cause discomfort is because we never forget that the actress is a woman wearing a prosthesis as artificial and harmless as a Greek statue's penis. Likewise, the fellatio Mia gives her boyfriend "spares" viewers any major shock or embarrassment, since frontal nudity is avoided and Mia's extremely sexy clothes highlight her womanly parts in contrast to the man's nudity [E3, 42:31]. Mia's fictional body would, then, represent but a partial success in the evolution toward a dissolution of strict gender lines.

But casting aside, the narrative is perhaps even more problematic. If we look back on the unraveling of the plot and the way the characters behave and evolve, we can see where the junction between the two parts of the initial proposal, the transgender and family issue on the one hand and the crime story on the other, misses the mark. When it comes to the murders, the classic binary order reappears, and the kills effected by the women remain justified. Riley is twice redeemed, since her act falls in the "natural" category, and she eventually gives herself up. As for Mia, her competence as a contract killer is endangered as she undergoes her metamorphosis: when she does her job well, her expertise assimilates her to a machine, a neutral contraption, but when she turns into a guardian, her responsibilities get in the way of a profession regarded as unsuitable for a woman.

This is not simply to suggest that the killings represent the male side of Mia and the family responsibilities the female one. My point is that the assumptions about how a woman should be and act tip the delicate balance precariously maintained in the construction and our responses to the character of Mia. Her acts must also be justified—by the imperative to preserve the farm as nest and cocoon. The choice of hits further justifies her acts, as they present a most unsavory range of disgusting macho behaviors in a very binary vision of manhood best epitomized in Riley's vile abuser and "victim." Riley, who fits the stereotype, stands out as a womanly model Mia wishes to emulate at one point, but that proves a dead-end, as illustrated by the fake pregnant belly she buys (Figure 3.2). The theatrical prop, a far cruder imitation than the penis prosthesis, reads as a synecdoche of Mia's impossible fate as a stable, unified character in a fiction that would tell the story of her metamorphosis into a "complete" woman, as well as a commentary on the murderous means used to obtain that result. The contradictory image of Mia trying on the fake belly while aiming her gun at a mirror reflects her desperate efforts to become this chimera, a being supposed to give life when her job is to kill [E5, 33:33].

Interestingly, the scenario of the "mother/grandmother" who pretends to be pregnant to usurp a much younger charge's baby happens to be a classic in popular culture, and especially melodrama and soap operas, as it involves mysterious origins and family secrets, the very stuff drama is made of. For example, in season 4 of *Desperate Housewives* (ABC, 2004–12),[12] perfection-freak Bree Van de Kamp, when faced with her young daughter's

Figure 3.2 *Hit & Miss* (Sky Atlantic, 2012): Mia with her makeshift belly and her guns, in a reference to *Taxi Driver* (1976).

illegitimate pregnancy, uses a series of fake bellies and manages to make her neighborhood believe she has given birth, thus concealing the blight on her family's reputation. The character of Bree caricatures middle-class assumptions of how a perfect housewife should behave. Mia, on the other hand, paradoxically cuts a far more realistic figure than Bree; Chloe Sevigny herself reveals in an interview[13] that she was very pleased with a challenging, almost impossible character, whom she did not wish to play as a preposterous one or a caricature. The stratagem, which answers more dramatic needs than Bree's as it is supposed to protect both the foetus's and Riley's lives, would have assimilated the series to yet another genre, that of the soap opera, which it contains definite elements of. More precisely, it may very well redefine the "feminine" nature of the series, since it seems to fit Tania Modleski's description of the soap opera as incapable of ending.[14] However, the prop is soon to be discarded and the scheme forgotten in the urgency of the final crisis aborting Mia's metamorphosis process, while the spectator's expectations are left unanswered in the interruption of the series.

The ambiguities and instability of a formula that is, perhaps, too rich may account for the series' interruption at the end of the sixth episode, a cliff-hanger that begs for a second season despite Sky Atlantic's claims that this was how the drama had been planned from the start.[15] The title would, then, quite ironically, sum up the series' fate, starting with a hit (the shock of the double revelation of Mia's "true nature") and ending on a "miss," that of a closure and maybe a redefinition of gender in the creation of an alternative to the traditional binary. The very last shot prevents an apparently transformed Mia from escaping the lethal retribution of her last breach of contract [E6, 43:58]. In transforming into a parenting figure, she has not performed the assassination she had been paid for, and her ex-boss has no other choice than to eliminate her. Yet as he holds her at gunpoint, he is stopped by Mia's own son Ryan, who completes and closes the Mexican standoff, aiming a gun at Mia's assailant and covering the latter's moves—moves we shall probably never be given to see as the series ends there. On the basis of the final shot, it would be possible to conclude that the decision to show a very feminine-looking Mia, complete with a *femme fatale*'s clingy red dress and blonde wig, being saved by her own son who now assumes the masculine part of gun-bearer, grounds the ending in a reassuring patriarchal framework. He is the one who is liable to kill now, while Mia as a woman no longer does. Yet in so doing, the ending would simultaneously confirm that Mia has become the image of "Woman" she longed for and highlight that her image of Woman is a patriarchal ideal, as opposed to a feminist or queer creation.

Should we see this last shot as a dead-end that admits to the defeat of deconstruction and ambiguity, or as an open ending that allows for new developments but also the acknowledgment of ever-shifting, precarious balances? After all, Mia's dress and wig are as much a disguise as her hood in the first shots, and the open conclusion could be that there is no such thing in postfeminist fiction as a clear and permanent definition of self in one specific gender. Mia's images change like her clothes or hair, and they are but transient stages and appearances that remind us of Calliope in Jeffrey Eugenides's 2002 novel *Middlesex*,[16] who runs away to escape the final operation that would cut off her/his vestigial penis to allow him/her to grow up as a girl. In the same way, the interrupted series may seem to lead nowhere in its suspension of choices, yet manages to create a hybrid, biased, oblique discourse sustained by the multiplication of mirrors and doubles. The reflected images and the different disguises would then compose a parody, in Greek a "discourse on the side," that puts us on the path to accepting the blurring and crossing of lines—and thus a queer position—while paradoxically wishing for hardly feasible closures and reconstructions. In that matter, suspension could well be an elusive yet somehow constructive solution to contradiction, and Mia's failure as a feminist heroine would allow for a qualified success in queering conventional figures of killing women and assassins.

Notes

1 Yvonne Tasker and Diane Negra, "Introduction: Feminist politics and postfeminist culture," in Y. Tasker and D. Negra (eds.), *Interrogating Postfeminism Gender and the Politics of Popular Culture* (Durham and London: Duke University Press, 2007), p. 1.
2 Queering is defined as "the process of making a given set of ideas strange, to destabilize dominant understandings and underlying assumptions" by C. B. Daring, J. Rogue, Deric Shannon, and Abbey Volcano in "Queer meet anarchism, anarchism meet queer," their introductory chapter to *Queering Anarchism: Addressing and Undressing Power and Desire* (Oakland, CA: AK Press, 2012), Kindle edition.
3 *Hit and Miss*, Bonus material, DVD, AbbottVision/Red Production Company, 2012.
4 Chris Holmlund, *Impossible Bodies: Femininity and Masculinity at the Movies* (New York: Routledge, 2001).
5 Gram Rabbit, "In the devil's playground," *Music to Start a Cult to* (Joshua Tree, 2004). Available at https://gramrabbit.bandcamp.com/track/devils-playground (accessed March 11, 2018).
6 Emma Saran Webster, "A troubling look at why men kill transgender women," *Teenvogue*, December 17, 2015. Available at http://www.teenvogue.com/story/transgender-women-killed-by-men (accessed March 11, 2018).

7 St Philip's Marsh Nursery School, "There's a tiny caterpillar." Available at
   http://stphilipsmarshnursery.co.uk/sounds/theres-a-tiny-caterpillar-3/
   (accessed March 11, 2018).

8 In his lecture on "Femininity," Freud forcefully inscribes the absence of the
   female spectator from theory in his notorious statement, "To those of you
   who are women this will not apply—you are yourselves the problem." Mary
   Ann Doane, "Film and the masquerade: Theorizing the female spectator,"
   Screen, 23/3–4 (September/October 1982), p. 74.

9 "The problem with Mr. Abbott's new show . . . isn't the premise but the
   solemnity with which it's approached . . . 'Hit & Miss' is so slow and earnest
   and teachy—several scenes involve Mia's young son exploring his own
   sexual identity by donning a dress and headband—that much of the show
   seems to be performed on tiptoe, and a giggle seems like the appropriate
   response." Mike Hale, *The New York Times*, July 10, 2012.

10 Lizzie Seal, *Women, Murder and Femininity: Gender Representations of
   Women Who Kill* (Basingstoke: Palgrave Macmillan, 2010).

11 "*Hit and Miss* Q&A session," The Mayfair Hotel, London, May 15, 2012, *Hit
   and Miss* DVD bonus, disk 1.

12 *Desperate Housewives*, Season 4, DVD, Disney (2008).

13 "[The summary] may sound preposterously camp and over the top but,
   thanks to Abbott's delicate script and a typically nuanced performance from
   Sevigny, the material proves unexpectedly moving." Sheryl Garratt, "Chloe
   Sevigny's interview for *Hit & Miss* on Sky Atlantic," *The Telegraph*, May 22,
   2012.

14 Tania Modleski, "The search for tomorrow in today's soap operas," *Film
   Quarterly*, 33/1 (Autumn 1979), pp. 12–21.

15 Morgan Jeffery, "'Hit & Miss' won't return for second series, confirms Sky
   Atlantic," *Digital Spy*, September 5, 2012. Available at http://www.digitalsp
   y.com/tv/news/a403924/hit-miss-wont-return-for-second-series-confirms-
   sky-atlantic (accessed March 11, 2018).

16 Jeffrey Eugenides, *Middlesex* (New York: Farrar, Straus and Giroux, 2002).

Filmography

Hit & Miss, created by Paul Abbott, written by Sean Conway, directed by
   Hettie MacDonald and Sheree Folks, produced by Juliet Charlesworth,
   performances by Chloe Sevigny, Peter Wright, Jonas Armstrong, Vincent
   Regan, Ben Crompton, Karla Crome, Reece Noi, music by Dickon Hinchliffe,
   cinematography by David Luther, edited by Celia Haining and Joe Randall-
   Cutler, AbbottVision/Red Production Company/British Sky Broadcasting
   Limited 2012.
DVD, AbbottVision/Red Production Company 2012.

4

Genre and Gender in *Sin City*: *A Dame to Kill For* (Frank Miller and Robert Rodriguez, 2014)

Christophe Gelly

When one considers the state of academic and public debate on gender issues in popular culture, the case of Frank Miller and Robert Rodriguez's *Sin City* (2005) and *Sin City: A Dame to Kill For* (2014) stands out. The critical reception of the 2005 film emphasized the direct, sometimes crude quality of gendered representations and the stereotypical references to male fantasies derived from the source text:

> On first viewing, the hookers looked like a boy's-own porn fantasy. Maybe porn nightmare is closer to the mark. Either way, these attack-mode lingerie models certainly hold their own with the menfolk in the mayhem department. But the effect is silly and tacky rather than scary or sexy.[1]
>
> This sexualization is much more implicit in the film, however, than it is in the graphic novels. Interestingly, almost all of the violence in the graphic novels remains intact in the film.[2]

Its crudity did not stop the 2005 film from grossing a considerable profit; the 2014 sequel, on the other hand, was a financial flop.[3] Although this study will not engage in a detailed comparison between both works, it will emphasize that the 2014 sequel articulates a different representation of gender issues compared to the 2005 film, which may account for its lack of public success—although the time gap between the two films is also often invoked as a motive for the sequel's failure.[4] The assumption is that *Sin City 2* targets a perceptibly different audience by dealing with Frank Miller's universe in a way that swerves away from the almost obsessive focus on sex and violence that characterizes *Sin City*. Attention will first be paid to how the treatment of the story, influenced by the source material from Miller's comics, offers a peculiar vision of gender issues in the film. The question of the specific gender constructs manifest in *Sin City 2* will then be examined as representative of the film's reliance on neo-noir conventions. Finally, I will argue that the representation of gender, and especially femininity, can be considered as a form of postfeminist parody.

Sin City 2: Comics, Adaptation, and Gender Constructs

Both *Sin City* adaptations develop a strategy based on the use of color as the sign of the intrusion of an alien element in the diegetic compound, a strategy that is directly drawn from the comics. In the initial scene of *Sin City 2*, Marv tries to remember how he got to the initial situation of the plot by swallowing a pill meant to treat him because he has "a condition" (of which nothing more specific will be said[5]). The vivid orange of the pill box [1:43] alerts the viewer to a running strategy in both films, which consists in highlighting the semantic value of certain diegetic elements (for instance, Junior's yellow blood in the first film) by contrasting their color with the black and white environment. This strategy pays tribute to the original noir model by recognizing the bichromatic backdrop of the plot as a necessary, significant reference and by devising a new mode of signification, in which the colored diegetic components stand out as obvious threats to the subject. This mode of representation not only departs from traditional noir or noirish black and white representations of ambivalence, but also graphically isolates elements of ambivalent behavior in the characters (the pills are a clue to Marv's drive to self-destruction) as external from the predominant color code. It thus adds a graphic element to the noir imagery, underlining that the filmic, diegetic universe is a fantasy world and not just a black and white film. As such, it acknowledges the comic books' origin and the way it influenced the aesthetics of *Sin City 2*. The relation between the color scheme and gender is visible through the association of one character who defends women (Marv) with one character who attacks them (Junior): both are characterized by this connection to a vivid color. The color scheme's ambivalent value thus mirrors the male characters' ambivalent attitude toward the female protagonists, and it highlights the uneasy relation between genders that is one of the essential points in the discourse of the source text and its adaptation.

Despite these connections, the debate over the nature of the films as real adaptations of the source texts is rather controversial. Much of the criticism in that regard revolves around the analysis of intermediality and on the "loss" of the comics syntax in the film;[6] many studies of the 2005 film focus on this point.[7] An examination of the sequel as a comics adaptation yields rather different conclusions concerning gender constructs. The central plot in *Sin City 2* revolves around the manipulation of Dwight McCarthy by Ava Lord in pure noir fashion, and the visuals related to Ava's appearance— especially her first—confirm the spellbinding quality of the *femme fatale*: Ava's image, what with the bright blue dress she is wearing, clashes with the setting of the bar where she meets Dwight (Figure 4.1). On the contrary, in the equivalent scene in the comic book, Ava's silhouette is partly masked by smoke, making her an indistinct figure to which Dwight is speaking. The hazy depiction of Ava comes back repeatedly throughout the source text. The blurring of Ava's image in the comic book and the central position Ava's face and body occupy in the film materialize the opposite takes adopted by the source text and the adaptation. While the comic book distances itself from the stereotype of the *femme fatale* by blurring her image and making her a not so central story element (she appears less frequently and less prominently in the book compared to the film), the adaptation foregrounds Ava's image as a visual "magnet" for Dwight, due to the treatment of colors. This is obviously heightened by the casting of Eva Green and the eroticization of her body in various scenes. It would be wrong to say that there is no emphasis on bodies in Miller's series, but the female bodies are often, like Ava's, seen through the distorting filter of shadows or smoke, while the film emphasizes the bodies' graphic quality—in the film, Nancy's video-like dance scenes differ from the

Figure 4.1 *Sin City: A Dame to Kill For* (Miller and Rodriguez, 2014): the seductive Ava Lord.

stylized depictions in the comics. If the comic book influence is obvious in the film's aesthetics, the representation of femininity differs significantly in the film and the comic book, both regarding the graphic quality attached to female bodies and, as we shall see, the roles that are ascribed to women characters.

Examining the construction of gender in *Sin City 2* necessitates a wider frame of references that is likely to account for the images of femininity that are prevalent in the film. This wider frame owes much to writings on postfeminism, inasmuch as the representations in the film are concerned with the fetishization of female bodies that essentially differs from first- and second-wave feminism and that contradicts the assumptions of earlier forms of feminism. This perspective corresponds globally to the outlook associated with postfeminism. According to Sarah Gamble:

> Because it is critical of any definition of women as victims who are unable to control their own lives, [postfeminism] is inclined to be unwilling to condemn pornography and to be skeptical of such phenomena as date-rape; because it is skewed in favour of liberal humanism, it embraces a flexible ideology which can be adapted to suit individual needs and desires. Finally, because it tends to be implicitly heterosexist in orientation, postfeminism commonly seeks to develop an agenda which can find a place for men, as lovers, husbands and fathers as well as friends.[8]

Rather than a continuation of second-wave feminism, postfeminism swerves away from the politically minded pursuit of equal rights.

> Instead, post-feminist discourse manifests as a series of contradictions and tensions, where the gains of earlier feminist movements are both taken for granted and undermined; the prevailing message being that feminism has been achieved, that it is a spent force, and as such is no longer needed.[9]

On this view, considering the film as postfeminist would account for how it combines two apparently incompatible claims: an empowering model of femininity (appearing through the murderous capacity of females in the plot, miles away from images of vulnerability) mixed with heavy reliance on sexual objectification. This is what Samantha Lindop suggests when, for instance, she refers to the depiction of the commodification of sex in the film as more "comfortable" than in noir and neo-noir. This contradiction appears for many authors, such as Gamble, as central to the cultural phenomenon of postfeminism: postfeminist discourses tend to acknowledge sexuality and seduction as tools to women's empowerment, and their growth to independence and action is not deemed incompatible with more traditional forms of gender and power struggle.

Two examples stand out in *Sin City 2*. The first has to do with the graphic depiction of the prostitutes in Old Town, which is clearly inspired by cartoonish male fantasies that associate the pin-up with popular culture artifacts (one girl even wears a Zorro mask). This portrayal (Figure 4.2) displays a contradictory vision of female empowerment typical of a postfeminist perspective, in the sense that it combines empowerment with the objectification of these women through their assimilation to male fantasies. The women characters are depicted in dominating positions, wielding weapons and endowed with autonomy (this is true of both *Sin City* films). Old Town is a neighborhood ruled by a gang of prostitutes headed by Gail, which the police do not enter in compliance with an implicit pact— namely, that the prostitutes enforce their own laws in that part of the city. The role played by these "kind-hearted" prostitutes, who rescue Dwight after his beating at Ava Lord's place, is determined by the performative quality their gear is endowed with. By dressing up like the male heroes of pop culture (like Zorro), they *become* invested with masculine power, as if their acting and looking like avengers were a guarantee of their power. This quasi-carnivalesque reversal of gender roles placing women in the role of justice-seekers rather than victims is, nonetheless, particularly ambivalent, as it aligns them with masculine stereotypes. Their empowerment thus relies not

Figure 4.2 *Sin City: A Dame to Kill For* (Miller and Rodriguez, 2014): the Girls of Old Town.

only on their identification to masculine roles, but also on the performance they make of this masculinization, combined with the eroticization of their bodies. The scene suggests that gender roles are, in effect, subject to redefinition and never stable—here, they are reversed in Grand Guignol fashion. This stress on the possible interplay of gender roles is typical of postfeminism not because of the reversal it operates, but because it does so by staging stereotypical gender roles and redistributing them among various female characters. The stereotypes include the involvement of these women characters in prostitution, an activity predominantly associated with women especially in the noir and neo-noir genre. *Sin City 2* as a postfeminist adaptation typically renegotiates the balance of power between males and females, while still relying on these stereotypes, thus steering a characteristic middle course between questioning gender roles and reproducing gender stereotypes. The centrality of performance also reminds us that the movie— and the comic books it is adapted from—also parodies the reduction of characters to cultural types.

Another example of this strategy is to be found in the graphic match visible when the shot of Gail bending over Dwight's wounded face segues to one of Lieutenant Mort's sleepless body next to his wife in bed [49:46]. The shift insists on the ambivalence of the film's gendered representations, since the two couples are connected by an implicit contradiction. Although Mort's wife will not play a major role in the plot, her presence serves to render more complex the representational strategies of female characters. The graphic match associates a first, unconventional couple living in violence with another conventional one steeped apparently in boredom and neurosis (Mort's decision to yield to Ava Lord's sexual advances is slow and guilt-ridden). The editing testifies to the contradictory portrayal of female characters that simultaneously partakes of the revenge motif and of the traditional couple, thus confirming that the postfeminist perspective is taking a middle course between opposite options. More largely, the image of Gail as a warrior princess,[10] while insisting on the autonomy of this female compound, points to the imagery of female exploitation and signifies the now established cultural comfort with which this imagery can be recycled without the previous intimations of a degrading commodification of the female image.

Considering how *Sin City 2* negotiates this postfeminist stance with its neo-noir aesthetics is the next necessary step in order to further understand the film's gendered representations. The connection between the generic influence of neo-noir on the film and the gender constructs revolves around the obvious recourse to the stereotype of the *femme fatale* that informs the character of Ava Lord. Initially, the figure was constructed by critics as a reaction to the cultural and economic emancipation of women in American post–Second World War society, but, of course, the noir label also indicates a number of aesthetic features, largely inherited from expressionism.[11] Neo-noir productions, emerging in the mid-1970s, articulate a more explicit social and political critique, and revisit the stereotypes of the hard-boiled detective and female manipulation from a distance. In typical postmodern fashion, neo-noir calls attention to the stereotypical quality of the generic traits that are used, as in *The Long Goodbye* (Robert Altman, 1973) where the detective's voice-over constantly and reflexively jokes about his own helplessness. The articulation between the treatment of gender in Rodriguez and Miller's films and neo-noir hinges on the centrality of the *femme fatale* figure. Yet the generic references in both films are also made problematic by the excess visible in the staging of the plot and in the screenplay itself, which both reproduce and outperform, in parodic fashion, the generic conventions. For instance, Christopher Pizzino argues that the 2005 film exhibits a level of adhesion to generic expectations that simplifies the plot into a mere moral confrontation between abusers and saviors of women, and deprives the spectators of the rich ambiguity of the noir intertext.[12] The question that is raised, here, is whether the neo-noir traits in the film concerning gender are dealt with in a significant fashion that may help to better understand representation. I shall examine this question through a survey of the main formal elements associated with the representation of female characters and influenced by noir and neo-noir conventions, giving way to a redefinition of the neo-noir perspective in *Sin City 2*, which has consequences on the implicit discourse held on gender issues in this film. It will also entail some general remarks on the overall visual style of the film that go beyond the issue of gender representation.

As far as form is concerned, it seems obvious that *Sin City 2* looks back to a number of the essential stylistic landmarks of noir filtered, as it were, through a neo-noir perspective. These landmarks include, according to film analyst James Naremore (among others), *chiaroscuro* lighting, voice-over narration, sometimes associated with flashbacks, and distorted angles inherited from German Expressionism.[13] Rodriguez and Miller's 2014 film begins with a black screen, a throwback to the numerous scenes in which noir characters pass out (for instance, in Edward Dmytryk's 1944 *Murder, My Sweet*), and continues with Marv's voice-over trying to recapture the flow of events that brought him to the initial situation. Within this tribute to the centrality of darkness in the genre, the film foregrounds a different use of colors; for instance, Pizzino analyzes the role of yellow in the first *Sin City* film, regarding the character of Junior Roark and the symbolical significance of the color that is associated both with him and detective Hartigan, after the latter kills Roark and is splattered with traces of his yellow blood:

Hartigan does not suggest that he must protect Nancy from his own desire, but the hand in which he holds his gun is notably spotted with the bright yellow of Junior's blood—a visual mark with an inescapable symbolic connotation. It suggests that Hartigan's very need to oppose Junior is driven by a fear that the two characters are similar. [. . .] In staining Hartigan yellow, Miller [. . .] implies that Hartigan has the same violent appetites as his counterpart.[14]

The moral ambivalence that becomes clear in the end is typical of a genre that stages noir detectives who experience the self-same mixed, protective, and aggressive feelings toward their protégées—the prototypical version of Sam Spade in *The Maltese Falcon* (John Huston, 1941) and his relationship with Brigid O'Shaughnessy come to mind. Whereas the noir version draws on aesthetics of contamination, suggesting through the omnipresence of darkness the moral decay that constantly threatens the characters, the *Sin City* films introduce a new, chromatic dimension that simultaneously complements, and comments on, the noir original. The visibility of Hartigan's contamination through the color yellow enhances the effect, making it highly salient in the film's graphic universe. It also makes the gender relationship more radically conflicting, since it provides a visual clue to the danger represented by male desire.

Camera angles function in a similar manner. True, the opening and especially final credit sequences play on the extreme high angles typical of film noir, for instance, when the camera zooms out rapidly to reveal the film title made up of a number of roofs from buildings viewed from high up [96:13]. This device recycles the frequent, distorted angles used in the expressionistic phase of the genre to signify either the characters' isolation from their environment or their feelings of subjection, among other possibilities.[15] But *Sin City 2* also radicalizes this strategy in the depiction of characters like Ava Lord who bathes naked in her swimming pool [62:25], in a shot that strikingly evokes a drowned body, whereas at this point in the narrative, she is about to try and manipulate Dwight McCarthy again by trying to get him to side with her when she realizes she is losing the game. These angles constitute another formal clue that beckons the spectator to consider conflicting interpretations of the film's relationship to noir, in the sense that it pays tribute to subjective, expressionistic visions of the characters' situation (Nancy Callaghan, for instance, is, in the end, seen as only a minor, disposable part of the savage universe that is Sin City when she slowly disappears through an extreme upward tracking shot) and renders this vision complex by choosing the exact same representational device for the killer female at the moment of her payback. The high angle, then, conveys the film's ambivalence toward the noir model as a reference whose undecidable visual features cannot be escaped in the neo-noir refashioning: it looks back to an unaccountable urban world that, as in film noir, is fraught with self-contradictory characterization, but it also makes this visual characterization so conspicuous as to question its very meaning and the meaning of the shooting angle attributed to the victim *and* the killer. As in the case of the treatment of colored inserts in the filmic texture, this reference makes the noir lineage both relevant and exaggerated, and it lends the film a singular parodic dimension, which recalls Fredric Jameson's description of postmodern "blank parody."[16] The meaning of the aesthetic reference to the noir model has become so involved and intricate that it cannot be identified univocally except as a stylistic throwback of sorts. The film uses these high angles specifically for women who appear first as victims then as aggressors, a fact very obvious in the case of Ava Lord but also in the case of a prostitute called Sally, who is shot from the terrace rooftop as she is tied to the bed by her client, before she is revealed to have manipulated him, in agreement with Dwight McCarthy, who took pictures of them to ground a petition for divorce lodged by Sally's client's wife [23:36]. The camera angle signals, here, the reversal in gender roles: it initially suggests a generically determined position of submissiveness before turning the tables on the male character. This redefinition of the generic, formal trait underlies a new configuration in characterization, distinguishing female empowerment from a stereotypical object position.

Voice-over is the third element among the significant noir devices that is essential in the generic interplay flaunted by *Sin City 2* in relation to gender constructs. The initial scene that presents Marv coming round after his fight with the frat boys exemplifies the classical treatment given to the voice-over flashback in reference to prototypical film noir, but another instance of voice-over dissociated from the flashback occurs in the scene where John Hartigan's ghost appears in the bar where Nancy Callaghan works as a dancer and witnesses her aiming her gun at Roark, commenting briefly on the scene with these words: "Someday she'll pull the trigger" [16:10]. This scene significantly resituates the use of voice-over in a hallucinatory context that disjoints the usual association between this device and the expression of a character's subjectivity—the device is a manifestation of Nancy's inner feelings of despair and longing for reunion with Hartigan, but it is also severed from the story development, unlike the usual function of noir voice-over flashback, and acts as a reminder of Nancy's previous relation with Hartigan. The device recurs when Nancy gets drunk and hallucinates Hartigan's presence again [81:42]. What also adds to the strangeness of this use of voice-over is that, in both cases, Nancy does not seem to be aware of Hartigan's presence near her, thereby further debunking the generic role of the voice-over as a voice issuing "from within" the character. In terms of gender constructs, these scenes stage a vision of Nancy as paradoxically unable to grasp reality, at the very moment when she is about to carry out her revenge on Roark. In contrast, the canonical use of voice-over in film noir relates to the conscious expression of the characters' experience, especially in confessional narratives like *Double Indemnity* (Billy Wilder, 1944).

These remarks point to a redefinition of generic markers that distance the film from its generic model, but they also highlight how irrelevant these markers have become in the diegetic universe. A world where none of these references apply is also a world where the classical references to interiority (voice-over) and moral landmarks (shooting angles, color) are failing. Similarly, the gender-related configurations set up by the sequel suggest a return to generic references *and* a manifest distance from them. This distance also appears through the film's discourse on sexuality. Critics like Frederick Luis Aldama, Torsa Ghosal, and Christopher González have remarked on the hypersexualized features of *Sin City 2*, but also on the general reluctance of explicit sexual representation, whereas sexualization remains implicit in classical noir. Of course, gender representations and sexual representations are far from equivalent, but the eroticized quality of gender roles is so obvious in the 2014 sequel that it needs to be examined as integral to these roles.

The film's sexual dimension relies mostly on the symbolical and explicit focus on the issue of castration. This focus recurs most visibly in the variety of cuttings and stabbings that lead to the protagonists' deaths, most strikingly when Senator Roark throws cards that cut his son into pieces [76:02]. This trope recurs each time the plot stages male bodies being penetrated, as when Marv tears Manute's eye out [41:49], or when "little deadly Miho" deals death to male opponents with variously shaped blades [60:40], or again when Lieutenant Mort kills his associate cop for trying to stop him from siding with Ava Lord by shooting him in the eye [57:48]. Of course, the origin of this focus is to be found with the literal emasculation suffered by Junior Roark in the first film, already present in the source texts. This excessively Freudian representational strategy is associated with a partly Oedipal configuration through a contrasted love/hate relationship: Johnny Roark wishes his father dead, while (in the first film) Nancy Callaghan flaunts her clearly incestuous attraction to John Hartigan. The interesting point in this strategy is that it emphasizes by accretion the excessive relevance of a common, psychoanalytical reading of the plot, based on the failure of repression and the omnipotence of the sexual imagery. Male characters are so obsessed with castration that they even try to inflict it on female characters, like Roark when he asks Nancy Callaghan: "Hartigan shot my son's pecker off so where should I shoot you next?" [94:08]. Of course, this is a tongue-in-cheek throwback to Freudian questions about the female version of the Oedipus complex. The excessive quality of such scenes of, and discourses on, emasculation not only literalizes the topic of female empowerment, as in the case of Miho, but it also opens the way for a reading of the film as a parody of this empowerment. The parodic dimension, which no doubt contributes to making the film enjoyable, can also be traced back to a post- or an anti-feminist approach that refuses to take "seriously" the symbolic connotations attached to the topic. One could also suggest that this discourse reproduces and satirizes the failure of male characters to conceive of female sexuality otherwise than in male terms, that is, the discourse on castration would represent an obsessive preoccupation with sex (as exemplified by Roark), characteristic of an ideal of male domination over women. This obsession participates in a rape culture that the heinous character's discourse often refers to, for instance, with Marcie, and that has been commented upon by scholars like Barbara Creed. What is essential in terms of gender representation in these examples is that the film consistently refers to this male domination through satire, but debunks it through the eventual revenge women characters are granted.

"Come on Dwight, You're No Fun At All": *Sin City 2* as Parody

The parodic dimension appears clearly in the scene where Nancy Callaghan disfigures herself with glass shards, the better to enlist Marv in her quest to take her revenge on Roark. The sequence could be construed as another example of the warrior stance that is imposed on a female character when she desires power, as in the case of Gail. But like the Old Town prostitutes, Nancy has to use her body to achieve her goal and manipulate Marv into compliance. Significantly, this scene was not taken from the comics, and the film here associates empowerment with self-mutilation in a contradictory manner. This contradictory association reasserts the "game" the film is playing with images, without complying with any stable vision of femininity. This is manifest in the motif of the double as well—a topic we understand as operating mainly through the various cases in which characters are confronted to their own reflected images. The primacy of appearances—and the criticism of it—thus appears clearly through the numerous occurrences of the motif of the double in the plot *and* in the representational choices of the filmic narrative (see [52:38], [33:27], and [94:58]). Whether we consider male or female characters, most are engaged in a dual relationship[17] with their own image or the reflection of this image, like Nancy Callaghan looking at herself in the mirror and seeing another image, Hartigan's body and face [79:20]. This recurrence of the motif of the double or the mirror image also derives from the high level of redundancy or repetition that occurs not in the representation but in the story itself: Johnny comes back after his fingers are broken by his father to be eventually shot dead by him; Dwight reinvades Ava Lord's property to kill her as he had done in the first place to kill her husband; and the dominant relationship Ava Lord initiates with Lieutenant Mort repeats the manipulation she previously exerted on Dwight to make him kill her husband. This plot structure based on repetition emphasizes the distanced reading that is required of it. If no appearances are reliable, if the story repeats itself in its diegetic development, it is because it represents an interplay of references whose ultimate meaning lies not within the plot itself but in its relation to its noir model. This device also points to the roles played by (mostly) female characters as artificial postures imposed on them and related to the world of appearances disjointed from reality.

Eventually, the stylistic and aesthetic choices evinced in the film also point to a similar determination, which becomes fairly obvious if we compare the 2005 and 2014 films. Concerning the former, Pizzino comments as follows on the scene where Nancy tries to seduce Hartigan in a motel after he gets out of prison [99:07]:

> The furnishings of the scene recall mid-century art (a table and sofa reminiscent of two or three different styles of the Eames era, a painting that seems like a cross between Kandinski and Mondrian), and the figures and the dialogue recall Lichtenstein, particularly a close-up image in which Nancy pleads "Sleep with me" and Hartigan responds "Stop it Nancy. You're talking crazy." Far from elevating this moment of potential seduction by furnishing it with allusions to respected traditions of art and design, this scene functions as a neutralizing gesture. [. . .] As with the other self-reflexive features I have considered, this moment is integrated into a narrative in which the moral temptation Nancy represents is quite real to the generically determined male self who must protect her from danger, including the danger of his own desire.[18]

The gist of this argument lies in the predominance of the generic frame over the aesthetic reference in this crucial scene, so that the characters' relationships appear to be "sifted" through the (neo-)noir genre, and are thus too simplified to allow any truly assumed, consistent aesthetic interplay with the "neutralized" art and design context. This concurs with Pizzino's view of the first *Sin City* film as constrained by generic rules.[19] If we compare this scene with a rather similar one from the 2014 film in which Nancy is visited by Hartigan's ghost (without her realizing it) while she is getting drunk in front of her television [81:06], we have a very different treatment of the aesthetic interplay. What immediately stands out is the fact that the design landmarks are much less specific aesthetically when compared to the first sequence from the 2005 film; the lampshade, for instance, could be a 1950s reissue, like the tufted sofa and footstool. If design clues are less significant, the film that Nancy is watching is central to the meaning of the scene [81:11]. In it, two apparently wounded characters (either tramps or more probably a battered down detective and his informer) are lying in a filthy street next to garbage cans and expressing their hatred of the town: "this rotten town. . . . It soils everybody it touches." This cue is taken up by Nancy who goes on speaking exactly at the same time as the (meta)-characters on screen: "This rotten town. Those it can't corrupt it soils." She then applies this dialogue to her own case by continuing thus: "It soiled you, John Hartigan." This overt reference to the noir genre through a film within the film (the scene which Nancy is watching on television was shot by Rodriguez and not extracted from any "classic") is part and parcel of the postmodernist practice of fictional quotes (a device examined among others by Linda Hutcheon[20]). But what differs in the treatment of this scene from the meeting between Hartigan and Nancy in the first *Sin City* film is the fact that the artistic quotes (the art and design trends presented in the furniture) serve to "neutralize" the scene through the lack of comment they elicit from the protagonists, whereas the *Sin City 2* sequence signals the metafilmic sequence both as artificial (it is not a real quotation) and as deeply significant for the subject—Nancy finds her self-expression through the dialogues of the scene she is watching on television. The aesthetic reference in this particular scene, compared with the 2005 film, realigns generic markers with Nancy's subjectivity, while still stressing the reflexive quality of the generic aesthetic traits in the sequence. The aim is to express the character's autonomous feelings within the generic frame recognized as such through the metafilm. Thus, *Sin City 2* not only inspires itself from noir references, but also materializes them in a made-up scene the better to present them as models. However, these models are not merely reproduced in the film; they are distanced through parody.

The parodic quality of the film appears as an excessive declension of the gruesomeness of criminal representations attached to the noir genre, far from any comical intent. This vision of the film as parody needs to be refined through another example, before it is applied to gender roles. Excess appears in several forms, through the repetitive quality of the plot structure in *Sin City 2* for a start. Some reviewers[21] blamed the 2005 film for using the same structure twice by ending two scenes in a revenge killing in a secluded farm. Such repetitions also appear in *Sin City 2* and can be accounted for by the motif of the double that informs, as we have seen, many of the characters' representations. But they also fulfill a function of their own, which is linked to parody. For example, in the case of the murder of Johnny, Roark's illegitimate son, by depicting how Johnny is killed by his father in the end of "The Long Bad Night" [74:23], in a scene that repeats the first confrontation with him in the gambling den, the script (an original script here, not drawn from the comics) thwarts a natural expectation that the subplot cannot end in the death of the innocent character. Repetition builds up suspense as to the outcome of this second confrontation, which bluntly ends with Roark shooting Johnny dead. The next episode where Nancy finally kills Roark is there to compensate for the frustration Johnny's death provokes, but the frustration remains, although we can also understand this episode as another sign that women are placed in a position of power compared to the 2005 film where they were more passive. This change indicates a postfeminist stance that associates women with resistance and men (Johnny, Roark's son) with both oppression and victimization. But more generally, the film deals playfully with the leads it gives to spectators, developing the confrontation to its deadly conclusion without the comfort of the criminal's punishment. This reversal of the outcome to the classical confrontation between a criminal mastermind and his victim is noir with a twist ending.

The parodic intent also appears in the reference to feminist assumptions. The fake autonomy the prostitutes from Old Town have gained is laced with open tribute paid to the commodification of the women's images through their reduction to pop culture artifacts, as in the case of Gail. Both the films and the comics redefine the female image according to the contradictory requirements of fetishization and empowerment, paradoxically presenting women as both objectified *and* placed in a controlling position, and thus highlighting the two opposite, noir components of female helplessness and manipulation. An example of this strategy occurs at the beginning of the already mentioned episode from *Sin City 2* taken from *A Dame to Kill For* [20:30]. Dwight McCarthy is presented as a detective spying on a business man sexually engaged with a prostitute called Sally and taking pictures of them for the man's wife who intends to file for divorce. Sally willingly asks this man to dominate her by handcuffing her, begging him to show her he is "the boss," thereby totally conforming to the stereotype of the submissive woman. When Dwight McCarthy interrupts the scene (the business man was about to kill Sally because she represents a threat to his economic safety if his wife discovers their affair), Sally takes off her wig and reveals her real, red hair (Figure 4.3). When she leaves the room with McCarthy, she hits her client in the groin as a gesture of revenge. This scene plays out two kinds of stereotypes: one linked to submissiveness; the other to a fantasy

Figure 4.3 *Sin City: A Dame to Kill For* (Miller and Rodriguez, 2014): Sally takes off her disguise.

of emasculation that comes back repeatedly in the plot and dialogues. By switching from one representation to the other so swiftly, the film insists on the artificial quality of both stereotypes. It uses the visual discrepancy between Sally as a blond, submissive prostitute and Sally as a dominant, Old Town resident as referring to equally misleading images. Vesting the female character with such opposite features points out the parodic quality of the roles these characters are made to play and ultimately calls our attention to the culturally constructed, artificial quality of these performances.

Conclusion

The parodic function of stereotypes in the 2014 sequel begs attention in relation to the difference between the two films (so far[22]) in the series. We began this chapter with a question bearing on a possible explanation for the lack of success (in terms of box office) of *Sin City 2*, rooted in the possibility that the treatment of gender issues and generic influence was somewhat less straightforward in the second production and addressed a more mature audience compared to the 2005 film. The first film does offer an image of women that is more traditionally associated with victimization. Obvious examples include the characters of Nancy, the young girl who is saved by detective John Hartigan, and Shellie, the waitress who is harassed by her abusive ex-boyfriend Jackie and rescued by McCarthy. Similarly, crime in *Sin City* (2005) is more classically attached to a depiction of male violence and to perverted killers like Cardinal Roark and his protégé Kevin. On the contrary, *Sin City 2* is centered on the *femme fatale* figure through the character of Ava Lord.[23] The focus on pure action is less visible in *Sin City 2*, and the film relies more clearly on generic references. This constitutes a departure from the strategy that appealed to the spectators of the 2005 film. More largely, the focus on violence and action scenes—that feature less prominently in *Sin City 2*—is also more adapted to the emphasis on CGI that characterized the first film's appeal and which, nine years later, appears to have lost its initial novelty. More pointedly, however, the *femme fatale*, who does *not* appear (or not so openly) in the 2005 film, orientates *Sin City 2* toward a more informed, sometimes tongue-in-cheek generic reference that was not so accessible in the action-packed 2005 film. The motif of the double that appears prominently in the 2014 sequel is a case in point. As a reference to classical film noir, and associated with Ava Lord's image when she dives in her swimming pool [33:27], it conjures up a whole generic lineage, which includes noticeably the celebrated, final mirror sequence in *The Lady from Shanghai* (Orson Welles, 1948). Such overt allusions are a far cry from how the first film referred to the genre, mainly through voice-over and expressionist aesthetics, without relinquishing a more direct emphasis on action. *Sin City 2*, by referencing female images more intricately to generic models and opening the possibility of reading these images as parody, somewhat departs from the approach developed in 2005.

Is it after all legitimate to consider *Sin City 2* as a more interesting, more valuable film than the 2005 release, both in terms of its representation of female characters and its parodic treatment of genre? And does this representation of women characters really tally with a postfeminist agenda? Despite its poor success in critical terms, the sequel deals more directly with genre and in a more distanced fashion, especially because it presents the roles attributed to women characters as stereotypes detached from any real connection to the characters' identity. The approach developed in the film calls attention both to the prevalence of stereotypes to which women are reduced (objectification or domination) and to the artificiality and inadequacy of those stereotypes. The arc of Nancy's resilience and final revenge on Roark seems to resolve the contradiction between stereotyping and empowerment of female figures and to foreground a final victory of women—but representation remains ambivalent in that respect. The excess in representations also presents these roles as constructed and artificial, as in the case of Sally, who is placed between the two extremes of domination and submission. Yet we should avoid exaggerating the film's metacritical dimension or its role as the medium of a critical discourse on the construction of female images. Its remains largely focused on entertainment through the playful and excessive quality of references to generic and gendered stereotypes. Thus, the extreme quality of the stereotypes the women characters are based on participates both in the criticism of received images on the one hand and on the spectacle that makes the film verge on sheer entertainment on the other. This middle course steered by *Sin City 2*, compared to the 2005 film more entirely devoted to entertainment, may account for its relative lack of success.

Notes

1 Peter Bradshaw, "Sin city," *The Guardian*, June 3, 2005. Available at https://www.theguardian.com/theguardian/2005/jun/03/1 (accessed October 30, 2018).

2 Lucas O'Connor, "A graphic nature: *Sin City*'s troublesome adaptation," *Film Matters*, 1/2 (Summer 2010), p. 27.

3 Oliver Gettell "'Sin City: A Dame to Kill For' bombs: 5 things that went wrong," *Los Angeles Times*, August 25, 2014. Available at http://www.latimes.com/entertainment/movies/moviesnow/la-et-mn-sin-city-a-dame-to-kill-for-20140825-story.html (link no longer working).
Concerning the profits made by the first film, see the following webpage: http://www.boxofficemojo.com/movies/?id=sincity.htm. (accessed October 6, 2017).

4 Betsey Sharkey, "Five things to know about 'Sin City: A Dame to Kill For'" *Los Angeles Times*, August 21, 2014. See also Luis Frederick Aldama, Torsa Ghosal, and Christopher González, "A world of sin: Conversations on Rodriguez & Miller's cinematic comic book film series," *Post Script: Essays in Film and the Humanities*, 33/3 (Summer 2014), pp. 106–16: "One of the critical factors in the disappointing performance of *Sin City 2* must be its nine-year remove from the first installment" (p. 108).

5 However, the spectator who remembers the 2005 film will relate these pills to Marv's mental treatment and his lesbian parole officer Lucille, who provides him with medicine prescribed by her girlfriend.

6 Christina Dokou, "Seen city: Frank Miller's re-imaging as a cinematic 'New Real,'" in A. A. Babic (ed.), *Comics as History, Comics as Literature: Roles of the Comic Book in Scholarship, Society, and Entertainment* (Madison, NJ: Fairleigh Dickinson University Press, 2014), pp. 178–79.

7 Pierre Floquet points out, for instance, how the 2005 film flaunts its own intertextual quality with the comic book series by explicitly quoting words and panels literally drawn from the source work. In a partly similar but contrasted perspective, Luke Arnott focuses in his paper on the semantic differences between onomatopoeia in the graphic novels and in the 2005 film. See "*Sin City* (Frank Miller et Robert Rodriguez, 2005): Les Improbables Rencontres de personnages incarnés et dessinés," in B. Mitaine,

D. Roche, and I. Schmitt-Pitiot (eds.), *Bande dessinée et adaptation (littérature, cinéma, tv)* (Clermont-Ferrand, France: Presses Universitaires Blaise Pascal, 2015), p. 273. See also Lisa Garibay on Rodriguez's own discourse regarding the inspiration he took from Miller's graphic novels and Schembri on the aesthetic meaning of neo-figurative technique in films by Rodriguez and Greenaway ("Finding redemption," in Z. Ingle (ed.), *Robert Rodriguez: Interviews* (Jackson, MS: University Press of Mississippi, 2012), p. 125).

8 Sarah Gamble, "Postfeminism," in S. Gamble (ed.), *The Routledge Companion to Feminism and Postfeminism* (London and New York: Routledge [1998] 2001), p. 44.

9 Samantha Lindop, "Jane postmillennial cinema and the avenging fatale in *Sin City, Hard Candy* and *Descent*," *Scope: An Online Journal of Film Studies*, February 26, 2014, p. 4.

10 This reference looks back to the 1950s pulps, which later inspired such characters as Xena in the 1990s TV serial, *Xena: Warrior Princess*. See Gary Westfahl, *The Greenwood Encyclopedia of Science Fiction and Fantasy, Themes, Works, and Wonders* (Westport, CT: Greenwood Press, 2005), p. 76.

11 James Naremore, *More than Night: Film Noir in Its Contexts* (Berkeley: University of California Press, [1998] 2008 (updated edition)), *passim*.

12 Christopher Pizzino, "Art that goes BOOM: Genre and aesthetics in Frank Miller's *Sin City*," *English Language Notes*, 46/2 (Fall–Winter 2008), pp. 117–18.

13 Naremore, *More than Night*, chapter 2, pp. 42 ff.

14 Pizzino, "Art that goes BOOM," p. 123.

15 Graham Fuller also suggests that the shooting angles in *Sin City 1* may be a homage to the famous crane shot that begins Welles's *Touch of Evil* ("Colour me noir," *Sight and Sound* 15/6 (2005), p. 16).

16 Fredric Jameson, *Postmodernism, or the Cultural Logic of Late Capitalism* (Durham, NC: Duke University Press, 1992), p. 17.

17 In Nancy's case, this duality refers to the opposition between her lost innocence as a child rescued by Hartigan and her present situation as a stripper.

18 Pizzino, "Art that goes BOOM," p. 122.

19 Ibid., pp. 124–25.

20 Linda Hutcheon, *A Poetics of Postmodernism: History, Theory, Fiction* (London and New York: Routledge, 1988), pp. 141–42.

21 Richard Alleva thus criticized the film for the "boredom" it exudes due to the repetition of violent scenes. See "Blood sport—*Sin City* & *Walk on Water*," *Commonweal*, May 6, 2005, p. 22.

22 Rodriguez has recently announced a *Sin City* TV series.

23 Interestingly, this last name suggests maleness, which tallies with a common critical conception of the *femme fatale*, in 1940s film noir, as the

embodiment of male anxiety triggered by the empowerment of women in
the post–Second World War period (see Naremore, *More than Night*, p. 37
and Andrew Spicer, *Film Noir* (Harlow: Longman, 2002), pp. 90–91). It
also evokes a connection with porn actress Tracy Lords and thus confirms
the importance of a discourse on sexuality in the film (often connected to
castration).

Filmography

Sin City, directed by Frank Miller, Robert Rodriguez, and Quentin Tarantino
(special guest director), produced by Elizabeth Avellan, Frank Miller, and
Robert Rodriguez, written by Frank Miller and Robert Rodriguez based
on *Sin City* by Frank Miller, performances by Jessica Alba, Benicio de
Toro, Brittany Murphy, Clive Owen, Mickey Rourke, Bruce Willis, Elijah
Wood, music by John Debney, Graeme Revel, and Robert Rodriguez,
cinematography by Robert Rodriguez, edited by Robert Rodriguez,
Troublemaker Studios/Dimension Films, 2005.

Sin City: A Dame To Kill For, directed by Frank Miller and Robert Rodriguez,
produced by Robert Rodriguez, Aaron Kaufman, Stephen L'Heureux, Sergei
Bespalov, Alexander Rodnyansky, and Mark Manuel, written by Frank
Miller based on *Sin City* by Frank Miller, performances by Mickey Rourke,
Jessica Alba, Josh Brolin, Joseph Gordon-Levitt, Rosario Dawson, Bruce
Willis, Eva Green, Powers Boothe, Dennis Haysbert, Ray Liotta, Jaime King,
Christopher Lloyd, Jamie Chung, Jeremy Piven, Christopher Meloni, Juno
Temple, music by Robert Rodriguez and Carl Thiel, cinematography by
Robert Rodriguez, edited by Robert Rodriguez, Dimension Films/Aldamisa
Entertainment/Demarest Films/Troublemaker Studios/Miramax/Solipsist
Films/A.R. Films, 2014.

5

Textbook *Femme Fatale,* De-eroticized Neo-noir Heroine or Postfeminist Woman Who Kills?

Genre Trouble in *Gone Girl* (David Fincher, 2014)

Cristelle Maury

Gone Girl, David Fincher's 2014 noir thriller, gave rise to controversy in the popular press. The plot revolves around Amy Dunne (Rosamund Pike), a manipulative woman who meticulously stages her own disappearance in order to punish her cheating husband (Ben Affleck) by having him accused of her murder. She then completely changes her mind and clears her husband of the very suspicion she had fabricated. She kills former lover Desi (Neil Patrick Harris), whom she had found refuge with, making it look like he had kidnapped and raped her. The highly ironic ending shows the married couple reunited. The plot led some reviewers to state that the film voices an anti-feminist discourse due to its malevolent female killer who falsely accuses her victims of rape. David Cox entitled his article "*Gone Girl* revamps gender stereotypes for the worse";[1] Dana Schwartz wrote: "Amy Dunne From '*Gone Girl*' Is Not a Feminist";[2] and Amanda Dobbins stated: "Yes, *Gone Girl* Has a Woman Problem."[3] For other reviewers, the film, on the contrary, articulates feminist discourses because it allows for the representation of a free powerful female character. Rhiannon Lucy Cosslett, for example, entitled her piece "Female villains and false accusations: a feminist defence of *Gone Girl*,"[4] while Todd VanDerWerff claimed that "*Gone Girl* is the most feminist mainstream movie in years."[5] What is striking about these reviews is that, although they hold diverging views, they all share a common desire to assign a firm univocal ideological stance to the movie. In doing so, they fail to acknowledge the film's project to "question the tyranny of images on which the manipulation exerted by Amy is based," as Christophe Gelly has shown.[6] Considering the movie's depiction of a fabricated accusation of rape as an endorsement of gender stereotypes, or conversely, considering that the film takes a feminist stand because it reverses the conventional role of woman as victim, tends to overlook the complexity of the representations it offers.

In this chapter, I want to argue that such a contrasted reception of the film and the discussions it entails about its gender politics reveal the fundamental ambiguity of the character of Amy Dunne, and that this ambiguity is, in turn, revealing of current feminist debates. By tracing the evolution of the *femme fatale* character and concentrating on the ways in which the archetypes of the classical and neo-noir *femme fatale* have been woven into the very fabric of the film, I will show that Amy Dunne embodies the complex, simultaneous, and conflicting presence of feminist and anti-feminist discourses—more precisely, what Rosalind Gill has called an "entanglement of feminist and antifeminist ideas"[7] after Angela McRobbie's "double entanglement"[8] logic—resulting in what Anthea Taylor has termed "contradictions and tensions that are constitutive of postfeminism *itself*."[9]

I will first examine the character in the light of classical film noir and will demonstrate that she combines the traits of three distinct female character types of classical film noir: (1) the unfathomable *femme fatale*; (2) her antithesis, the "nurturing woman," described by Janey Place as "the opposite female archetype [. . .] also found in film noir";[10] and (3) the psychotic heroine of a subcategory of films noirs, which explore the psyche of unbalanced and obsessive women who commit murder with a domestic motive that can be found in films such as *Possessed* (Curtis Bernhardt, 1947), *Angel Face* (Otto Preminger, 1952), and *Sunset Boulevard* (Billy Wilder, 1950). I will then compare *Gone Girl* to two commercially successful neo-noir films that made a lasting impression due to their powerful erotic charge, *Fatal Attraction* (Adrian Lyne, 1988) and *Basic Instinct* (Paul Verhoeven, 1992). This comparative study will foreground how the film transforms "the orgasmic femme fatale"[11] of neo-noir into a de-eroticized version of the character, thereby completely undermining the *femme fatale* archetype—whatever its subtype—and making Amy a mere woman who kills. In the process, I will show that, although Fincher has often voiced his rejection of film theory[12] and refused to resort to "allusionism,"[13] a practice that was in vogue among the directors of 1980s and 1990s neo-noir, the film itself fully integrates the theses developed by feminist film studies on the significance of the *femme fatale* in noir and neo-noir. Tapping at once into classical noir, neo-noir as well as into their scholarship results in a character full of contradictions, Amy Dunne thereby perfectly illustrating the contradictory nature of postfeminism: as a seductress, she is in keeping with the codes of heterosexual attractiveness and runs counter to the values of second-wave feminism, while as a killer she violates "norms of femininity such as nurturance, gentleness and social conformity," and troubles "the masculine/feminine gender binary by transgressing its boundaries," as Lizzie Seal has shown.[14] As such, Amy Dunne both complies with and challenges the patriarchal allocation of gender roles and is an example of Gill's description of postfeminism as the site where "feminist ideas are both articulated and repudiated, expressed and disavowed."[15]

The Classical Film Noir *Femme Fatale* Revisited

A "Textbook"[16] *Femme Fatale*

Judging by the deceitful scenario she devises to frame her husband for her alleged murder, Amy Dunne has a lot in common with the mischievous and manipulative *femme fatale* as she has consensually been described in film scholarship from 1946 until very recently.[17] The very short opening sequence displays many aural and visual references to classical film noir, which endow Amy Dunne with the aura of a *femme fatale* [0:20–0:50]. The eerie soundtrack and Nick's voice-over create a strong noir atmosphere. His introspective discourse in which he muses over the enigmatic nature of his wife is in line with the typical noir voice-over of the male protagonist who expresses his existential angst, tells about his failures and/or confesses his difficulties in resisting the alluring *femme fatale*, in what J.P. Telotte called "a case of self-exploration and discovery":[18]

> When I think of my wife, I always think of her head. I picture cracking her lovely skull, unspooling her brain. The primal questions of a marriage: What are you thinking? How are you feeling? What have we done to each other? [0:24-0:50]

With this graphic fantasy of penetrating his wife's secret thoughts, Nick ponders over the woman's inaccessibility. His reflection on his wife is itself in keeping with what a number of critics have noted about the mystery of the *femme fatale*.

Visually, the film opens on a black screen that fades in to a chiaroscuro close-up of the back of Amy's head, which "carries connotations of the mysterious and the unknown,"[19] in accordance with Janey Place and Lowell Peterson's seminal article on film noir's visual style. By highlighting Nick's hand stroking Amy's blonde hair, the composition gives a distorted sense of space typical of noir mise-en-scène, "designed to unsettle, jar and disorient the viewer in correlation with the disorientation felt by the *noir* heroes."[20] The last shot provides a visual confirmation of Nick's thoughts about the inaccessibility of his wife: Amy's face is lit in "direct, undiffused light [which] create[s] a hard statuesque surface beauty that seems more seductive but less attainable, at once alluring and impenetrable."[21] Amy is thus represented as a typical—maybe even a stereotypical—*femme fatale*.

Besides being conjured up visually and aurally, the sense of mystery surrounding Amy is reinforced through the casting. Rosamund Pike was cast in the role precisely because she looked mysterious, as Fincher himself indicated: "I never got a sense of who she was. [. . .] There was an opacity there and it was interesting."[22] Opacity is a recurring word when it comes to defining the typical *femme fatale*. And with her blonde hair, regular features, and cold beauty, Pike is reminiscent of another type of *femme fatale*, equally or even more mysterious than the classical *femme fatale*: the sophisticated, mysterious Hitchcockian blonde. Pike especially takes after Kim Novak, whose double role as a fabricated heroine in *Vertigo* (Alfred Hitchcock, 1958) was clearly an inspiration for the character of Amy. Like Judy/Madeleine, Amy lends herself to several changes of identity. She also exerts fascination on the male protagonist and the spectator, especially as she submits herself to his voyeuristic gaze. The close-up of Amy thus complies with what Laura Mulvey described about Hitchcock "go[ing] into the investigative side of voyeurism" where "the beauty of the woman as object and the screen space coalesce: she is [. . .] a perfect product, whose body, stylized and fragmented by close-ups, is the content of the film and the direct point recipient of the spectator's look."[23] The pleasure in looking felt by Nick, what Mulvey calls "scopophilia,"[24] may also be felt by the spectator as our gazes are often aligned.

Most of the stylistic conventions of film noir, identified by film critics, are accumulated in this liminal sequence, which illustrates Place's contention that "the source and the operation of the sexual woman's power and its danger to the male character is expressed visually both in the iconography of the image and in the visual style."[25] Amy is the epitome of the classical film-noir *femme fatale* and, as such, represents the danger of using her sexuality as a weapon, in keeping with feminist film scholars who conclude that femmes fatales represent a threat to male domination; Gledhill, for instance, speaks of "the perennial myth of woman as threat to male control of the world and destroyer of male aspiration,"[26] while Place states that women "derive power, not weakness, from their sexuality,"[27] and Kaplan that "the female characters [. . .] represent a challenge to [the male order]."[28] All these ideas are contained in the opening of *Gone Girl* and point at once to Amy's closeness to the *femme fatale* archetype and to the filmmakers' and the novel's author's familiarity with film noir itself, as it is described in feminist film theory. This familiarity is made clear as Fincher also incorporates another noir archetype into the Amy character: the nurturing woman.

A Nurturing *Femme Fatale*

Besides stressing the mysterious, unfathomable intentions of the *femme fatale*, Nick's voice-over ruminates on a common domestic concern about the lack of communication between husband and wife, thereby casting the narrative against a background of dysfunctional married life and domesticity. In doing so, Nick asserts Amy's status as a wife and, therefore, as a potential "nurturing woman," one of the secondary characters of film noir that Janey Place identifies as the antithesis of the *femme fatale*:

> The opposite female archetype is also found in film noir: woman as redeemer. She offers the possibility of integration for the alienated, lost man into the stable world of secure values, roles and identities. She gives love, understanding (or at least forgiveness), asks very little in return (just that he come back to her) and is generally visually passive and static.[29]

Not only does Amy comply with the archetype of the *femme fatale*, but she is also very close to the nurturing woman, as her romantic aspiration to find true love, her constant domestic concern to save her marriage, and her desire to become a mother suggest. Toward the end of the film, in the final interview the couple gives for the Ellen Abbott Show, Amy is sitting in just the sort of "passive and static" position Place describes [137:39–138:19]. She is wearing her wedding ring and a very conventional white blouse with a Peter Pan collar, connoting prudishness, and is holding hands with her husband. She quietly waits for him to do the talking, including announcing that they are "going to be parents." Although the staged nature of this recovered marital bliss makes no doubt—it is based on an artificial insemination she undergoes without Nick's consent and preserved only because of threats she makes against her husband—she is definitely represented as a wife and potential mother.

But Amy wants more than just to represent a nurturing woman; she aspires to *be* one. While the classical *femme fatale* has her husband killed by her lover out of venality, Amy does exactly the contrary: she kills her lover to reclaim both her husband and her marital life. This twist can be read as a skewed reference to the famous classical film-noir love triangle established by James Damico, in which a man is induced by "a not-innocent woman [to] actually murder a second man to whom the woman is unhappily or unwillingly attached."[30] Amy uses all the strategies typical of the *femme fatale*—duplicity and manipulation—but she does so to remain a domestic, nurturing woman. Indeed, she cannot stand that her stereotypical life has been violated (her husband has cheated on her), and she kills a man in order to become a happily married woman *again*, as well as a mother as she plans to get herself inseminated with her husband's sperm. Thus, the character of Amy Dunne paradoxically combines incompatible elements of the mysterious *femme fatale* and the nurturing housewife, or as Place puts it, "the deadly seductress" and "the rejuvenating redeemer,"[31] two character types she identified in a feminist attempt to question the traditional representation of women in film, but not for the same woman. In *Gone Girl*, these two archetypes are fused in one single character and are presented right away in the opening sequence and consistently built up throughout the film. It even runs the risk of compromising the consistency in terms of characterization by integrating yet another subtype of *femme fatale*: the psychotic heroine.

A Psychotic *Femme Fatale*

Amy's deranged persona is given full vent as she engages in a psychotic staging of rape and murder. The last shot of the opening sequence already foreshadows her psychotic personality. As Amy turns her head and faces the camera (Figure 5.1), the Mulveyan "scopophilia" the viewer may have been indulging in is broken by the look-to-the-camera that calls into question our identification with the diegetic male viewer, her husband. Her gaze echoes the Hitchcockian psychotic gaze, such as the one Norman Bates directs at the audience as he waits at the police station at the very end of *Psycho* (1960). The shot also prefigures a close-up with a similar gaze in the scene where she slits Desi's throat, thereby proleptically announcing her status as a psychotic heroine (Figure 5.2).

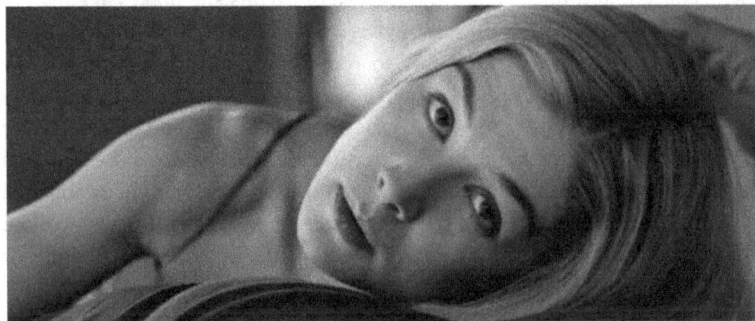

Figure 5.1 *Gone Girl* (Fincher, 2014): close-up of the mysterious Amy Dunne.

Figure 5.2 *Gone Girl* (Fincher, 2014): Amy Dunne's psychopathic gaze, on the brink of murder.

Amy's characterization is influenced by the psychotic heroines of a subcategory of films noirs in which women commit crimes of passion. Like Louise Howell (Joan Crawford) in *Possessed*, who remains obsessed with a man who has fallen out of love with her, Amy feels rejected by the man she loves. Like Diane Tremayne (Jean Simmons) in *Angel Face*, who provokes a car accident to kill herself and her husband, Amy refuses the idea that her marriage is falling apart. Like Norma Desmond (Gloria Swanson) in *Sunset Boulevard*, who has been fashioned by the Hollywood star system and cannot bear to no longer be a silent film diva, Amy has become a prisoner of the image of perfection imposed on her by her parents through the children's book series "Amazing Amy." As a sociopathic victim of excessive media coverage, contemporary Amy is in keeping with classical film-noir psychotic victims whose "psychological illness represents social disorder,"[32] and for whom disease is the vector translating the oppression sustained. But her characterization is all the more complex as, unlike Louise Howell who is committed to a psychiatric hospital, Diane Tremayne who dies at her own hands, and Norma Desmond who is arrested by the police, Amy Dunne remains alive, goes unpunished, and recovers her status as a married woman and a mother-to-be. Feminist film scholars have shown that, in classical film noir, psychosis is a way for the heroines to rebel against patriarchal order. Janey Place explains that the "dangerous lady of film noir" is transgressive because she is ambitious, and "this ambition is inappropriate to her status as a woman and must be confined"; she cites Norma Desmond, who "wants to be a star, not a recluse," and Diane Tremayne, who "wants to win an uninterested lover,"[33] as examples. Likewise, according to Julie Grossman, "the women in these films are, in narrative terms, mentally unstable, but their instability reflects a rebellion against patriarchal rules that not only deny them value in psychosocial realms but make them crazy, ready to act and react violently to the authority figures and patriarchal institutions that govern their lives."[34] On the contrary, Amy is compelled by external pressure to fit into the patriarchal system at all costs. As such, Amy is a victim of an oppressive patriarchal order, but unlike the psychotic heroines of classical film noir, there is nothing rebellious about her as she longs to return to her golden cage. Such a twist establishes an ironic distance with the feminist discourses on film-noir heroines. Representing Amy and Nick as the couple who has saved their marriage and can live up to their idyllic public image could be read as the ironic postfeminist conclusion that "the time for feminism is past"[35]—and, for Amy, it is indeed.

Gone Girl meticulously breaks down the archetype of the noir *femme fatale* by fusing it with two other character types: the nurturing woman and the psychotic heroine. It reflects an awareness and mastery of the codes of classical film noir as established by (feminist) film critics, rather than a lack thereof, as the director likes to claim. This unusual combination is furthered by Amy's being alternately represented as a childlike woman (Amazing Amy) and as a "sexually potent"[36] seductress who uses her charms to get her way in the scene where she kills. The fact that she plays the role of the perfect housewife and of the irresistible seductress could be put down to her duplicity as a *femme fatale*, but the combination of these contradictory characteristics, in addition to her psychotic personality, results, in effect, in an incongruous mix that destroys her sexual potency: what we have, here, is a mere woman who kills. The dismantling of the *femme fatale* as an archetype of noir and neo-noir is finalized by a process of de-eroticization.

From Neo-noir *Femme Fatale* to Mere De-eroticized Woman Who Kills

Gone Girl explicitly refers to two famous prototypical big-budget neo-noir erotic thrillers, *Fatal Attraction* and *Basic Instinct*, which, Linda Ruth Williams observes, have left a "legacy [that] would be seen throughout the following decade and beyond."[37] These neo-noir hypotexts immediately place Amy in the category of the "hypersexualised version of the *femme fatale*":[38] in other words, the neo-noir *femme fatale*. *Gone Girl*, however, transforms some of the ingredients of these two erotic thrillers by including references to two other film genres that are at odds with the neo-noir erotic thriller: the romantic comedy and the horror movie. As we shall see, the central female character of *Gone Girl* ends up, in effect, de-eroticized.

The "First Night"

The night of Nick and Amy's romantic encounter at a New York party [3:21–6:42] echoes the famous elevator scene of *Fatal Attraction*, in which Alex Forrest (Glenn Close) and Dan Gallagher (Michael Douglas) engage in wild sex [19:39–21:49]. In both films, the newly formed couple leaves the party, walks the busy New York streets at night, and ends up at the woman's trendy apartment for a night of passionate sex. Both films make use of low-key lighting and take advantage of the urban setting and of the elevator to create a shadowy universe. Given the fact that there is no sex scene in the novel, this addition corresponds to a clear intention on the part of the director and screenwriter (the author herself) not so much to eroticize the encounter, as to comment on eroticism. Indeed, framed within a similar action, setting, and cinematography, the slight differences serve to undermine the erotic charge of the neo-noir erotic thriller.

The first difference concerns the order of the events. In *Gone Girl*, Nick and Amy leave the party together and find themselves in an elevator in which Nick makes a romantic commitment to Amy. They then walk into the New York streets before having sex at Amy's. In *Fatal Attraction*, the couple formed by Alex and Dan is first seen walking at night in the busy streets after leaving the party, and then and only then does the couple enter an elevator where the passionate sex scene takes place. The order of the events is designed to build up sexual tension before reaching a climax, as the illegitimate couple leaves the public space for the confined, erotically charged elevator. In *Gone Girl*, the sequence of events is reversed, thereby reducing the elevator to a mere means of transportation. The conventional place for sex for legitimate couples—the bedroom—has been retained, so that the erotic potential created by the enclosed space and forced intimacy of the elevator is lost.

In terms of setting, both couples walk the New York streets arm in arm, chatting and laughing. In *Fatal Attraction*, the imminence of carnal love is signaled by the fact that it takes place in the Meatpacking District. As Alex and Dan are going to her place to have sex, they are shot walking among butchers who carry animal carcasses and in the middle of fires, burning along the street. In *Gone Girl*, instead of the hellish bustling of the butchers and carcasses, sacks of powdered sugar are being funneled into a bakery, creating a sugar snowstorm. The sugar floats all around them as Nick gently kisses Amy, endowing the scene with a romantic, fairy tale and even Christmassy atmosphere. The possibility of fleshly desire strongly suggested in *Fatal Attraction* is totally ruled out from *Gone Girl* in favor of sugary romance. Thus, the use of similar settings with a twist participates in debunking the sexual tension, and the sexual potency of the *femme fatale* is completely lost.

Finally, the erotic charge is totally lost because of the way in which the sexual act itself is filmed. The sex scene of *Gone Girl* comes down to a very short sequence shot (sixteen seconds long) that takes place in a bed and in the dark. There is no undressing and no nudity. The camera is placed behind Amy's head so that we can see her head dangling from the bed. The shot segments her body in a composition that is more typical of horror films than of erotic thrillers. Moreover, the lighting techniques also contribute to defusing the erotic tension. Chiaroscuro lighting is used in an unconventional manner. While in neo-noir, this trope is used to endow bedroom scenes with a heavy erotic charge, here, it creates exactly the opposite effect in that it prevents the viewer from seeing the two lovers in bed. To top it off, Amy's words after sex, "Nick Dunne I really like you," sound very prosaic and out of step with the alleged intensity of the moment they have just experienced; it deflates the erotic charge created by the prospect of the sexual encounter. *Fatal Attraction*'s sex scene, on the contrary, relies on quick editing from different points of views to favor voyeurism and arouse the spectator's desire. The elevator scene is composed of a series of shots that detail the positions of the lovers: high angles offering a bird's-eye view of the couple and highlighting their brisk passionate movements; inserts of their restless feet and legs, indicative of their ardent jostle; two shots to depict their fervent kisses; head and shoulder shots to show the man violently tearing off her dress and kissing her naked breasts. No nondiegetic music is used to endow the scene with a romantic tone or create a music video aesthetic. Instead, the absence of music draws attention to the quickening breathing and moaning of the couple and brings out the signs of sexual arousal. Nick and Amy's first night is thus constructed as the polar opposite of this scene of erotic adultery and is characterized by the invisibility of their sexual attraction.

The *Fatal Attraction* hypotext draws the audience's attention to the apparent absence of "fatal attraction" between Amy and Nick, thereby underlining the discrepancy between announced eroticism and the lack thereof. The viewer's expectations are thus thwarted, reinforcing the feeling of "missing out on" eroticism. In the postfeminist era, the *femme fatale* has lost her power of attraction and has become a mere woman who kills. In addition, the first night of *Gone Girl* is placed under the aegis of corny romanticism. The scene opens on Amy's voice-over expressing overgrown-teenage-like excitement as she reads out loud the words she is writing in her diary: "I'm so crazy, stupid, happy. I met a boy." She uses a very girlish pen topped with pink feathers, while the soundtrack plays a soft, syrupy melody. It places Amy in the Bridget Jones type of role (Pike played Jane Bennet in the 2005 adaptation of *Pride & Prejudice*)—single woman in desperate search of the right man—and, as such, she seems to be a character from a chick-flick comedy, not from an erotic thriller. Amy's "infectious girlishness"[39] precludes her sex appeal and ultimately de-eroticizes her. In typical postfeminist fashion, and like Bridget Jones in McRobbie's reading, Amy is a liberated woman who enjoys "sexual freedom, the right to drink, smoke, have fun in the city, and be economically independent," but who "despite feminism [. . .] wants to pursue dreams of romance, find a suitable husband, get married and have children."[40] In effect, the strong erotic component of *Fatal Attraction* has been turned into mere girlish aspirations of romance and marriage. Both Amy's sexual potency and identity as a *femme fatale* are undermined by the parodic inclusion of some of the conventions of the romantic comedy.[41] While *Fatal Attraction* has been read as a critique of second-wave feminism because the character of Alex is a progressive career woman who is punished for her independence,[42] *Gone Girl* can be read as a critique of the effects of postfeminist ideology because Amy is turned into a deranged product of postfeminism. Like Alex, she is a successful career woman, an affluent, independent woman who makes financial decisions on her own, including deciding to return the money from her trust fund to her parents without her husband's consent. But her success is brutally brought to a halt by the recession, which shakes the very foundations of her "neoliberal feminism," one of the ways in which postfeminism provides, in Gill's words, "an acceptable face of feminism."[43]

The Murder Scene

Amy is further de-eroticized through the introduction of elements of the horror film within an allegedly erotic scene. The sequence in which she kills Desi [117:57–120:26] echoes the famous highly erotic opening of *Basic Instinct*, in which a mysterious blonde woman stabs her victim with an ice pick as he reaches orgasm [2:54–4:29]. In *Gone Girl*, Amy kills her lover in the same manner, using a box cutter instead, but the scopophilic erotic charge is entirely obliterated by the gory killing.

The universe of *Basic Instinct* is clearly conjured up in *Gone Girl* through the use of similar decor, action, and even visual style. Both scenes take place in a luxurious bedroom with a huge bed in the middle of which the lovers are having sex. Both women wait for their lovers to reach orgasm before killing them. The two scenes are filmed in sepia colors with soft, indirect, orange lighting and make use of high-angle shots to show the action on the bed, and of inserts on the women's hands when they seize the weapon hidden on the bed. Yet the erotic charge of *Basic Instinct* is totally absent from *Gone Girl*. In the 1992 film, the woman's naked body and blonde hair are fetishized and fragmented through a variety of close-ups. The action itself recalls soft-core pornography: Catherine Tramell straddles her lover and ties him up to the cast-iron headboard of the bed. The camera offers a variety of angles from which the woman's body can be admired, including one from behind the headboard, which, along with the white bondage scarf, are typical soft-porn props. The murder, which constitutes the surprise conclusion of the scene, does not defuse the eroticism.

Although the action is exactly the same in Fincher's film, the murder scene is staged as a murder scene. The presence of shots of Amy looking offscreen indicates that she is faking her pleasure. Instead of actively engaging in foreplay, she remains aloof and emotionless, as a reverse shot in which she avoids Desi's gaze indicates. What is clear is that she has staged the entire scene and that sex is just a means to kill. While *Basic Instinct* relies on surprise—providing erotic pleasure by giving the audience the opportunity to indulge in "scopophilia" before the killing—*Gone Girl* relies on suspense, thereby focusing the spectator's attention on the impending murder instead of the erotic potential of the scene, since the audience is made aware of the outcome from the outset. Interestingly enough, viewers of *Basic Instinct* never find out whether Catherine Tramell, the *femme fatale*, is the killer or not. In *Gone Girl*, there is no such doubt. The absence of mystery further contributes to dismantling eroticism. Moreover, while in *Basic Instinct*, the two lovers are naked, in *Gone Girl*, the costumes play an important role by not being congruent with the codes of eroticism. Amy unzips her white dress, and the camera reveals her perfect body in chaste white underwear in keeping with her self-portrait as a pure, innocent, and abused victim; Desi is wearing plain cotton boxer shorts. The camera is placed behind the protagonists so that we get an external and totally nonerotic perspective on the action. As they are sitting on the bed, we can see Amy's back, and then Desi's buttocks, while Amy puts her arm in his crotch to grab his bottom. A high-angle shot reveals Desi in a somewhat unflattering position: he is on all fours, his shorts half way down, giving an image of a first-timer that verges on comedy. In no way does the sequence abide by the codes of the erotic thriller, where murder occurs during highly charged sex scenes.

In the novel, Desi's killing is not a scene. It is mentioned by several characters after the killing, so that it is up to the reader to imagine the event. Although the descriptions are all very bloody, the fact that they are a posteriori accounts has a distancing effect. The film's graphic and explicit murder scene, on the other hand, taps directly into horror film conventions. Unlike the musical score of *Basic Instinct*, which is mysterious and enticing, the pulsating heartbeat of Trent Reznor's soundtrack evokes both the emotional and visceral quality of the scene. The viewer remains an outside observer of the sex scene: it is a murder scene where there happens to be sex and where the viewer is made to be an active participant in the crime. The low-angle shot of Desi when Amy slits his throat makes it look as though the blood is going to fall directly onto the viewer, giving the impression that we are actively taking part in the murder, either as killers or as victims.

A Postfeminist Woman Who Kills

By invoking *Fatal Attraction* and *Basic Instinct*, *Gone Girl* promises to project an image of Amy as a "hypersexualized" neo-noir *femme fatale*, offering, as Andrew Spicer contended, "the postfeminist image of a strong and attractive woman who is both feminine and feminist, if utterly ruthless."[44] But instead of fulfilling this promise, eroticism is lost to corny romanticism and gory killing. The film seems to represent Amy as a "do-me feminist," that is to say, a "feminist wom[a]n who like[s] sex,"[45] thus "celebrat[ing] the pleasures of feminine adornment and sexuality,"[46] when it suggests that sexual freedom is one of the keys to female independence and emancipation.[47] But ultimately, as the sexual tension is defused, *Gone Girl* only presents the contradictions inherent in postfeminism. The de-eroticization of Amy, therefore, functions as a political comment on the politics of pleasure that has been key to third-wave feminism and on the present state of feminism.

By fusing three character types into one—the *femme fatale*, the nurturing woman, the psychotic heroine—and by de-eroticizing the neo-noir *femme fatale*, *Gone Girl* achieves a step-by-step implosion of the *femme fatale* archetype of both classical noir and neo-noir. The transformation of the *femme fatale* into a mere, albeit complex woman who kills echoes the current debates about the present state of feminism. The viewer is faced with the entanglement of incompatible traits. This brings to mind some of the inconsistencies of postfeminism, as described by Gill, who states that "what makes contemporary media culture distinctively postfeminist, rather than prefeminist or antifeminist, is precisely this entanglement of feminist and antifeminist ideas,"[48] or by Anthea Taylor for whom postfeminism consists in "'suturing' of feminism and antifeminism."[49] The contradictions and tensions that have been mapped around the figure of Amy are indicative of the contradictions that are constitutive of postfeminism itself. Like postfeminism, Amy simultaneously endorses and disavows feminism, according to the logic of "double entanglement" that is at the core of Angela McRobbie's definition of dominant postfeminist discourse:

[P]ostfeminism positively draws on and evokes feminism as that which can be taken into account, to suggest that equality is achieved, in order to install a whole repertoire of new meanings which emphasize that it is no longer needed, it is a spent force.[50]

Amy is at once a mysterious *femme fatale*, a passive homemaker, a de-eroticized neo-noir heroine, a do-me feminist, a chick-flick heroine, a psychotic heroine, and a woman who kills. She embodies these contradictions and is, as such, an ironic product of postfeminism.

Besides blurring Amy's identity, the accumulation of persona gives way to a succession of performances that never unveil her core identity. As a victim of the media and of public image, she is only what she represents. Her identity consists in the accumulation of all her contradictory traits, rather like Michel Serres's Harlequin's color-strewn mantle metaphor.[51] She is not a homemaker and is a *femme fatale* only in *trompe l'oeil* style. The scene of her transformation is but another indication that she plays multiple roles. The most obvious instance of performativity is when she decides to "kill" her Amazing Amy character. She cuts her hair, dyes it brown, stuffs herself with food to put on weight, and buys glasses. Then under Desi's supervision, she transforms back to her older self. In any case, it seems that she has no other identity apart from the ones she plays out, illustrating, in a sense, Judith Butler's thesis that identity is a construct. Amy has no "stable identity." Her (gender) identity is "tenuously constituted in time, instituted in an exterior space through a *stylized repetition of acts*."[52] But the only reality behind Amy's contradictory postfeminist acts is the fact that, like gender, they are only real to the extent that they are performed. Beyond the host of postfeminist debates, it is the performativity of identity that prevails. Through this complex characterization of Amy as a postfeminist woman who kills, it seems that *Gone Girl* has sought to debunk noir and neo-noir codes in an effort to critique the effects of postfeminist ideology and with the clear intention to take ironic distance with theories altogether.

Notes

1 David Cox, "*Gone Girl* revamps gender stereotypes—for the worse," *The Guardian*, October 6, 2014.
2 Dana Schwartz, "Amy Dunne from '*Gone Girl*' is not a feminist," *The Observer*, June 9, 2016.
3 Amanda Dobbins, "Yes, *Gone Girl* has a woman problem," *Vulture*, October 3, 2014.
4 Rhiannon Lucy Cosslett, "Female villains and false accusations: A feminist defence of *Gone Girl*," *The New Statesman*, October 7, 2014.
5 Todd VanDerWerff, "*Gone Girl* is the most feminist mainstream movie in years," *Vox*, October 6, 2014.

6 Christophe Gelly, "*Gone Girl* (David Fincher, 2014) médias, mensonges et manipulation," *Revue Française d'Études Américaines,* 150 (1er trimester 2017), p. 74, my translation.

7 Rosalind Gill, "Postfeminist media culture: Elements of a sensibility," *European Journal of Cultural Studies,* 10/2 (2007), p. 161.

8 Angela McRobbie, "Post-feminism and popular culture," *Feminist Media Studies,* 4/3 (2004), p. 255.

9 Anthea Taylor, *Single Women in Popular Culture: The Limits of Postfeminism* (Houndmills Basingstoke: Palgrave Macmillan, 2012), p. 13.

10 Janey Place, "Women in film noir," in E. Ann Kaplan (ed.), *Women in Film Noir* (London: British Film Institute, 1978), p. 50.

11 Chris Straayer, "*Femme fatale* or lesbian femme: *Bound* in sexual *différance,*" in E. A. Kaplan (ed.), *Women in Film Noir,* expanded edition (London: British Film Institute, 1998), p. 153.

12 Fincher bears a clear grudge against film scholars (see Todd McCarthy, "HBO directors' dialogues New York Film Festival—*The Social Network,* part 3 of 6," September 25, 2010). Available at https://www.youtube.com/w atch?v=4VCuLT6SV7c (accessed June 29, 2017).

13 See Noël Carroll, "The future of allusion: Hollywood and the seventies (and beyond)," *October,* 2 (Spring 1982), p. 52.

14 Lizzie Seal, *Women, Murder and Femininity Gender Representations of Women Who Kill* (Houndmills Basingstoke and New York: Palgrave Macmillan, 2010), p. 1.

15 Gill, "Postfeminist media culture," p. 163.

16 Reference to the expression Gillian Flynn uses to describe Amy's staging of her murder in her fabricated diary in *Gone Girl* (London: Weidenfeld & Nicolson, 2012), p. 383.

17 See Jean-Pierre Chartier, *La Revue du cinema* 2e série 2 (novembre 1946), pp. 67–70; Raymond Borde and Etienne Chaumeton, *A Panorama of American Film Noir 1941–1953* (San Francisco: CityLight Books, 2002 [1955]); A. Silver and J. Ursini (eds.), *Film Noir Reader* (New York: Limelight, 1996), Foster Hirsch, *The Dark Side of the Screen: Film Noir* (San Diego: A.S. Barnes, 1981), Thomas Schatz, *Hollywood Genres: Formulas, Filmmaking, and the Studio System* (Boston: McGraw-Hill, 1981), Alain Silver and Elizabeth Ward, *Film Noir: An Encyclopaedic Reference to the American Style* (Woodstock: The Overlook Press, 1979), Kaplan (ed.), *Women in Film Noir;* Mary Ann Doane, *Femmes Fatales: Feminism, Film Theory, Psychoanalysis* (New York and London: Routledge, 1991); Yvonne Tasker, "Women in film noir," in A. Spicer and H. Hanson (eds.), *A Companion to Film Noir* (Chichester, West Sussex: Wiley-Blackwell, 2013), pp. 353–68.

18 J. P. Telotte, *Voices in the Dark, the Narrative Patterns of Film Noir* (Urbana and Chicago: University of Illinois Press, 1989), p. 94.

19 Janey Place and Lowell Peterson, "Some visual motifs of *film noir*" [1974], in Silver and Ursini (eds.), *Film Noir Reader* (New York: Limelight, 1996), p. 66.

20 Ibid., p. 68.
21 Ibid., p. 66.
22 Jeff Labrecque, "*Gone Girl*: Why David Fincher cast Ben Affleck and Rosamund Pike," *Premiere*, September 27, 2014.
23 Laura Mulvey, "Visual pleasure and narrative cinema" [1975], in L. Braudy and M. Cohen (eds.), *Film Theory and Criticism: Introductory Readings* (New York: Oxford University Press, 1999), p. 841.
24 Ibid., p. 835.
25 Place, "Women in film noir," pp. 43–44.
26 Christine Gledhill, "Klute 1: A contemporary film noir and feminist criticism," in Kaplan (ed.), *Women in Film Noir*, expanded edition (London: British Film Institute, 1998), p. 19.
27 Place, "Women in film noir," p. 35.
28 E. Ann Kaplan, "The place of women in Fritz Lang's *The Blue Gardenia*," in Kaplan (ed.), *Women in Film Noir*, expanded edition (London: British Film Institute, 1998), p. 83.
29 Ibid., p. 50.
30 James Damico, "Film noir: A modest proposal," [1978], in Silver and Ursini (eds.), *Film Noir Reader* (New York: Limelight, 1996), p. 103.
31 Place, "Women in film noir," p. 52.
32 Julie Grossman, *Rethinking the Femme Fatale in Film Noir, Ready for Her Close-Up* (Basingstoke, Hampshire, and New York: Palgrave Macmillan, 2009), p. 122.
33 Place, "Women in film noir," p. 46.
34 Grossman, *Rethinking the Femme Fatale*, p. 70.
35 Sarah Gamble, "Postfeminism," in S. Gamble (ed.), *The Routledge Companion to Feminism and Postfeminism* (London and New York: Routledge, 2001), p. 44.
36 Hirsch, *Dark Side of the Screen*, p. 20.
37 Linda Ruth Williams, *The Erotic Thriller in Contemporary Cinema* (Bloomington: Indiana University Press, 2005), p. 163.
38 Tasker, "Women in film noir," p. 358.
39 Angela McRobbie, *The Aftermath of Feminism: Gender, Culture and Social Change* (London and New York: Sage, 2012), p. 12.
40 Ibid.
41 This parodic use is an instance of what Abbott and Jermyn noted about the romantic comedy as a genre: "a parody-able commodity, demonstrating the manner in which its conventions are part of a shared cultural landscape" (Stacey Abbott and Deborah Jermyn), "Introduction—a lot like love: The romantic comedy in contemporary cinema," in S. Abbott and D. Jermyn (eds.), *Falling in Love Again, Romantic Comedy in Contemporary Cinema* (London: I.B. Tauris, 2009), p. 3.
42 Susan Faludi takes it as an example to illustrate her backlash theory (*Backlash: The Undeclared War against American Women* (New York: Three Rivers Press, 1991), p. 3.

43 Rosalind Gill, "Post-postfeminism? New feminist visibilities in postfeminist times," *Feminist Media Studies,* 16/4 (2016), p. 618, pp. 617–18.

44 Spicer, Andrew, *Historical Dictionary of Film Noir* (Lanham, MD: Scarecrow Press, 2010), pp. 330–31.

45 Tad Friend, "Yes: Feminist women who like sex," *Esquire,* February 1994.

46 Stéphanie Genz and Benjamin Brabon, *Postfeminism: Cultural Texts and Theories* (Edinburgh: Edinburgh University Press, 2009), p. 93.

47 Ibid., p. 91.

48 Gill, "Postfeminist media culture," p. 161.

49 Taylor, *Single Women in Popular Culture,* p. 13.

50 McRobbie, "Post-feminism and popular culture," p. 255.

51 Michel Serres, *Atlas* (Paris, Julliard, 1994), p. 210.

52 Judith Butler, *Gender Trouble Feminism and the Subversion of Identity* (New York and London: Routledge, 1999), p. 179.

Filmography

Basic Instinct, directed by Paul Verhoeven, produced by Alan Marshall, written by Joe Eszterhas, performances by Michael Douglas, Sharon Stone, George Dzundza, Jeanne Tripplehorn, music by Jerry Goldsmith, cinematography by Jan de Bont, edited by Frank J. Urioste, Carolco/Le Studio Canal+, 1992. DVD Studiocanal, 2000.

Fatal Attraction, directed by Adrian Lyne, produced by Stanley R. Jaffe and Sherry Lansing, screenplay by James Dearden based on *Diversion* by James Dearden, performances by Michael Douglas, Glenn Close, Anne Archer, music by Maurice Jarre, cinematography by Howard Atherton, edited by Michael Kahn and Peter E. Berger, Jaffe/Lansing Productions, 1987. DVD Paramount Home Entertainment, 2002.

Gone Girl, directed by David Fincher, produced by Arnon Milchan, Joshua Donen, Reese Witherspoon, and Cean Chaffin, screenplay by Gillian Flynn, based on *Gone Girl* by Gillian Flynn, performances by Ben Affleck, Rosamund Pike, Neil Patrick Harris, Tyler Perry, music by Trent Reznor and Atticus Ross, cinematography by Jeff Cronenweth, edited by Kirk Baxter, Regency Enterprises/TSG Entertainment, 2014. DVD 20th Century Fox 2015.Nobis alique sitistio ma net min es res eos es ea quamet as corissit volo omnis est etur res rem eossita tecersp elendae coribus, sum secture cullis a idem. Nam, offic tem reium in cum volorru mquiae eost vel ipis maximus andigenis alis sit facea quaepel eri antiori corporp orehend itatior estruntis ad mi, id modi ut quibus quid que cum endes vella voluptibus doluptur moluptatat.

Neque odit il et essequam nam que paribus rem veligenis ad etur re nam aut de vel eos ditate nobitaquist evelendunt que ma con re non num aut

Part Two

Action Babes

6

From Sarah Connor 2.0 to Sarah Connor 3.0

Women Who Kill in the *Terminator* Franchise

Marianne Kac-Vergne

Sarah Connor has become one of the most famous embodiments of the gun-toting action heroine since the release of *Terminator 2: Judgment Day* (James Cameron, 1991), where she is played by the muscular, stone-faced Linda Hamilton. So iconic is the character that she was given her own television series—*Terminator: The Sarah Connor Chronicles* (Fox, 2008–09)—before reappearing in the latest installment of the *Terminator* franchise—*Terminator Genisys* (Alan Taylor, 2015)—as a young mother-to-be played by Emilia Clarke. *Terminator Genisys* reboots the first film of the franchise, where Sarah Connor was an inexperienced waitress terrified of the Terminator, by taking into account the character's subsequent avatars, as well as the changing representations of women in the context of postfeminism and its "Girl Power" version. In this chapter, I wish to examine the evolution of Sarah Connor through the lens of postfeminism to see how, in the franchise, "feminism is decisively aged and made to seem redundant" by connecting "the tropes of freedom and choice [. . .] with the category of young women."[1] Conjuring up the "spectre of feminism,"[2] the franchise thus invokes second-wave feminism while casting it in the shadows as outdated and ineffective, celebrating instead the possibilities offered to younger women by postfeminism. As Stéphanie Genz and Benjamin A. Brabon note, "critics have claimed and appropriated the term [postfeminism] for a variety of definitions,"[3] but I want to focus here on the "aftermath of feminism" implied by the prefix "post-" and the distancing (albeit not always for the same reasons) of second-wave feminism by third-wave feminists and Girl Power advocates alike.

My argument is that Sarah Connor in *Terminator 2* represents a negative retrospective version of second-wave feminism that the rest of the franchise both adverts to and takes its distance from. Declared dead in *Terminator 3: Rise of the Machines* (Jonathan Mostow, 2003), which features a glamorous Terminatrix instead, she is resuscitated as the central character in the eponymous *Terminator: The Sarah Connor Chronicles*, where she is nevertheless overshadowed by the legacy of the postfeminist Terminatrix and the rise of Girl Power embodied by the female cyborg Cameron. Finally, I will argue that the 2015 reboot of the franchise owes as much to the series as to the previous films in its depiction of Sarah Connor as a girl, in a celebration of Girl Power that tends, in the end, to adhere to patriarchal structures of power, negating the legacy of the 1991 Sarah Connor.

Rejecting Second-Wave Feminism

Terminator 2 insists on the transformation of Sarah Connor from harassed waitress in pink to gun-toting action heroine by turning her into a "phallic woman," "a woman with allegedly masculine traits."[4] The first shot of Sarah includes clearly hypermasculine attributes: she is presented working out in her cell, sweating in an undershirt that reveals her bulging muscles [14:00]. The fragmentation of her body (the camera does not show her face but only her left shoulder) and the close-up of her biceps evoke the extreme close-ups of body parts that often introduce hypermasculine action heroes, for instance, in the opening scenes of *The Terminator* (Cameron, 1984) and *Rambo: First Blood, Part II* (George P. Cosmatos, 1985). Sarah Connor is thus masculinized not only through her mastery of weapons (she handles many guns throughout the film and even keeps an impressive cache in the middle of the desert), but also through the transformation of her body, marking her as a true action heroine. Indeed, the film's promotional material insisted on Hamilton's months of training, notably in traditionally masculine fields, prior to the shooting: running, cycling, and swimming, but also weight lifting, judo, and heavy-duty military training with an Israeli commando.[5] Julie Baumgold's description of her in *New York* magazine insists on her defeminization: "the power body—the arms and shoulders packed with muscle, the straight thick waist, the boy's hips, no ass, the bosom so small it doesn't require a bra [. . .] the arms have rivers of veins rising above the bulging muscle."[6] The two references to muscle and the absence of waist, hips, buttocks, or bosom paint her almost as a biological male.

Terminator 2 tends, in effect, to negate Sarah Connor's femininity, invalidating even her motherhood, since any maternal tenderness has all but disappeared. When David Ansen writes in his review for *Newsweek*,

"Hamilton's sinewy Sarah, a fanatical matriarchal warrior, is a wonderfully gaga heroine, as ferocious as a lioness protecting her cub,"[7] he is insisting on her masculine traits, making of Connor a warrior more than a mother, so that in the end she is discredited as "fanatical" and "gaga." Connor appears devoid of traditional feminine characteristics, and the film tends to portray her as a bad mother, concerned only with her son's physical well-being rather than his emotional happiness. Her lack of tenderness and emotional intelligence is apparent in the scene that follows her escape from the psychiatric hospital with her son John and the Terminator [59:24–60:32]. When she asks him how he is and opens her arms, John rushes to her in search of affection but is disappointed when she starts palpating him frenetically to make sure he has not been wounded. John's disappointment with, and rejection of, his mother highlights Sarah's inability to behave as a "normal" feminine mother would, expressing feelings and emotions. Sarah is thus depicted as lacking in femininity, as suggested by the end of the scene, which contrasts her cold and stern expression not only with John's tears, but also with the Terminator's concerned reaction to the teenager's tears. Several reaction shots in extreme close-up of his perplexed expression in the rearview mirror insist on his concern for John, as opposed to Sarah, who turns away from her son and is relegated to the background in the following shot when she converses with the Terminator [60:28].

Moreover, in the same scene, Sarah yells at John for risking his life to rescue her, asserting that "[she] can take care of [her]self," the film connecting her fierce independence to her lack of emotions in an increasingly negative light. Indeed, her unilateral decision to kill Dyson, the computer scientist who will develop Skynet, is presented as terribly mistaken, thus calling into question her judgment and rationality, especially since she herself breaks down and is unable to carry out her plan. Consequently, her status as heroine is seriously compromised, while her female point of view is challenged, as emphasized by the contrast between her cold and cynical voice-over about Dyson—"It's not every day that you find out you're responsible for three billion deaths. He took it pretty well."—and the image, focused on Dyson's distressed expression as he mumbles: "I feel like I'm gonna throw up" [83:50–84:48]. Set apart from the others by the staging (she is sitting on a kitchen counter while Dyson, his wife, the Terminator, and John are all sitting together at the same table) and emotionally detached, smoking her cigarette in the background, and out of focus, Sarah is set at a distance by the film, so that her response to Miles Dyson, a feminist diatribe against "fucking men like you [who] built the hydrogen bomb," is debunked as extreme and unwarranted, the wounded black man appearing more like a victim than an oppressor. In addition, the harsh light and gray geometrical background contribute to dehumanizing the overly aggressive Sarah, further discrediting her simplistic speech, which denounces men as destructive while praising women as life-giving ("You don't know what it's like to really create something, to create a life. All you know how to create is death and destruction"), a comment that becomes ironic in view of her own lack of compassion.

Sarah Connor can thus be considered as a caricature of the "women's libber" or "bra burner" (she does not wear a bra, as Baumgold notes), those second-wave feminists who supposedly rejected femininity and constantly vituperated against men, making everyone ill-at-ease. During Sarah's speech, John covers his face and finally interrupts her, asking her to be more "constructive," that is, less rigidly intolerant and counterproductive. From then on, Sarah is, in fact, sidelined. Her last voice-over before the conclusion occurs a few minutes later and announces the end of her status as omniscient narrator, since she no longer knows what the future holds ("The future, always so clear to me, had become like a black highway at night"). The last third of the film does not use her voice-over and favors the Terminator's point of view, so that she is replaced in the narration as well as in the diegesis by the machine, who outshines her both as warrior and parent and is the film's true hero.[8]

Sarah's portrayal as a brutal and unfeeling mother disconnected from femininity and unproductively hateful toward men thus echoes the criticism directed against second-wave feminism by the mass media[9] and some postfeminist writers such as Naomi Wolf in *Fire with Fire* or Rene Denfeld in *The New Victorians*,[10] who rejected the previous generation's feminism as an outdated sexually repressive "victim feminism" that denigrated female (hetero)sexual pleasure, feminine glamour, and any other form of overtures to men. She represents the "spectre of [second-wave] feminism" that, Angela McRobbie and Rebecca Munford[11] argue, is invoked and disallowed by postfeminism, as underlined by the camerawork throughout the scene of her attempted murder of Dyson. She first appears at night, out of focus behind the lens of her sniper rifle and is then set apart, again out of focus, during the discussion in Dyson's kitchen. It comes as no surprise, then, that Sarah Connor disappears from the next installment of the franchise, where she is simply declared dead.

Indeed, in *Terminator 3*, the woman with the gun becomes the antagonist, a female Terminator known as the Terminatrix. The name of the character immediately denotes her hypersexualization, marking the transition to a postfeminist media culture where action heroines are routinely commodified and fetishized.[12] The Terminatrix is played by a model, Kristanna Loken, who appears naked in a shop window among mannequins who melt away, playfully highlighting the commodification of the female figure. She is clearly fetishized through her tight-fitting maroon leather outfit and her high heels, and even dons a police uniform to have access to classified information. Her fetishization is a way of both highlighting her power and containing her. As Charles-Antoine Courcoux underscores, the Terminatrix embodies from the outset "the archetype of the sexually and financially independent woman," with her sexy leather outfit, sports car, and enhanced breasts.[13] Female victimhood is rejected, as symbolized by the murder of the woman who offers to call 911, having misconstrued the Terminatrix's nakedness as the result of sexual assault. The Terminatrix does not need her help but wants her car: she is no victim but, rather, a powerful female machine able to take what she wants, magnified by static low-angle close-ups and the editing of the soundtrack, which juxtaposes her desire ("I like this car.") and its fulfillment (the roar of the sports car engine) [6:53–7:09]. Furthermore, the Terminatrix uses her female attributes to gain power over men, as exemplified when she enhances her breasts for the policeman who stops her for speeding. The scene humorously plays with gender codes, since the Terminatrix's answer, "I like your gun," could be read as an enticing sexual innuendo intended to appease a dominant male but expresses, in effect, her indomitable will and the policeman's impending death [8:28-8:55].

The Terminatrix's castrating power is most explicitly developed in her fight scene against the Terminator in the toilets of the Skynet headquarters [76:09–76:56]. His efforts at destroying her, by crushing a urinal on her head, for instance, are fruitless, and she defeats him by grabbing him by the crotch and ramming him through walls, then wrapping her legs around him and decapitating him with her high heels. However, her fetishization enables a playful self-consciousness that disavows castration anxiety all the while explicitly evoking it. The bathroom combat scene highlights the contrast between her feminine appearance and her brutal demeanor by emphasizing the incongruity of her perfect looks and figure as she catwalks through a bathroom in ruins and looks at herself in the mirror. This feminine self-consciousness contains the threat embodied by the Terminatrix. The film explicitly plays with gender codes so as to alleviate the anxiety triggered by powerful women who kill. It thus heralds the franchise's turn to postfeminism, first by featuring women who have power, denying feminist demands for more women at the top.[14] Secondly, female power is circumscribed through the use of irony, a well-worn postfeminist trope.[15] Finally, the film opposes the powerful woman who kills to a gentler female character of inferior status and power, Kate Brewster (Claire Danes). It is the supporting female character who openly rejects the Terminatrix and expresses the anxiety she provokes, exclaiming: "Just die, you bitch!" These three strategies—giving power to female characters, tempering it through self-conscious irony, and offering divergent models of femininity—are reprised in *Terminator: The Sarah Connor Chronicles*.

Two Models of Killer Women in *Terminator: The Sarah Connor Chronicles*

The iconic Sarah Connor was resuscitated in 2008 and given her own television series, where she is played by Lena Headey in clear homage to Linda Hamilton from *Terminator 2*; both Sarah Connors are in their thirties and have to deal single-handedly with a teenage son, John Connor, played in the series by Thomas Dekker. Sarah Connor appears prominently in the marketing of the show, since her name is in the title, and is presented from the outset as a tough action heroine. The series' trailers show her reloading a machine gun, while the voice-over announces that "a mother will become a warrior."[16] The opening of the first episode condenses Sarah Connor's transformation from *The Terminator* to *Terminator 2*—Headey is dressed in a waitress outfit with a pink apron, drives a car alone on a desert road (a reference to the end of *The Terminator*), and barks orders at her son. They are immediately arrested by the police, but Sarah Connor manages to uncuff herself, kneeing a policeman in the face, escape from the police car, and rescue her son. Headey's Sarah Connor thus inherits Hamilton's characteristics as a "matriarchal warrior" and "ferocious lioness."[17] She is a protective mother who constantly gives orders, handles guns and money, negotiates with gangsters, and eludes the police. In the very first episode, she takes a bullet in the shoulder and is operated on without any anaesthesia or even any ice, a feat that is repeated and amplified in season 2 since the operation (a bullet in the leg that is removed again without anaesthesia) takes up a whole episode (S2E14).

Sarah Connor drives the action: she decides what to do and when, and is looked up to by her son, who is certain that she can stop Judgment Day. She is regularly shot in low angle from John's point of view, standing, whereas he is sitting (for instance, S1E1, [0:54; 7:38]). She is a single mother who heads an extended family without male interference—Derek Reese (Brian Austin Green), John's uncle, is rescued and included in the family as a helper in a subordinate position, as his girlfriend scornfully remarks: "Sarah running you around?" (S2E17, [6:18]). Furthermore, as in *Terminator 2*, Sarah Connor controls the narration through her voice-over, which introduces and concludes every episode. We have access to her subjectivity through her dreams, which are recurrent throughout the series, with an episode in season 2 entirely devoted to one long dream (S2E16), which ends with a poetic monologue affirming women's supernatural power over men: "She is a nightmare, a demon woman, the oldest and most enduring story told by man. [. . .] She is a bad dream, she is a bad bitch" [41:22–41:46].

Yet what looks like an ode to Linda Hamilton and radical second-wave feminism—notably its empowerment of women, its celebration of feminine subjectivity and imagination, and its challenge to patriarchy through the promotion of matriarchal structures[18]—is fraught with joylessness and distress. Many of Sarah's dreams are, in fact, nightmares in which she is unable to protect her son or accomplish her mission. The opening of the first episode is exemplary in this respect, since the tough Sarah Connor who rescues her son from the police is actually a dream that turns into a nightmare when she fails to protect him from a Terminator and ends up crying in anguish over his dead body (S1E1, [3:46]). Sarah Connor's emotional anguish and human weakness are thus played up in the series. For instance, Hamilton's rant in *Terminator 2* against men who bring death and destruction is pictured and developed in another dream sequence where Sarah Connor dreams about killing the nuclear scientists who invented the bomb, "the fathers of our destruction" (S1E3, [1:43–3:03]). As the voice-over wonders whether she would have the courage to stop them, Sarah Connor finds herself in the middle of a room full of men only and shoots them all. But the men get back up on their feet and turn into large robots who encircle her and raise their weapons against her (Figure 6.1). The sequence shows both the difficulty of fighting against patriarchy as a woman, with patriarchal oppression pointedly

Figure 6.1 *Terminator: The Sarah Connor Chronicles* (Fox, 2008-9): Sarah Connor dreams she is surrounded by terminators.

captured in a high-angle shot of tall robots holding large guns and closing in on a lone woman, and Connor's anguish through many close-ups of her pained face.

Indeed, throughout the series, Sarah Connor rarely smiles and expresses concern or distress instead. Her emotional anguish is often conveyed by shots of her in profile, part of her face in the shadows—Lorrie Palmer notes that Lena Headey conveys this anxiety "by turning her head slightly off-center and sliding her eyes to one side while she is speaking to others, never holding her gaze in one place for very long."[19] Constantly worried, often harsh, Sarah repeatedly acknowledges her limits as a parent; for instance, she is afraid she will lose her son if they keep running (S1E2), does not know how to help him after he sees a girl commit suicide at school (S1E3), and has trouble dealing with his girlfriend in season 2.

Sarah is thus limited as a parent but also, and more importantly, as a warrior. As her failure to kill in the dream with the nuclear scientists underlines, Sarah cannot kill in cold blood, even if it is necessary to protect her son. For instance, she is unable to kill her friend Enrique in S1E2 even though he is about to give her up to the FBI, and she lets a young robber go in S2E7, resulting in his giving their address to the Terminator, leading the latter to her son. Sarah only kills one man in the whole series, in self-defense (S2E13), and is actually saved by her son when they are kidnapped by ruthless gangsters (S2E1), a revelation that comes as a shock six episodes later, when John lashes out at his mother for not protecting him (S2E7). Sarah repeatedly leads killers to her son, as when nefarious Skynet-linked attackers locate John thanks to a tracker implanted in her breast, a symbol of her maternal failings (S2E20). This censure of the mother figure can be linked to a dismissal of second-wave feminism by a new generation who sees it as outmoded—Sarah Connor does not know how to use a cell phone (S1E3) and is generally bad with technology, unlike her son and her pretend daughter, Cameron the Terminator, who repeatedly accesses data in her mission to protect John. In fact, Sarah Connor tends to fail as a woman who kills, too vulnerable to match Cameron's cyborg strength and skills. Whereas Cameron kills neatly, most often standing at a distance from her victims, Sarah kills her only victim after being shot in the leg, lying down and at point-blank range, so that the man falls on top of her and her hands are smeared with his blood. The successful woman who kills is thus a cyborg, whose clean and precise movements offer an ironic take on the perfect girl conjured by Girl Power postfeminism.

Terminator: The Sarah Connor Chronicles seems to favor Cameron over Sarah Connor, showing, in third-wave feminist fashion, an "eagerness to signal a break from an earlier feminist generation—a break that is embedded in [third-wave feminist texts'] celebration of girl culture and an understanding of feminist history framed by the mother-daughter metaphor."[20] Sarah Connor's second-wave legacy is literally outshone by her postfeminist "daughter" and her Girl Power attributes. Cameron benefits from the kind of "luminosity" mentioned by McRobbie when talking about girls in the aftermath of feminism.[21] When Sarah, John and Cameron appear naked in the middle of a highway after time traveling at the end of the pilot episode, Sarah appears first, her face half-hidden behind her hair, John second, but it is Cameron who steals the limelight as she gets up in front of them, her face lit up in an extreme frontal close-up, her eyes staring back at the astounded onlookers, including a grinning young male (S1E1, [42:32–42:54]). Drawing on the postfeminist Terminatrix of *Terminator 3*, Cameron looks back at the male gaze and reverses women's "to be looked-at-ness"[22] into a stare. Cameron's lit-up face and powerful stare can be contrasted with Sarah Connor's more shadowy presence, as she is caught, stunned, and bewildered, on a grainy cell phone video (S1E1, [43:02]), an image that reappears throughout the first season and contributes to making her presence feel antiquated, like the old photographs and videos of her that are repeatedly dug up by FBI agent James Ellison (Richard T. Jones).

Benefiting from a delayed appearance in the pilot episode, Cameron is given the famous rescue line that runs through the franchise, "Come with me if you want to live" [19:41]. She is the female avatar of Schwarzenegger's Terminator in *Terminator 2*, a much more effective protector than Sarah Connor, since she can take bullets for John, kill in cold blood (she kills Enrique and three of the robbers), and store information. Furthermore, whereas the character of Sarah Connor is single-minded, unwavering in her mission to protect her son and thus lacking any possibility of evolution, Cameron's character is given a more interesting narrative arc, as she struggles between her initiation into human thoughts and feelings and her mechanical condition. Cameron's struggle is at the heart of season 2, after she turns on John when her chip is damaged by an explosion (S2E1), and we are given access to her memories of both the past and the future (S2E4). The end of the series confirms that Cameron thus belongs to the future and Sarah Connor to the past, as John decides to time travel to the future to find Cameron, leaving his mother behind—Sarah steps outside the lightning bubble, into the shadows of the past, while in the future, Cameron walks out of the shadows into the light, filmed in slow motion to emphasize John's joy and relief at finding her.

Sarah Connor and Cameron embody, in effect, "the mother-daughter metaphor" and its emphasis on a generational gap that is recurrent in third-wave or postfeminist writings. The lack of trust between the two women produces constant tension. As early as the pilot episode, Cameron rebukes

Sarah for not having changed her alias, to which Sarah replies, "Go to hell." In the following episodes, Cameron is repeatedly told off by Sarah for failing in her duty to protect John or having inappropriate behavior, for instance, walking around the house in her underwear (S1E3). Contrary to Sarah, who never appears undressed, Cameron is continuously fetishized, appearing half-naked in colorful bras or wearing revealing outfits, most often mini-skirts and low-cut tank tops.[23] Like postfeminist action heroines, she embraces glamour, learning to put makeup on (S1E3) and paint her nails (S1E8). Cameron can, indeed, be associated with Girl Power and its "re-appraisal of femininity (through symbols like Barbie dolls, make-up and fashion magazines) as a means of female empowerment and agency."[24] She appears fully madeup for the first time when she kills Enrique and repeatedly uses makeup to blend in and hide her cyborg nature. Consequently, Cameron becomes the more marketable character, appearing both on the front and on the back cover of the DVD of the second season, while Sarah appears only on the front. Cameron's Girl Power-inflected postfeminism ends up overshadowing Connor's second-wave brand of feminism.

Indeed, the cyborg embodies the ideal girl, "the glamorous high-achiever" described by McRobbie,[25] who excels at everything she does. McRobbie insists on the importance in contemporary culture of the figure of the "girl," associated with "capacity, success, attainment, enjoyment, entitlement, social mobility and participation."[26] Similarly, Sinikka Aapola et al. adopt a view of Girl Power that offers young women an image of femininity that is about "possibility, limitless potential and the promise of control over the future."[27] Lorrie Palmer thus underlines that "[Cameron's] ability to pass as a normal teenage girl" is a form of power that helps her destabilize her enemy and carry out her mission of protection.[28] As a teenage girl, Cameron represents the future and the possibility of change. The series emphasizes her learning process, for instance in the case of makeup, which she learns about in S1E2, applies to herself in S1E3 and to another girl in S2E4—in both cases her learning process is appreciatively commented on by John ("You're getting pretty good at that.") and by the girl ("Nice! Where did you learn to do that?").

Yet the fact that Cameron learns how to behave like a girl, explicitly mimicking a female gang member's posture in S1E2 and adopting teenage slang used by school girls in S1E3 ("It's tight"), reveals the constructedness of gender, or, to use Joan Riviere's expression, that womanliness is a masquerade.[29] She embodies the positive aspect of Girl Power's politics of femininity "that implies using the signs and accoutrements of femininity to challenge stable notions of gender formations."[30] For instance, in S1E7, Cameron takes a ballet class, learning so quickly that the ballet teacher confides in her and invites her to see her wanted brother, leading to their deaths. The episode juxtaposes

Cameron's emotional detachment—she does not care that they have died because of her—and the gracefulness of her movements, creating a jarring effect that is most manifest at the very end of the episode when Cameron practices ballet alone in her room to the melancholy sound of Chopin's *Nocturnes*, watched by Derek with both fear and wonder [38:34]. One could argue, with Riviere, that Cameron's masquerading conceals "a wish for masculine identity,"[31] although the two identities are juxtaposed rather than superimposed. As in *Terminator 3*, the show repetitively cultivates a contrast between Cameron's masculine characteristics (physical strength and lack of emotions) and her feminine looks and pursuits, exposing the unnaturalness of both gender identities.

In fact, Cameron's gender instability is the source of much of the show's humor, with the contrast creating irony that can be read, along with Jeffrey Brown, as a form of feminine self-awareness that reveals the social construction of gender roles.[32] This is apparent in the fight scene between Cameron and another young female cyborg (Rosie) in S2E6 [35:02–39:20]. The two cyborgs are presented as girls, both wearing low-cut tops, Rosie in pink. They walk in the door at the same time, hips swaying with a feminine gait, and proceed to fight in a graceful choreographed dance-like sequence, rolling their shoulders back in a same fluid move when passers-by enter the elevator they are fighting in. Cameron finally uses Rosie's femininity against her, bending her flexible leg around her head in a vice and piercing her eye with her high-heeled boot. The scene's self-reflexive irony on gender norms is underlined by the editing, since the brutal fight begins just after John, in a humorous understatement, tells a psychotherapist that "[his] sister [Cameron] is stronger than [him]," opposing John's feminine emotional expressiveness and Cameron's masculine combat skills. The incongruity of the feminine combatants is further highlighted when a little boy stares at the two injured cyborgs in the elevator, wondering at the cuts and bruises on the faces of these two pretty girls. By bringing humor, gender instability, and narrative change into *Terminator: The Sarah Connor Chronicles*, Cameron thus eclipses Sarah Connor in the series that bears her name, influencing the next installment of the franchise with her brand of Girl Power postfeminism.

Postfeminism Wins the Day

Indeed, the same type of self-reflexive irony can be found in *Terminator Genisys*. The film contrasts how the adult John Connor (Jason Clarke) presents his mother to Kyle Reese (Jai Courtney) before sending him into the past to protect her—"She'll be scared and weak. She won't be a warrior.

[. . .] She will need you but she won't know it."—and Sarah Connor's first appearance, in medias res, driving a truck into a supermarket and shooting at a Terminator to rescue Kyle [27:09]. Kyle's subsequent attempts at protecting her prove entirely futile, since he tries to kill her protective Terminator (Arnold Schwarzenegger) and is knocked down by him immediately, then laid unconscious in the back of the truck. In *Terminator Genisys*, Sarah is clearly distinguished from the young waitressing Sarah Connor of *The Terminator* and inherits some of the characteristics of the 1991 Sarah Connor: our first glimpse of her is a figure in the dark and a POV shot through the lens of a rifle, recalling Sarah's sniper attack on Miles Dyson in *Terminator 2*. Yet second-wave feminism is invoked in its most spectral form, and the 2015 Sarah Connor owes much more to Cameron's portrayal in *Terminator: The Sarah Connor Chronicles* than to the legacy of Sarah Connor. Her first appearance reprises Cameron's rescue of John in a pick-up truck in the *Chronicles'* pilot episode, and she is, in turn, given the famous line, "Come with me if you want to live." Young and childless, she can be considered as an embodiment of Girl Power's "new girl": "assertive, dynamic, and unbound from the constraints of passive femininity (Figure 6.2)."[33]

Sarah Connor is thus recast as a rebellious postfeminist Riot Grrrl type who listens to the Ramones and wears a black combat outfit, boots, and wristbands, as well as the franchise's iconic black leather jacket. Unlike Cameron, however, she is not fetishized—even though she is played by Emilia Clarke, well known for her nude scenes in *Game of Thrones* (HBO, 2011–)—and makes no use of the "signs and accoutrements of femininity."[34] She appears as a tomboyish, sexually inexperienced "Daddy's girl," still under the control of a father figure, her Terminator tellingly nicknamed "Pops."

Figure 6.2 *Terminator Genysis* (Paramount, 2015): Sarah Connor reprises the franchise's famous line, "Come with me if you want to live!"

According to Brown, this recurrent pattern among action heroines allows "male authority to revel in female sexuality, and to control it."[35] Indeed, "Pops" repeatedly reminds Sarah that she has to "mate" with Kyle in order to give birth to the famous John Connor. Furthermore, the film explicitly adheres to the patriarchal structure described by Claude Lévi-Strauss, whereby women are given in exchange to other men to cement alliances[36]—Pops the Terminator commands Reese to "protect [his] Sarah" when they leave him behind to time travel and then validates Sarah's choice by overseeing their kiss with a smile, appearing in the middle of the shot [117:16]. Eventually, the three of them get in a car together at the end of the film, ready to face the future as a united family.

Sarah's postfeminist rebelliousness is, in effect, equated with teenage rebellion and thus deprived of any threatening power. The film repeatedly insists on her status as a girl, diminutive and sentimental, and thus unthreatening. First, Clarke is very short, as underlined in the mugshots taken by the police where Sarah Connor barely reaches the 5'4 bar, struggling to make it into the shot, while Pops and Kyle tower above at 6'6 and 6'3, respectively [91:06–91:10]. Her girlishness can also be seen in her desire for romance and her rejection of "mating" for "love," as she explains when first meeting Kyle ("So you're the one I'm supposed to fall in love with?"). She consequently covers her naked body with Kyle's coat before entering the time-traveling device and accepts his love by choosing to kiss him. In fact, Sarah Connor repeatedly claims her desire to make her own choices, a postfeminist trope that insists on the importance of choice as an individual form of empowerment to the detriment of political action and female solidarity.[37] Indeed, there are no other women with whom to bond in *Terminator Genisys*, and Sarah's choice is restricted to that of choosing a father for her son, a rather limited political act. Finally, given an open destiny with the expiration of Judgment Day, Sarah prefers heterosexual love to action and chooses the man who has been sanctioned by her adoptive father and prospective son. As Bitch Flicks puts it, "perhaps a more interesting, and more feminist, ending would be her choosing to not be with Reese at all."[38]

Conclusion

The evolution and persistence of the character of Sarah Connor can be read as emblematic of the ambiguities of postfeminism, which recognizes the achievements of second-wave feminism and the heroism of feminist ancestors— Linda Hamilton's 1991 Sarah Connor is a constant reference—while keeping its distance from the braless libbers' movement through irony and a focus on girly girls, suggesting that old-style feminism is a thing of the past. The old Sarah Connor becomes more and more spectral as the franchise goes by[39] and even loses her voice-over in the 2015 installment. We can also notice a striking change in bodily representations: while the 1991 Sarah Connor and even the Terminatrix are older, taller, and more muscular, the 2015 Sarah Connor and Cameron are small and slim, emphasizing their youthfulness. Here, I would disagree with Lorrie Palmer, who commends such feminine slim builds for "evading the expected cinematic category of the spectacle."[40] Indeed, as adult warrior women, Sarah Connor and the Terminatrix were presented as equals to the Terminator, whereas the focus on 2015 Sarah Connor's and Cameron's girlishness subordinates them to men, Pops the Terminator and John Connor, who can remove Cameron's chip and is later able to terminate her at will in *Terminator: The Sarah Connor Chronicles*. Sarah Connor and even the female killer cyborg have thus become much less threatening as girls, especially since the contrast between the girls' diminutive bodies and their physical abilities is a source of humor in both productions. Even if this irony highlights the social construction of gender norms, girlishness allows killer women to be appealing without challenging patriarchy. While Girl Power gives the impression that women are in control and herald a new future, in all productions, it is John who leads the resistance in the future, with most flash-forwards being male-dominated (by Derek Reese in *Terminator: The Sarah Connor Chronicles* and by Kyle in *Terminator Genisys*). Furthermore, the emphasis on young women tends to sideline mothers, since Sarah Connor is criticized and finally left behind in the series and is not yet a mother in *Genisys*, to the benefit of father figures. There is no intergenerational female solidarity, so that women who kill appear like lone phenomena lacking greater political agency and wider support: *Terminator: The Sarah Connor Chronicles* was canceled after two seasons while *Terminator Genisys* was a failure at the box office.

Notes

1　Angela McRobbie, *The Aftermath of Feminism: Gender, Culture and Social Change* (Los Angeles: Sage, 2009), p. 11.
2　Ibid., p. 1. See also Rebecca Munford and Melanie Waters, *Feminism and Popular Culture: Investigating the Postfeminist Mystique* (New Brunswick: Rutgers University Press, 2014), p. 17.
3　Stéphanie Genz and Benjamin Brabon, *Postfeminism: Cultural Texts and Theories* (Edinburgh: Edinburgh University Press, 2009), p. 1.
4　Jean Laplanche and Jean-Bertrand Pontalis, *The Language of Psycho-Analysis* (London: Hogarth, 1985), p. 311.

5 Margot Dougherty, "A new body of work," *Entertainment Weekly*, July 12, 1991.
6 Julie Baumgold, "Killer women: Here come the hardbodies," *New York*, July 29, 1991, p. 26.
7 David Ansen, "Conan the humanitarian," *Newsweek*, July 8, 1991.
8 According to David Ansen, a large part of the film's enormous budget was spent on Arnold Schwarzenegger ($12 million, "because he can pack movie houses all over the world"), while Linda Hamilton was paid only $1 million. On the Terminator's parenting and warrior skills, see Marianne Kac-Vergne, "Losing visibility? The rise and fall of hypermasculinity in science fiction films," *InMedia*, 2, 2012. Available at http://inmedia.revues.org/491#toctoln3 (accessed August 7, 2017).
9 For more on the negative stereotyping of feminists in the mass media, see Susan J. Douglas, *Where the Girls Are: Growing up Female with the Mass Media* (London: Penguin, 1995).
10 Naomi Wolf, *Fire with Fire: The New Female Power and How It Will Change the 21st Century* (New York: Random House, 1993); Rene Denfeld, *The New Victorians: A Young Woman's Challenge to the Old Feminist Order* (New York: Warner Books, 1995).
11 See note 2.
12 Jeffrey A. Brown, *Dangerous Curves: Action Heroines, Gender, Fetishism and Popular Culture* (Jackson: University Press of Mississippi, 2011), p. 68.
13 Charles-Antoine Courcoux, "D'une peur de la modernité technologique déclinée au féminin," in Laurent Guido (ed.), *Les peurs de Hollywood* (Lausanne: Editions Antipodes, 2006), p. 238, my translation.
14 On women of power as antagonists, see Marianne Kac-Vergne, *Masculinity in Science Fiction Cinema: Cyborgs, Troopers and Other Men of the Future* (London: I.B. Tauris, 2018).
15 McRobbie, *The Aftermath of Feminism*, p. 17.
16 https://www.youtube.com/watch?v=xbVj9UdEHjg; https://www.youtube.com/watch?v=GVhElUwt4Tw (accessed July 29, 2017).
17 Ansen, "Conan the humanitarian."
18 Imelda Whelehan, *Modern Feminist Thought: From the Second Wave to "Post-Feminism"* (New York University Press, 1995), p. 73; Jill Johnston, *Lesbian Nation: The Feminist Solution* (New York: Simon & Schuster, 1973), p. 248.
19 Lorrie Palmer, "She's just a girl: A cyborg passes in *The Sarah Connor Chronicles*," in J. Telotte and G. Duchovnay (eds.), *Science Fiction Film, Television, and Adaptation: Across the Screens* (New York: Routledge, 2012), p. 92.
20 Munford and Waters, *Feminism and Popular Culture*, p. 23.
21 McRobbie, *The Aftermath of Feminism*, p. 54.
22 Laura Mulvey, "Visual pleasure and narrative cinema," *Screen*, 16/3 (1975), p. 11.

23 Here I disagree with Lorrie Palmer's analysis. Even if "Cameron is not positioned as sexually threatening" and dresses less excessively than the Terminatrix, the fact that she is repeatedly shown in underwear does involve a certain measure of "spectacle." Palmer, "She's just a girl," p. 87.

24 Genz and Brabon, *Postfeminism*, p. 76.

25 McRobbie, *The Aftermath of Feminism*, p. 15.

26 Ibid., p. 57.

27 Sinikka Aapola, Marnina Gonick, and Anita Harris, *Young Femininity: Girlhood, Power and Social Change* (Houndsmill Basingstoke: Palgrave Macmillan, 2005), p. 39.

28 Palmer, "She's just a girl," p. 89.

29 Joan Riviere, "Womanliness as masquerade," in V. Burgin, J. Donald, and C. Kaplan (eds.), *Formations of Fantasy* (London: Methuen, 1986 [1929]).

30 Genz and Brabon, *Postfeminism*, p. 78.

31 Riviere, "Womanliness as Masquerade," p. 35.

32 Brown, *Dangerous Curves*, p. 154.

33 Marnina Gonick, "Between 'Girl Power' and 'reviving Ophelia': Constituting the neoliberal girl subject," *NWSA Journal,* 18/2 (Summer 2006), p. 2.

34 Genz and Brabon, *Postfeminism*, p. 78.

35 Brown, *Dangerous Curves*, p. 14.

36 Claude Lévi-Strauss, *Les Structures élémentaires de la parenté* (Paris: Mouton, 1967 [1947]).

37 McRobbie, *The Aftermath of Feminism*, p. 1.

38 Bitch Flicks, "Terminator Genisys: Not my Sarah Connor," July 27, 2015. Available at http://www.btchflcks.com/2015/07/terminator-genisys-not-my-sarah-connor.html#.WYSmlek682x (accessed August 4, 2017).

39 The article was written before the release of Terminator: Dark Fate (Miller, 2019).

40 Palmer, "She's just a girl," p. 94.

Filmography

The Terminator, directed by James Cameron, produced by Gale Anne Hurd, written by James Cameron and Gale Anne Hurd, performances by Arnold Schwarzenegger, Michael Biehn, Linda Hamilton, Paul Winfield, music by Brad Fiedel, cinematography by Adam Greenberg, edited by Mark Goldblatt, Hemdale/Pacific Western Productions, 1984. DVD by TF1 vidéo, 1999.

Terminator 2: Judgment Day, directed by James Cameron, produced by James Cameron, written by James Cameron and William Wisher, performances by Arnold Schwarzenegger, Linda Hamilton, Robert Patrick, Edward Furlong, Joe Morton, music by Brad Fiedel, cinematography by Adam Greenberg, edited by Conrad Buff, Mark Goldblatt, and Richard A. Harris, Carolco Pictures/Pacific Western Productions/Lightstorm Entertainment/Le Studio Canal+ S.A., 1991. DVD by Gaumont Columbia Tristar home vidéo, 1999.

Terminator 3: Rise of the Machines, directed by Jonathan Mostow, produced by Hal Lieberman, Colin Wilson, Mario F. Kassar, Andrew G. Vajna, Joel B. Michaels, screenplay by John Brancato and Michael Ferris, based on characters by James Cameron and Gale Anne Hurd, performances by Arnold Schwarzenegger, Nick Stahl, Claire Danes, Kristanna Loken, music by Marco Beltrami, cinematography by Don Burgess, edited by Neil Travis and Nicolas de Toth, Intermedia/C2 Pictures, 2003. DVD by Gaumont Columbia Tristar home vidéo, 2004.

Terminator: The Sarah Connor Chronicles, created by Josh Friedman, based on characters by James Cameron and Gale Anne Hurd, performances by Lena Headey, Thomas Dekker, Summer Glau, Brian Austin Green, Garret Dillahunt, Shirley Manson, Richard T. Jones, Leven Rambin, music by Brad Fiedel, and Bear McCreary, Sarah Connor Pictures/Bartleby Company/C2 Pictures/The Halcyon Company (season 1)/Warner Bros Television (season 2)/ Fox, 2008–09. Blu-ray DVD of season 1 by Warner home video, 2010; Blu-ray DVD of season 2 by Warner home video, 2011.

Terminator Genisys, directed by Alan Taylor, produced by David Ellison and Dana Goldberg, written by Laeta Kalogridis and Patrick Lussier, based on characters by James Cameron and Gale Anne Hurd, performances by Arnold Schwarzenegger, Jason Clarke, Emilia Clarke, Jai Courtney, J.K. Simmons, Dayo Okeniyi, Matt Smith, Courtney B. Vance, Lee Byung-hun, music by Lorne Balfe, cinematography by Kramer Morgenthau, edited by Roger Barton, Skydance Productions, 2015. Blu-ray DVD by Paramount home entertainment France, 2015.

7

Girls against Women

Contrasting Female Violence in Contemporary Young Adult Dystopias

Adrienne Boutang

Most writers concerned with feminism and representations praised the recent trend of young adult dystopian fictions featuring teenage heroines who resort to violence to defend their freedom and protect the ones they love. The success of the film adaptations of the *Hunger Games*[1] and *Divergent*[2] novels, and the charisma of young actresses Jennifer Lawrence and Shailene Woodley, enhanced the iconic seduction of these updated incarnations of "girl power," which somehow rejuvenated a notion that had been depoliticized since the 1990s. As Jessica Taft writes, what "began as an explicitly political concept" has "been deployed by various elements of popular culture and the mainstream media in a way that constructed a version of girlhood that excludes girls' political selves."[3] Indeed, researchers exploring the complexities of commodified feminism in pop culture have unveiled how ambivalent these teenage characters are, maintaining that the narratives perpetuated "implicit assumptions about what constitutes 'normal' bodies and desires."[4]

By studying three popular young adult fictions, *The Hunger Games*[5] (Gary Ross, 2012; Francis Lawrence, 2013–15), *Divergent*[6] (Neil Burger, 2014; Robert Schwentke, 2015; Robert Schwentke, 2016), and *The 5th Wave*[7] (Jonathan Blakeson, 2016), I intend to expand this defiant interpretation by shifting the focus onto other recurrent fictional figures that have been neglected by academic analyses: namely the female villains of the stories. Indeed, most analyses stop short of taking into account these powerful forty-to-sixty-year-old female characters, who are eventually killed, either symbolically or literally, by younger heroines in climactic epilogues.

A "revenge" pattern tends to direct the young girls' hostility toward their adult counterparts and is reminiscent of famous "backlash" narrative patterns that emerged in earlier decades, such as the famous ending of *Fatal*

Attraction (Adrian Lyne, 1987), in which the female villain played by Glenn Close was eventually shot by the "good wife." This chapter will thus analyze the tension between conflicting representations of strong femininities. This striking opposition between two types of "women who kill"—girls on the one side, and women on the other—and the inevitable brutal sacrifice of the old by the young will be investigated as a manifestation of the ambiguities of postfeminism. The presence of these characters, as I will attempt to show, not only undermines the narratives' alleged feminism but also exemplifies the contradictions inherent to postfeminist culture, highlighting the contradictions of the so-called girl culture in its mainstream version.

First, I will examine the implicit double standard that allows teenage girls to be androgynous but denies the same gender fluidity to older female characters. These portrayals exemplify the ambivalences of postfeminist culture, caught between essentialist and more constructivist models.[8] I will then focus on the treatment of violence, before concentrating on the narrative and visual motifs of the symbolical killing scenes, and attempting to analyze how these climactic scenes work to contain the subversion and ultimately reassert more traditional gender norms.

Contrasting Liminalities

Although these films allow young girls to explore a liminal position at the crossroads between gender and identity, they tend to treat their female adult characters with much less leniency. The contrast between two women—an "older woman" (either a witch or a "wicked stepmother") and a "younger, nubile female" with whom the older one competes—is a classic fairy tale trope. But the peculiarity of these dystopian narratives stems from the fact that this conservative pattern of competition between female characters is combined with a more progressive construction as far as the teenage characters are concerned.

The Hunger Games, notably, was widely praised for its portrayal of a "tough-minded young woman who [. . .] challenges authority to become a central figure."[9] Author Suzanne Collins has been applauded for "boldly flout[ing] literary stereotypes [. . .] and proclaim[ing] that girls can do anything boys can do, including strategize, make demands, and even hunt and kill."[10] They have been compared to previous young adult literature tomboys, "from early twentieth century fiction, such as Louisa May Alcott's Jo March (*Little Women*) and Harper Lee's Scout Finch (*To Kill a Mockingbird*)," among other "classical examples of literary tomboys."[11] According to Meghan Gilbert-Hickey, gender is "muddled to the point that masculine and feminine are temporarily indistinguishable";[12] for Jessica Miller, "Collins has given us characters who invite us to reflect on the categories of sex and gender."[13] Academic excitement was shared by more mainstream reviewers, quick to cast "Katniss Everdeen's value as a feminist heroine" and eager to "encourage [their] daughter to read this series."[14] Indeed, the girls possess gender-fluid features, and Katniss has, according to Collins, been inspired by male mythological figures, an androgyny that is replicated in the young girls' attire. Cassie is wearing her survival outfit when we first meet her in *The 5th Wave*, while Katniss, as related in the first page of the book, sports her father's old hunting jacket when she first goes out hunting in the book—and even though the jacket is more becoming and trendy in the opening sequence of the film, it still conveys her tomboyish persona [2:37]. Interestingly enough, Tris becomes more tomboyish as the story progresses and she takes off her old, feminine but austere, clothes; as the series unfolds, especially in *Insurgent*, she increasingly resembles the ambiguous model of the Final Girl as defined by Carol Clover[15]: her short, androgynous haircut and rather masculine attire contrast with voyeuristic moments in which her body is deliberately eroticized.

However, these young characters have the ability to behave in stereotypically feminine ways when called upon to do so. Strikingly, all three narratives tend to contrast their heroines with an even more tomboyish young female character as a way to highlight their potential for a more conventional femininity. In *Hunger Games*, the narration complacently alternates between visions of a boyish Katniss and more seductive appearances, after she has been properly groomed, through the topical motif of the makeover. This only goes to show that these gritty science-fiction universes remain closely linked to the Cinderella model. In accordance with postfeminist girl culture, which stresses the notion of choice,[16] the young heroines treat their femininity as an item they can choose to activate or not, according to circumstances. The makeover pattern evokes the ambiguity of the "rhetoric of girlhood in contemporary culture."[17] Their ambiguities link them directly to former models of tough femininity, which have been analyzed by both Clover and Yvonne Tasker. The shifting back and forth between masculine, warrior clothes, and more traditional feminine attire echoes Tasker's remarks about female action heroines: "The sense of a transitional state is sometimes played for eroticism—as if the 'masculine' clothing forms a disguise behind which the 'real' figure of the woman is glimpsed."[18]

A closer look at their characteristics shows how all the gender-fluid qualities the girls are praised for become irredeemable flaws when associated with the older female characters. Contrary to their younger counterparts, the women in these stories clearly lack the ability to play with the codes of femininity. First, they renounce any kind of private identity altogether, and at least two of them are deprived of first names; Alma Coin is only referred to by her function, "President Coin," and the same is true of Sergeant Reznik in *The 5th Wave*. Much less fluid than the young heroines, these women are stuck in a single, clearly defined outfit, which connects each of them to their stable and even rigid identity. As President Coin, Julianne Moore wears an austere outfit, and the actress's flamboyant red hair gives way to gloomy gray that emphasizes her paleness. From her first appearance in *Mockingjay: Part 1*, [5:06], the character wears what will become her defining outfit: namely loose, buttoned up, grayish overalls, designed to conceal her figure. Her obvious desire to erase, or even repudiate, any trace of femininity becomes a metaphor for her rigidity, with obvious negative connotations. Conversely, Kate Winslet's elegant clothing as erudite faction leader Jeanine Matthews is reminiscent of 1980s working girl villains, more specifically, of the "wicked SWW" ("single working woman") or "monster-career woman" identified by critic Judith Williamson in several 1980s films;[19] it also recalls Patricia Clarkson's outfit in *The Maze Runner* (Wes Ball, 2014). Maria Bello, as Sergeant Reznik, embodies the complex function of the "military woman," who, according to Tasker, tends to represent "a particular sort of gender trouble."[20] This character is a very interesting example of the deliberate construction of a negative female counterpart to the young heroine. Reznik, a Czech word meaning "butcher," is a man in the book, yet the film adaptation changed the gender of the cruellest and most negative character in the book, a striking example of the casting of females in negative roles. Instead of alternating feminine with masculine attire, Reznik combines both: glossy lipstick with a strict military uniform. Of the three villains, she is the one who best fits the category of the "phallic woman." However, her hard, "masculinized" and "muscular" body, echoing strong female characters, such as Ripley and Sarah Connor in the *Alien* and *Terminator* movies, carries a much more negative connotation.

The merging of male and female attributes in these adult women is treated as a sign of monstrous aberration. The liminal space occupied between male and female roles becomes a fully negative trait, reminiscent of archetypal representations of the bitch, "often portrayed in literature as the manipulating, domineering, scheming woman."[21] Whenever these women behave in a way that might be associated with feminine archetypes, such as tender physical contact or caring words, the films lay bare the ugly truths they attempt to conceal: duplicity and manipulation, reminiscent of the cliché of the *femme fatale*. Many scenes feature moments of intimacy that will later be revealed as attempts, on the part of the female villains, to manipulate the young and candid heroines, such as Reznik caressing Cassie's hair in *The 5th*

Wave [90:56], or when Coin and Katniss, or Tris and Jeanine, have intimate conversations [*Mockingjay Part 1* 05:26]. These scenes are carefully captured in close shots; they evoke the disturbing relationship between Carrie and her neurotic mother in Brian de Palma's 1976 film and quickly give way to a relation based on competition and defiance. In addition to the themes of manipulation and hypocrisy, the stories also subtly suggest, in typical backlash fashion, that the powerful position these women occupy might be the product of usurpation. The narratives emphasize the girls' reluctance to endorse active positions and powerful functions; many aspects of *The Hunger Games*' plot revolve around Katniss's reluctance to become a leader. Conversely, we are never given any details concerning the powerful women's pasts; the means by which they reached a high political function, in what appears to be a largely male-dominated world, remains unknown. While this might be viewed as a feminist stance—female power being deemed to be "natural" enough not to require any justification—the lack of a backstory could also be seen as a way to stress their lack of legitimacy because (1) they are depicted as hubristic, and (2) they are castigated for it, publicly or not, through a very clear political revolutionary pattern, as we shall see.

The confrontation between women and girls is grounded in the motif of motherhood, be it actual or symbolical. Katherine R. Broad observes that "the final image of complacent adulthood suggests that Katniss's instances of rebellion are permissible for girls, but not women."[22] Sara K. Day similarly argues that many young adult narratives "ultimately link sexual awakening not only to rebellion but also to eventual acquiescence to conventional women's roles."[23] The three girls in the series are usually allowed only a brief stage of tomboyishness, coinciding with their teens. While Tris is the only one to be elevated to high political office, she eventually pays the ultimate price for it and is shot. The two other heroines quickly and happily distance themselves from any sort of public fight and turn into more maternal figures. Cassie eventually plays the role of surrogate mother for her young brother, and Katniss conforms to a very traditional type of domesticity. To quote Broad again, "the final image of complacent adulthood suggests that Katniss's instances of rebellion are permissible for girls, but not women."[24] Meanwhile, the three older women, presented as childless, would fit perfectly into the category of the "wicked stepmother." Even the character played by Naomi Watts, for instance, throughout the *Divergent* series, is described as a bad mother and resented by her son. It should come as no surprise that Collins claimed the Amazonian model for Katniss, since, as Elizabeth Schreiber-Byers explains, "Amazons are women who are equal parts warrior and mother."[25] To the contrary, the villainesses exemplify a more negative embodiment of the Amazonian model: the "cruel and sadistic woman."[26] As we can see, the plots oppose two types of female warriors: on the one hand, the young girl akin to the "virginal warrior maiden in keeping with the Amazonian tradition," and on the other, a "masculine strongwoman and animal tamer."[27]

The clear-cut distribution of roles, with the young heroines—unlike the career women—eventually renouncing their fights in order to focus on rebuilding a private family, evokes what Susan Faludi described as a "you-can't-have-it-all message."[28] The distinction between caring heroines, endowed with motherly qualities, and cold female characters giving up their femininity altogether elucidates the way these films represent the characters' relationship to violence. For the young heroines, violence is considered as an extension of a more general and altogether positive protective impulse. For the older villains, violence appears as a gratuitous impulse stemming from a fundamentally perverse personality.

Unnatural Born Killers

The desire to absolve the young girls from any attraction toward physical violence, while asserting their "toughness," ends up producing somewhat contradictory portrayals, as the sagas both highlight and deny their abilities as warriors. Critics tended to downplay these contradictions, with analyses relying mostly on the iconic static images displayed on the promotional posters: Katniss notching her arrow, Cassie holding her weapon. Strikingly, though, it is worth noticing that this image from *The 5th Wave* was replaced, in other posters, by a much less martial picture showing Cassie tenderly holding her little brother in her arms instead of a weapon. As we shall see, this image foreshadows the emphasis on the sacrificial caretaker, which competes with that of the active warrior.

Indeed, all three characters exhibit agency, courage, and determination, traits that are particularly obvious in their ability to defend both themselves and the ones they care for. When requested, all girls shift to "survival mode," enabling them to shoot and kill when needed. Moreover, they all tend to distance themselves from weaker female characters, such as Katniss's own mother. The film adaptation of *Divergent* even subverts the original description of Tris as a "petite" heroine by casting the tall and athletic Shailene Woodley in the role. The three girls share many common features with their already mentioned precursor, the "final girl," with her "competence, strength of character, and force of will,"[29] as well as the "turn-of-the-millennium tough girl,"[30] all being examples of "a girl power feminist icon for many girls and women."[31]

Yet even though the films show that the girls adapt fast and easily to more masculine behaviors, their combat skills are hardly presented as innate qualities. Because this ability for violence is generally coded as male,[32] the narratives try to minimize the young characters' violent impulses. The narratives attempt, rather contradictorily, to underline both the natural gifts of their characters, in accordance with more general patterns of young adult fiction, and the difficulties they encounter, which lead them to be put under close protection of male mentors. The fictions thus stress the unnaturalness of their violent behavior. Even though their physical strength and aptitude are highlighted, their reluctance to put them to use in fights is equally so. These qualities are always the product of very specific circumstances, and, in at least two cases, the ultimate stage in the requisite training process under the tutelage of a male mentor—although it is blurred by the nonlinear structure in *The 5th Wave*. Both Cassie and Tris need the help of male trainers who seem more at ease wielding lethal weapons than they are. The men also routinely come to their rescue, thereby contradicting the apparent agency and autonomy of the heroines, diminishing their status as tough girls, and demoting them to mere damsels in distress—a familiar model that returns with a vengeance when the rescuers become love interests.

The three protagonists of young adult dystopias share a clear distaste for violence, which the storylines eagerly emphasize. This is exemplified by Katniss's first hunt [4:08–4:17]. What starts off as a scene reminiscent of *The Deer Hunter* (Michael Cimino, 1978) almost turns into a remake of *Bambi* (1942), as the teenager is too moved by a cute baby deer to even notch her arrow. This unwillingness to kill may even lead the protagonists to self-sacrifice. In a significant scene from *Divergent*, Tris chooses to turn her weapon on herself rather than having to kill her partner [124:36–124:44]. The situation recurs again in *Insurgent*, when she threatens to kill herself and points a shotgun at her own face in order to compel the villainess to save her friends; shortly after this attempted sacrifice, she spares the life of an enemy who just betrayed her [72:37]. Eventually, the film sets up a complex staging, aligning three different levels of victims and shooters; Tris is seen pointing a gun at a man as he is targeting someone, and she herself becomes the target of a third weapon as a guard turns against her [108:50–108:54]. The narrative thus produces an entangled setup, which makes her both victim and aggressor, and tends to dissolve her active position into a more defensive pattern. This sacrificial pattern is, to a certain extent, present in *The Hunger Games* as well.

When the killings do take place, the stories tend to moralize them by presenting them as inevitable and dramatizing the moral throes experienced by the characters. Both the overarching plots and the individual scenes are organized in a way that allows viewers to witness the protagonist's dilemmas. *The 5th Wave* opens with what will later be revealed to be Cassie's first killing

[0:55–3:20]. This original killing, which turns out to be pointless since the man was harmless, is presented so that the viewer shares her panic and understands the necessity to kill. This is reinforced by the fact that Cassie comments in voice-over on her actions as they unfold, thereby helping the viewer understand that she is not really a murderer and was forced to toughen up due to special circumstances. In *Mockingjay: Catching Fire*, Katniss is interrupted right before shooting another prey in the forest, as the memory of a killing from the previous installment resurfaces through a traumatic flashback [2:34–2:39]. By highlighting remorse and guilt, the film reaffirms its heroine's morality and tends to disconnect her from the violent acts she was forced to commit. The *Divergent* series equally dramatizes the agonies Tris endures after being responsible for the death of innocent victims; ultimately, her death will appear as the culmination of a sacrificial process that had started much earlier and is repeatedly re-enacted throughout the different episodes.

On a deeper level, the characters' violent actions appear to be motivated by a fundamental nurturing instinct, which the narratives present as a "natural" feminine impulse. As Meghan Gilbert-Hickey and Lindsey Issow Averill have shown, Katniss's behavior is closely linked to the ethics of care, a "feminine" vision of the world and of ethics, which was theorized and developed by Carol Gilligan. To quote Gilbert-Hickey, "the difference [. . .] between Katniss and Coin is that Coin engages on the act in order to promote her own interests, while Katniss's motives more closely align with the 'feminine' care ethic."[33] One could go even further by noting how much these stories, and in particular the films, emphasize the emotional reactions of their young characters. Their actions are almost always presented as reactive, and these reactions, always triggered by intense emotions, are clearly manifested by the shedding of tears. Tris is described as a "walking bleeding heart" [*Insurgent*, 60:15]. All three franchises repeatedly insist on the sensitivity of their teenage protagonists, the camerawork enhancing the young actresses' expressivity by lingering on their faces deformed by grief and anger. The recurrent sight of these pretty faces deformed by tears and sorrow draws on the traditional association between women and emotions, and contradicts, on some level, the statement that the characters have been "written for a generation that has become desensitized to violence in a way no other has before" and that "these new tomboys have to be able to keep up with boys in that realm as well. They can defend themselves, and have little regard for human life as their male counterparts in other series."[34] The narratives thus merge, as Sonya Sawyer-Fritz argued,[35] a traditional feminine trait—hypersensitivity— with a progressive one—the ability to convert emotions into action—thus blurring the distinction between the heroines of classical melodramas and contemporary action movies. To quote Jessica Taft, "they simultaneously replicate and reconfigure powerful, and often quite conventional narratives about girlhood and girls' cultures. They assert that girls are, indeed, more emotional, more caring, more sensitive."[36]

As opposed to these archetypal caring, maternal girls, the women are not only childless (or apparently so); they appear to be incapable of empathy altogether. In contrast to the warm and impulsive, emotional young protagonists, they represent cold rationality and disembodied intelligence, devoid of emotion. President Coin's ever-unruffled composure betrays an inability for empathy that will increasingly reveal itself as cold-hearted pragmatism, before it turns into moral monstrosity. In *Mockingjay Part 1*, President Coin coldly claims that "individuals don't make demands at (District) 13" [25:49], before making her point by launching bombs on innocent children [110:50–112:50]. In contrast to the more intuitive demeanor of their young counterparts, these women share a tendency to objectify individuals, neglecting humanity because they are too absorbed in abstract views, even for a good cause, adopting a "patriarchal, competitive model of selfhood and ethics."[37]

The narratives of *The Hunger Games* and *The 5th Wave* end with a form of return to a state of nature that tends to connect their protagonists with primitive power (this is less true of *Divergent*). Katniss's association with the Amazon, her connection with nature and the wilderness, her ability to survive in the mock primary jungle of the Games, as well as Cassie's wanderings into the woods, re-establish a topical "intimate bond between nature and woman."[38] Paradoxically, the young heroines are associated with traditional craftsmanship, whereas the older characters are linked to the use of state-of-the-art technology. Katniss uses a rather old-fashioned weapon—her iconic bow and arrow—that requires physical strength. The nature versus culture opposition is foregrounded, in various ways, throughout the narratives and is contrasted with the high-tech equipment used by the enemies. By resorting to "survival" tropes, the plots frequently insist on the need to return to a more archaic state of nature—as is made clear, for instance, at the end of *The 5th Wave* when Cassie joins a community of nature-loving outcasts and takes care of her little brother [103:50–end].

Conversely, adult women are associated with science and technology, and disconnected from nature not only as an external environment but also as an internal instinct, eventually becoming cold-blooded murderers. Contrary to the girls, the women villains are surrounded by technological devices, through which most of their plans are carried out. Their prosthetic use of technology, which is present in the source works, has been expanded in the films. This is patent, for instance, in a sequence from *Mockingjay: Part 2* that

Figure 7.1 *The Hunger Games: Mocking Jay—Part 2* (Lawrence, 2015): Katniss sees President Alma Coin on a screen.

opposes, in a typical shot/reverse shot, Katniss, standing alone, to President Coin, seen on a screen (Figure 7.1) [61:07–61:53]. Coin's multiple avatars, spreading over an ever-expanding number of screens, express not only her growing hubris but also her dehumanization. Even more striking is the opening sequence of *Insurgent*, showing an almost disembodied Jeanine, pixelated, featured on every electronic billboard in the area, both displayed and panoptical, staring at the viewer in a terrifying close-up as the credits roll [0:43–2:54]. If intimacy with nature has, in the past, been one of the features of archetypal negative female figures, such as the witch, the construction of villainesses disconnected from nature is consistent with more modern visions connecting women with "insensate and brutal machines,"[39] and more generally "destructive technologies."[40] Through their young characters who represent a more traditional vision of femininity, the narratives indulge in an old-fashioned "longing for reconciliation with nature,"[41] while condemning, through their more mature female protagonists, the use of destructive technologies.

The women almost become cyborgs, as they are either portrayed through a technological device or operating screens or other surveillance systems, which in turn distance them from others and dehumanize them. These traits highlight their alienated nature, in other words, the fact that they are separated from both outer and inner "nature." Kate Winslet's Jeanine sums up the general code of conduct adopted by the empowered women of these works when she says: "I think human nature is the enemy. . . . And I want to eradicate that" [81:11]. Their appeal for science at the expense of "nature" is connected with their proneness to violence, a logical association, given the cultural "genderization of science" and the "association of scientific thought with 'masculinity' and 'violence.'"[42] Yet this conventionally masculine attribute, usually connected with agency and power, is offset by what might be considered female flaws: cowardice and lack of self-control.

The sacrificial heroism of the young female protagonists is contrasted with the recurrent pattern of the vicariousness of the women's murderous actions. While the girls put themselves at risk by reluctantly fighting with their own weapons, the women kill either by ordering others to do it for them or by using sophisticated devices that can be operated at a distance. In *Divergent,* Jeanine Matthews creates a serum that allows her to control young members of her faction and make them kill her opponents. President Coin launches the bombs from the safety of her bunker without ever appearing on the battlefield in person. *The 5th Wave* and *Divergent* feature very similar scenes in which the women kill or torture helpless victims standing behind a screen or a tinted window. This physical separation is emphasized by the fact that the women never pull the trigger and keep delegating the responsibility to others. Reznik, for instance, indoctrinates the young teenagers she recruits and tricks them into shooting other teenagers.

Instead of the immediate reactions of the young girls, the women move from cold, almost inhuman rationality, to a more complex—and always negative—range of emotions. As the stories unfold, their lack of feelings gives way to an attraction to violence and suffering. The shift from coldness to straightforward sadism is obvious in *Insurgent,* which features several scenes that show Jeanine eagerly contemplating, from behind a glass partition, the torture of a victim (Figure 7.2) [47:25–48:02]. While her goal seems to be only utilitarian—she is looking for information—her expression reveals in close-up a genuine fascination verging on sadism. In the particular scene opposing Jeanine to Tris [74:50–83:50], the contrast between the helpless girl, held prisoner in what looks like a sophisticated cobweb, and the disturbing

Figure 7.2 *Insurgent* (Schwentke, 2015): Jeanine eagerly contemplates, from behind a glass partition, the torture of her young victim.

resolve of her torturer evokes not only the traditional wicked woman of fairy tales, but more specifically the topical "exploitation cinema" figure of the sadistic woman, such as the infamous *Ilsa: She Wolf of the SS* (Jess Franco, 1975). With Reznik, the two figures, the doctor and the officer, are merged into one to offer a particularly bloody example of sadistic feminine impulse. She is seen implanting a tracking device in a young boy's neck; the close-up of the boy's wound, after the device has penetrated him, emphasizes Reznik's sadism [34:52]. The sacrificial executions of the women in the fictions represent, as we shall see, both a return of the repressed and a restoration of a supposedly "natural" order that had been transgressed.

Making Sense of Ritual Executions

The climactic epilogue is the culmination of parallel arcs established throughout the series. No matter how complicated the plots, the narratives always find a way to set up a direct confrontation between the two female characters, emphasized by a careful narration designed to produce striking effects of symmetry, notably with the use of shot/reverse shots. Throughout the *Divergent* series, the editing aims to create a close connection between the two female protagonists, even when they are physically apart. In *Insurgent*, for instance, a shot of Jeanine declaring, "We need to find that very special one," is immediately followed by a close-up of Tris [48:44]. The most obvious and systematic example of visual symmetry to depict the two female antagonists face to face occurs in *The Hunger Games*, especially in the final installment, *Mockingjay Part 2*. As President Snow, the male villain, is gradually replaced by President Coin, the antagonism becomes conspicuous, most notably during the sequence concerning the vote on holding the murderous games yet again, where the two women are facing each other at the roundtable [105:25–109:00]. A more solemn confrontation occurs during the execution, with the shot/reverse shot technique, combined with high and low angles, highlighting the personal nature of the conflict opposing the two women [111:49–112:23]. This violent ending is presented as the only possible outcome for the two women, since their arcs deny them the possibility of transformation. While the young characters are given a chance to evolve to some degree, the women are never allowed to develop except toward an ever-greater thirst for power and domination. This appears more clearly if we compare them to a very similar villain from another dystopian film, *The Girl with All the Gifts* (Colm McCarthy, 2016). This postapocalyptic zombie film features a classical adult bitch, played by Glenn Close: Dr. Caroline Caldwell, a military doctor who heartlessly experiments on zombie children.

Yet if she is presented as a heartless and rigid woman, one might still think that her actions are motivated by the desire to save humanity, rather than caused by mere sadism. Even though her character uses zombified children in cruel experimental research, Close's complex performance conveys more humanity and empathy than the other women under study; she, at least, seems capable of remorse. Moreover, she comes across as more trustworthy, given the context of the story. Indeed, the ending proves her right and tends, on some level, to confirm her viewpoint, as ruthless as it sounds. The survival of the zombified children has occurred at the expense of the human species, and several of her predictions ("You cannot save everybody" or "This is the end of the world," for instance) actually come true.

The univocal condemnation of these "bitch" characters is all the more interesting in an era that has actually recognized and valued what Sarah Appleton Aguiar calls the "Millennium Bitch," a trendy figure who has gained positive recognition in several fields, from music to bestseller lists, comics to websites. Aguiar claims that "bad women" have given way, in third-wave feminist fiction, to a new set of characters, as female writers recently reclaimed traditional "embodiments of female evil," from a feminist, or at least feminine, perspective. As Aguiar remarks, the key feature of these new female villains is the fact that they are given "motivation" for their behavior.[43] By contrast, young adult dystopian narrations never provide an explanation for the villainesses' moral aberrations, and they are never given the opportunity to "bid for sympathy,"[44] through a confession that might "explain and thereby normalize" them, contrary to what happens, for instance, with femmes fatales in noir and neo-noir films. While these confessions might have shown that their conduct was "a product of culture rather than a moral choice," as would have been perfectly coherent with their dystopian premises, the narratives deny these women a voice. They are not provided a backstory, making them quite atypical "villain" characters, since "contemporary feminist renderings of the bitch suggest that she is not born a bitch [. . .] she is, instead, created by specific circumstances and, more importantly, by herself."[45] Instead of these arguably "rhetorical" confessions, the narratives rely on a quite different climax: the highly symbolic killing of a woman by another woman. Just as the revised ending of *Fatal Attraction* had "the wife shoot the single woman," contrasting "bad and good women, with traditional women represented as good,"[46] the narratives achieve closure by killing off the villains.

In *The 5th Wave*, a highly violent fight, which is set apart from other such scenes, shows Cassie brutally attacking and eventually strangling Sergeant Reznik [91:29–92:00]. The scene emphasizes the resemblance between the two blondes, but also the very physicality of hand-to-hand combat. The *Divergent* films somewhat complicate the situation by having Jeanine executed twice. A first symbolical fight occurs in *Divergent*, opposing Tris to Jeanine in hand-to-hand combat. The scene opens with a motif strikingly similar to the fight between Carrie and her mother in De Palma's movie; just like Carrie, Tris throws a knife at Jeanine, piercing her hand [126:07]. She then proceeds to inject a serum in her, penetrating her with a device not dissimilar to the one used in *The 5th Wave*. This symbolic murder deprives her of the ability to think and make decisions, turning her into an obedient body with a vacant gaze. In *Insurgent*, the actual execution is accomplished by another ambiguous woman character, when Naomi Watts's Evelyn shoots Jeanine from behind in a last-minute twist [107:49]. *The Hungers Games'* execution best exemplifies how the narratives choose to concentrate all their hostility on the female villain, instead of the male villains. While Katniss was supposed to execute President Snow, she ultimately decides to kill the woman instead, literally diverting her arrow's trajectory to target her, in what is arguably the most ritualized sequence of the whole series [112:23].

In all these examples, not only do the girls restore what appears to be a traditional, natural order by toppling the empowered women from their positions, but, on a more symbolic level, they also embody a kind of return of the repressed. The villains from these stories lack archetypal female qualities, a trait that, significantly, differentiates them not only from nice girls but also from the set of negative archetypes constitutive of the "monstrous-feminine" as defined by Barbara Creed. However, their death throes turn these cold-hearted, robotic monsters into more traditional representations of "abject," out-of-control females. In so doing, figures who were, up to that point, estranged from nature and completely disconnected from "biological bodily functions"[47] are brought back to the "physical states and bodily wastes" that characterize the monstrous-feminine.[48]

Conclusion

How can one interpret the repeated slaughtering of a woman by a girl? While these works are obviously polysemic and open to multiple interpretations, one might nevertheless attempt to make sense of this repeated pattern by putting the fictions in the perspective of both contemporary popular young adult culture and a wider cultural context. The pattern might be seen as the manifestation of the Electra complex: namely a young girl's fantasy of eliminating her mother and taking on the motherly role. Transposed to the cultural context of young adult culture, the need to put adult women at a distance might be traced back to the claiming of subjectivity and the refusal to endorse any influence from previous generations.[49] This conflict may be explained by a theme that is ubiquitous in young adult cultures: the inevitable conflict between generations. This would explain why, in other contemporary works featuring powerful female characters, whether teenage or adult, that do not directly target teenage girls, the emphasis is on more traditionally feminist topics of sisterhood and matrilinear transmission; these ideas are at the core of *Wonder Woman* (Patty Jenkins, 2017) and appear at the end of the postapocalyptic zombie movie *The Girl with All the Gifts*, two films that highlight the possibility of female intergenerational transmission.

In terms of gender politics, the villainesses have given rise to contrasting interpretations as to whether they exemplify a kind of patriarchal or even postfeminist backlash. The univocal condemnation of these characters by the narratives, the fact that female power is unambiguously associated with evil, exemplifies the process of patriarchal punishment against empowered women "displaying the very same traits a male hero might be lauded for possessing: assertiveness, command and leadership, an acquisitive nature, intellect, persistence, ambition and self-preservation instinct."[50] The oppositions that this chapter attempted to bring to light seem to indicate that empowered girls are more easily accepted than empowered women. The representation of the women brings us back to the contradictions of both "girl culture" and postfeminism, since it shows that these fictions are not able to consider the possible transition of their transgressive, bold, and empowered teenage characters into womanhood. By emphasizing conflict rather than transmission, through the paradoxical motif of girls killing women, the fictions foreground the generational gap between two waves of feminism: on the one side, second-wave feminists, of whom the wicked women of the fictions seem to be a particularly negative caricature; and on the other, girls who illustrate the ambiguities of postfeminist girl culture, begrudgingly endorsing the role of collective hero because of special circumstances, but secretly longing for a more traditional, private, and maybe even conservative destiny. While these narratives, "in conjunction with girl-power rhetoric [. . .] lead us to believe that girls can do, and be, and have anything they want,"[51] they nonetheless condemn women who avoid the traditional mission of motherhood. Thus, like previous generations, contemporary girls need to eliminate this burdensome model, the mother, thus somehow reversing the previous connotations of girlhood during second-wave feminism[52]. *Hunger Games*, *Divergent*, and *The 5th Wave* exemplify a version of postfeminism that can, at least to some extent, be interpreted as an anti-feminist backlash, endorsing an essentialist stance and punishing the overt transgressions of its powerful females. Meanwhile, outside youth culture, other works, like *Wonder Woman* (2017), offer a more positive version of postfeminism: on the one hand, such films still ambiguously commodify feminism, through the eroticization of their female heroines, and perpetuate the "belief in a matriarchal past or a contemporary 'matristic realm,'"[53] but on the other, they offer the possibility of a peaceful intergenerational transmission and allow their heroines a chance to play the lead without being punished for it.

Notes

1 Suzanne Collins, *The Hunger Games* (New York: Scholastic, 2008); *Catching Fire* (New York: Scholastic, 2009); *Mockingjay* (New York: Scholastic, 2010).
2 Veronica Roth, *Divergent* (New York: HarperCollins Publishers, 2011), *Insurgent* (Katherine Tegen Books, 2012), *Allegiant* (HarperCollins and Katherine Tegen Books, 2013).
3 Jessica K. Taft, *Rebel Girls: Youth Activism and Social Change Across the Americas* (New York and London: Routledge, 2011), p. 69; Sonya Sawyer-Fritz, "Girl power and girl activists in the fiction of Suzanne Collins, Scott Westerfeld, and Moira Young," in S. K. Day, M. A. Green-Barteet, and A. L. Montz (eds.), *Female Rebellion in Young Adult Dystopian Fiction* (London and New York: Routledge, 2016 [2014]), pp. 35–36.
4 Sara K. Day, "Docile bodies, dangerous bodies: Sexual awakening and social resistance in young adult dystopian novels," in Day, Green-Barteet, and Montz (eds.), *Female Rebellion in Young Adult Dystopian Fiction* (London and New York: Routledge, 2016 [2014]), p. 96.
5 The trilogy *The Hunger Games* became a major motion picture franchise only a couple years after its publication.
6 *Divergent* was also adapted, with less success, with the third installment, *Allegiant*, going directly to video.
7 Rick Yancey, *The Fifth Wave Trilogy* (*The Fifth Wave, The Infinite Sea The Last Star*) (G. P. Putnam's Sons, 2013–2016). So far, only the first installment has been adapted for the screen.
8 Anita Harris, *All About the Girl: Culture, Power and Identity* (New York and London: Routledge, 2004); Clare Bradford and Mavis Reimer (eds.), *Girls, Texts, Cultures* (Waterloo, ON: Wilfrid Laurier University Press, 2015).
9 Katherine R. Broad, "'The dandelion in the spring: Utopia as romance in Suzanne Collins's *The Hunger Games* Trilogy," in B. Basu, K. R. Broad, and C. Hintz (eds.), *Contemporary Dystopian Fiction for Young Adults: Brave New Teenagers* (London and New York: Routledge, 2013), pp. 117–30.
10 Ibid., p. 117.
11 Hannah Smith, "Permission to diverge: Gender in young adult dystopian literature," *Gender Studies Research Papers* (2014), p. 6.
12 Meghan Gilbert-Hickey, "Gender rolls: Bread and resistance in *The Hunger Games* trilogy," in B. Basu, K. R. Broad, and C. Hintz (eds.), *Contemporary*

Dystopian Fiction for Young Adults: Brave New Teenagers (New York:
Routledge, 2013), p. 3.

13 Jessica Miller, "'She has no idea. The effect she can have': Katniss and the
politics of gender," in G. A. Dunn and N. Michaud (eds.), *The Hunger
Games and Philosophy: A Critique of Pure Treason* (Hoboken, NJ: John
Wiley and Sons, 2012), p. 116.

14 Quoted in Broad, "The dandelion," p. 117.

15 Carol Clover, *Men, Women, and Chain Saws: Gender in the Modern Horror
Film* (Princeton, NJ: Princeton University Press, 1992).

16 Harris, *All About the Girl*, p. XV.

17 Sawyer-Fritz, "Girl power," p. 18.

18 Yvonne Tasker, *Spectacular Bodies: Gender, Genre and the Action Cinema*
(London and New York: Routledge, 1993), p. 81.

19 Judith Williamson, "Nightmare on Madison Avenue," *New Statesman*
(1988), p. 29; Charlotte Brunsdon, *Screen Tastes: Soap Opera to Satellite
Dishes* (London: Routledge, 1997), p. 101.

20 Yvonne Tasker, *Soldiers' Stories: Military Women in Cinema and Television
Since World War II* (Durham: Duke University Press, 2011), p. 3.

21 Ibry Theriot, "The bitch archetype," *Journal of Dramatic Theory and
Criticism*, 9/1 (1994), p. 121, quoted in Sarah Appleton Aguiar, *The Bitch Is
Back: Wicked Women in Literature* (Carbondale and Edwardsville: Southern
Illinois University Press, 2001), p. 7.

22 Broad, "The dandelion," p. 126.

23 Day, "Docile bodies," p. 91.

24 Broad, "The dandelion," p. 126.

25 Elizabeth Schreiber-Byers, "Amazon, goddess, and Valkyrie: Re-reading
the roots of female sadism in Krafft-Ebing's Psychopathia Sexualis," in L.
Fallwell and K. Williams (eds.), *Gender and the Representation of Evil* (New
York and London: Routledge, 2016), p. 49.

26 Ibid., p. 54.

27 Ibid., p. 49.

28 Susan Faludi, *Backlash: The Undeclared War Against Women* (New York:
Three Rivers Press, 2010 [1992]), p. 162.

29 Rosalind Sibielski, "What are little (empowered) girls made of?: The
discourse of girl power in contemporary US popular culture," Dissertation
Thesis (Bowling Green State University, 2010), pp. 130–31.

30 Ibid., p. 162.

31 Ellen Riordan quoted by Sibielski, "What are little (empowered) girls," p.
163.

32 Teresa de Lauretis, *Technologies of Gender, Essays on Theory, Film and
Fiction* (Bloomington and Indianapolis: Indiana University Press, 1987), p.
42.

33 Ibid., p. 104.

34 Smith, "Permission to diverge," p. 6.

35 Sonya Sawyer-Fritz, "Girl power," pp. 17–32.

36 Taft, *Rebel Girls*, p. 79.

37 Mary J. Moran, "The three faces of Tally Youngblood: Rebellious identity-changing in Scott Westerfeld's '*Uglies*' series," in Day, Green-Barteet, and Montz (eds.), *Female Rebellion in Young Adult Dystopian Fiction* (London and New York: Routledge, 2016 [2014]), p. 130.

38 Silvia Bovenschen, Jeannine Blackwell, Johanna Moore, and Beth Weckmueller, "The contemporary witch, the historical witch and the witch myth: The witch, subject of the appropriation of nature and object of the domination of nature," *New German Critique*, 15 (1978), p. 105.

39 Eduard Fuchs, quoted in Bovenschen, Blackwell, Moore, and Weckmueller, "The contemporary witch," p. 91.

40 Ibid., p. 111.

41 Ibid., p. 114.

42 Evelyn Fox Keller, *Reflections on Gender and Science* (New Haven: Yale University Press, 1985), p. 20; De Lauretis, *Technologies*, p. 42.

43 Aguiar, *The Bitch*, p. 57.

44 Anna McHugh, "Demanding an explanation, rhetorical apologia and the construction of evil in Victorian literature," in L. Fallwell and K. V. Williams (eds.), *Gender and the Representation of Evil* (New York and London: Routledge, 2016), p. 30.

45 Aguiar, *The Bitch*, p. 98.

46 Fox Keller, *Reflections*, pp. 84–85.

47 Barbara Creed, *The Monstrous-Feminine, Film, Feminism, Psychoanalysis* (London and New York: Routledge, 1993), p. 38.

48 Ibid., p. 36.

49 Roberta Seelinger Trites, *Disturbing the Universe: Power and Repression in Adolescent Literature* (Iowa City: University of Iowa Press, 2000), p. 61.

50 Aguiar, *The Bitch*, pp. 7–8.

51 Shauna Pomerantz and Rebecca Raby, "Reading smart girls, post-nerds in post-feminist popular culture," in C. Bradford and M. Reimer (eds.), *Girls, Texts, Cultures* (Waterloo, ON: Wilfrid Laurier University Press, 2015), p. 13.

52 Angela McRobbie, *The Aftermath of Feminism: Gender, Culture and Social Change* (London: Sage, 2009).

53 De Lauretis, *Technologies*, p. 21.

Filmography

Divergent, directed by Neil Burger, produced by Douglas Wick, Lucy Fisher, and Pouya Shahbazian, screenplay by Evan Daugherty and Vanessa Taylor based on Veronica Roth *Divergent*, with Shailene Woodley, Theo James, Ashley

Judd, Jai Courtney, Ray Stevenson, Zoë Kravitz, Miles Teller, Tony Goldwyn, Maggie Q, Kate Winslet, music by Junkie XL, cinematography by Alwin H. Küchler, edited by Richard Francis-Bruce and Nancy Richardson, Red Wagon Entertainment, Summit Entertainment, 2014. Blu-ray disk Summit Entertainment, Lionsgate 2014.

The Divergent Series: Insurgent, directed by Robert Schwentke, produced by Douglas Wick, Lucy Fisher, and Pouya Shahbazian, screenplay by Brian Duffield, Akiva Goldsman, and Mark Bomback based on *Insurgent* by Veronica Roth, performances by Shailene Woodley, Theo James, Octavia Spenser, Jai Courtney, Ray Stevenson, Zoë Kravitz, Miles Teller, Ansel Elgort, Maggie Q, Naomi Watts, Kate Winslet, music by Joseph Trapanese, cinematography by Florian Ballhaus, edited by Nancy Richardson and Stuart Levy, Red Wagon Entertainment/Summit Entertainment/Mandeville Films, 2015. Blu-ray disk Summit Entertainment, Lionsgate 2015.

The Divergent Series: Allegiant, directed by Robert Schwentke, produced by Lucy Fisher, Pouya Shahbazian, and Douglas Wick, screenplay by Noah Oppenheim, Adam Cooper, and Bill Collage based on *Allegiant* by Veronica Roth, performances by Shailene Woodley, Theo James, Jeff Daniels, Ansel Elgort, Zoë Kravitz, Maggie Q, Miles Teller, Ray Stevenson, Bill Skarsgard, Octavia Spencer, Naomi Watts, music by Joseph Trapanese, cinematography by Florian Ballhaus, edited by Stuart Levy, Red Wagon Entertainment/ Mandeville Films, 2016. Blu-ray disk Summit Entertainment, Lionsgate.

The 5th Wave, directed by Jonathan Blakeson, produced by Graham King, Tobey Maguire, Lynn Harris, and Matthew Plouffe, screenplay by Susannah Grant, Akiva Goldsman, and Jeff Pinkner based on *The Fifth Wave* by Rick Yancey, performances by Chloë Grace Moretz, Nick Robinson, Ron Livingston, Maggie Siff, Alex Roe, Maria Bello, Maika Monroe, Zackary Arthur, Live Schreiber, music by Henry Jackman, cinematography by Enrique Chediak, edited by Paul Rubell, Columbia Pictures/GK Films/LStar Capital/Living Films/ Material Pictures, 2016. Blu-ray disk Sony-Columbia 2016.

The Hunger Games, directed by Gary Ross, produced by Nina Jacobson and Jon Kilik, screenplay by Suzanne Collins, Gary Ross, and Billy Ray, based *on The Hunger Games* by Suzanne Collins, performances by Jennifer Lawrence, Josh Hutcherson, Liam Hemsworth, Woody Harrelson, Elizabeth Banks, Lenny Kravitz, Stanley Tucci, Donald Sutherland, music by James Newton Howard, cinematography by Tom Stern, edited by Stephen Mirrione and Juliette Welfling, Color Force, 2012.

The Hunger Games: Catching Fire, directed by Francis Lawrence, produced by Nina Jacobson and Jon Kilik, screenplay by Simon Beaufoy and Michael Arndt based on *Catching Fire* by Suzanne Collins, performances by Jennifer Lawrence, Josh Hutcherson, Liam Hemsworth, Woody Harrelson, Elizabeth Banks, Lenny Kravitz, Philip Seymour Hoffman, Jeffrey Wright, Stanley Tucci, Donald Sutherland, music by James Newton Howard, cinematography by Jo Willems, edited by Alan Edward Bell, Color Force, 2013 (Lionsgate). DVD Warner Home Video 2017.

The Hunger Games: Mockingjay—Part 1, directed by Francis Lawrence, produced by Nina Jacobson and Jon Kilik, screenplay by Danny Strong and Peter Craig based on *Mockingjay* by Suzanne Collins, performances by Jennifer Lawrence, Josh Hutcherson, Liam Hemsworth, Woody Harrelson, Elizabeth Banks, Julianne Moore, Philip Seymour Hoffman, Jeffrey Wright, Stanley Tucci Donald Sutherland, music by James Newton Howard, cinematography by Jo Willems, edited by Alan Edward Bell and Mark Yoshikawa, Color Force, 2014. Itunes HD, Lionsgate 2016.

The Hunger Games: Mockingjay (Part 2), directed by Francis Lawrence, produced by Nina Jacobson and Jon Kilik, screenplay by Danny Strong and Peter Craig based on *Mockingjay* by Suzanne Collins, with Jennifer Lawrence, Josh Hutcherson, Liam Hemsworth, Woody Harrelson, Elizabeth Banks, Julianne Moore, Philip Seymour Hoffman, Jeffrey Wright, Stanley Tucci, Donald Sutherland, music by James Newton Howard, cinematography by Jo Willems, edited by Alan Edward Bell and Mark Yoshikawa, Color Force/Studio Babelsberg, 2015. Blu-ray disk Summit Entertainment, Lionsgate 2016.

8

Motherhood, Domesticity, and Nurture in the Postapocalyptic World

Negotiating Femininity in *The Walking Dead* (AMC, 2010–)

Marta Suarez

The Walking Dead is a postapocalyptic series that deals with the collapse of civilization and its aftermath, following the spread of a virus that raises the dead and transforms them into predatory hunters of flesh. The narrative follows Rick Grimes, a deputy from a small town in Georgia. Having been in a coma during the outbreak, he wakes up to find walkers[1] roaming the streets. He joins some survivors, reunites with his family, and eventually becomes the leader of the group (S1E3). It is during this initial reunion that we are introduced to the first of the female characters discussed in this chapter, Carol. The second, Maggie, is introduced at the start of the second season when Rick arrives at her father's farm (S2E2). The third character, Michonne, appears briefly at the end of season 2, with a more extended introduction at the start of season 3. The three are the longest-surviving female characters and are still alive at the time I am writing.[2] All three evolved from a pre-outbreak life connected to domestic spaces and distanced from acts of killing to a post-outbreak life as warriors and protectors of the group. Their portrayal differs from that of the three male protagonists introduced in the early seasons (Rick, Shane, and Daryl), whose skills to kill evolve from their pre-outbreak occupations as deputies or hunters.

This chapter explores the characterization of Carol, Maggie, and Michonne, in relation to nurturing, motherhood, and their involvement in domestic tasks, and will discuss how these elements connect them to (post-) feminist goals. These characters evolve from a reductive representation of femininity based on gendered and racial stereotypes, toward a more complex characterization where stereotypically feminine and masculine traits combine to construct richer and layered characters. At the start of their journeys, each character embodies a particular archetype of femininity that relates them to passivity and weakness (Carol), youthful sexual empowerment (Maggie), or the "angry black woman" (Michonne). However, they all overcome these reductive representations within their particular arc, which leads them to positions of trust and power by challenging these stereotypes and transforming into new selves. Their transformations are motivated by dramatic conflicts related to gendered ideas of motherhood, nurturing, and their place in the domestic space. Yet by the end of season 8, these gendered categories have not been entirely discarded, only redefined. In doing so, these women who kill are able to embrace signifiers of "mother" and "nurturer" alongside those of "leader," "fighter," or "protector." Additionally, their presence in domestic spaces is not in conflict with their public figures, and instead of containing their femininity to domestic chores, these domestic spaces provide comfort and solace in hard times.

The Female Heroine and Motivations to Kill

In this postapocalyptic world, audiences are encouraged to accept the characters' potential need to kill walkers and humans in self-defense. Whereas killing humans is common for male action heroes, heroines who kill are often given a justification for their violent behavior. Mary Jo Lodge concludes in her work that the "protection of a child becomes an acceptable reason for a female action hero to emerge,"[3] and Sherrie A. Innes affirms that on the rare occasions that an action hero has a child, "her aggression is shown as only a manifestation of her desire to save him or her."[4] Rikke Schubart distinguishes between the "good mother" and "bad mother"[5]: the first "symbolizes the patriarchal family and raises her children in a self-sacrificing manner," while the second "abandons her post" and follows "her desire to do what men do."[6] The two types confine action heroines within a patriarchal system in which they fight due to their maternal desire to protect the child. If their desire to fight falls outside this justification, or if the heroine does not revert to a patriarchal feminine role after winning the fight, she is usually punished through loss, violence, or death. Revenge after a man's betrayal[7] or sexual violence[8] is also a motivator for a female action hero to emerge, argues Carol Clover. Even the figure of the Final Girl, who kills the villain and survives the narrative, is more victim than hero, Clover argues that, despite her heroic characteristics, she often survives thanks to some "element of last-minute luck."[9]

Another characteristic often associated with female action heroes is the presence of signifiers of masculinity. This has led some scholars to understand the figure within a binary coding of masculinity and femininity. For example, Hilary Neroni suggests that the female action hero adopts violence in a process of masculinization in times of need, but that the narrative suggests that she will "retreat back into her more feminine self."[10] Other scholars, however, have emphasized a discourse of inclusion, whereby these masculine traits do not masculinize the character, but make the heroine more complex by integrating both feminine and masculine traits. This argument recurs in the works of Charlene Tung[11], Jeffrey Brown,[12] Elizabeth Hills,[13] Jacinda Read,[14] Yvonne Tasker,[15] and Barbara Creed.[16]

Female Heroines in *The Walking Dead*

Although Carol, Maggie, and Michonne evolve over the seasons, they all share characteristics of the bad mother at the start of their journeys. Carol initiates her character arc defined within the bad mother archetype because she has not protected her daughter from her husband or the walkers. Despite opportunities to become a mothering figure to other children (Lizzie, Mika, Sam, and Henry), she imposes limitations on their bond and refuses to fully embrace the motherly role by preventing them from calling her "mom." Maggie embodies the "bad mother" archetype by leading battles despite her pregnancy. Michonne is positioned in her origin story as the bad mother because she had left to gather supplies when her son died.

These characters' femininities are positioned continuously as sites of struggle in which they have to negotiate, embrace, or transform ideas of motherhood, domesticity, and nurture. By situating these characters in more traditional gendered roles, the series provides the audience with a background conforming to patriarchal roles, over which the justifications to kill are implemented afterward. Each character's transformations connect with notions associated with both postfeminism and feminist theory. Carol embodies first- and second-wave feminism through a narrative arc that leads her to obtain voting rights as part of the council, addresses issues of domestic violence, and makes her become an equal to other members of the group, including the male lead. Maggie, however, embodies postfeminism by starting her character arc from a position of equality, where she voices her opinion and has control over her body and sexuality. Portrayed as in control and also as "having it all," Maggie is associated with both leadership and motherhood. Michonne, however, cannot be defined in simple terms, since the intersectionality of gender and race complicates her arc. Her initial embodiment of the "angry black woman" makes her a volatile outsider that must become more nurturing before she can join the group. Her arc emphasizes her transformation into both a motherly figure and a romantic interest. Although these are not goals of white feminism, they can be correlated to black feminism, such as debunking the "angry black woman" figure or the possibility of being a romantic interest without exoticizing the black woman's body.

Carol: From Survivor to Warrior

Carol's introduction is marked by invisibility. During the opening credits of S1E3, she appears in the background of a long shot in which Lori is cutting Carl's hair [5:07]. Often obscured in the sequence yet present throughout, Carol is barely visible in the top-right corner of the frame alongside her daughter, Sophia. Though she appears on screen several times after that, it is not until almost fifteen minutes into the episode that Carol speaks for the first time at the campfire [12:35]. The scene [11:30–12:52] sets up the power dynamics within Carol's family by portraying her as submissive and compliant, and her husband Ed as arrogant and domineering, a characterization emphasized later on in the episode when Ed hits her during an argument [36:39–41:48]. In this scene, the camerawork suggests notions of vulnerability through high angles that serve to conceal her partially or relegate her to the sides of the frame [40:15–40:53]. The tension and impact of the scene are heightened by the introduction of a nondiegetic score just before Ed hits Carol [40:41], increasing in volume as the scene develops. As Shane starts beating Ed in retaliation, Carol's cries are muffled, and her lines are inaudible. The sound of the beating directs the focus on the violence, while the visuals show her despair. She is then shown comforting Ed after the beating, when her apologetic lines are heard once again [41:48].

Although the roles of mother and wife are not exclusive to Carol at this point in the narrative, she is representative of a kind of femininity that is stereotyped as passive, accommodating, in need of protection, and unskilled when it comes to weapons and defense. During the first season, most of the women in the group are defined by their relationships or contained within scenes linked to domestic tasks. Framing the female characters within these relationships and tasks is a portrayal that has attracted criticism regarding the representation of gender in *The Walking Dead*, as in works by Simpson[17] or Baldwin and McCarthy.[18] However, it is worth noting that the serialization of a narrative that had over six years' worth of comics at the time of filming allows for long-term planning of character evolution, an argument also defended by Brown in relation to action heroines in serialized narratives.[19]

Thus, although the critics of the first season are right in pointing out that the portrayals conform to gender stereotypes, it is also true that the latter are challenged from season 3 onward.

Season 3 is also the season in which Carol undergoes a symbolic rebirth after managing to fight walkers all by herself. Unlike the comics (her character dies at this point), the TV show turns her into a female fighter in a move that is reminiscent of Barbara in the remake of *Night of the Living Dead*,[20] who "not only survives" but also performs the "unpleasant but necessary task(s)" that leads to that survival.[21] In the post-outbreak world, damsels in distress are a burden and are thus required to aid in their own rescue. Even though Carol's transformation includes acquiring skills that are stereotypically masculine, her full character arc highlights the assumption of a more "adequate femininity" that uses fighting skills for protective nurturing, thus aligning her with the "good mother."

One of the events that significantly impacts Carol's toughening up is Lizzie's death. After a period of exile, Carol reunites with Tyreese, baby Judith, and the young sisters with whom Carol had developed a close bond, Lizzie and Mika [S4E10 17:33]. Upon returning from getting supplies, Carol and Tyreese arrive to find that Lizzie has killed her sister [S4E14 28:46]. Concluding that Judith is not safe around Lizzie, Carol takes Lizzie outside and asks her to look at the flowers before shooting her [36:11], echoing Mika's words of comfort to Lizzie in a previous episode. In a reversal of stereotypical gender roles on screen, it is Tyreese who stays indoors with Judith, while Carol is the one who takes Lizzie's life. Tyreese and Carol regularly perform these roles during their time in the woods, with Tyreese often carrying baby Judith or doing basic childcare, and Carol taking the role of fighter; for instance, when Carol rescues Rick's group at Terminus [S5E1 13:34], she assumes the role of heroic leader, a role also granted by Rick when he asks her "Will you have us?"

Following Terminus's rescue, Carol's feminine behavior becomes a conscious performance of nonthreatening femininity. Upon arriving at Alexandria (S5E12), Carol suddenly acts as if she were not proficient with weapons, handling the guns awkwardly [09:35–09:54]. Whereas she rarely smiles in the previous season, at this point, she adopts an unguarded posture with arms to the side, a big grin, and a soft voice. As part of her performance, Carol describes herself to the town mayor as a lucky housewife who was protected by the rest of the group in exchange for domestic tasks and some mothering; she even refers to her abusive husband as "that stupid wonderful man" [S5E1 27:23–28:09] Carol plays this double act between the arrival at Alexandria (S5E12) and the attack of the Wolves (S6E2), presenting herself to the new group as a harmless and innocuous housewife or, in her own words, as "invisible" [S5E13 12:06]. Some time after revealing to the community her fighting skills during the Wolves' episode and Alexandria's defense against walkers (S6E9), Carol shows a desire to merge the fighter and the nurturer, which is visually conveyed during the opening sequence of S6E12 [0:00–3:01]. The editing shows Carol choosing ingredients, baking, killing a walker, choosing a patterned "housewife" shirt, and handing cookies to Alexandrians [2:10]. Combining signifiers associated with both the nurturer and the killer, an upbeat song links the scenes, suggesting a reconciliation of both roles, metaphorically represented by her "housewife" outfit accessorized with her gun and her knife, clearly visible at the waist (Figure 8.1).

The balance between the two roles is short-lived, as a plan for a preemptive attack on the Saviors makes her question her role in the group, triggering feelings of guilt that are visually conveyed on a list count of those she has killed. Tobin, conversing with Carol shortly afterward, deems her both maternal and scary,[22] linking her to what Barbara Creed describes as the monstrous-feminine and the terrible mother.[23] Recalling Laura Mulvey's remarks on the guilt of the female heroine,[24] Carol is guilty of having usurped phallic power and abandoned her mothering duties to the group. Since protecting loved ones involves killing, she resolves that the only solution lies in a self-imposed exile that lasts the whole of season 7 [S6E14 40:13–41:45]. Even when she rejoins the group, Carol is portrayed as taciturn; she avoids the children, and when she joins the battles, a sense of unpassionate duty to the group defines her actions. It is not until she rescues Henry that her emotions return, in a scene of healing that closes her character arc, as we shall see.

Figure 8.1 *The Walking Dead* (AMC, 2010–): Carol distributing cookies, trying to resolve her inner conflict.

The invisibility that the pre-outbreak world imposed has now become a choice that allows Carol to mask her fighting skills. The difference between Carol's two roles is emphasized by the costumes: comfortable loose clothing in dark, earthen tones when representing the "killer"; light-colored cardigans and flowered patterns when portraying the "housewife." The use of flowers is a recurring motif linked to Carol's mothering and nurturing nature, but it also evokes grief. The first instance in which Carol is connected to the image of the flower is during S2E4, when Daryl gives her a Cherokee rose and explains its meaning of hope, through a legend about Native American Mothers who lost their children during the Trail of Tears [S2E4 34:36–36:50]. Blending meanings of nurture and grief, the motif outlines her arc: Carol destroys the field of blossoming roses upon finding Sofia dead [S2E8 14:19–14:49]; she refers to flowers when killing Lizzie; she is framed within flowered patterns when Morgan tries to convince her to rejoin the fight [S7E8 20:46–23:06]; a flower graffiti is next to her during the opening battle of S8E1; and The Kingdom's citizens she co-leads are given a small bunch of flowers before combat, where all but her and two other characters die. The flowers serve as a reminder of the signifiers of grieving motherhood that Daryl's Cherokee rose evoked, those that Carol has to embrace as part of the resolution of her character arc, which involves forgiving herself for Sophia's death. This redemption does not take place until season 8 when she saves Henry, a child of a similar age,[25] who was also lost alone in the woods. Finding Henry under the tree roots[26] that recall Sophia's disappearance [S8E14 40:24–41:47], Carol sobs and apologizes to Henry. Her narrative arc and the editing connect both sequences with the meanings of motherhood, grief, healing, and hope that the flowers symbolized. Using her skills as a fighter to track and save Henry realigns Carol with a more conforming femininity—that of the protective mother—yet it does not detract from her identity as a fighter or relegate her back to domestic space.

Maggie: From Having-it-All to Pregnant Widow

Maggie is introduced in S2E2 [4:33–05:33]. As Rick carries an injured Carl toward her farm, Maggie appears, a figure on a porch, in the blurry background of a medium long shot of Rick [4:40]. The editing alternates between a POV shot of Rick from Maggie's perspective before her face is revealed, thus aligning the audience with Maggie's gaze. While the POV shot can suggest a threat, its combination with medium close-ups allows the audience to infer that she is a young woman, alone in clear sight, with no visible weapons [4:53]. After she alerts them, her family walks out of the house just as Rick arrives. Her posture is nonthreatening, while the composition, which abides by the rule of thirds, makes her the center of attention, highlights her place in the family, and announces her importance in the narrative [5:20]. Introducing both Carol and Maggie from a distance underscores their nonthreatening position in space. At the same time, by presenting their characters within a family, the composition articulates the power dynamics in the private space. Maggie is defined from the start as an independent young woman who appears equal to her father. By positioning her on the porch in the front line with her father, yet not physically connected to him, the framing asserts these qualities, which become more evident as the episode unfolds.

Maggie is rarely involved in cooking or childcare, but rather, in gardening and farming activities. Planting crops and discussions of land fertility suggest notions of reproduction, which are embodied in her later pregnancy. She is soon introduced as the initiator of sex [S2E4 29:21] and shown in control of her sexuality, notions that connect her to "do-me feminism."[27] The character is thus representative of postfeminist discourses on femininity and sexuality, where empowerment is connected to choice and agency in sexual encounters. She is thus initially portrayed in accordance with contemporary representations of the female action hero; her primary value is her "irresistible sexuality" despite being as "tough as the guys,"[28] blending "sexuality with assertiveness" and "tough-girl strength, allowing her to transcend the patriarchal limits of female identity/femininity."[29] By the end of season 2, her sexual encounters evolve into a romantic relationship with Glenn, who finally tells her he loves her [S2E13 20:15]. From this point on, their arcs often involve forced separation and the strong desire to return to each other.

Her fertile sexuality is threatened via plots of rape [S3E7 29:25] and of endangered pregnancy [S6E15 40:54]. In doing so, the viewer is reminded of the feminine fragility of her sexual body. After Maggie and Glenn are rescued following the governor's sexual violence, Glenn takes on the role of Maggie's protector. This is furthered when Glenn takes a picture of a sleeping Maggie (Figure 8.2) [S4E2 07:51], which he cherishes. During a forced separation (S4E8) and until they reunite [S4E15 32:18], Glenn finds comfort with this picture. Her body, once more, is the object of the gaze, connecting it to notions of scopophilia[30] on two levels, that of the narrative and that of the audience. Maggie destroys the picture as soon as they reunite [S4E15 37:10], reclaiming her right to be in control of how and when her body is looked at.

Protecting Maggie's body is a central concern of season 6, this time to protect her pregnancy, which is directly threatened on two occasions: first, when a prisoner in a Saviors' outpost (S6E12), and later when she becomes

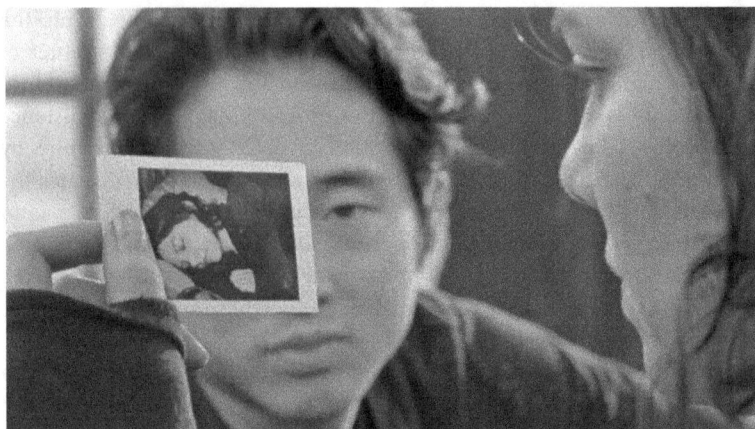

Figure 8.2 *The Walking Dead* (AMC, 2010–): Maggie, taking control of her image.

critically ill due to *placenta previa* (S6E16). The sudden awareness that something is wrong takes place after Maggie decides to cut her long hair (a visible feminine trait) to go to war [S6E15 41:17]. The efforts of the group to take her to a nearby doctor lead to their capture by the Saviors and the subsequent murder of Glenn by Negan.[31] After their release, and although Maggie's pregnancy is still in jeopardy, compositions do not suggest weakness but intense pain. With low angles and central framing, her suffering is emphasized and contrasted to the group's sorrow. Sobbing, Maggie is seen standing up with effort, yet refusing anyone's help. As the group carries away the dead bodies, connotations of isolation and pain are suggested by a high-angle establishing shot of her alone in the empty field, next to the spilled blood [S7E13 43:31].

The characterization of Maggie as a strong woman is further stressed in S7E5 [15:58–19:38], in which she becomes the de-facto leader of the Hilltop. Still recovering, Maggie wakes up in the middle of the night to a Saviors' attack. Climbing on top of her caravan to see what is happening, she organizes the defense. The low angle, combined with low-key lighting, emphasizes her power and authority [S7E5 17:41]. A similar shot is used when she addresses the whole community at the end of season 7 and the start of season 8, in speeches that take them all to war[32] and that identify her as the chosen leader at the Hilltop.

The desire for revenge after her husband's death underlies her arc in subsequent seasons and comes to the fore at the end of season 8. At this point, Maggie is known as "the widow," a nickname that associates her identity with her husband's death and her thirst for revenge. At the end of the season and in a scene reminiscent of *The Godfather* (Francis Ford Coppola, 1972),[33] Maggie sits behind a desk in low-key lighting demanding revenge on Negan, Rick, and Michonne. In doing so, she not only reinforces her position as leader of the Hilltop, but also embraces her role as antagonist. It will be interesting to see whether season 9 will allow her to reach full leadership of both groups without jeopardizing her motherhood, or whether her desire to continue the fight will once again be punished by death.

Maggie thus starts out as a confident and independent postfeminist character who is soon involved in a normative relationship with goals of marriage, parental approval, and reproduction. These heteronormative goals conform to hegemonic ideas of femininity. Yet when Maggie chooses actions linked to hegemonic masculinity, such as willfully attacking another community or dethroning the leader of the Hilltop, the narrative punishes her with a loved one's death. Throughout the seasons, her narrative arc tends to reward actions that lead to family pursuits; for instance, when Maggie decides to stay behind because of her pregnancy instead of looking for Glenn, he reappears even though he was believed to be dead (S6E7). Yet the narrative punishes fighting actions that could have been prevented and are not carried out in the name of the family: attacking Woodbury brings retaliation that ends with the death of her father; joining a trip to Washington instead of looking for her sister ultimately leads her to Beth's dead body; and her decision to attack the Saviors leads to her husband's death. The trope of the guilty woman is here linked to her transgressions, which pursue masculine pursuits instead of conforming to feminine ones, pursuits that must be either controlled or disciplined, thereby linking her character to Shubart's "bad mother." Yet despite all these deaths, Maggie stands as a proud leader of her community and derives strength from her anger, still balancing the notions of motherhood and leadership, which are visually symbolized when at her office desk she holds her bump protectively while looking at baby Gracie [S8E11 16:41].

Michonne: From Lonely Angry Warrior to Partner and Mother

The character of Michonne cannot be reduced to (post)feminist goals but begs for an intersectional analysis that takes into account race and gender. Second-wave feminism has often been criticized for its tendency to speak for "all women" when, in reality, it has focused on the needs and equality goals of

Western white middle-class women.[34] Postfeminist theory, asserts Kimberly Springer, highlights the absence of women of color in influential positions but generally fails to interrogate white privilege and the importance of race.[35] In fact, postfeminism commodifies race by making it consumable through ethnic fashion and bodily characteristics.[36]

Although Michonne's appearance evokes some ethnic elements, more significant is her initial portrayal as the "angry black woman" archetype. Unlike Carol and Maggie, Michonne is not introduced from a distance in a nonthreatening position, but abruptly and in an aggressive context [S2E13 36:54–37:49]. She is revealed first through her katana, and thus her capacity to castrate. As a walker is beheaded while approaching a defenseless Andrea, its body drops offscreen, revealing a mysterious figure with a chained walker to each side; Michonne's face is concealed under a hood, and her body is wrapped in darkness (Figure 8.3) [S2E13 37:47]. By introducing her character through violence and delaying the revelation of her face, her character is associated with danger and menace.

Unlike Carol and Maggie, then, Michonne appears for the first time in a narrative cliff-hanger at the end of a season. Pointedly, her face is not revealed until S3E1, where we encounter her via a back close-up that emphasizes her dreadlocks, before seeing her features [S3E1 30:00–33:27]. Though no longer anonymous, her face expresses anger, an element that characterizes her throughout most of season 3. Introduced as the angry outsider, Michonne's character arc connects to notions of opening up, being accepted in the group, and toning down her attitude by acquiring traditional feminine traits related

Figure 8.3 *The Walking Dead* (AMC, 2010–): Michonne's first appearance.

to (surrogate) mothering. If Maggie and Carol were required to harden up before taking on leadership positions, Michonne's journey requires her to become more nurturing. Her character arc starts with stereotypes that align the black heroine with the "angry black woman"[37] lacking "lady-like femininity."[38] Her transformation, which implies a sort of softening, has been discussed by Caroline Brown in relation to Michelle Obama, who placated criticism on her aggressive "unfemininity" through the use of fashion and an emphasis on her role as a mother.[39] As with sexism, racial stereotypes and tokenism populate the first seasons of *The Walking Dead*, despite the in-narrative claims of a post-racial world.[40]

Characterized as fierce and distant upon meeting the group [S3E6 41:47–42:25], she is told she must leave once she has recovered from her injuries. Whereas the comics link her mistrust, anger, and isolation to the trauma of having been tortured and raped, the TV series does not explain her behavior other than as a means to survive. Her reckless and violent attitude thus conjures up images of the Sapphire and the Crazy Black Bitch.[41] Patricia Hill Collins asserts that negative stereotypes are "designed to control assertive Black female behavior," and that "aggressive Afro American women are threatening because they challenge white patriarchal definitions of femininity."[42] The solution, Collins argues, is not to change "their behavior to become meek, docile, and stereotypically 'feminine,'"[43] but to value this assertiveness to transcend and control this "externally-defined controlling images."[44] Michonne's transformation and acceptance in the group are affected through her alignment with the roles of mother and wife. Yet this status does not affect her sword-fighting skills, intuition, or bravery; instead, she uses these skills to protect her new family unit without compromising her assertiveness and independent thought.

Michonne is accepted in the group after bonding with Carl in a mission to collect a family picture for him and a cot for his baby sister, both family-related objects (S3E12). For Michonne, gaining trust is associated with nurture and protection. This turn is not a radical change but a rediscovery of her mothering-self, a journey that becomes apparent when Michonne softly sobs and cuddles Judith when they are alone [S4E2 32:23–33:58]. Cradling the baby is embracing not only her mothering nature, but also the group and her role in it. Nurturing aspects of her personality are also revealed through a dream sequence that depicts fragments of her family before the outbreak [S4E9 13:30–16:08] and where her hardening, like Carol's, is connected to a failure to protect her child. Shortly after this dream, Michonne turns around and joins Rick and Carl [S4E9 31:49–34:14]. For a brief period, Michonne expresses a desire to settle down and stop fighting, her goals thus conforming to the "new traditionalism,"[45] which "articulates a vision of the home as women's sanctuary from the stresses of their working lives."⁴⁶ Yet it will become apparent that she cannot put down her weapons even in periods of apparent peace, after the sword that she had hung on the wall [39:41–40:14] is used to kill the Major's husband. Subsequently, Michonne comes to terms with the fact that her desire for a peaceful home requires her to defend it, thus carrying the sword once again and removing it permanently from the wall.

Michonne's position as mother in Rick's family unit becomes complete in S6E10. First, Carl tells Michonne that he would stop her from reanimating out of love, as he did for his mother. Later that night, Rick and Michonne watch Judith on the baby monitor. As their fingers touch, they hold hands and smile before sharing their first kiss [S6E10 41:51]. The full sequence [S6E10 38:20–42:09] focuses on romantic elements but leaves the sexual act in ellipsis, cutting to Michonne and Rick sleeping naked in bed. Their bodies occupy the center of the composition, their legs intertwined, and their weapons at each side. With a balanced composition, the framing suggests that these characters have become whole in each other's company. The way Michonne is portrayed in this sequence breaks with common portrayals of black female sexuality after Blaxploitation cinema, where the black female character is either exoticized sexually or coded as masculine and desexualized,⁴⁷ with narratives suggesting that the black heroine "does not fall in love"⁴⁸ or where she is "depicted as sexual predator(s)."⁴⁹ Instead, this sequence makes Michonne the object of love, and not just desire, first framing her in a domestic setting, then focusing on romantic elements, and finally skipping the sexual encounter in favor of gentle intimacy.

The more Michonne's relationship with Rick evolves, the less she is involved in fight scenes. This could be understood as a negative representation of a female character who submits to traditional femininity; from an intersectional perspective, however, her characterization as a skillful motherly fighter, as well as a romantic interest who is not objectified, breaks negative stereotyping and constitutes positive representation.⁵⁰ Feminization takes place through her mothering relationship with Carl and her romantic relationship with Rick. This relationship empowers her by allowing her influence over the male lead. Instead of weakening her as a warrior, Michonne acquires a more domestic and nurturing role without detriment to her warrior skills. By season 8, Michonne has attained the postfeminist ideal of "having it all" by debunking the "angry black woman" and "loveless black heroine" tropes. In so doing, her character counters the lack of "multi-faceted roles routinely available to black women in American films with which to counterbalance their 'sexual' images."⁵¹

Conclusion

If the arcs of Carol, Maggie, and Michonne follow different paths, all acquire survival, fighting, and leadership skills, which characterize them as female warriors. However, each of them is marked distinctly in connection to notions of femininity, domesticity, and motherhood. Carol's initial mothering role is perceived as inadequate because she cannot protect her child in this world, so that her journey also involves mastering the warrior skills that will allow her to protect those she loves. Maggie's femininity is associated with her fertile sexuality, and her journey aims toward leadership and family. While she is still pregnant by the end of season 8, the narrative has constructed a strong leader that has in mind the protection of those under her guardianship, including her child. Michonne's femininity is initially contained, in line with stereotypical representations of nonsexual black female characters. As she engages in a romantic relationship with the main lead, her portrayal avoids exoticizing or sexualizing her body, the narration focusing instead on romantic gestures evoking tenderness and closeness. If the start of the show associated these female characters with stereotypical traits, their evolution as resourceful, authoritative, and skilled is essential in a genre where women warriors often follow narratives of the Final Girl, the dangerous bombshell, or the crazed avenger. Instead, these representations offer portrayals based on developing skills, becoming protectors of the group, and gaining positions of trust and power within it. In doing so, the series challenges patriarchal notions of femininity and offers alternatives to hegemonic discourses. Overall, and despite character arcs linked to motherhood and guilt, the series moves beyond the gender stereotypes it initially set up to create rich and complex action heroines that combine both masculine and feminine traits, moving away from the "figurative male" and approaching Hills's notion of transformation and becoming.[52] Their embodiment of different feminist goals creates a multifaceted universe that asserts their individuality and gives them narrative arcs that do not confine them to the realms of the mother and wife, even though they embrace these roles at some point during the narrative.

Notes

1 I refer to the raised undead as "walkers" in line with the series, which makes a point of not using the word "zombies."
2 Season 8.

3 Mary Jo Lodge, "Knocked up, not knocked out," in L. M. DeTora (ed.), *Heroes of Film, Comics and American Culture: Essays on Real and Fictional Defenders of Home* (Jefferson: McFarland and Company, 2009), p. 230.

4 Sherry A. Inness, "Boxing gloves and bustiers," in S. A. Innes (ed.), *Action Chicks: New Images of Tough Women in Popular Culture* (New York: Palgrave Macmillan, 2004).

5 Rikke Schubart, *Super Bitches and Action Babes: The Female Hero in Popular Cinema, 1970-2006* (Jefferson: McFarland and Company, 2007), pp. 169–245.

6 Ibid., p. 181.

7 Carol J. Clover, *Men, Women, and Chain Saws: Gender in the Modern Horror Film* (Princeton, NJ: Princeton Classics, 2015), Kindle edition, p. 29.

8 Ibid., p. 144.

9 Ibid., p. x.

10 Hilary Neroni, *The Violent Woman: Femininity, Narrative, and Violence in Contemporary American Cinema* (New York: State University of New York Press, 2005), pp. 84–86.

11 Charlenne Tung, "Embodying and image: Gender, race, and sexuality in *La Femme Nikita*," in A. S. Inness (ed.), *Action Chicks: New Images of Tough Women in Popular Culture* (New York: Palgrave Macmillan, 2004), pp. 103–6.

12 Jeffrey A. Brown, *Beyond Bombshells: The New Action Heroine in Popular Culture* (Jackson: University of Mississippi Press, 2015).

13 Elizabeth Hills, "From 'figurative males' to action heroines: Further thoughts on active women in the cinema," *Screen*, 40/1 (1999), p. 40.

14 Jacinta Read, "'Once upon a time there were three little girls . . .': Girls, violence, and *Charlie's Angels*," in S. J. Schneider (ed.), *New Hollywood Violence* (Manchester: Manchester University Press, 2004), p. 205.

15 Yvonne Tasker, "Action heroines in the 1980s: The limits of musculinity," in G. Turner (ed.), *The Film Cultures Reader* (London: Routledge, 1993), pp. 308–10.

16 Barbara Creed, "Horror and the monstrous-feminine: An imaginary abjection," in B. K. Grant (ed.), *The Dread of Difference: Gender and the Horror Film* (Austin: University of Texas Press, 2015).

17 Philip L. Simpson, "The zombie apocalypse is upon us!: Homeland insecurity," in D. Keetley (ed.), *"We're All Infected": Essays on AMC's The Walking Dead and the Fate of the Human (Contributions to Zombie Studies)* (Jefferson: McFarland and Company, 2014), Kindle edition, Loc. 719.
   For similar conclusions in relation to differences in gender roles related to either the TV show or the comic series, see Jessica Murray, "A Zombie apocalypse: Opening representational spaces for alternative constructions of gender and sexuality," *Journal of Literary Studies*, 29/4 (2013), pp. 1–19; Tammy Garland, Nickie Phillips, and Scott Vollum, "Gender politics

and *The Walking Dead*: Gendered violence and the reestablishment of patriarchy," *Feminist Criminology*, 13/1 (2018), pp. 59–86; and Stephen Olbrys Gencarella, "Thunder without rain: Fascist masculinity in AMC's *The Walking Dead*," *Horror Studies*, 7/1 (2016), pp. 125–46. While Cynthia Vinney and Caryn Wiley-Rapoport do comment on this division, they also discuss gender transgressions. See "'Look at the Flowers': Female evolution in the face of the zombie hordes of *The Walking Dead*," in B. Brodman and J. E. Doan (eds.), *The Supernatural Revamped: From Timeworn Legends to Twenty-First-Century Chic* (London: Fairleigh Dickinson University Press, 2016).

18 Martina Baldwin and Mark McCarthy, "Same as it ever was: Savior narratives and the logics of survival in *The Walking Dead*," in M. Balaji (ed.), *Thinking Dead: What the Zombie Apocalypse Means* (Plymouth: Lexington Books, 2013), p. 86.

19 Jeffrey A. Brown, "Gender, sexuality and toughness: The bad girls of action film and comic books," in S. A. Innes (ed.), *Action Chicks: New Images of Tough Women in Popular Culture* (New York: Palgrave Macmillan, 2004), pp. 70–71.

20 Tom Savini, *Night of the Living Dead* (1990).

21 Barry Keith Grant, "Taking back the *Night of the Living Dead*: George Romero, feminism, and the horror film," in B. K. Grant (ed.), *The Dread of Difference: Gender and the Horror Film* (Austin: University of Texas Press, 2015), pp. 231–34.

22 *Not Tomorrow Yet*, [11:36–13:34] "(Tobin:) Worried about tomorrow. (Carol:) You going? (Tobin:) No, you are . . . You can do things that . . . that just terrify me. (Carol:) How do you think I do those things? (Tobin:) You're a mom. (Carol:) I was. (Tobin:) You are. It . . . It . . . It's not the cookies or the smiles. It's . . . it's the hard stuff. The scary stuff. I's how you can do it. It's strength. You're a mom to most of the people here. (Carol:) To you too? (Tobin:) No. You are something else to me. (Carol:) Well, it's not tomorrow yet."

23 Barbara Creed, *The Monstrous-Feminine: Film, Feminism, Psychoanalysis* (New York: Routledge, 1993).

24 Laura Mulvey, "Visual pleasure and narrative cinema," in L. Braudy and M. Cohen (eds.), *Film Theory and Criticism: Introductory Readings* (New York: Oxford University Press, 1975).

25 The actor is also the real-life brother of the actor who plays Sophia.

26 Same shooting location, different locations in the narrative.

27 Stéphanie Genz and Benjamin A. Brabon, *Postfeminism: Cultural Texts and Theories* (Edinburgh: Edinburgh University Press, 2009), pp. 90–92.

28 Brown, *Beyond Bombshells*.

29 Genz and Brabon, *Postfeminism*, p. 150.

30 Mulvey, "Visual Pleasure."

31 From S6E16 [52:23] to S7E1 [20:07].

32 In S7E16 [58:55–59:22] and more clearly in S8E1 [04:31–05:12].

33 [S8E16 41:12–42:37].

34 Benita Roth, *Black, Chicana, and White Feminist Movements in America's Second Wave* (Cambridge: Cambridge University Press, 2004), p. 2.

35 Kimberly Springer, "Divas, evil black bitches, and bitter black women: African-American women in postfeminist and post-civil rights popular culture," in Charlotte Brunsdon and Lynn Spigel (eds.), *Feminist Television Criticism: A Reader* (Berkshire: McGraw-Hill, 2008), p. 72.

36 Ibid., p. 74.

37 J. Celeste Walley-Jean, "Debunking the myth of the 'angry black woman': An exploration of anger in young African American women," *Black Women, Gender & Families*, 3/2 (2009), pp. 66–86.

38 Springer, "Divas, evil black bitches, and bitter black women."

39 Caroline Brown, "Marketing Michelle: Mommy politics and post-feminism in the age of Obama," *Comparative American Studies an International Journal*, 10 (2012), pp. 239–54.

40 Dawn Keetley, "Introduction," in D. Keetley (ed.), *"We're All Infected": Essays on AMC's* The Walking Dead *and the Fate of the Human (Contributions to Zombie Studies)* (Jefferson: McFarland and Company, 2014), Kindle edition.

41 Wendy Reynolds-Dobbs, Kecia M. Thomas, and Matthew S. Harrison, "From Mammy to Superwoman: Images that Hinder Black women's career development," *Journal of Career Development*, 35/2 (2008), p. 136.

42 Patricia Hill Collins, "Learning from the outsider within: The sociological significance of black feminist thought," *Social Problems*, 33/6 (1986), p. S17.

43 Ibid., p. S18.

44 Ibid.

45 Genz and Brabon, *Postfeminism*, pp. 51–53.

46 Ibid., p. 52.

47 Norma Manatu, *African American Women and Sexuality in the Cinema* (Jefferson: McFarland and Company, 2002), p. 44.

48 Ibid., p. 11.

49 Ibid., p. 66.

50 Dwight E. Brooks and Lisa P. Hébert, "Gender, race, and media representation," in B. J. Dow and J. T. Wood (eds.), *The SAGE Handbook of Gender and Communication* (Thousand Oaks: Sage, 2006).

51 Manatu, *African American Women*, p. 43.

52 Hills, "From 'figurative males' to action heroines."

Filmography

The Walking Dead, based on the comic book by Robert Kirkman, Tony Moore, and Charlie Adlard, developed by Frank Darabont, produced by Jolly

Dale, Caleb Womble, Paul Gadd, and Heather Bellson, performances by Andrew Lincoln, Jon Bernthal, Sarah Wayne Callies, Laurie Holden Jeffrey DeMunn, Steven Yeun, Chandler Riggs, Norman Reedus, Lauren Cohan, Danai Gurira, Michael Rooker, David Morrissey, Melissa McBride, music by Bear McCreary, cinematography by Rohn Schmidt, David Boyd, Michael E. Satrazemis, Stephen Campbell, David Tattersall, edited by Julius Ramsay, Hunter M. Via, Avi Youabian, Dan Liu, Nathan Gunn, Rachel Goodlett Katz, Kelley Dixon, Idiot Box Productions circle of Confusion, Skybound Entertainment/Valhalla Entertainment/AMC Studios, 2010–present. Amazon Prime Streaming.

9

An Audience Studies Approach to Tarantino's Violent Heroines in *Kill Bill* (2003–04) and *Death Proof* (2007)

Connor Winterton

Introduction

In November 2016, I presented at a conference on the topic of Tarantino's heroines in *Death Proof* (2007) in relation to homage and the representation of gender. When I joined the panel afterward, I was greeted, as usual, by a range of questions. These questions did not directly relate to the talk I had just given, but focused more broadly on the political and gendered ramifications of Tarantino's heroines. One delegate made a comment about the poor quality of female dialogue in Tarantino's films, while another ignited an interesting debate around the lap-dance scene in *Death Proof* and what it says about female sexual agency, feminism, spectatorship, and the male gaze.[1] After the questions and panel finished, a fellow presenter made a comment regarding the relationship between texts and audiences that stuck with me and also somewhat inspired this chapter. They said, and I roughly quote, "often critical discourse that examines female heroines does not align with what people actually think—who is to say that the women in *Death Proof* are, or are not, empowering?" I pondered over this question for a while, which led me to ask myself some other questions: who is to say these heroines are not powerful or empowering representations of violent women? Has anybody conducted this research before to find out? What do spectators actually think of these heroines?

Unfortunately, very few academics within the study of action heroism and cinema have undertaken audience research to attempt to discover what audiences think of Tarantino's controversial killer women, and more generally of women in the action genre. Jennifer McClearen's "Unbelievable Bodies: Audience Readings of Action Heroines as a Post-Feminist Visual Metaphor" (2015) is, in this respect, one of the few exceptions. This chapter will specifically focus on audience reception in relation to Tarantino's violent women by providing primary research that shows (some) spectator opinions in relation to the representations of the heroines. It will delineate what the heroines mean for and to spectators by primarily surveying discussions on the online forum "The Quentin Tarantino Archives Community" (QTAC for short), as well as comments on relevant Reddit threads.[2] Diverting away from a more rigidly formal approach to Tarantino's heroines provides a new approach to understanding both the violent women *and* how audiences react to them, outside of critiques that rely solely on theoretical observations.

This chapter is divided up into three key sections. First, it will outline key terms of reference, such as "feminism," "postfeminism," and "empowerment," concepts that are at the heart of the celebration or critique of Tarantino's violent women, and in this same section, I will also outline the academic literature that has analyzed Tarantino's women who kill. Following this, I will outline and synthesize my findings with secondary literature, suggesting that the audience responses to Tarantino's women who kill ultimately point to the fact that the women are a site of *interpretative conflict*. My conclusion will also point to the fact that gender and gendered readings are central to the enjoyment of these texts, as they are also central to the criticism of these texts.

Methodology

As mentioned earlier, the main approach (so far) of analyzing Tarantino's women who kill has been through a formal or theoretical approach, which typically examines, for example, the women's corporeality, their violent actions, the representation of femininity and motherhood, through either a "feminist" or a "postfeminist" lens. While these critiques have their merits and are standardized frameworks in film studies, they often focus exclusively on the films themselves, eluding issues of audience reception or gratification. Very few academic texts, in response to either Tarantino's heroines or action heroines in general, have taken an audience studies approach that puts audiences and reception at the forefront of an investigation.[3] It was because of this that I decided to survey two online forums to try and discover what other people think of Tarantino's violent women outside of academic debates steeped in theory. The two forums I surveyed were "The Quentin Tarantino Archives," a free online website that provides news on the director and his upcoming projects and has a community forum where members can write posts and others can comment on them, and Reddit threads that discuss the films and the heroines.[4] QTAC has over 18,260 posts devoted to *Kill Bill* with 658 topics and has 11,636 posts on *Grindhouse* (which is a feature that includes *Death Proof*), spanning the years 1999 to the present day (although the chats on the website appear to have stagnated over the last few years). The website chat forum also has a handy "search" option, which enabled me to find posts that discussed the representation of women and violence with more ease. While QTAC does provide fertile ground for this type of research, Reddit is a more neutral site for considering what spectators "liked" or thought about *Kill Bill* and *Death Proof.*

The limitations of conducting this kind of research particularly center on the fact that online forums can be saturated with individuals who spam or write offensive comments. However, they are online spaces where people can openly share their (often honest) opinions and connect with like-minded individuals from all across the globe, for free. This kind of research is often labeled "virtual ethnography" (and has some ethical considerations and conundrums, which are too many to fully delineate here). Coinciding with the rise of the internet in the 1990s, "virtual ethnography" was initially seen as groundbreaking but was also criticized as being a "fast ethnography," a "cheap-and-easy way to reach [new] worlds."[5] Christine Hine was "among the first advocates of virtual ethnography in the early to mid-1990s"[6] and critically discussed this newer way of researching certain (online) cultures; she notes that it was (and still is) an adaptive and flexible research method.[7] Emma Hutchinson, however, states in relation to the ethical considerations of virtual ethnography that "it is important to examine the ethics of studying forums since they can be easy pickings for the novice social researcher looking to quickly grab data for a project";[8] the ease with which it is possible to copy and paste comments is often an attractive element of this kind of research, but is to a certain degree unethical as users are not always conscious that their comments will be used and possibly scrutinized elsewhere.[9] The research I have undertaken would not necessarily be seen as a formal "virtual ethnography," as I mainly engaged in "covert observation" to find comments[10] and did not fully submerge myself in these online environments. Even this carries some ethical burdens, particularly regarding how researchers sift through such vast amounts of information to then use in academic works, usually with the aim of supporting their own arguments.[11] Before I delineate my findings and their implications, it is useful to outline what some key terms mean and discuss other academic works that have focused on Tarantino's women who kill.

Terms and Academic Discourse

Terms

I have three terms in particular I think are worth pragmatically delineating, instead of taking it for granted that they are clearly defined and ubiquitous.

The first is "feminism." I use feminism here as shorthand for Western feminism. Feminism is, without recounting its entire history, an ideology that advocates women's rights, equality of the sexes as well as dismantling and removing patriarchy from society. My second term of reference is one that branches from but ultimately counters a feminist ideology: "postfeminism." Postfeminism has been a term and a "cultural sensibility" since the 1990s;[12] it "broadly encompasses a set of assumptions, widely disseminated within popular media forms, having to do with the 'pastness' of feminism, whether that supposed pastness is merely noted, mourned or celebrated."[13] Moreover, a postfeminist ideology or view is often more evident through narrative and representation in contemporary Western cinema and television than it is through spoken discourse. In other words, people do not say, "I am a postfeminist," like they would say, "I am a feminist." This is also where the divide between academia and general audience reception lies, with feminism being predominant in the humanities and in nonacademic works and discourses, whereas postfeminism is typically a media-specific term that relates to how women have been represented in mainstream visual culture. The tension between feminism and postfeminism (or between feminist and postfeminist representations) is evident in both *Kill Bill* and *Death Proof*, which will be discussed as follows.

My final term of reference that needs defining is "empowering." Describing a representation as "powerful" is different from describing it as empowering. If a representation of a woman who kills is seen as powerful, then this typically connotes that she is a physically and mentally "strong" individual who holds power in some way.[14] A powerful representation of a woman who kills could also relate to the affect she has on the spectator—a fictional, strong woman may be powerful because she moves audiences to tears, joy, excitement, anger, and so on. An "empowering" representation also closely relates to affect, but differs from the affect a "powerful" representation may have. An empowering representation can be seen as more active or even extreme. If an image is empowering, then it means it either literally or even metaphorically *gives* power to the subjects, moving them in a way that makes them feel stronger and more confident, particularly in controlling their lives and claiming their rights. The following films are often included in lists such as "20 Female Empowerment Movies You Need to Watch Right Now" or "33 Feminist Films Every Girl Should See In Her Lifetime": *All About Eve* (Joseph L. Mankiewicz, 1950), *Coffy* (Jack Hill, 1973), *Nikita* (Luc Besson, 1990), *Thelma and Louise* (Ridley Scott, 1991), *A League of Their Own* (Penny Marshall, 1992), *Erin Brockovich* (Steven Soderbergh, 2000), *Kill Bill, Death Proof*, and *Mad Max: Fury Road* (George Miller, 2015).[15] Such films have an affective quality that empowers women to be "stronger," more confident, more socially mobile, to be inspired, and so on.[16] However, there are, of course, other more negative ramifications of calling certain films "empowering." For instance, who do certain films empower? Is this ability to be empowered, dominated, or influenced by intersections such as race, class, sexuality, and ethnicity? These are not questions that are necessarily answered within this chapter but are still important to consider when discussing *how* films empower spectators and *who* they actually empower.

When researching for this chapter, I did spend some time focusing on posts that explicitly or implicitly discussed the powerful or empowering elements of both *Kill Bill* and *Death Proof*, and I focused more specifically on those that thought the films were "empowering," as this relates closer to my object of study.

Academic Discourse

Kill Bill and *Death Proof* explore and celebrate their violent heroines and their often redemptive actions. In true Tarantino-esque style, both are decidedly postmodern films that employ spectacular violence, bodies, and set pieces to showcase the women who kill. Both films are often discussed in relation to feminism and postfeminism, and while Tarantino seems to try and celebrate the violent heroine in *Kill Bill* and *Death Proof*, his heroines have divided critics and scholars. Lisa Coulthard notes that, on *Kill Bill*'s release, for example, "media, critical, and audience responses to [the film] consistently refer to its excess, attacking or celebrating the film's extreme and arguably gratuitous use of blood and gore; its stylistic referentiality; its lack of character depth, emotion, or psychology; and its use of female figures (and young female figures in particular) as both agents and victims of violence," with The Bride's (Uma Thurman) exceptional redemption only being aimed at re-establishing a family unit.[17] Other feminist critics have also criticized Tarantino's version of violent femininity. Lisa Purse states that *Kill Bill* "present[s] us with a protagonist who seems readily to correspond to the sexualized object/active subject dualism of the action heroine,"[18] with Emma Wood adding that *Death Proof*'s representation of women is "bullshit" and that these types of films are "still predicated on the eroticization of killing."[19] Tarantino's entire filmography, ranging from *Reservoir Dogs* (1992) to *The Hateful Eight* (2015), also presents violence and gore in a hyperbolic and spectacular manner, with blood spraying from victims' wounds, splattering the environment around them. The spectacular violence inflicted by The Bride in *Kill Bill* (which is in itself an homage to Japanese samurai films), for instance, was both shocking and unfamiliar to some Western spectators on release, and this was made even more surprising as a (vengeful) female was inflicting the pain.[20]

A. O. Scott's initial review of *Kill Bill* in *The New York Times* is emblematic of this kind of shocked or disgusted reaction that some spectators felt; he writes that Tarantino's violence is "fundamentally cartoonish," but he also sometimes "crosses the line" with sequences that are "jolting and sickening."[21] Nonetheless, these images of aggressive and violent women, also prevalent in *Death Proof*, challenge gender stereotypes, while at the same time, nearly all of these heroines (in both Tarantino's films and others) are "depicted as young and unmarried,"[22] as well as being "predominately white, heterosexual, sexualized, affluent, normatively feminine." This is particularly the case in *Kill Bill*.[23]

The Bride, alongside Zoe (Zoe Bell), Kim (Tracie Thomas), Abernathy (Rosario Dawson) in *Death Proof*, likewise fit the "action babe" brand of heroism, as they are, arguably, both normatively attractive *and* powerful. Marc O'Day writes that in "action babe" films, "the emphasis is on beautiful feminine bodies combined with masculine strength," and the term itself is "intended to capture the yoking together of the 'soft' and 'hard' elements which comprise this fantasy figure."[24] In short, the "action babe" is a heroine who has a combination of "masculine" and "feminine" traits; these women usually have curvy, slim, or beautiful bodies, which are then united with the (stereotypical) strength or integrity seen in male heroes. However, this representation of heroism also comes with a plethora of issues, particularly in relation to the "male gaze" and eroticization of the (female) body, and this is where feminist and postfeminist critiques of the films clash. As Jeremi Szaniawski states, "Tarantino's filmography boasts female characters who can be related to a postfeminist ethos [. . .] [t]hey are attractive, trendy and young";[25] however, scenes such as Butterfly's (Vanessa Ferlito) lap dance in *Death Proof* visually undermine (even if just for that scene) the powerfulness of the characters through an eroticization of the body, because the whole point is that the female characters of the first half of the movie consciously subject themselves to the male gaze.[26] These characters are arguably "undermined" in other ways as well; most of the heroines' violent actions are spurred on by revenge and vengeance (which is in itself a long tradition in American and East Asian cinema, particularly in the rape-revenge subgenre), and as stated before, The Bride's redemptive actions are all, as some scholars argue, inspired by rebuilding a (nuclear) family unit rather than pure or even unmotivated revenge.

Jennifer McClearen's "Unbelievable Bodies" is one of the only studies that focuses primarily on action heroism and audience reception. McClearen used a qualitative method and interviewed "11 young women who enjoy watching action heroine films to understand how they make sense of feminine representations of physicality and power."[27] Her study focused more particularly on women who actively enjoy "watching action heroine films," as opposed to fan communities or participatory cultures.[28] Through the interviews that were conducted, McClearen concludes that the female viewers of action heroine films tended to find the women's bodies and their actions "physically unbelievable," but ultimately the "unbelievable" elements act as visual metaphors for women's success in modern (Western) society. McClearen states: "I argue that participants in this study undertake a complex negotiation of action heroine texts and draw from ambivalent post-feminist notions about limits and possibilities for women in society."[29] The women in the study never consciously knew that their comments were relating to postfeminist notions, but, as McClearen notes, "such displacement of assumed female strength from the body to the mind illustrates the post-feminist trend of celebrating women's intellectual opportunities while disciplining feminine bodies."[30] In many ways, my study complements but also extends McClearen's journal article, as it approaches the subject of audiences and action heroism with internet research as opposed to qualitative interviews, and with less of a sole focus on female spectators, providing a broader overview of what spectators think of Tarantino's women who kill. However, McClearen's argument that spectators read action heroines through a postfeminist lens is both challenged and reinforced through my findings.

It is clear from my delineation of academic discourses surrounding these killer women that they are a site of what I call interpretative conflict—the women are simultaneously seen, by critics, scholars, and audiences, as being sexualized and objectified or powerful/empowering/strong, and this leads to the women's overall representation and impact being paradoxical. More broadly, this interpretative conflict also pertains to the division between feminism and postfeminism, as we shall see.

Findings

The findings presented in both sections are indicative examples, and I have only included comments from online users that relate to my object of study. On IMDb, for instance, there was such a rich array of reviews that sifting through information was difficult for two reasons: first, because there was simply so much to read and pick from, and secondly, not all reviews dealt with the representations of the women (this is why IMDb has been eluded from this chapter in favor of QTAC and Reddit, which had more specific discussions regarding Tarantino's women who kill). The findings are, therefore, condensed for the sake of my study and should be taken as indicative samples rather than being definitive. However, after reading so many reviews and posts, a study of this kind could be replicated, but the focus could instead center on the films' gratuitous violence, their "cartoonish" violence (especially in *Kill Bill*), their film style, as well as how strongly a sense of authorship is exuded from them.[31]

Kill Bill

To begin, I have drawn on two posts on the QTAC website and some discussions on Reddit pages/threads that primarily caught my attention when researching as the conversations almost directly fitted in with this chapter.

In the *Kill Bill* chat room on the QTAC website, a post entitled "Male Uma Thurman???"[32] led a debate on gender and how the film would have been different if it was male-led. The conversation was instigated by the user Todd MacG, who wrote: "Does anyone think that *Kill Bill* would have been better if Uma Thurman's role was done by a man?" The chat was posted in 2007 (four years after the release of Vol. 1) and was commented on by several users, which created a lively debate. One of the first responses was written by "El Ray Cannibal," who commented:

> A male in the role would have added nothing to the drama of the story. There is nothing more heart wrenching then [*sic*] a mother having her child taken away from her—[this] relates directly to the idea that *Kill Bill* is ultimately about re-establishing a mother-daughter relationship.[33]

Instantly, El Ray picks up on an issue central to feminist critiques of *Kill Bill*, some of which I have already mentioned.[34] This is reverberated in other comments as well. For example, on a Reddit page that discusses fan theories of *Kill Bill*, the user analogkid01 writes that "QT crafted a masterful film around the concept of maternal instinct . . . you could almost draw a line from *Aliens* [James Cameron, 1986] to *Kill Bill*." Whereas this connection may be seen as a reiteration of the "maternal stereotype," the maternal element can instead be a positive thing for spectators; the user "Beahabib" on QTAC adds:

> The bride was beaten down, got back up, and got even. That is why I loved it. It also tapped into the nature of a mother to love her baby, Men will never truely [*sic*] know that feeling.

"Beahabib's" comment points to an issue eluded from academic discussion. Whereas scholars such as Coulthard state that *Kill Bill* emphasizes "a nostalgia for [a] nuclear family unity,"[35] instead for spectators like El Ray and Beahabib, the fact that The Bride is a vengeful mother who wants to re-establish a family is both gratifying and a pivotal element to the narrative, which only adds to their enjoyment and appreciation of the film. Often critical discourse labels the mother-daughter relationship as a somewhat limiting element to The Bride's characterization, as it is both stereotypical and normative; however, this is not an issue for these spectators, on the contrary.

Moreover, the mother-daughter bond may act as an element of identification for many female viewers, as Beahabib suggests. While this comment promotes the idea that women can only ever "truly" love a child, it nonetheless suggests that the mother-daughter bond may be a source of identification for some spectators, rather than being an "issue." However, from a feminist perspective, the suggestion that fathers can never truly love a childlike mothers is a very essentialist view and thus not as "positive" as Beahabib perhaps seems to think. Moreover, while the supposed death of The Bride's daughter spurs on her violent vengeance (in soap opera fashion, we find out at the end of Vol. 1 that this is not true), for some spectators, this heightens The Bride's humanity. Later on in the conversation on the QTAC forum, Todd MacG rejoins and writes:

> The following titles show that she [The Bride] is a number of other roles as well: Beatrix Kiddo AKA The Bride AKA Balck [*sic*] Mamba AKA Mommy. This demonstrates that she is three dimensional and does not occupy one role.

Todd MacG recognizes that the role of "The Bride" is multifaceted: Uma Thurman in *Kill Bill* is playing a character who is not *just* a mother who aims to re-establish a family unit, but instead is also an assassin (Black Mamba), a kick-ass heroine (The Bride), and a flawed but seemingly "normal" woman (Beatrix Kiddo). This supposed three-dimensionality can arguably add an extra element of enjoyment for spectators like Todd MacG, who realizes that The Bride is not just one type of character/heroine. Danish scholar Rikke Schubart also discusses the multidimensionality of The Bride in *Super Bitches and Action Babes* (2007): "The Bride is not one archetype, but [. . .] a fusion of every one of them," which includes the figure of the "Amazon" woman, the "dominatrix," and the "mother."[36] This fusion of archetypes fits in with Tarantino's homage to previous action heroines (in Japanese samurai films, exploitation and blaxploitation movies), but also, as Schubart notes, makes The Bride an ambivalent figure, whose identity and femininity are "different from the self-absorbed sulky teen narcissism of Lara Croft and from the girlish teen narcissism of the angels [in *Charlie's Angels*]."[37] The Bride's contrast to other heroines such as Lara Croft or Charlie's Angels is once again picked up on within the QTAC discussion board. Plunderbunnie says:

> It's not about her being a women, or a sex object, she clearly isn't any more then [sic] any of the men in the story in *Kill Bill*. If she was[,] the fights with the chicks would be full of sexual sounding moans, and she wouldn't be smeared in disturbing amounts of blood (fight with Elle. Not exactly sexy stuff). She'd also be wearing sexually appealing clothing, having ridiculously pointless shots of her bod, etc.

For Plunderbunnie, the fact that The Bride's fight scenes are violent and visceral, and (arguably) "non-sexualized," furthers their enjoyment of the film and the representation of a strong heroine, who unlike Lara Croft and Charlie's Angels, is not aestheticized or fetishized since she does not wear "sexually appealing clothing" or "have ridiculously pointless shots of her bod[y]." This also pertains to the way in which a spectator like Plunderbunnie reads the fight scenes through a feminist lens, where they appreciate the representation of aggression and violence as being "non-sexualized," which, essentially, is a feminist tenet.

Furthermore, one of the most poignant and nuanced comments in the discussion on the QTAC comes from BKiddo:

> Challenging QT's representation of women is irresponsible because no matter how much he loves & respects women he'll always be representing them from a man's point of view. And that's OK because he's honest in is [sic] approach to movie making and his films are just plain fun.

BKiddo acknowledges the issues of gender within filmmaking and the more limiting aspects of the violent women, tying this to the issue of a masculinized lens/viewpoint. Nonetheless, even when we do get a comment that recognizes these issues, they are forgiven because the film is "just plain fun," and, because of this, challenging their representations would seem "irresponsible," or in other words, a waste of time.

It is apparent from the examples I have provided so far that, while some spectators tend to offer a feminist understanding of the film (for instance, the "non-sexualized" violence), most offer postfeminist readings. This is apparent in comments about it being "okay" that Tarantino will "always be representing them [the women] from a man's point of view," as well as comments about mother-daughter bonds and the Bride's potential to be beautiful and strong (see earlier comments about three-dimensionality), a duality that is often at the heart of postfeminist discourses.

Death Proof

In the *Grindhouse* chat room on QTAC, a discussion was posted in
November 2007, with the title "Feminists in Britain Attack Grindhouse and
Tarantino."[38] The user Ladysnow initiated the forum, writing: "I'm not sure
if this has already been posted but I was very discouraged by this article.
It was posted in a feminist blog called, the F-Word." Ladysnow is referring
to Emma Wood's piece on the *F-Word* website, entitled "Is Tarantino really
feminist?," posted on November 2007. In her article, Wood states that "not
quite everyone 'on planet Earth' believes that *Death Proof* empowers women,"
that the female cast "are shot in an extremely sexualized, objectifying way[s],"
and finally that "the women only get to kick ass when a sufficient number of
women have already met their gory, eroticized end [. . .] this male version
of women's empowerment is bullshit." It was interesting to find a forum that
directly responded to a feminist critique of the film, and while some users
did construct sexist or derogatory responses (toward feminists), there were
also some nuanced comments. Pete, for instance, replied: "What makes the
ending of *Death Proof* uncomfortable to men I think is the fact the women
who kill Mike are not the typical slasher film virginal types, they are sexually
active, strong archetypes." This resonates with another user's comment,
Roulette67, who says:

> I don't understand the attack on QT. I find his female characters to be
> secure in their sexuality, themselves and strong. [. . .] Being a woman, a
> strong woman who can kick ass and be sexually in control of her body
> and who she chooses to share it with is strength, power. There are no
> flaky, bimbo's [*sic*] running in heels who don't fight back, because they
> are "just women" in his movies.

What both Pete and Routlette67 pick up on here, maybe unintentionally,
is the postfeminist version of femininity and heroism that Tarantino often
represents and endorses. Their reactions recall what McClearen observed
through her interviews with women who watch action heroine films. The
ending of *Death Proof*, which sees the three heroines beat Stuntman Mike
(Kurt Russell) to death, arguably escapes phallocentric methods of killing
often present in "action babe" films. More often than not, action heroines
use guns, knives, or swords (like The Bride in *Kill Bill*) to defeat their
enemies (which are all popularly seen as phallic objects); as Jeffrey Brown
argues, "the masculinization of the character's performed gender role is most
visible through her possession of the most eminent of male icons: guns and
muscles."[39] For spectators such as Pete and Routlette67, the pure aggression

the heroines in *Death Proof* exhibit makes them strong, independent, and "sexually in control" of their bodies (Routlette67), elements that constitute a postfeminist view. On a Reddit chat, there was a similar discussion entitled "Can we talk about Quentin Tarantino's *Death Proof?*"[40] which was concerned with the heroines and their feminist status. The user monsieurxander wrote that *Death Proof* shows "the two schools of feminism" with "the girls in the second half" being "total badasses, grown up women with their own jobs, goals, and lives . . . [t]hey ditch the one example of traditional femininity. And this time, when going up against this predator, they take control of the situation and kick his ass." Other users agreed with monsieurxander and also acknowledged Tarantino's homage to 1970s exploitation; stoltesawa wrote: "not many exploitation films pass the Bechdel Test to begin with . . . I think there's more than enough social justice value [in *Death Proof*]—not to mention entertainment value and juicy aesthetic." A number of spectators, then, enjoy the coupling of a postfeminist representation of action heroism and the gendered and aesthetic homage to exploitation genres, which was arguably Tarantino's aim.

While the majority of users involved within the discussions on QTAC and Reddit reacted positively to the women in *Death Proof*, some others did not, with the split, on average, being a 75 percent positive response and a 25 percent "negative" response. The user Nonstop in the QTAC discussion wrote: "I loved *Kill Bill*, where the lead character was a women [*sic*], same with JB [*Jackie Brown*], but I really just couldn't stand the feminist ending of DP," with Pete replying: "QT ends the film with three strong, intelligent women kicking the psycho killers ass. What's the problem?" On Reddit, FearAndLoathing122 also wrote: "I feel like he [Tarantino] really, really tried to replicate his favorite films with *Death Proof* and it just came out cheesy, and not in a good way." The user wowdotcom in the QTAC forum added:

Not only am I offended by his portrayal of women though, but his portrayal of men is really disgusting too. A lot of leading men in his films aren't really what real men are like. Sure there are rapists and perverts out there and guys who practice violence out there—but where are his characters in his movies that treat women with real respect? They're mostly pigs, which I don't consider to be "real men" just as I don't consider the bimbo prostitute characters to be "real women."

For a spectator like wowdotcom, gender again appears to be a central issue in Tarantino's films, and this extends both to the representation of masculinity and femininity, men and women, protagonists and antagonists. While Tarantino attempts to offer a violent and also "positive" version of femininity, he also depicts an equally violent but dystopian form of masculinity; as wowdotcom notes: "where are his characters in his movies that treat women with real respect?" By presenting strong, active, and violent women, Tarantino, then, offers men as the opposite of these women: the men are still strong and violent but are instead evil and cruel; masculinity is often represented as hegemonic, heteronormative, gross, but ultimately destructible.

Conclusion

What wowdotcom's comment shows, along with nearly all of the comments cited in this chapter, is that gender is a key element not only within academic discussion of Tarantino's works but also for fans and audiences. I would like to conclude on three points.

First, while it may seem obvious that there are differences in opinion between academics and spectators, this division has rarely been delineated in studies of action heroism and cinema. Scholarly analysis of film or popular culture often aims to succinctly examine representations, and therefore often discovers more "negative," "regressive," or limiting elements to films, rather than just accepting or enjoying the styles, images, and narrative(s). This chapter was born out of a question, but also out of intellectual curiosity—a curiosity as to why so many feminist critiques of Tarantino's works seemed to obsess with the heroines' limiting elements, but not their relationship with audiences. The findings delineated in this chapter show that a range of spectators finds Tarantino's heroines empowering, inspiring, and enjoyable, and recognition of the limiting factors does not entirely ruin these individuals' experiences. If the users on QTAC and Reddit could be completely biased and favorable toward Tarantino, I have displayed a range of comments that demonstrates how spectators do still notice nuances and other more "negative" or regressive factors.

Secondly, the issue of gender is central to the enjoyment of these films as it is also central to criticism. The discussion boards used in this chapter demonstrate that gender, feminism, and the figure of the action heroine are a key element to the enjoyment of the films, while remaining a problematic feature. Here, then, we can see a direct correlation between academia and the reception of *Kill Bill* and *Death Proof*. However, while a number of feminist responses to these films carve out the limiting elements to suggest the heroines are not as "progressive" as they may first appear, for spectators, this is not a resounding issue. While academics may be blinded by theoretical frameworks, it seems that spectators also notice some of the limiting discourses the films offer, but enjoy them nonetheless. This could be seen as a postfeminist way of reading and watching films, as most spectators do not feel as if the films were damaging to women; instead, they are problematic but equally fun/enjoyable/empowering.

My final conclusion is that the women in both *Kill Bill* and *Death Proof* are beyond the "sexualized/empowering" binary and are a site of interpretative conflict. Tarantino's women are not simply sexualized or empowering, objectified or inspiring—they are all of these things. While some viewers read the women through a feminist lens, more often than not they are understanding these killer women through a postfeminist lens, where limiting elements do not distract from the fact that the women can still be empowering, powerful, or inspiring. McClearen's study concludes that female spectators read the "unbelievable bodies" of contemporary action heroines as visual metaphors for economic and societal success, and that the "powerful feminine body is lost in translation" for some female spectators.[41] My study has found that, if some spectators do not necessarily read contemporary action heroines as visual metaphors for economic and societal success, they do understand the women primarily through a postfeminist lens. The representation and the reception of the killer women in *Kill Bill* and *Death Proof* are paradoxical, or in other words, they are a site of interpretative conflict, a conflict that closely relates to that between feminism and postfeminism.

Notes

1 Laura Mulvey, "Visual pleasure and narrative cinema," *Screen*, 16/3 (1975), pp. 6–18.

2 "*Kill Bill* fan theory—Beatrix doesn't actually Kill Bill," *Reddit*. Available at https://www.reddit.com/r/movies/comments/15rgga/kill_bill_fan_the ory_beatrix_doesnt_actually_kill/ (accessed April–June 2017); "Male Thurman???" *QTAC*. Available at http://forum.tarantino.info/viewtopic.ph p?f=4&t=7966&hilit=GENDER&sid=6cb8291a679bd911023bc903c0f272 58 (accessed between April and June 2017); "Can we talk about Quentin Tarantino's *Death Proof?" QTAC*. Available at https://www.reddit.com/r/ TrueFilm/comments/24u5g0/can_we_talk_about_quentin_tarantinos_dea th_proof/ (accessed April–June 2017).

3 With the exception being Jennifer McClearen, "Unbelievable bodies: Audience readings of action heroines as a post-feminist visual metaphor," *Continuum: Journal of Media & Cultural Studies*, 29/6 (2015), pp. 833–46.

4 Reddit is a free and popular social media website that allows people to share GIFs, photos, theories, and ideas, and others can comment on them, creating dynamic discussions and debates.

5 David Bell, *An Introduction to Cybercultures* (London: Routledge, 2001), p. 195.

6   Catherine Driscoll and Melissa Gregg, "My profile: The ethics of virtual
    ethnography," *Emotion, Space and Society*, 3/1 (2010), p. 13.
7   Christine Hine, *Virtual Ethnography* (London: Sage, 2000).
8   Emma Hutchinson, "Researching forums in online ethnography: Practice
    and ethics," in Martin Hand and Sam Hillyard (eds.), *Big Data? Qualitative
    Approaches to Digital Research Studies in Qualitative Methodology* (Bingley:
    Emerald Publishing, 2014), p. 92.
9   While not all researchers do so, I did contact the website facilitators of
    QTAC and they agreed to let me use comments and posts for this chapter;
    however, individuals who posted specific threads or comments were not
    contacted.
10 This is as opposed to "lurking," which as a term carries more negative
    connotations.
11 To try and remedy this issue, I only focused on posts or reviews that
    thoroughly discussed, for example, gender and/or feminism and/or
    the representation of the violent heroines as sexualized *or* powerful/
    empowering. This narrowed down my focus and allowed me to only read
    the most relevant pieces that align with my research.
12 Joel Gwynne and Nadine Muller, "Introduction: Postfeminism and
    contemporary Hollywood cinema," in J. Gwynne and N. Muller (eds.),
    Postfeminism and Contemporary Hollywood Cinema (Houndmills
    Basingstoke: Palgrave Macmillan, 2013), p. 2.
13 Yvonne Tasker and Diane Negra (eds.), *Interrogating Postfeminism: Gender and
    the Politics of Popular Culture* (Durham: Duke University Press, 2007), p. 1.
14 This can extend to women holding economic, social, or cultural power, as
    well as physical and mental strength.
15 If you look closer, all of these films, alongside *Kill Bill* and *Death Proof*, are
    predominately directed by (straight) men, which is another, entire debate,
    but is problematic when you consider who is constructing representations
    of "strong" and "empowering" women.
16 See Ellie Bate, "33 feminist films every girl should see in her lifetime," July
    8, 2016. Available at https://www.buzzfeed.com/eleanorbate/grrrrrrrrl-p
    ower?utm_term=.ykg4PRQNa#.edq95MGJZ, and Odyssey Online's "20
    female empowerment movies you need to watch right now." Available at
    https://www.theodysseyonline.com/20-films-to-watch-if-you-need-dose-of
    -girl-power.
17 Lisa Coulthard, "Killing Bill," in Y. Tasker and D. Negra (eds.), *Interrogating
    Postfeminism: Gender and the Politics of Popular Culture* (Durham: Duke
    University Press, 2007) pp. 153–72.
18 Lisa Purse, *Contemporary Action Cinema* (Edinburgh: Edinburgh University
    Press, 2011), p. 85.
19 Emma Wood, "Is Tarantino really feminist?" *The F Word*, 2007. Available at
    https://www.thefword.org.uk/2007/11/is_tarantino_re_1/ (accessed January
    15, 2018).

20 I say "some Western spectators" as the vengeful female is a prominent figure in East Asian cinema and was especially prominent by the time *Kill Bill* was released.

21 A. O. Scott, "Film review: Blood bath & beyond," *The New York Times*, 2003. Available at http://www.nytimes.com/movie/review?res=9804e6d7163ff93 3a25753c1a9659c8b63 (accessed June 5, 2017).

22 Katy Gilpatric, "Violent female action characters in contemporary American cinema," *Sex Roles*, 62/1 (2010), pp. 734–46.

23 Purse, *Contemporary Action Cinema*, p. 85.

24 Marc O'Day, "Gender, spectacle and action babe cinema," in Yvonne Tasker (ed.), *Action and Adventure Cinema* (London: Routledge, 2004), pp. 203–5.

25 Jeremi Szaniawski, "Laisse tomber les filles: (Post)Feminism in Quentin Tarantino's *Death Proof*," in Marcelline Block (ed.), *Situating the Feminist Gaze and Spectatorship in Postwar Cinema* (Newcastle Upon Tyne: Cambridge Scholars, 2008), pp. 169–85.

26 David Roche, *Quentin Tarantino: Poetics and Politics of Cinematic Metafiction* (Jackson: University Press of Mississippi, 2018), pp. 90–91.

27 McClearen, "Unbelievable bodies," p. 833.

28 Ibid.

29 Ibid., p. 834.

30 Ibid.

31 Nearly all reviews on IMDb discussed, if only briefly, the presence of Tarantino in both films and whether his stylistic intentions (homage, parody, pastiche) paid off or failed.

32 "Male Thurman???" *QTAC*. Available at http://forum.tarantino.info/viewtop ic.php?f=4&t=7966&hilit=GENDER&sid=6cb8291a679bd911023bc903c 0f27258 (accessed between April and June 2017).

33 It is as if "El Ray Cannibal" took the words straight out of Coulthard's mouth (or book)!

34 Purse, *Contemporary Action Cinema* for instance.

35 Coulthard, "Killing Bill," p. 169.

36 Rikke Schubart, *Super Bitches and Action Babes: The Female Hero in Cinema, 1970–2006* (London: McFarland, 2007), pp. 307–11.

37 Ibid., p. 307.

38 "Feminists in Britain Attack *Grindhouse* & Tarantino," *QTAC*. Available at http://forum.tarantino.info/viewtopic.php?f=79&t=8717&hilit=Objectific ation (accessed between April and June 2017).

39 Jeffrey Brown, *Dangerous Curves: Action Heroines, Gender, Fetishism, and Popular Culture* (Jackson: University Press of Mississippi, 2011), p. 30.

40 "Can we talk about Quentin Tarantino's *Death Proof*?" *QTAC*. Available at https://www.reddit.com/r/TrueFilm/comments/24u5g0/can_we_talk_abo ut_quentin_tarantinos_death_proof/ (accessed April–June 2017)

41 McClearen, "Unbelievable bodies," p. 843.

Filmography

Death Proof, directed and written by Quentin Tarantino, produced by
Quentin Tarantino, Robert Rodriguez, Elizabeth Avellan, Erica Steinberg,
performances by Kurt Russell, Rosario Dawson, Vanessa Ferlito, Jordan
Ladd, Rose McGowan, Sydney Poitier, Tracie Thoms, Mary Elizabeth
Winstead, Zoe Bell, cinematography by Quentin Tarantino, edited by Sally
Menke, Troublemaker Studios, 2007.

Kill Bill, written and directed by Quentin Tarantino, produced by Lawrence
Bender, performances by Uma Thurman, Lucy Liu, Vivica A. Fox, Michael
Madsen, Daryl Hannah, David Carradine, Sonny Chiba, Julie Dreyfus,
Chiaki Kuriyama, Gordon Liu, Michael Parks, music by The RZA, Robert
Rodriguez, cinematography by Robert Richardson, A Band Apart, edited by
Sally Menke, 2003.

10

Licensed to Kill?

Arming and Disarming Female Killers in Action Film and Parody in *Mad Max: Fury Road* (George Miller, 2015) and *Spy* (Paul Feig, 2015)

Elizabeth Mullen

Traditionally, female killers on screen fall into several distinct types: the *femme fatale*, the hot girl with a gun, the revenge killer, or the monster.[1] As Monica Michlin argues, such portrayals often tend to support eroticized patriarchal fantasies of female "deadliness."[2] Neither film to be discussed here fits into any of those categories: both main characters, Furiosa in *Mad Max: Fury Road* and Susan Cooper in *Spy*, represent a different kind of killer, one motivated not solely by psychological trauma or a desire for revenge but by missions centered on preserving life and reclaiming agency.

Much of *Fury Road*'s critical acclaim involved the portrayal of Imperator Furiosa, the dystopian dictator Immortan Joe's female lieutenant, who betrays him by commandeering a War Rig and freeing his Wives, women forced into sexual slavery and kept as breeding stock. With her shaved head, mechanical arm, and military-style clothing, Furiosa defies the sexualizing gaze, while at the same time avoiding the fetishized, stereotypically masculine "butch" portrayal of the action heroine. As Scott and Dargis have pointed out,[3] she is an intelligent, resourceful killer who uses the elements at her disposal (leaning on Mad Max's shoulder to steady her shot; launching, then releasing her own prosthetic arm to rip off Immortan Joe's face) to ensure the success of her mission.

Spy's Susan Cooper is also a trained killer. A CIA operative whose deadly fighting skills are put to use when she is assigned on a mission to recover a nuclear bomb from enemy hands, Cooper is a spy, not a hired assassin— yet the bodies keep piling up as she (mostly) deliberately wipes out enemy forces to defend herself and protect her team. Like Furiosa, Cooper adapts to her environment and uses her head as well as her training to eliminate the enemy.

While both films merit detailed analysis of their respective politics of gender representation, this chapter focuses primarily on each film's critical reception along gender lines. An examination of online and mainstream criticism reveals relatively little tension between feminist and postfeminist interpretations of both films. However, distinct differences in the ways men's rights groups reacted to each film seem to reflect current gendered attitudes toward female killers.

The postapocalyptic action extravaganza *Mad Max: Fury Road* was made by acclaimed Australian filmmaker George Miller, director of all three earlier *Mad Max* films starring Mel Gibson (*Mad Max*, 1979; *Mad Max 2*, 1981; *Mad Max: Beyond Thunderdome*, 1985). Featuring well-known British actor Tom Hardy and South African megastar Charlize Theron, *Fury Road* was produced for a budget of $150 million and netted more than double that worldwide, grossing nearly $400 million in the three months following its May 15, 2015 release. The film received ten Oscar nominations including Best Picture and Best Director, and it won six; it is worth noting that *Fury Road* was the first film of the *Mad Max* franchise to be nominated for an Academy award.[4]

Released just two weeks later, on June 5, 2015, *Spy* achieved somewhat similar success within the comedy genre. Written and directed by the American filmmaker Paul Feig, known for comedies such as *Bridesmaids* (2011) and *The Heat* (2013) and for the cult series *Freaks & Geeks* (NBC, 1999–2000), *Spy* is a parody of action spy thrillers like the James Bond and Jason Bourne franchises. Featuring comedy stars Melissa McCarthy, Miranda Hart, and Rose Byrne, as well as a number of famous action and drama stars (Allison Janney, Jude Law, and Jason Statham, among others), *Spy* was made for a budget of $65 million; by November 2015, it had grossed nearly $236 million worldwide. The film also met with critical acclaim in the comedy world and was nominated for several awards, including two Golden Globe awards.[5]

In short, within the same time frame and in widely different genres, we can observe two box office and critical successes that both feature strong female protagonists and story lines. Given these factors, it is all the more surprising to note that while women reacted positively overall to both films, male audience reception could not have been more different: Theron's portrayal of Furiosa sparked eruptions of betrayed shock and outrage among certain male viewers, while McCarthy's parody provoked barely a blip on those same viewers' radar. A close examination of the timing and scope of these reactions before and during the each film's release will shed light on twenty-first-century gender dynamics.

Mainstream and Feminist Reception
of *Mad Max: Fury Road*

Reviews of *Mad Max: Fury Road* in the mainstream media were overwhelmingly positive (a 97 percent Fresh rating on *Rotten Tomatoes*, full marks from *The Los Angeles Times*, *The New York Times*, and *Rolling Stone*).[6] Feminist media outlets responded favorably to the film, citing the development of strong female characters, the nonsexual partnership between Mad Max and Furiosa, and more generally, the undercutting of patriarchal norms. While there was some criticism of the film's predominantly white cast (Furiosa, the Many Mothers, and all but one of the Wives are white) and its mixed messages about disability (the positive portrayal of Furiosa's lack of an arm is undermined by that of Immortan Joe's band of deformed grotesques), many applauded Miller's decision to consult extensively with *Vagina Monologues* author Eve Ensler on sex trafficking and violence against women to inform the development of female characters, particularly the Wives.[7] On the since-defunct feminist blog *Gender Focus*, Jessica Crichter acknowledges the role misogynist backlash played in increasing female viewership of the film before pointing out the contemporary relevance of the film's basic feminist message:

> Furiosa is not just a "strong female character" (a weak phrase I personally detest and wish we could officially retire because it's usually code for a "fighting fuck-toy" or used to excuse the fact that there is only one woman in a film opposite dozens of men). Furiosa rescues women from slavery, and their final act of defiance to their captor is to scrawl messages on the walls of their cell, most notably: "We are not things." I'll admit I got chills.

> Yes! Women are not things! It's true! I was so thrilled to see this as the driving force behind an action film. But "women = things" is not just the stuff of fantasy, believed only by comically evil people. We're treated like things all the time. Our images are hacked apart in the media or in advertisements that we're forced to look at every day. Our politicians compare us to animals and try to take away our reproductive rights. We're beaten and sexually assaulted at appalling rates across the world. This film had a lot of feminist themes, and the parts of it that I enjoyed, I enjoyed for feminist reasons.[8]

Crichter lauds the representation of women's rejection of commodification in a postapocalyptic world precisely because in 2015, women were still being commodified in violent ways. Other feminist media outlets framed the film's feminist message in less direct ways. On the website *Bustle*, Anna Klassen praises Miller's representation of the women in *Fury Road* working together and expressing agency without (for the most part) catering to the male gaze or established norms:

> When the ultimate battle between good vs. evil, Joe vs. the girls plus Max, plays out, it's the women—old, young, inexperienced, strong—who risk their lives for their fellow woman. They are capable and angry, weathered and weak, but entirely real. They aren't carved out of the same material that formed Lara Croft or her unnaturally sexy and tough counterparts. Yes, the wives appear in barely-there getups, but only because Joe adorned them with his male gaze. There are no push-up bras or lipgloss for women in the desert landscape.[9]

Like Klassen, Sasha James of *The Mary Sue* applauds Miller's film for its innovative approach to female characters in the action genre, particularly its refusal to portray strong women as exceptional or anomalous:

> But what's interesting about *Fury Road* is that its feminism isn't pulling focus. It's not saying, "Hey! Look at this Strong Female Character!" The film's feminism is a utilitarian result of the plot's mechanics [. . .] *Fury Road* is a feminist film *because it's not* outright "feminist propaganda." It uses gender and sex in a utilitarian, matter-of-fact manner, allowing its females to use their womanhood as a weapon against its universe's established norms, but neither heroizing or demonizing that action. *Fury Road* radically allows its female characters to enact as much agency as its men. They are allowed to survive by whatever means are available to them.
>
> *Fury Road* isn't trying to say that Furiosa is better than Max or that female-led action films are the new status quo. Instead, George Miller's fourth *Mad Max* film is a gentle reminder—amongst blood-lust and post-apocalyptic madness—that men and women are equal, and that we shouldn't still have to make such a big f***ing deal about it.[10]

Klassen, James, and other feminist critics blend third-wave feminist and postfeminist discourses in their reviews of *Fury Road*, acknowledging Furiosa's power not as a singular, "badass" heroine alone against her enemies, but as an integral element of a four-part alliance with Mad Max, the Many Mothers, and the Wives. They acknowledge how the female characters of the film "use their womanhood as a weapon against its universe's established norms," noting, for instance, a scene where one of the Wives uses her pregnant belly, the literal embodiment of her former objectified status, to shield Furiosa from Immortan Joe. Significantly, while openly celebrating *Fury Road*'s feminist message, critics across the spectrum pointed to its "utilitarian, matter-of-fact" feminism and its broad target audience as part of the key to its success. Rarely have feminist and mainstream media been in such agreement about an action film.

Reactions within the extremist fringe of the "manosphere," however, were quite different. Before dissecting these reactions, a further look is required to understand the contours of those spaces where a broad spectrum of like-minded anti-feminists and men's rights activists share information and rage.

Malaise in the Manosphere

In their analysis of the manosphere—a loose network of blogs, Twitter accounts, YouTube channels, and Reddit-type message boards and forums that "rest on the ideological foundation calling for men's reclaiming of societal power to [*sic*] which they believe they have lost and are entitled to be based on their male status"[11]—Rachel M. Schmitz and Emily Kazyak outline two main rhetorical strategies with which these platforms reflect and propagate anti-feminist backlash and actively work to undermine gender equality. Among participants on Men's Rights Activist sites (or MRAs), "Cyber Lads in Search of Masculinity" seek to reassert (mostly white) straight masculine hegemony by decrying the evils of feminism, policing homosocial activity, and portraying women as sexual commodities.[12] The spontaneous, anonymous nature of the internet creates an ideal environment for virulent commentary on sites such as *Return of Kings, Alpha Game, Men Going Their Own Way*, or *Angry Harry*, allowing for the spread of misogynistic and homophobic ideas and opinions.

The rhetorical strategies of those Schmitz and Kazyak call "Virtual Victims in Search of Equality" are subtler: these groups use more neutral, inclusive language than do their Cyber Lad counterparts and focus on perceived injustices linked to "unrealistic societal stereotypes" in issues like (heterosexual) dating, men's health, fathers' rights in child custody cases, and undocumented violence against men. Schmitz and Kazyak point out, however, that by assertions such as anti-male bias in alleged "false" rape accusations and in the prosecution of men who don't pay child support, "this cherry-picking of evidence used to support these groups' claims of men's victimization serves to legitimate their viewpoint and provide indirect support for hegemonic masculinity by reinforcing their sense of social entitlement."[13]

While both groups employ strategies designed to affirm straight white masculine hegemony, neither group perceives itself to be particularly empowered: quite the contrary. As Faludi, Kimmel, and Bird have noted, the discourse of many straight white men is marked by feelings of *failure* to meet hegemonic standards and by a sense that the world no longer conforms to these hegemonic codes.[14] It is in this context that blog posts like "A Beginner's Guide to the Pussification of American Men," "The Trojan Horses of Feminism," "The Good Men Project Wants Men to be Blubbering Manginas or Outright Homosexuals," or even more disturbingly, "How to Beat Your Girlfriend or Wife and Get Away With It"[15] reveal the intensity of this phenomenon. In an atmosphere so rife with misogyny and masculine malaise, it is not surprising that *Mad Max: Fury Road* provoked such outrage within the MRA universe.

Furious about Furiosa

Interestingly, the first strains of anti-feminist internet backlash against Miller's *Mad Max: Fury Road* appeared before the film was actually released in theaters. For example, four days before the film's opening, *Return of Kings* blogger Aaron Clarey published a now-infamous diatribe entitled "Why You Should Not Go See 'Mad Max: Feminist Road'":

> If you were like me, the explosions, fire tornadoes, even the symphonic score surrounding "Fury Road's" first trailer made your attendance a foregone conclusion. It looked like a straight-up guy flick. No fucking around. [. . .]
>   But then my spidey senses started noticing a couple things.
>   Charlize Theron kept showing up a lot in the trailers, while Tom Hardy (Mad Max) seemed to have cameo appearances. Charlize Theron sure talked a lot during the trailers, while I don't think I've heard one line from Tom Hardy. And finally, Charlize Theron's character barked orders to Mad Max.
>   Nobody barks orders to Mad Max.
>   [. . .] The real issue is not whether feminism has infiltrated and co-opted Hollywood, ruining nearly every potentially good action flick with a forced female character or an unnecessary romance sub-plot to eek [*sic*] out that extra 3 million in female attendees.
>   It has.
>   And the real issue is not whether Hollywood has the audacity to remove the name sake [*sic*] of a movie franchise called *MAD FREAKING*

MAX, and replace it with an impossible female character in an effort to kowtow to feminism.

It has.

It's whether men in America and around the world are going to be duped by explosions, fire tornadoes, and desert raiders into seeing what is guaranteed to be nothing more than feminist propaganda, while at the same time being insulted AND tricked into viewing a piece of American culture ruined and rewritten right in front of their very eyes.

The truth is I'm angry about the extents [*sic*] Hollywood and the director of Fury Road went to trick me and other men into seeing this movie. Everything VISUALLY looks amazing. It looks like that action guy flick we've desperately been waiting for where it is one man with principles, standing against many with none.

But let us be clear. This is the vehicle by which they are guaranteed to force a lecture on feminism down your throat. This is the Trojan Horse feminists and Hollywood leftists will use to (vainly) insist on the trope women are equal to men in all things, including physique, strength, and logic. And this is the subterfuge they will use to blur the lines between masculinity and femininity, further ruining women for men, and men for women.[16]

According to this and other MRA posts,[17] *Fury Road* betrays hegemonic masculinity on multiple levels by reversing the "natural" order: insertion of an "impossible" (read: physically strong) female character, an "unnecessary romance subplot" (which is, in the movie, absent between Mad Max and Furiosa and only briefly hinted at between two minor characters), and sneaky use of car chases and explosions to lure otherwise manly men into swallowing feminist propaganda. Clarey's message on behalf of the extremist masculinist fringe is clear: by her very filmic existence, Furiosa—a female killer—is killing more than an iconic symbol of patriarchy; she is subjugating the all-American (straight male) viewer and destroying American culture— quite a feat for a South African star in an Australian film.

Clarey expresses, here, what De Coning identifies as evidence of the ongoing crisis of American masculinity and of fissuring hegemonic norms.[18] The language used is one of panic and dismay bordering on the grotesque: a world the author thought he knew and understood (the world of straight white male privilege) has become something else, something other; codes he thought were implicit reveal themselves to be unstable and untrustworthy.[19] On a more physical note, Clarey and his followers use the language of physical vulnerability to voice an intense fear of penetration: Hollywood has been "infiltrated" by feminists who lure men into a sense of cinematic complacency through manly tropes before ramming feminism "down [their] throat[s]."

As evidenced in this excerpt, the subtext of MRA outrage is fear, shame, and humiliation rooted in a deep sense of entitlement. In his book *Angry White Men: American Masculinity at the End of an Era*, feminist sociologist Michael Kimmel points out the link between what he calls "aggrieved entitlement" and masculine vulnerability in his discussion of physical violence inflicted on women:

> Masculinity is about impermeability, independence. [...] But the defense against vulnerability and exposure [...] seems to be activated only when something else breaks down. If masculinity is based on impermeable defenses and the feeling of being in control, then violence may be restorative, returning the situation to the moment before that sense of vulnerability and dependency was felt and one's sense of masculinity was so compromised.
>
> But still, one needs an additional ingredient: the feeling of right, or entitlement. One must feel entitled to use violence as a means of restoring what was experienced as threatened, that part of the self that is suddenly made vulnerable. If you don't feel entitled to use violence, then all the vulnerability in the world won't lead you to hit somebody.[20]

The same arguments apply to violent language within the manosphere. Ultimately, MRA extremists see *Mad Max: Fury Road* as a threat to "their" filmic universe, and this combination of vulnerability and "aggrieved entitlement" sparked a backlash so severe a number of mainstream media outlets[21] reported on extremist manosphere reactions. In the wake of this backlash, though not necessarily because of it, trending topics like "Masculinity is So Fragile" on Tumblr and #MasculinitySoFragile on Twitter began calling out examples of toxic masculinity across the media spectrum, triggering, in certain cases, another wave of violent backlash.[22]

Disarming Feminism in *Spy*

Surprisingly, spectators of all genders reacted differently to a trained female killer in a James Bond–like universe. At first glance, Paul Feig's Bourne/Bond parody seems like perfect fodder for anti-feminist backlash: it features a strong female cast in key roles (the titular spy, her boss, the villain, and the sidekick); it specifically mocks stereotypical masculine tropes—Jason Statham, as rogue

CIA agent Rick Ford, gleefully parodies his own *Transporter* (2002–08) and *Fast and the Furious 6* (2013) and *7* (2015) personae; and there is no romantic (read: heteronormative) happy ending at the end of the film. In addition, much of the film's humor stems from the multiple ways in which everyone involved— from her female superior and male coworkers at the CIA to her villainous adversaries—repeatedly underestimates and misrepresents CIA agent Susan Cooper. This underplaying includes Cooper's CIA-issued spy paraphernalia, from her secret identities (a series of pathetic cat ladies) to her spy gadgets disguised as embarrassing hygiene products; even her ultra-sophisticated laser watch has a picture of Bette Midler and Barbara Hershey from *Beaches* (Gary Marshall, 1988) on it. Finally, Cooper's character does not fully correspond to the parodic fish-out-of-water trope found in films like *Austin Powers* (1997–2002), *The Pink Panther* (1963–2006), or *The Naked Gun* (1988–94); whereas in those films an inept main character somehow manages to succeed, in *Spy* we find a trained killer using her skills to defeat the forces of evil and save the day, much to the (unjustified) astonishment of nearly everyone involved.

Though there was nothing like the social media storm that surrounded *Fury Road*, mainstream and feminist media outlets covered *Spy's* release extensively and lauded the film's entertaining-yet-feminist approach, commenting at length on the solidarity among female characters and the film's refusal to give in to fat shaming for laughs at the expense of actress Melissa McCarthy. Stassa Edwards of the feminist blog *Jezebel* gleefully praises *Spy's* crushing box-office defeat of the bro-comedy *Entourage* (Doug Ellin, 2015),[23] while *Bitch Flicks* writer Ren Jender applauds the way the film sidesteps common satirical sendups of those outside the norm to take on genre stereotypes instead:

> In a world where "satire" is used as a descriptor for works like *Entourage*, the word might not have much meaning, but *Spy*, in the tradition of the best satire, makes fun of conventions we might not have realized we were sick of—like the cat-lady typecasting. Also, while male action heroes like 007 and Jason Bourne never make a wrong move, no matter how extreme the situations they find themselves in and shoot and kill others with all the sensitivity of a giant swatting at flies, two of the women in *Spy* who kill react more like the rest of us might: neither plays it cool.
>
> I kept on waiting for the film to go wrong, for someone to humiliate Susan for her size, which miraculously never happens.[24]

Jender's reading of the film nonetheless points out some of its feminist and postfeminist contradictions; she comments, for example, on a scene where, shedding her cat-lady disguise, Susan embarks on a spending spree and is rewarded for her glamorous new look by catcalls from a previously indifferent group of Italian men. *Nerdy Feminist's* A. Lynn addresses this scene (as well as the continuous attentions of Cooper's handsy Italian liaison, Aldo) from a postfeminist fat person's perspective, commenting that aggressive harassment of fat women is not uncommon both in person and online; she references online comments to the effect that plus-sized women should be "grateful" for any sexual attention, whether or not it is wanted. Lynn's own reaction to such scenes in the film is mixed: "McCarthy is dealing with the overly aggressive gross harasser while she's kicking ass and taking names as an awesome fat lady. It felt simultaneously disgusting and also surprisingly on point."[25]

From a more mainstream point of view, A. O. Scott's review in *The New York Times* highlights the disarming nature of *Spy*'s feminism:

Even better [than the film's "cheeky surrealism"] is the blithe feminism that makes "Spy" feel at once revolutionary and like no big deal. It's not just that the movie aces the Bechdel test[26]. It didn't even need to study. The movie isn't uplifting; it's buoyant. While Susan at first clearly has a lot to prove—that she's a skilled professional and a ruthless adversary, everyone else's doubts to the contrary—Mr. Feig doesn't make her proving it the central arc of the narrative.[27]

Scott pinpoints the paradoxical nature of the film's feminist success: Feig puts female characters and their interactions at the core of the film while simultaneously employing a kind of cinematic sleight of hand to draw focus away from their accomplishments—"disarming" his female killer by focusing viewer attention away from her skills as a killer.

Surprisingly, across MRA websites, *Spy* caused barely a ripple. Of course, this may be in part because fewer MRA followers planned to see it. *The Guardian* puts the film's opening weekend audience at 60 percent female and 65 percent over the age of twenty-five—both out of the range of typical MRA demographics, which heavily feature straight white working- and middle-class men.[28] There was one lonely account (since deleted) called "How to Be an Alpha Male," which disparaged the film to its twelve followers, but otherwise the manosphere remained largely unperturbed by the spy parody: no outraged blog posts lamenting a feminist takeover of the parody genre; no negative reactions to a female CIA leader or to a tough-yet-feminine female villain.

While it may be tempting to attribute this clemency to a greater tolerance within the more mixed audience terrain of the comedy genre, the outpouring of misogynistic online hatred and violence for Feig's follow-up film, an all-female reboot of *Ghostbusters* (2016), would suggest the opposite: *Return of Kings* blogger J. D. Unwin's prerelease rant voiced attitudes similar to those expressed about *Fury Road*: "the feminists and their mangina accomplices in the media once again demonstrate their need to forcibly intrude upon any perceived male bastions."[29] More disturbingly, the sustained online harassment of African–American actor Leslie Jones, one of the film's stars, revealed unprecedented levels of violent and racist misogyny as a response to the gender-flipping of the original films.[30] Generic conventions aside, why, then, do reactions to *Spy* and *Fury Road* vary so widely?

Conclusion

It seems clear that audience expectations are a key factor in determining gendered reactions. Much of *Spy*'s marketing strategy centered on underscoring the laughable, "harmless" nature of its female protagonist. The trailer heavily features physical comedy showing McCarthy at a disadvantage, and posters distributed before the film's release emphasized these aspects; one showed an ample, bewigged McCarthy drenched in gold, a parodic take on the 1964 Bond classic, *Goldfinger* (Guy Hamilton), while another featured a goofy, smiling McCarthy sandwiched between Jude Law and Jason Statham in traditional "Bond" poses, underscoring her secondary status. This "disarming" approach, based on deliberately underplaying feminist narratives for marketing purposes, points to subtle tensions between feminism and postfeminism in twenty-first-century cinema. Beyond the marketing campaign, within the film, McCarthy's character's agency stems as much from her newfound freedom to dress in sexy clothes and attract the good-looking guy (though she ends up turning him down), as it does from her validation as a bona fide field agent, mirroring what Yvonne Tasker and Diane Negra refer to as "a commodified image of female agency."[31] In this sense, *Spy*'s satiric subversion of generic and gender conventions flies further under the radar than does *Fury Road*'s outspoken rejection of commodification in general and of the commodification of women in particular. And yet, as critics of both films have noted, these movies owe their success in part to a refusal to focus on a single, exceptional feminist heroine. Cooper and Furiosa represent a new kind of woman who kills: one who works as part of a team to get the job done.

Several factors combined to create the virulent anti-feminist backlash to *Mad Max: Fury Road* within the manosphere. First, by their very nature, sequels, remakes, and reboots create strong expectations in viewers and invite comparisons based on their "original" counterparts;[32] Clarey references the power of this association in gendered terms when he expresses outrage that a film franchise called "*MAD FREAKING MAX*" would draw focus away from its eponymous hero in favor of a female character. The tendency to measure follow-up films in light of their adherence to former versions can especially be seen in genres traditionally defined as focusing on male audiences: action, horror, sports drama, police procedural, war films, and so on.[33] Until recently, with many franchises, audiences could "trust" follow-up films to run true to formulas established in the originals: for example, main characters and story arcs in *Rocky* (John G. Avildsen, 1976) and in *Rambo: First Blood Part II* (George P. Cosmatos, 1985) differ little from their subsequent iterations or even represent more quintessentially reactionary versions of what Clarey refers to as "one man with principles, standing against many with none." In her analysis of gender, genre, and the action cinema, Yvonne Tasker points out that it is the representation of this principle that appeals to popular audiences:

> Increasingly the powerful white hero is a character who operates in the margins, whilst in many senses continuing to represent dominance. This is an important trait in many action pictures and is central to the pleasures of the text.[34]

When this traditional role is taken on by a character who does not "represent dominance"—a woman, for instance—audience reactions can change. Negative reactions to nonconforming films within a given genre are not limited to sequels, remakes, and reboots, however; one example of this would be the anti-feminist hysteria generated by *G.I. Jane* (Ridley Scott, 1997), a film explicitly marketed as a female empowerment film within the traditionally male genres of action and war.[35]

In gendered terms, for some, these audience expectations can be seen as a kind of hegemonic entitlement; any deviation from the formula provokes strong negative reactions triggered by what I would call "toxic nostalgia." Toxic nostalgia, as the name implies, frames audience expectations in terms of a normalizing worldview, a regressive vision of the way things "should" be: male characters embody traditional (straight white) masculine tropes, female characters fit into prescribed roles, and in the course of the narrative, to quote MRA website *Return of Kings*, "one man with principles [is] standing against many with none." Across various film genres, toxic nostalgia dictates that cowboys should be straight, Stormtroopers should be white, and Ghostbusters should be men.[36] And, needless to say, Mad Max should never, ever play second fiddle to and enter into a nonsexual alliance with a strong female character. As with toxic masculinity, toxic nostalgia relies on a sense of entitlement to fuel the violence it spreads: for the men of the manosphere,

Furiosa and her sisters are guilty of encroaching on an (imagined) past—one that clearly belonged to straight white men.

Of course, all audiences are far from single-gendered or monolithic, and the manosphere in no way represents all men; the relative lack of backlash within the "nerdosphere" at the recent naming of Jodie Whittaker as the 13th Doctor in the *Doctor Who* franchise (BBC, 1963–89, 2005–) attests to this reality.[37] Recent box office and critical successes of female-centered blockbusters like *Wonder Woman* (Patty Jenkins, 2017) and *Atomic Blonde* (David Leitch, 2017), as well as a spate of strong female-centered television series, also point to increasingly varied and accepted representations of women on film or television, with or without the disarming strategies noted in *Spy*. This increased on-screen representation of women also makes economic sense—in fact, the streaming giant Netflix now lists "Shows featuring a strong female lead" as one of its categories designed to lure viewers.

Nevertheless, gendered twenty-first-century audience reception among extreme men's rights groups seems increasingly darker and more vitriolic as online communities continue to find new and more brutal ways to spread misogyny. As Leo Braudy points out, "allowing us to know the way we see and have seen ourselves has been one of film's greatest contributions to culture."[38] In this context, the violence of MRA reactions to the questioning of straight white male hegemony in *Mad Max: Fury Road* seems all the more troubling. This chapter was first presented as a conference talk at a time when the first female president of the United States seemed a foregone conclusion. Since then, Donald Trump, former reality TV star and symbol of toxic masculinity for many, has become president, unleashing waves of pent-up toxic nostalgia within the darkest corners of the manosphere and beyond; violent demonstrations by white supremacist groups who, according to Ku Klux Klan leaders marching on Charlottesville, Virginia, were determined to "take [straight white male] America back"[39] fade into the background as the raw hatred of incel groups spawns a terrorist attack in Toronto.[40] At the same time, the rapid and dramatic changes within the media industry brought about by the rise of the #MeToo movement[41] and other similar calls against toxic masculinity seem to indicate that the manosphere is right to tremble: it turns out that "We [women] are not things" is, in fact, a terrifying idea.

Notes

1 Mary Anne Doane, *Femme Fatales: Feminism, Film Theory, Psychoanalysis* (New York: Routledge, 1991); Carol Clover, *Men, Women, and Chainsaws: Gender in the Modern Horror Film* (Princeton: Princeton University

Press, 1992); Barbara Creed, *The Monstrous-Feminine: Film, Feminism, Psychoanalysis* (London and New York: Routledge, 1993); Lynda Hart, *Fatal Women: Lesbian Sexuality and the Mark of Aggression* (London: Routledge, 1994); Jacinda Read, *The New Avengers: Feminism, Femininity and the Rape-Revenge Cycle* (Manchester: Manchester University Press, 2000).

2 Monica Michlin, "*Monster*: Ambiguous depiction of the female killer," *Cycnos*, 23/2 (2006). Available at http://revel.unice.fr/cycnos/index.html? id=721 (accessed April 4, 2017).

3 A. O. Scott and Manohla Dargis, "Heroines triumph at box office, but has anything changed in Hollywood?" *The New York Times*, July 3, 2015. Available at https://www.nytimes.com/2015/07/05/movies/heroines-triu mph-at-box-office-but-has-anything-changed-in-hollywood.html (accessed April 22, 2018).

4 *IMDb* (*The Internet Movie Database*), "Mad Max: Fury Road (2015)." Available at http://www.imdb.com/title/tt1392190/ (accessed September 9, 2016).

5 *IMDb*, "Spy (2015)." Available at http://www.imdb.com/title/tt3079380/ (accessed September 9, 2016).

6 A. O. Scott, "Review: 'Mad Max: Fury Road:' Still angry after all these years," *The New York Times*, May 14, 2015. Available at https://www.nytimes.com/ 2015/05/15/movies/review-mad-max-fury-road-still-angry-after-all-these-years.html?partner=rss&emc=rss (accessed September 9, 2016). See also Peter Travers, "Mad Max: Fury Road: Tom Hardy and Charlize Theron take on the apocalypse in this breathtaking reboot," *Rolling Stone*, May 14, 2015. Available at https://www.rollingstone.com/movies/movie-reviews/mad-max-fury-road-250978/ (accessed September 9, 2016). Finally, see Kenneth Turan, "'Mad Max' kicks a post-apocalyptic extravaganza into overdrive," *The Los Angeles Times*, May 14, 2015. Available at http://www.latimes.com/ entertainment/movies/la-et-mn-mad-max-review-20150515-column.html (accessed September 9, 2016).

7 Eliana Dockterman, "*Vagina Monologues* writer Eve Ensler: 'How *Mad Max: Fury Road* became a 'Feminist Action Film,'" *Time Magazine*, May 7, 2015. Available at http://time.com/3850323/mad-max-fury-road-eve-ensler-feminist/ (accessed September 9, 2016).

8 Jessica Critcher, "Who killed the world?—The complicated feminism of Mad Max: Fury Road," *gender-focus.com*, May 26, 2015. Available at http://www.gender-focus.com/2015/05/26/who-killed-the-world-the-complicated-feminism-of-mad-max-fury-road/ (accessed April 24, 2018)

9 Anna Klassen, "Mad Max is a feminist masterpiece, because 'Fury Road' is all about Furiosa . . . & her sidekick Max," *Bustle*, May 12, 2015. Available at https://www.bustle.com/articles/82751-mad-max-is-a-feminist-masterpiece -because-fury-road-is-all-about-furiosa-her-sidekick (accessed April 15, 2018).

10 Sasha James, "*Mad Max: Fury Road*: George Miller's feminist answer to his own franchise?" *The Mary Sue*, May 16, 2015. Available at https://www.the marysue.com/george-miller-feminist-answer-franchise/ (accessed June 15, 2017).

11 Emily Kazyak and Rachel Schmitz, "Masculinities in cyberspace: An analysis of portrayals of manhood in men's rights activist websites," *Social Sciences*, 5(2)/18 (2016). Available at http://www.mdpi.com/2076-0760/5/2/18/htm (accessed June 6, 2017).

12 Ibid., p. 6.

13 Ibid., p. 9.

14 Susan Faludi, *Stiffed: The Betrayal of the American Man* (New York: Harper Collins, 1999). See also Michael S. Kimmel, *Manhood in America: A Cultural History* (New York: Oxford University Press, 2006), and Sharon R. Bird, "Welcome to the men's club: Homosociality and the maintenance of hegemonic masculinity," *Gender & Society*, 10/2 (April 1996), pp. 120–32.

15 Kazyak and Schmitz, "Masculinities in cyberspace," pp. 14–15.

16 Aaron Clarey, "Why you should not go see 'Mad Max: Feminist Road,'" *Return of Kings*, May 11, 2015. Available at http://www.returnofkings.com/63036/why-you-should-not-go-see-mad-max-feminist-road (accessed April 4, 2016).

17 For an extensive look at antifeminist backlash within the manosphere, see Alexis De Coning, "Recouping masculinity: Men's rights activists' Responses to *Mad Max: Fury Road*," *Feminist Media Studies*, 16/1 (2016), pp. 174–76. Available at http://www.tandfonline.com/doi/abs/10.1080/14680777.201 6.1120491 (accessed May 5, 2016).

18 Ibid.

19 For more on alienation and the grotesque, see Wolfgang Kayser, *The Grotesque in Art and Literature* (New York: Indiana University Press, 1963), p. 37.

20 Michael Kimmel, *Angry White Men: American Masculinity at the End of an Era* (Philadelphia: Nation Books, 2013), p. 177.

21 See, for example, Matilda Battersby, "Mad Max: Fury Road enrages Men's Rights activists who claim they are being duped by action sequences into watching 'feminist propaganda,'" *The Independent*, May 14, 2015. Available at http://www.independent.co.uk/arts-entertainment/films/news/mad-ma x-fury-road-enrages-mens-rights-activists-who-claim-they-are-being-dup ed-by-explosions-into-10249443.html (accessed June 6, 2016), Jessica Valenti, "Sexists are scared of Mad Max because it is a call to dismantle patriarchies," *The Guardian*, May 27, 2015. Available at https://www.the guardian.com/commentisfree/2015/may/27/sexists-are-scared-of-mad-max-because-it-is-a-call-to-dismantle-patriarchies (accessed June 6, 2016), and also Cristina Maza, "'Mad Max: Fury Road': Why are anti-feminists so angry about action film?" *The Christian Science Monitor*, May 14, 2015.

Available at https://www.csmonitor.com/USA/Society/2015/0514/Mad-Max
-Fury-Road-Why-are-anti-feminists-so-angry-about-action-film (accessed
June 6, 2016).

22 The first post on masculinityissofragile.tumblr.com dates back to June 17,
2015. Anthony Williams began tweeting about #MasculinitySoFragile in
July 2015. See his article, "Why I started tweeting and helped popularize
#MasculinitySoFragile," *The Independent*, September 27, 2015. Available at
http://www.independent.co.uk/voices/why-i-started-tweeting-and-helped-
popularise-masculinitysofragile-a6669101.html (accessed July 7, 2017).

23 See Stassa Edwards, "*Spy* beats *Entourage* at box office because women don't
hate themselves," *Jezebel*, June 7, 2015. Available at https://jezebel.com/spy-
beats-entourage-at-box-office-because-women-dont-ha-1709647650?utm
_campaign=socialflow_jezebel_facebook&utm_source=jezebel_facebook
&utm_medium=socialflow (accessed July 9, 2018).

24 Ren Jender, "'Spy': Truly funny and truly feminist," *Bitch Flicks*, June 4, 2015.
Available at http://www.btchflcks.com/2015/06/spy-truly-funny-and-truly-f
eminist.html#.WudwihSFgfE (accessed June 6, 2016).

25 A. Lynn, "A few thoughts on *Spy* and being a fat lady," *Nerdy Feminist*, June
4, 2015. Available at http://www.nerdyfeminist.com/2015/06/a-few-thought
s-on-spy-and-being-fat-lady.html (accessed July 9, 2018).

26 First appearing in Alison Bechdel's 1986 comic, *Dykes To Watch Out For*
(Ann Arbor: Firebrand Books, 1986), the tests references the Bechdel–
Wallace rule for choosing a film:

  The movie has to have at least two women in it,
  who talk to each other,
  about something besides a man

  See Bechdel's blog about the comic here, http://alisonbechdel.blogspot.
  com/2005/08/rule.html (accessed August 8, 2017).

27 A. O. Scott, "In 'Spy', Melissa McCarthy is a C.I.A. Drudge who goes rogue,"
The New York Times, June 4, 2015. Available at https://www.nytimes.com/
2015/06/05/movies/review-in-spy-melissa-mccarthy-is-a-cia-drudge-
who-goes-rogue.html?mcubz=0 (accessed August 8, 2017).

28 Phil Hoad, "Women's trouble: Did *Spy* suffer in the US from femme-centric
targeting?" *The Guardian*, June 10, 2015. Available at https://www.the
guardian.com/film/2015/jun/10/global-box-office-spy-san-andreas-insidi
ous-chapter-three-entourage (accessed August 20, 2017). For more on the
demographics of the manosphere, see Michael Kimmel, *Angry White Men:
American Masculinity at the End of an Era* (Philadelphia: Nation Books,
2013), p. 17.

29 J. D. Unwin, "The new Ghostbusters movie will be ruined by the feminist
agenda," *Return of Kings*, February 19, 2015. Available at http://www.retu
rnofkings.com/56056/the-new-ghostbusters-movie-will-be-ruined-by-the-
feminist-agenda (accessed July 11, 2018).

30 See, for example, Andrew Marantz, "The shameful trolling of Leslie Jones," *The New Yorker*, August 26, 2016. Available at https://www.newyorker.com /culture/cultural-comment/the-shameful-trolling-of-leslie-jones (accessed July 11, 2018).

31 Yvonne Tasker and Diane Negra, "In focus: Postfeminism in contemporary media studies," *Cinema Journal*, 44/2 (Winter 2005), pp. 107–10 (accessed April 22, 2018).

32 See, for instance, Steffen Hantke's remarks in *American Horror Film: The Genre at the Turn of the Millennium* (Jackson: University of Mississippi Press, 2010), pp. ix–xi.

33 For a more in-depth look at how genre and gender intersect, see Christine Gledhill (ed.), *Gender Meets Genre in Postwar Cinemas* (Chicago: University of Illinois Press, 2012).

34 Yvonne Tasker, *Spectacular Bodies: Gender, Genre and the Action Cinema* (London: Routledge, 1993), p. 98.

35 See, for instance, Phyllis Schlafly, "GI Jane is a role model for evil," *Eagle Forum.org*, September 10, 1997. Available at http://eagleforum.org/col umn/1997/sept97/97-09-10.html (accessed April 30, 2018).

36 MRA websites roundly criticized homosexuality in *Brokeback Mountain* (Ang Lee, 2005), the presence of a black stormtrooper in *Star Wars: The Force Awakens* (J. J. Abrams, 2015) and the all-female cast in *Ghostbusters* (Paul Feig, 2016).

37 Note, for instance, Anna Menta, "The 15 best tweet reactions to 'Doctor Who' casting a woman doctor," *Elite Daily*, July 17, 2017. Available at http://elitedaily.com/entertainment/best-tweet-reactions-doctor-who-wo man/2019179/ (accessed August 8, 2017).

38 Leo Braudy, *The World in a Frame: What We See in Films* (Garden City: Anchor Press, 1976).

39 Joe Heim, Ellie Silverman, T. Rees Shapiro, and Emma Brown, "Chaos in Virginia as white supremacist rally takes deadly turn," *The Toronto Star*, August 12, 2017. Available at https://www.thestar.com/news/world/2017/ 08/12/white-supremacists-clash-with-protesters-in-virginia-college-town. html (accessed August 25, 2017).

40 For more about the incel (involuntarily celibate) movement and the links between its philosophy of toxic entitlement and the April 23 terrorist attack in Toronto, see Zoe Williams, "'Raw Hatred': Why the 'incel' movement targets and terrorises women," *The Guardian*, April 25, 2018. Available at https://www.theguardian.com/world/2018/apr/25/raw-hatred-why-ince l-movement-targets-terrorises-women (accessed April 30, 2018).

41 For a general idea of the origins of the #MeToo movement, see *Time* magazine's double issue, "Person of the year: The silence breakers: The voices that launched a movement," *Time*, December 18, 2017. Available at http://time.com/time-person-of-the-year-2017-silence-breakers/ (accessed July 13, 2018).

Filmography

Mad Max: Fury Road, directed by George Miller, written by George Miller, Brendan McCarthy, Nico Lathouris, produced by Doug Mitchell, George Miller, P.J. Voeten, performances by Tom Hardy, Charlize Theron, Nicholas Hoult, Hugh Keays-Byrne, Rosie Huntington-Whiteley, Riley Keough, Zoë Kravitz, Abbey Lee, Courtney Eaton, music by Junkie XL, cinematography by John Seale, edited by Margaret Sixel, Village Roadshow Pictures/Kennedy Miller Mitchell/RatPac-Dune Entertainment, 2015.

Spy, written and directed by Paul Feig, produced by Peter Chernin, Paul Feig, Jessie Henderson, Jenno Topping, performances by Melissa McCarthy, Jason Statham, Rose Byrne, Miranda Hart, Bobby Cannavale, Allison Janney, Jude Law, music by Theodore Shapiro, cinematography by Robert Yeoman, edited by Brent White and Melissa Bretherton, Chernin Entertainment/Feigco Entertainment/TSG Entertainment, 2015.

Part Three

Monstrous Women

11

The Women Who Killed Too Many

Contagion (Steven Soderbergh, 2011) and Female Virality

Julia Echeverría

As opposed to their male counterparts, female murderers in the cinema tend to be portrayed and classified attending to the psychological drive and intentionality of their crimes.[1] We tend to speak of the female psycho-killer dominated by her irrational emotions,[2] of the revenge-murderer who has been victim of a previous crime such as rape,[3] and of the evil, oversexualized *femme fatale* and the "super-bitch killer beauties"[4] whose main aim is to tempt men. The academic literature devoted to this figure typically focuses on the film genres where these murderous women most frequently appear—namely, horror, melodrama, and film noir—and on the specific historical times where each type proliferates. Regardless of the film genre and typology of the murderer, one constant is the binary dynamics under which these female killers operate, systematically oscillating between nurturer and castrator, victim and perpetrator, and inspiring both repulsion and erotic desire.[5] This dualism is present in feminist film criticism as well. One of the sustained quandaries in critical discussions is whether women killers may be read as projections of patriarchal anxieties—what Barbara Creed calls the "monstrous phantasy of woman as castrator"[6]—or, on the contrary, as agents that contest patriarchy, subverting the traditional "feminine" roles ascribed to women as passive victims.[7]

In this chapter, I propose a reading of a yet underexplored staple character in a yet underexplored film genre—the Patient Zero in virus narratives—that brings together these opposing meanings and that, for reasons that will be addressed below, tends to be characterized as female. Even though it may appear counterintuitive to speak of crime or murder when dealing with a virus carrier, contagion films have a tendency to criminalize the first infected person or originator of the epidemic—what is popularly known as the Patient

Zero or, in scientific jargon, the "index patient"—by personifying the killer virus through them. These peculiar types of murderers blur and problematize questions of intentionality, as they frequently kill their victims unknowingly and are themselves victims of the virus. Yet they are constructed as serial killers who share traits with the classic types of female murderers and are even associated with the same generic conventions.

Focusing on this figure through a diachronic approach that ranges from two real-life Patients Zero, Mary Mallon and Gaëtan Dugas, to three film incarnations of female index patients in *The Killer that Stalked New York* (Earl McEvoy, 1950), *Rabid* (David Cronenberg, 1977), and *Contagion* (Steven Soderbergh, 2011), this chapter aims to provide a new perspective on the female killer. The films, a classical film noir, a Canadian exploitation movie, and a contemporary Hollywood blockbuster, reveal the evolution of the female Patient Zero with relation to different discourses and views on feminism. The last section focuses on the character of Beth Emhoff (Gwyneth Paltrow) in the more recent *Contagion*, analyzing the meanings that the controversial star persona of Paltrow adds to this figure and endeavoring to assess to what extent it complicates discussions on postfeminism. By means of this historical overview, I aim to draw attention to this singular killer, while disclosing the fruitful meanings that the "fertile" terrain of viruses offers in relation to questions of gender.

The Female Carrier in *The Killer that Stalked New York* and *Rabid*

Mary Mallon and Gaëtan Dugas are perhaps the most infamous super-spreaders in the recent history of epidemics. Mallon was an Irish immigrant who worked as a cook in New York in the early 1900s—an asymptomatic carrier who unknowingly spread typhoid fever in every household for which she worked, thus earning the title of "Typhoid Mary." Dugas, a French-Canadian flight attendant, was, in the 1980s, wrongly accused, as a recent study demonstrates,[8] of being the Patient Zero of the AIDS epidemic in the United States.[9] In spite of the eighty-year gap, the stories of Mallon and Dugas share the same narrative of criminality and stigmatization ascribed to the figure of the Patient Zero. Even if typhoid is not a venereal disease, Mallon was coded by the media and health authorities as an unclean, "fallen woman,"[10] condemned for her sexual activity and unmarried status. Similarly, Randy Shilts's 1987 novel and the subsequent HBO adaptation *And the Band Played On* (Roger Spottiswoode, 1993) portrayed Dugas as a callous and extremely promiscuous homosexual man who, even after being aware of his sickness, continued to sleep with men, and thus disseminated the disease, in the multiple cities he traveled to as a steward. Both Mallon and Dugas were pictured by the media as murderers and transgressors who acted either out of maliciousness or on account of their reckless practices and plain ignorance. Moreover, as itinerant workers and part of minority groups, one an immigrant woman, the other a homosexual man, both were instantly cast as embodiments of otherness, their disease serving to simultaneously manifest and punish their deviance, understood in both cases in sexual terms of promiscuity and depravity.

Epidemic film narratives tend to reify the connotations of Mallon's and Dugas's stories by commonly picturing their Patients Zero through gender, sexual, and/or national markers of alterity. The three following case studies will serve as examples of how these meanings converge particularly well with representations of gender.

Set in 1947 and based on an actual smallpox scare that took place that year in New York,[11] *The Killer that Stalked New York* tells the story of Sheila Bennet (Evelyn Keyes), a woman doubly betrayed by her criminal husband Matt (Charles Korvin), a diamond smuggler who cheats on her with her sister and runs away with the diamonds Sheila had smuggled from Cuba on his behalf. In her journey from Cuba, Sheila unknowingly "smuggles" smallpox as well and disseminates the disease while wandering about the streets of New York, looking for Matt to exact revenge on him.[12]

Coded as a classic *femme fatale*, Sheila is *doubly* characterized as a criminal—both a diamond smuggler and a killer-virus carrier. The film's male voice-over narrator makes sure to stress this idea by using a moralizing and outright sexist tone when describing her in the opening scene [1:03–3:30]. He dubs Sheila "Death" and "the killer" and objectifies her by overemphasizing her looks, while claiming that "*it* was something to whistle at" and "*its* name was Sheila Bennet: A pretty face with a frame to match, worth following [my emphasis]." He continues:

The odd part about the whole thing is the customs cop [. . .] never suspected the blonde target was a killer. Oh no, she didn't deal death out of the end of a gun or off the point of a knife. She delivered it wholesale. Just by walking through a crowd [. . .] Better than wholesale. For free. No charge. The tragedy was she didn't know she was Death, either.

Sheila is presented as the title character: a large-scale killer of the Typhoid-Mary kind who puts the city of New York in danger. As the film progresses and Sheila gets sicker, she seemingly becomes proportionally more evil, apparently possessed by the maliciousness of the virus, which she seems to impersonate. She shoots at the doctor who tries to help her, is described as having "murder burning in her eyes" [41:27], and her wardrobe gets darker by the end of the film. Her thirst for revenge connects her with the long list of female avengers in the cinema, a vengeance the virus helps her exact, as when, for instance, she indirectly "kills" the bar owner who had previously attempted to force himself upon her.

Yet at the same time, Sheila's double criminality is rendered as a twofold victimization. She is subjected, on the one hand, to her criminal husband and, on the other, to the virus, whose destructive power she cannot control either. In fact, neither she nor the virus succeeds in killing Matt, who eventually dies by falling off a building, thus problematizing Sheila's actual agency in her revenge plans. All in all, the film seems to warn us that Sheila's transgression, fueled by her love for the wrong kind of man, leads to a flawed model of womanhood that is punished by the virus, which ultimately kills her. In a conversation with a young girl at a hospital [9:57–11:20], Sheila confesses her desire to be a mother. However, the film makes sure to emphasize how, instead of giving life, Sheila infects and "kills" (as the doctor later tells her) that same girl, as well as many other children, with her poisonous touch. Her criminal behavior—her apparently active and mobile role in the film—is presented as a destructive force that annihilates the nurturing traits stereotypically associated with femininity, a fact that the perverse reproductive capacity of the virus and its pregnancy-like expansion inside her body aptly convey.

With its correlation between crime and infectious disease, *The Killer that Stalked New York* casts a reactionary look on gender roles in keeping with its times. Sheila's "transgressive" behavior is actually based on a relation of submission to her husband. Moreover, her body becomes an object to be contained, monitored, and surveilled by the (male) health and police authorities who relentlessly chase and finally "hunt" her down, preventing her from committing suicide in a final chivalric scene [73:20–74:37]—a frustrated attempt that confirms once again her actual lack of freedom and even control over her own body. In the end, Sheila, who is described by the voice-over as a "sick animal" [65:42], is trapped either by iniquitous male forces that precipitate her downfall or by normative male authorities that attempt to control and correct her disruption of the status quo. With her mixture of virus-impersonator *femme fatale*, passion-fueled avenger, and unintentional serial killer on the one hand, and of suffering victim on the other, Sheila brings together a multiplicity of meanings that ultimately become a call for the restoration of patriarchal order celebrated by the male voice-over. In her study of women killers, Sylvie Frigon argues that murder committed by women "contradicts their socialized roles, which depict them as being naturally loving and nurturing."[13] In *The Killer that Stalked New York*, this unnatural monstrosity has, like the virus, no cure and no turning back (only preventive measures such as vaccination can be taken against it), and so, the only possible ending for Sheila is her death, which miraculously restores order in the city, as if she were, quite implausibly, the only infectious agent in the narrative.

This cautionary and reactionary message connects the film with traditional readings of the *femme fatale* in classical film noir as being a "symptom of male fears about feminism."[14] Thus, despite driving the narrative, the female protagonist in *The Killer that Stalked New York* is filtered through a male perspective and, literally, through a male voice-over that acts to contain her. The narrator is in keeping with Kaja Silverman's discussion of the "disembodied voice-over" in classical cinema, which "speaks from a position of superior knowledge, and which superimposes itself 'on top' of the diegesis," an authoritative role reserved for "an exclusively male voice."[15] Sheila's role as Patient Zero advances the multiplicity of forms and meanings this figure will be capable of adopting in future instances of the genre (as the following example from a 1970s exploitation film proves), while at the same time converging here with the gender ideology of classical Hollywood cinema as described by classical feminist film theory.[16]

Rabid, one of David Cronenberg's early films, introduces the character of Rose (Marilyn Chambers), a woman who has the urge to feed from people's blood by stinging them with an appendix grown in her armpit as a result of an experimental surgery. Every time she attacks a new victim, she infects them with a rabies-like disease that eventually spreads throughout the city of Montreal. Like Typhoid Mary, Rose is an asymptomatic carrier, the Patient Zero of a disease whose symptoms she does not suffer as such and of which she is completely unaware. Much like Sheila, she is depicted as oscillating between the roles of perpetrator and victim. Her appendix looks, in fact, like a combination of male and female genitalia, her body fluctuating between normative parameters of gender. Her attacks evoke not only sexual penetration (an idea reinforced by Chamber's fame as a porn star, which the film reverses here by picturing her in the position of penetrator) but also function as a displaced representation of the virus's own urges to invade the healthy cells of her victims. The sexual innuendoes make her multiple attacks on men, women, and even animals hint at a promiscuity that, as she claims, she cannot help, and which enrages her boyfriend [77:21–78:31]. The disease is, therefore, coded as a sort of sexually transmitted ailment in a context where the most infamous and dreaded venereal disease, AIDS, had not yet emerged.

Rose claims she feels strong and powerful as her new murderous self. Her sting becomes an empowering weapon that even protects her in situations where she would have otherwise felt vulnerable, like in a lonely barn at night when a drunken farmer attempts to sexually assault her [22:16–23:19]—a scene that resonates with Sheila's own sexual assault and, more generally, with the rape-revenge genre. Yet at the same time, she is profoundly disgusted at her own abject body and deeply conflicted about her acts. Even more so than Sheila, Rose's characterization shows a bipolarity that William Beard refers to as a "schizoid state,"[17] a dualistic alternation between a "monster and a person,"[18] between a sexualized object of desire and a suffering human subject.[19] Her personality does, in effect, oscillate between that of a cold-blooded murderer who lures men in order to attack them, and that of a remorseful, even childish, victimized woman. She eventually dies at the hands of one of her rabies-infected victims while trying to prove her innocence—somehow punished, as in Sheila's case, by her own destructive forces.

Rose's role has inspired contradictory gender-related readings on the film. Most famously, Robin Wood has criticized the sexual politics behind Cronenberg's first films, arguing that they are reactionary patriarchal nightmares that project "horror and evil onto women and their sexuality, the ultimate dread being of women usurping the active, aggressive role that patriarchal ideology assigns to the male."[20] Wood argues that, in films like *Rabid*, chaos and horror result from the male scientists' attempt to change society, but that, tellingly, it is the women, in this case Rose, that are ultimately blamed for the ensuing mayhem. He interprets this as an attack on second-wave feminism and the sexual liberation of women.[21]

Other scholars refute Wood's reading by claiming that the male scientist's primary responsibility can point to the existence of a "lurking patriarchal culprit,"[22] while others hold that the actual horror derives from technology and from the "nightmare of human behavior reduced to the mechanical activity of propagation."[23] I would indeed argue that Rose's adoption of an active and transgressive role endows her with an empowering agency that can be understood as a form of subversive revenge on patriarchy itself, especially in those scenes where she attacks men who attempt to rape or take advantage of her.

In any case, the binary way in which Rose is portrayed—as both a vulnerable victim and a cold vampire "huntress"—hinders the simplistic interpretation of her role as either active or passive, rebellious or monstrous, transgressive or reactionary. In the end, the true villain of the film can be said to be the infectious disease. Rose's body, very much like Sheila's, becomes a weapon (a flesh and blood machine) for the virus to use at its own will, urging her to penetrate other bodies so that it can replicate and survive. Rose's feelings of satisfaction when she stings a new victim may be read, after all, as voiced manifestations of the virus itself, which is physically embodied in her new morphed self. Cronenberg himself stands by this position in what has become one of his legendary quotes, soliciting spectators to "see the movies from the point of view of the disease."[24] Rose is, like Sheila, at the mercy of forces she cannot truly control—her body manipulated by a Frankenstein-type scientist and by the virus—even though she assumes a much more active and conscious role in her killings. Thus, horror derives from her abject body and from the pathogen that invades and transforms organic life.

Both *The Killer that Stalked New York* and *Rabid* offer relevant examples of the way the Patient Zero type facilitates the articulation of questions of gender that traverse different film genres, discourses, and contexts. The duality of this staple character helps to offer a rumination on difference and otherness that the disease brings out and renders visible. This connects with Linda Williams's well-known notion of the likeness between the monster and the female victim in classical horror films, the monster being a mirror or a "double for the women,"[25] as both pose a potential threat to patriarchy through their otherness. The interplay that the virus establishes between sexuality, reproduction, death, and bodily transformation is fittingly embodied in the criminal/victim body of the female Patient Zero, suggesting a confrontation between conventional gender roles of femininity and motherhood, and these characters' continuous trespassing of normative lines. The following section will attempt to provide a more contemporary look on this figure, aiming to highlight both the continuities and points of difference with respect to these earlier versions of the female Patient Zero.

The Postfeminist Super-Spreader in *Contagion*

Unlike Sheila and Rose, the Patient Zero character in *Contagion*, Beth, appears on screen for a total amount of barely six minutes of the film's run-time.[26] The movie, a multi protagonist story about the global outbreak of a highly lethal microorganism—the fictional MEV-1 virus—narrates the running-against-the-clock efforts of health authorities to trace the original carrier, contain the epidemic, and develop a vaccine against the virus. The multiple narrative strands attempt to offer a holistic and scientifically accurate vision of epidemiology, as director Steven Soderbergh himself explained.[27] And like the virus, these narrative lines, each led by a renowned star, spread and multiply in a sometimes intersecting network.

Among the many science-related characters, one of the storylines focuses in particular on the family of the first infected victim: the index patient, Beth Emhoff; her husband, and then widower, Mitch Emhoff (Matt Damon); Mitch's teenage daughter from a previous marriage, Jory (Anna Jacoby-

Heron); and Beth's six-year-old son from a previous marriage, Clark (Griffin Kane). The film opens precisely with a short prologue that introduces an already sick-looking Beth sitting at a bar in O'Hare International Airport in Chicago [0:41–2:01]. The virus manifests itself in the form of ominous coughs that anticipate the ensuing disaster, while Beth eats peanuts from a shared bowl and then passes her credit card to the bartender. The narration underscores the virus's intangible presence through its ill-omened fixation on the contaminated objects touched by Beth, documenting through extreme close-ups the quick process of transmission in a way that invites us to imagine, rather than actually see, viruses traveling from Beth's mouth to her hand, from her hand to the peanut bowl and credit card, from her credit card to the bartender's hand, and from the bartender's hand to the cash register screen (Figure 11.1). In a few seconds, germs pervade Beth's surrounding space, waiting for the next unsuspecting victim to catch them.

As we can infer from her phone conversation, Beth is returning home to Minneapolis from a business trip in Hong Kong. During her layover in Chicago, she has taken the opportunity to have an extramarital tryst with an old boyfriend, John Neil (Robert G. Beck). Unaware of the deadly virus she has contracted in Hong Kong, she infects (and kills) no less than six people in a short period of time. Her international mobility and multiple social interactions facilitate the simultaneous outbreak of different global clusters of which she is held responsible. Taking into account the reproductive rate of the virus, which at the beginning of the story is R-2—meaning that each carrier is prone to infect an average of two people—Beth's astonishing levels of infectiousness instantly situate her as a super-

Figure 11.1 *Contagion* (Soderbergh, 2011): Gwyneth Paltrow in the role of the victim/killer Patient Zero.

spreader that inevitably brings to mind the characterization of Dugas as a promiscuous and itinerant host.

However, and despite her A-list star persona and her major opening appearance, Paltrow's character does not stay alive for long. Some eight minutes into the narrative, she is already dead, and the film hurries along without apparently giving it a second thought, even unglamorously displaying her peeled scalp over her face, while medical examiners peer inside her skull in a passionless autopsy. Her early death and the negative light in which her character is portrayed were read by various film critics as a nod to the acrimony stirred up by the actress.[28] Wesley Morris even suggested that the "entire movie is a kind of joke whose punch line is 'Gwyneth Paltrow makes the whole world sick,'" and added: "I don't know what this woman has done to win the schadenfreude of so many, but Soderbergh has turned her into a 21st century Veronica Cartwright."[29]

Like Chambers in *Rabid*, Paltrow's star persona adds a specific set of meanings to her Patient Zero, and the film definitely plays on them. Usually deprecated by the press and the public, Paltrow was even ranked as the most hated celebrity in a poll carried out by the tabloid *Star Magazine* in 2013. The reasons given for this animosity are the actress's self-proclaimed role as a "healthy lifestyle" guru in her business/website *Goop* and her elitist, frivolous, unfortunate, and sometimes pseudoscientific advice and remarks on issues such as nutrition and parenthood, which have been described as showing a "Marie Antoinette-esque detachment from reality."[30] Paltrow's image has, in effect, been inscribed within what scholar Jorie Lagerwey calls a postfeminist "brand mom": a white, upper-class celebrity who uses her fame and motherhood as a brand in order to sell her products to her "fan-consumers"[31] in an "individualist, neoliberal, and brand-saturated culture."[32]

It can be argued that the postfeminist model that Paltrow incarnates is based on an image of entrepreneurial success and libera(liza)tion that seems to imply the idea that feminism is no longer necessary or that equality has been already attained, while at the same time displaying and demanding, from a clear position of privilege, a woman's success in every professional, personal, and physical area of her life—thus falling into a pernicious model of femininity much criticized by feminist scholars like Angela McRobbie.[33] In an article in *The Guardian*, however, Elizabeth Day claims that Paltrow is a "curiously polarizing figure"[34] that is either extremely loved or loathed. Paltrow's fixation with health issues, her pseudoscientific well-being remedies, her defense of open relationships, and, more generally, her controversial star persona ironically come into play in a film that cherishes science and the crucial role of scientists, appropriately casting her as the equally demonized and victimized stock character of the sick Patient Zero.

The film introduces Beth as a successful woman who flawlessly balances her work and family lives. She is the Global Marketing Operations Manager at the AIMM Alderson firm in Minneapolis and seems to be the provider for her family, as her husband is apparently unemployed. However, from the very opening scene to the final revelatory coda, Beth is marked as disruptive and morally dubious. On a personal level, she is unfaithful to her loyal husband with a man who practically does not appear on screen and who dies right at the beginning, thus hampering any chance of sympathy with, let alone interest in, him or their love affair. Her family is not a "traditional" one either, in the sense that both Clark and Jory are children of previous relationships. The fact that she prefers to delay her flight home in order to be with her lover also seems to call into question her motherhood. Meanwhile, Mitch, played by a sympathetic Matt Damon, the epitome of the Nice Guy in Hollywood, is depicted as a devoted husband and father who spends most of the film mourning the loss of his wife and appalled by her infidelity. Quarantined at home, he jealously safeguards Jory's health and, metaphorically, her virtue, from her teenage boyfriend, whom he forbids her to see. Mitch's efforts to control Jory may, indeed, be read as an expression of his frustration and repressed anger over the lack of control he had over his wife's life. Only when he comes to terms with her death at the very end of the film does he allow Jory to come into physical contact with her now vaccinated (and, therefore, prophylactic) boyfriend, even if this occurs at home and under his careful supervision [99:36].

Unlike the rest of the female characters in the film, who all have active roles outside their homes, Mitch assumes a static, domestic role that subverts traditional gender stereotypes. The film seems to highlight Mitch's castrated role in their marriage and, therefore, Beth's empowered role as castrator. The fact that she unintentionally infects (and kills) both her lover and her son Clark speaks both of her predatory praying mantis skills and her horrific Medea-like motherhood (Figure 11.2). Compared with Sheila's and Rose's crimes, Beth's are judged as being much more execrable, especially the "killing" of her son. It is, perhaps, for this reason that the movie does not allow her to remain alive for more than a few minutes of screen time.

Despite Soderbergh's insistence on the idea that the virus in *Contagion* is not a metaphor,[35] the film relies on the long-standing myths that surround epidemics. The idea of punishment—or of exoneration in the case of Mitch, who is, coincidentally, immune to the virus—looms over the narrative. The film activates the conventions of the disaster genre through its set of stock types like the profiteer, its emphasis on the traditional family (dis)unity, and its cautionary subtext of moral retribution. The fact that Beth, John, and her son Clark die, whereas Mitch and his daughter Jory are spared from the

Figure 11.2 *Contagion* (Soderbergh, 2011): Beth Emhoff's monstrous motherhood epitomized by her lethal hug.

plague, invites us to inevitably think of a sort of divine sentence, as several critics duly noted.[36] One of the most common questions raised by journalists in press conferences was whether Beth's disease was a retribution for her infidelity, which both Soderbergh and Paltrow categorically denied.[37]

And yet, on a professional level, Beth is also representative of destructive late-capitalist practices. Her corporation's outsourcing and environmental damage in rural China is the explanation the film gives for the virus's inception in a final revelatory scene. The coda shows an AIMM Alderson bulldozer cutting down trees in the Chinese rainforest. Bats are driven out of their habitat as a result, and one of them, presumably infected, comes into contact with a pig, which is later used by the restaurant chef where, coincidentally, Beth eats dinner, becoming, in a rather implausible way, the index patient. This corroborates that, even if Beth's infidelity and castrating role in her marriage may not be the actual (at the most, the metaphorical) trigger of the epidemic, she is literally to blame for it as the corporation's leading manager of the exploitative practices for which she travels to Hong Kong. Her damaging influence, misbalancing both her family and the world's ecosystem, translates perfectly well into the deterministic role of the Patient Zero.

The film thus brings together in one single character a representative of late capitalism, globalization, and postfeminism, all cast in a negative light. Beth stands for a new emancipated femininity that is in tune with neoliberal discourses of individualism, empowerment, and an ethos of success associated with agency and global mobility. Authors Rosalind Gill and Christina Scharff contend that postfeminism and neoliberalism cannot be understood separately, as the former is "not simply a response to feminism but also a sensibility that is at least partly constituted through the pervasiveness of neoliberal ideas."[38] The film's toying with the mythical idea of individual and collective retribution both unveils our preconceived need to read plagues (and narratives) following a causal pattern, and confirms the prevalence of hierarchical top-down structures of power that determine the economic, environmental, and social inequities of the world. This top-down exploitative influence can be read as being turned against itself, as symbolized by Beth's status as the literal victim of her own (family-, corporate-, and epidemic-related) "sins."

In so doing, the film offers a problematic vision of (post)feminism. Unlike Sheila and Rose, who were at the mercy of male superior forces, Beth appears to occupy a liberated position. However, her assumption of what has been traditionally presumed to be the male patriarchal role of provider seems to be, as in previous cases, castigated by the film through its virus and, especially, through the casting of the much-execrated Paltrow in the much-demonized character of the Patient Zero. Beth is informed by Paltrow's incarnation of a postfeminist discourse of choice that encourages women "to embark on projects of individualized self-definition and privatized self-expression exemplified in the celebration of lifestyle and consumption choices."[39] As the film seems to convey, this model cannot possibly escape the global structures of power that are capitalist and patriarchal in nature, and of which Beth is at once the representative and victim. The film makes clear that getting infected is not simply a matter of accidental exposure and bad luck; geographical, gender, racial, political, social, and especially economic factors play a fundamental part in the process. By exposing its greater incidence on the Chinese rural areas, for instance, the film's epidemic not only ascertains that we are living in an interconnected global world, but it also brings to light the unbalanced order of that world, the unequal distribution of wealth that results in a corresponding unequal distribution of disease and of other natural and human disasters.

The rest of the main female characters featured in the movie corroborate this idea. They are actually celebrated as devoted scientists ready to sacrifice their lives for the sake of humanity, but they appear to have no family lives, no (illicit) sex lives, and no positions of power, which are reserved for their male colleagues who stay safely in their offices. The film seems to offer a critical commentary on questions of gender and privilege, even if it is never explicit about its own position, nor does it present itself clearly as an ironic subversion—as a "joke," as Morris suggested—of the conventions of the disaster genre, a genre that has been characterized by some as being inherently reactionary.[40]

What is certain is that Beth bears the heavy burden of the Patient Zero and that, unlike Sheila and Rose, whose destruction was restricted to the cities of New York and Montreal, respectively, hers is a large-scale massacre. Her greater libera(liza)tion and trespassing of normative patriarchal customs seem to cause an even superior form of damage. Like Sheila and Rose, Beth kills unknowingly, but she is criminalized through the connotations of sexual license, faulty motherhood, and unruly entrepreneurship that the virus helps to unveil. The fact that she privileges her career and sexual desires over her family is rendered as a form of monstrosity. As Ann Jones claims, maternity has been traditionally linked to self-sacrifice, and any trace of "self-interest [is] condemned as unnatural and monstrous."⁴¹ In this respect, Beth does not last long as a killer because she is soon punished by the virus, but her sins and bedlam linger for the rest of the film.

Conclusion

The Killer that Stalked New York, *Rabid*, and *Contagion* reveal the contradictory meanings the figure of the female Patient Zero helps to bring out in relation to feminism. Fluctuating between murderer and victim—and sometimes sharing conventions with the rape-revenge heroine-victims, the femmes fatales, and the passion-led killers—this figure activates discourses on gender and sexuality through the virus's penetrating, reproductive, and body-transforming qualities. More often than not, these infected and infectious women are presented as transgressors associated with sexual promiscuity and with a deadly form of procreation and motherhood that draws connections with the also infectious and, in some cases, infected economic system of consumer-capitalism.

Ranging from the blatantly objectified character of Sheila or, as the narrator calls her, "the blonde death" [65:38], to the porn-star implications of Chambers and the feminist movements of the 1970s to, finally, the brand-mom star persona of Paltrow in the postfeminist era, these three characters provide a diachronic vision of the female index patient and their ongoing subjection to, and fight against, the structures of patriarchal/capitalist power. Even though each of these examples belongs to three different time periods and genres, and thus, each of them translates the Patient Zero differently, the narrative of the fallen woman and the mythical idea of retribution and penitence surface in all of them, each picturing attractive but threatening characters and actresses who get punished for and by their transgressions. These women's destructive capacities succeed, at least, in momentarily overturning the existing system for the duration of the epidemic. The annihilation they provoke becomes, after all, not only the result but also the mirror of their own subversion of the status quo, a subversion that lingers far beyond the realm of each film.

Notes

1 I would like to thank the two blind reviewers for offering their insights and providing me with some very good ideas for improving this manuscript.
2 Steven J. Schneider, "The madwomen in our movies: Female psycho-killers in American horror cinema," in A. Burfoot and S. Lord (eds.), *Killing Women: The Visual Culture of Gender and Violence* (Waterloo: Wilfrid Laurier University Press, 2006), pp. 237–50; Helen Birch, "Introduction," in H. Birch (ed.), *Moving Targets: Women, Murder, and Representation* (Berkeley: University of California Press, 1994), p. 4.
3 Alexandra Heller-Nicholas (ed.), *Rape-Revenge Films: A Critical Study* (Jefferson, NC: McFarland, 2011).
4 Karlene Faith, *Unruly Women: The Politics of Confinement and Resistance* (New York: Seven Stories, 2011 [1993]).
5 Sylvie Frigon, "Mapping scripts and narratives of women who kill their husbands in Canada, 1866–1954: Inscribing the everyday," in A. Burfoot and S. Lord (eds.), *Killing Women: The Visual Culture of Gender and Violence* (Waterloo: Wilfrid Laurier University Press, 2006), p. 3.
6 Barbara Creed, *The Monstrous-Feminine: Film, Feminism, Psychoanalysis* (London: Routledge, 2007 [1993]), p. 7.
7 Jacinda Read, *The New Avengers: Feminism, Femininity and the Rape-Revenge Cycle* (Manchester: Manchester University Press, 2000), p. 4; Susan Lord, "Killing time: The violent imaginary of feminist media," in A. Burfoot and S. Lord (eds.), *Killing Women: The Visual Culture of Gender and Violence* (Waterloo: Wilfrid Laurier University Press, 2006), p. 177; Sylvie Frigon, "Mapping scripts and narratives of women who kill their husbands in Canada, 1866–1954," in *Killing Women*, p. 18; Steven Jay Schneider, "The madwomen in our movies: female psycho-killers in American Horror Cinema," in *Killing Women*, p. 240; Jyotika Virdi, "Reverence, rape—and then revenge: Popular Hindi cinema's 'women's film,'" in *Killing Women*, pp. 251–72.
8 Michael Worobey et al., "1970s and 'Patient 0' HIV-1 genomes illuminate early HIV/AIDS history in North America," *Nature*, 539 (2016), pp. 98–101.
9 "Patient Zero" is a coinage that originated fortuitously in relation to Dugas. As Worobey et al. explain, Dugas was initially labeled Patient "O," an abbreviation that stood for "Outside-of-California." The letter was misread as a "zero" and the captivating expression soon caught on, inaccurately employed from then on to refer to the index patient.

10 Priscilla Wald, *Contagious: Cultures, Carriers and the Outbreak Narrative* (Durham, NC: Duke University Press, 2008), pp. 84–94.

11 Jeff Stafford, "The killer that stalked New York," *Turner Classic Movies Blog*. Available at https://goo.gl/aDm7X5 (accessed June 7, 2017).

12 Susan Sontag remarks that there is a "need to make a dreaded disease foreign." Most virus films situate the origin of the disease in a distant land. The fact that, in *The Killer*, this land happens to be Cuba adds political innuendoes in tune with a context of growing anxieties regarding the territorial and ideological invasion of communism. These anxieties are similarly enunciated by other epidemic films of the time, as is the case of Kazan's *Panic in the Streets* (1950), where an Eastern European migrant introduces pneumonic plague in the United States. The medieval undertones of some of these sicknesses not only indicate territorial distance but also, in most cases, evoke primitiveness, suggesting a kind of temporal distance as well.
       Susan Sontag, *Illness as Metaphor: AIDS and Its Metaphors* (London: Penguin, 1991 [1977, 1988]), p. 133.

13 Frigon, "Mapping scripts and narratives," p. 18.

14 Mary Ann Doane, *Femmes Fatales: Feminism, Film Theory, Psychoanalysis* (London: Routledge, 1991), pp. 2–3.

15 Kaja Silverman, *The Acoustic Mirror: The Female Voice in Psychoanalysis and Cinema* (Bloomington: Indiana University Press, 1988), p. 48.

16 Laura Mulvey, *Visual and Other Pleasures* (Houndmills, Basingstoke: Palgrave, 2008 [1989]).

17 William Beard, *The Artist as Monster: The Cinema of David Cronenberg* (Toronto: University of Toronto Press, 2001), p. 63.

18 Ibid.

19 Ibid., p. 52.

20 Robin Wood, "An introduction to the American horror film," in B. K. Grant and C. Sharrett (eds.), *Planks of Reason: Essays on the Horror Film* (Lanham, MD: Scarecrow, 2004), p. 136.

21 Ibid., p. 135.

22 Gaile McGregor, "Grounding the countertext: David Cronenberg and the ethnospecificity of horror," *Canadian Journal of Film Studies*, 2/1 (1992), p. 51.

23 Mary B. Campbell, "Biological alchemy and the films of David Cronenberg," in B. K. Grant and C. Sharrett (eds.), *Planks of Reason: Essays on the Horror Film* (Lanham, MD: Scarecrow, 2004), p. 334.

24 Kim Newman, *Nightmare Movies: Horror on Screen since the 1960s* (London: Bloomsbury, 2011 [1988]), p. 156.

25 Linda Williams, "When the woman looks," in B. K. Grant (ed.), *The Dread of Difference: Gender in the Horror Film* (Austin: University of Texas Press, 2015 [1996]), p. 22.

26 See Ondrej Pavlik's shot measurement of the film *Contagion* at the *Cinemetrics* database. Available at http://www.cinemetrics.lv/movie.php ?movie_ID=10716 (accessed June 7, 2017).

27 Claudette Barius, "*Contagion* consultants talk about the movie's scientific accuracy," *Washington Post*, September 12, 2011. Available at https://goo.gl/6tUegF (accessed February 5, 2017).

28 Wesley Morris, "*Contagion*," *Boston Globe*, September 9, 2011. Available at https://goo.gl/hDBJUR (accessed February 10, 2017); J. R. Jones, "Reach out, touch somebody, and die," *Chicago Reader*, September 8, 2011. Available at https://goo.gl/LgjM7V (accessed February 10, 2017); Marc Savlov, "*Contagion*," *Austin Chronicle*, September 9, 2011. Available at https://goo.gl/AXN3tD (accessed February 22, 2017).

29 Morris, "*Contagion*." Veronica Cartwright starred in the 1978 version of *Invasion of the Body Snatchers* (Philip Kaufman), as well as in other horror and science-fiction movies.

30 Elizabeth Day, "Gwyneth Paltrow: Loved, loathed, but never ignored," *The Guardian*, May 5, 2013. Available at https://goo.gl/eJfDKP (accessed June 12, 2017).

31 Jorie Lagerwey, *Postfeminist Celebrity and Motherhood* (New York: Routledge, 2017), p. 19.

32 Ibid., p. 30.

33 Angela McRobbie, "Post-feminism and popular culture," *Feminist Media Studies*, 4/3 (2004), pp. 255–64.

34 Day, "Gwyneth Paltrow."

35 Jason Solomons, "Steven Soderbergh: I need a break to recalibrate," *The Guardian*, October 16, 2011. Available at https://goo.gl/rVXtkp (accessed February 5, 2017).

36 Morris, "*Contagion*"; Peter Travers, "*Contagion*," *Rolling Stone*, September 8, 2011. Available at https://goo.gl/yzPufs (accessed February 10, 2017).

37 Mark Brown and Jason Solomons, "Venice film festival: *Contagion* is not the final reel for Steven Soderbergh," *The Guardian*, September 4, 2011.

38 Rosalind Gill and Christina Scharff, "Introduction," in R. Gill and C. Scharff (eds.), *New Femininities: Postfeminism, Neoliberalism and Subjectivity* (Houndmills Basingstoke: Palgrave Macmillan, 2011), p. 7.

39 Shelley Budgeon, "The contradictions of successful femininity: Third-wave feminism, postfeminism and 'New' femininities," in R. Gill and C. Scharff (eds.), *New Femininities: Postfeminism, Neoliberalism and Subjectivity* (Houndmills Basingstoke: Palgrave Macmillan, 2011), p. 281.

40 Michael Ryan and Douglas Kellner, *Camera Politica: The Politics and Ideology of Contemporary Hollywood Film* (Bloomington: Indiana University Press, 1988).

41 Ann Jones, *Women Who Kill* (New York: Feminist Press, 2009), p. 156.

Filmography

Contagion, directed by Steven Soderbergh, written by Scott Z. Burns, produced by Michael Shamberg, Stacey Sher, Gregory Jacobs, performances by Marion

Cotillard, Matt Damon, Laurence Fishburne, Jude Law, Gwyneth Paltrow, Kate Winslet, Cliff Martinez, music by Cliff Martinez, cinematography by Steven Soderbergh, edited by Stephen Mirrione, Participant Media/Imagenation/Abu Dhabi Double Feature Films, 2011. DVD. Warner Home Video, 2012.

The Killer that Stalked New York, directed by Earl McEvoy, written by Harry Essex and Milton Lehman, produced by Robert Cohn, with Evelyn Keyes, Charles Korvin, William Bishop, Dorothy Malone, music by Hans J. Salter, cinematography by Joseph F. Biroc, edited by Jerome Thoms, Robert Cohn Productions, 1950. DVD. Sony Pictures Home Entertainment, 2010.

Rabid, written and directed by David Cronenberg, produced by John Dunning, with Marilyn Chambers, Frank Moore, Joe Silver, Howard Ryshpan, cinematography by René Verzier, edited by Jean LaFleur, Dunning/Link/Reitman, 1977. Via Vision Entertainment, 2016.

12

"Always Take Care of Ganja"

Intersectional and Postfeminist Contradictions in *Da Sweet Blood of Jesus* (Spike Lee, 2014)

Hélène Charlery

Lisa Coulthard argued that "[interrogations] of violence and gender have always been a significant part of film, feminist theory, and film criticism."[1] However, discussing the filmic representations of black women who kill is complicated, first, because in spite of Hollywood's fascination for women who kill,[2] there are few examples of such characters in American mainstream cinema. Thus, few, if any, of the referenced publications on women who kill in film include an intersectional approach that would consider the specific characterization of black women. In their introduction to *Killing Women*, Annette Burfoot and Susan Lord have positively acknowledged the recent "shifts [in popular culture] in the characterization of women who kill."[3] However, the examples they refer to are all white: "Ripley from the film series *Aliens*[,] Lara Croft, Buffy, and *Kill Bill*."[4] Feminist film theorists of the 1980s, Barbara Creed and Carol Clover, have developed valuable theories on female monsters in horror movies.[5] But Diana Adesola Mafe has confirmed in her book, relevantly entitled *Where No Black Woman Has Gone First*, that "[there] are few works that explicitly tackle both race and gender in speculative cinema."[6]

Kinitra Brooks acknowledges turning to black independent filmmaking because of the "erasure of black women in mainstream horror."[7] Excepting Bill Gunn's *Ganja & Hess* (1973), discussed in this chapter, there are few other examples of black female leads in American vampire or horror movies or in films that could be labeled as such. In 1974, *Abby* (William Girdler) and *Sugar Hill* (Paul Maslansky) featured black female characters turned into demon-possessed or revengeful voodoo monsters. Katrina in *Vamp* (Richard Wenk, 1986) sucks the blood of a fraternity student in an eroticized scene before she is killed by his friend. The list would also include Michael Rymer's 2002 adaptation of Anne Rice's novel *The Queen of the Damned*, featuring a black female vampire, Akashi, who is turned into a marble statue at the end of the film.[8] One cannot forget that black and white womanhood have been represented differently in popular culture, and in the horror genre, because of race: black female sexuality was not presented as monstrous because they could kill, but because they were black, notwithstanding representations of violence or murder.[9] Thus, an act of violence that could be seen as liberatory because transgressive from a white-gendered perspective might seem all the more oppressive from an intersectional perspective.

Similar remarks can be made regarding the articulation between intersectionality and postfeminism. Linda Mizejewski has portrayed the postfeminist female character as a "savvy woman who no longer needs political commitment, who enjoys consumerist choices, and whose preoccupations are likely to involve romance, career choices, and hair gels."[10] Yet Mizejewski's examples—Clarice Starling in *The Silence of the Lambs* (Jonathan Demme, 1991) or Karen Sisco in *Out of Sight* (Steven Soderbergh, 1998)—do not involve an analysis of the female protagonists' racial and ethnic characterization. The few works that discuss intersectionality and postfeminism point at their antagonism,[11] whether postfeminism is understood "as an epistemological shift, a historical transformation [or] a backlash against feminism."[12] As a historical break, postfeminism implies a fracture from second-wave feminism's focus on gender equality and interpersonal politics. The latter would have been replaced by a third-wave or postfeminist

> gender politics relevant for a context in which women's cultural and economic enfranchisement was accepted, and where, for example, women could enjoy participating in traditionally feminine beauty practices free of their patriarchal past associations.[13]

This vision of postfeminism runs counter to Rebecca Walker's vision of the third wave in her 1992 essay in *Ms. Magazine*, in the aftermath of Clarence Thomas's confirmation hearings.[14] Walker precisely demonstrated that gender equality was not fully reached, that sexism was still institutional and not solely personal, and that feminism, like violence against women, was not *passé*. This chapter considers postfeminism as a cultural sensibility, as defined by Rosalind Gill, particularly its reference to sexuality. Among the "interrelated themes" that Rosalind Gill has used to conceptualize the term "postfeminist sensibility" is the "shift from sexual objectification to sexual subjectification, where women's participation in apparently sexually objectifying practices was understood as the outcome of an agentic, knowing sexuality."[15] This shift, we shall see, is relevant to the analysis of Ganja, the black female killer of Spike Lee's *Da Sweet Blood of Jesus* (2014), Lee's loose remake of *Ganja & Hess*.

Although *Da Sweet Blood of Jesus* follows Gunn's film quite closely, in a promotional interview, Lee considered *Ganja and Hess* as a "source" that he chose to "contemporize."[16] *Da Sweet Blood of Jesus* is not Lee's first attempt at discussing black female sexuality in film. His first film *She's Gotta Have It* (1986) raised legitimate criticisms from black feminists, most famously from bell hooks, who challenged the assumption that the film's lead character, Nola Darling, "[embodied] the liberatory ideal of African American female sexuality."[17] Notwithstanding the fact that Nola is punished by sexual assault at the end of the film, the film suggests that Nola is the own architect of her objectification.[18] Ten years later, Lee's discourse on black female sexuality had changed. In *Girl 6* (1996), the objectification of the black female central character was not self-inflicted; rather, the film's opening and concluding scenes reveal the "oppressive industries and institutions" that continue to objectify a sexualized "ideal" of African American women.[19] If Gunn's 1973 film is now praised for its feminist approach,[20] how does Lee, 41 years after *Ganja & Hess* and 18 years after *Girl 6*, contemporize the original film's discourse on black female sexuality and the characterization of its blood-drinking black woman?

In this chapter, I discuss two major changes from Gunn's original story in particular. First, in both films, Ganja's monologue displays her rationale to always "take care of Ganja," thereby justifying her choices, including murder. But in the 2014 film, the monologue is rewritten with a more overt intersectional approach, which, paradoxically, objectifies the character. The fact that Ganja's lover and victim is a woman in Lee's film, instead of a man as in the original movie, is also a noteworthy change. The new homoerotic context in which the murder is framed may lead to reaffirm Kimberley Springer's view of postfeminism as a practice "directed at a female audience, even while covertly acknowledging male viewers/voyeurs."[21] I will show how Lee's narrative and aesthetic choices render such a reading more complex.

Rewriting Ganja's Intersectional Monologue: Discussing the Enduring Woman

Analyzing blaxploitation films of the 1970s, Robin Means Coleman adapted Clover's "Final Girl" to the films' black heroines and conceptualized the figure of the "Enduring Woman." In her analysis of the black female character in *Chloe, Love Is Calling You* (Marshall Neilan, 1934), Means Coleman wrote that black women are "much more than 'final.'" They "must be resilient battlers of evil who not only live, but live on to *continue to fight* monstrous forms of systemic (racial) injustices."[22] Contrary to the Final Girl, the Enduring Woman's killing impulse is not geared toward her own survival but toward her racial community's. *Sugar Hill*'s lead character perfectly illustrates this definition, even more so than Ganja.[23] As Means Coleman has noted,

> Ganja not only survives her encounter with the monster, but happily chooses to become one. [As] an Enduring Woman she is sexy and sexual, she finds her victory in the death of her two husbands, and now, fully independent [. . .], [she] is no longer bound or terrorized; rather, she happily terrorizes (men) herself.[24]

Although I agree with this analysis of Ganja, I nonetheless think that she stands out from other Enduring Women. Contrary to Sugar Hill and other blaxploitation black heroines, Ganja's killing impulse is driven by a condition that Hess imposes upon her body and life.[25] By making Ganja's vampirism a consequence of Hess's narcissism, the 1973 film emphasizes her status as a black woman subjected to male domination. Ganja does endure, but not to continue fighting for others, but for her own pleasure. She is not the self-sacrificing black woman whose resilience is only collective. This is featured in Ganja's monologue before she becomes a blood-drinking murderer.

The monologue intervenes after Ganja is faced with Hess's embodiment of the abject, a subject who turns human life into object and mere commodity and who does not show any remorse for it. The previous scene, in which he is seen leaving the room of one of his victims, while her baby can be heard crying in the background, reinforces this construction of Hess as abject [63:21]. The monologue intervenes after she has discovered her late first husband's body in Hess's wine cellar. As Ganja suspects that he killed her husband, she does not flee, but directly demands an explanation, when the couple faces each other across the dining room table. Without a proper answer to her question, she leaves the room, infuriated. The following scene shows that Ganja has still not left Hess's mansion [66:57]. Rather, at the end of the scene, the narration cuts to another setting in Hess's house where she delivers the monologue in which she relates a childhood memory involving her mother. The editing suggests that Ganja has accepted Hess's abject nature. Both Means Coleman and Jeffrey Weinstock have interpreted Ganja's reaction as part of her rationale: she "would rather be married to an extremely wealthy crazed man than the widow of a poor one."[26] In other words, Ganja explains away Hess and his freakiness into another one of her moves to take care of herself, now that her first husband is gone. However relevant, I think, like Lindop, that Ganja's acceptance of Hess's abject nature is part of a different "rationalizing" logic, according to which "everyone she knows is 'some kind of a freak.'"[27] Although the black actress Marlene Clark, who plays Ganja in the film, made up the monologue,[28] the content of her speech suggests that she herself was constructed as freak and abject.

Interestingly, no shot during the monologue frames Ganja and Hess together; rather, Ganja is constantly singled out. Because the camera lingers on the black female character's face as she tells her story, the viewer must focus on the content of her speech. Visually, the scene starts as Ganja's voice can be heard over the consecutive close-ups of two busts of women in a dark background. The camera pans, and Ganja's face appears in the same shot as the busts. The repetition of these compositions illustrates the way Ganja handles the positive way she saw herself ("I was in the best snowball fights, and I always won") and the way she was seen—or rather not seen, or misseen—by others ("Someone said they saw you being chased by a boy."/"You are a liar . . . and a slut"). Thus, if Ganja accepts Hess's abject nature because "everyone she knows is 'some kind of a freak,'" she includes herself in the construction of the freak/abject by an outside gaze. Her concluding rationale to "provide for Ganja always" can be read as the character's asserting agency and self-empowerment to accept her construction as abject as she chooses to define it in order to better reject her construction as objectified Other. This is illustrated by the shift in the monologue's syntax, from "it was as if I was a disease," to "I decided I was a disease," and by the imperative forms in the last part of the monologue. The sound of drumming that serves as the transition to the next scene, from the close-up of her face and concluding resonating voice to the images of the new couple's playful relationship and wedding, celebrates the character's credo.

Yet, at this stage in the film, Ganja, unlike Hess, has not killed yet. This temporality dissociates the construction of her as abject from his. He is abject because he commodifies others for his thirst for blood. She was constructed as abject because she was not wanted. While he struggles with his abjection as killer and commodifier, from Ganja's monologue on, everything that happens is to be read as Ganja's rationale; this illustrates how the 1973 film integrates and prioritizes her narrative authority.[29] If Ganja is to be read as an Enduring Woman, her strength and enduring black womanhood come from the fact that she rejects the objectification of her beauty and abjection by an outside gaze. How does Spike Lee adapt the monologue and its importance in establishing Ganja's self-empowerment and -determination, and what does this imply in terms of a postfeminist sensibility?

Figure 12.1 *Da Sweet Blood of Jesus* (Lee, 2014): Ganja asks Hess about her ex-husband's corpse in his freezer.

In *Da Sweet Blood of Jesus*, the monologue intervenes in the same part of the narrative as in *Ganja & Hess* [64:12]. The 2014 Ganja discovers her first husband's dead body in Hess's freezer and asks Hess for an explanation, as the couple sit at the living-room table (Figure 12.1). Similarly, Hess is shown leaving one of the victims' rooms between the moment Ganja discovers the body and the moment she questions him. However, Hess is seen playing with the child of his dead victim before the camera pans to disclose the dead mother. Similarly, the 2014 couple's dinner conversation is depicted in shot/reverse shot, whereas, in the original film, Hess, Ganja, and Archie, Hess's butler, were framed in the same static shot. Although this may seem to be a mere aesthetic choice, the larger shot sizes alter the characterization. The construction of Hess as abject in the 1973 film is transferred onto the shift from the bloodied body that Hess left in the previous scene to the close-up of the piece of roast that the 2014 butler, Senechal, cuts provocatively. The camera's focus on Senechal as he leaves the dining room displays a medium shot in which Hess is seen eating in the left fore/mid/background dressed in a black shirt, with the picture of a strong, half-naked black warrior in the background [62:48]. And yet, at that moment, Hess provides an explanation as to why the dead body is in his basement: "Your ex-husband committed suicide." His words are accompanied by a music that heightens the romantic tone of the character's discourse: "I wouldn't do anything to hurt you." Ganja's answer suggests that her husband's suicide is not a surprise to her, thereby eliminating Hess's construction as an abject killer from her point of view. Instead, he appears as the romantic savior.

In the 2014 monologue, the multiple grammatical forms Ganja employs do not emphasize a dichotomy between how she viewed herself and how she was seen by others, as in the original film; they emphasize her sole status as victim: "My three brothers used to gang up on me. Beat me up when I was little. [. . .] I had a rough time growing up." Lee therefore reproduces Gunn's discourse on the relationship between representation and its manifestation through physical violence ("she slapped my face [. . .] Someone said they saw you being chased by a boy [. . .]" "You are a liar . . . and a slut"), but the monologue reinforces Ganja's victimization. Although the screenplay shows that she tried to move away from that status, as it shifts to more active verbs involving the I-subject ("finally, I'd had enough. I was fed up. I started throwing hands"), the empowerment is only temporary, when her brother punched her in the stomach. She is further victimized because her elder brothers looked, cheered, and did not stop her from being beaten down by her younger brother, Baby Jesus. Ganja's parents, then, take over her narrative. While the mother bitterly reminded Brother Jesus not to "ever hit a woman again, especially in her stomach," it is Ganja's father who teaches her the lesson of how "this world is a cruel, harsh place, especially for a black woman": "And you're going to have to learn to deal with the double whammy. You're gonna be a woman one day soon, and you were born black. Ganja's got to learn to take care of Ganja."

Thus, in Lee's film, Ganja's motto "to take care of Ganja" is the application of rules she was bitterly taught by men, whether by force or by reasoning. Paradoxically, while the 2014 monologue acknowledges black women's multiple oppression ("the double whammy"), it reinforces Ganja's powerless acceptance of, and accommodation to, her condition as a black woman and belittles the role of the monologue in the black female protagonist's empowerment before she commits her first murder. Because the 2014 film does not include a discourse on the abject, it constructs Ganja as just a victim. The music that accompanies her monologue further dramatizes her status as victim when she tells her story. The filmic choices in the 1973 monologue scene mark Ganja's self-subjectification and her authority over the narrative before she becomes a killer: Ganja's choices were to be interpreted throughout the film according to her motto. In spite of the fact that the 2014 monologue acknowledges "the unique positionality of black women, most specifically in the simultaneity of oppressions that aids in defining black women's identities,"[30] it fails to establish Ganja's subjectification.

The fact that *Da Sweet Blood of Jesus* visually includes Hess during Ganja's monologue also modifies his characterization. If her oppressed status as a black woman is institutional ("this world is cruel"), her rationale with Hess is built into an interpersonal relationship due to Hess's love-twisted confession. From abject in the 1973 film, Hess becomes a savior and protector. Once Ganja's monologue is over and she asks again for an explanation as to why her ex-husband's body is in his freezer, the narration cuts back to Hess at the other side of the table. This time, however, the medium shot that brought together Hess in his black shirt and the savage half-naked man on the picture behind him has disappeared. It is replaced by a shoulder shot of Hess's face, eliminating the previous visual association of Hess as a warring and savage monster. The shoulder shot prepares the rest of the scene in which Hess confesses his addiction to blood *and* his love for Ganja [64:16–67:54]. His addiction is compared with other addictions, including nicotine, which is interesting considering the way the scene builds Ganja's heavy smoking as one of her ways to deal with pain, stress, or discomfort. The couple's abjection is, here, not dissociated.

In addition, by the time the dialogue begins, shot sizes have decreased to close-ups. So while the 1973 monologue excludes Hess from Ganja's character development and rationale, the 2014 film tends to highlight both characters, Ganja as victim and Hess as romantic savior and partner. In spite of its overt intersectional construction, the 2014 monologue ends up giving more prominence to the film's male protagonist. The screenplay concludes, in effect, on Hess defining himself to Ganja: "What I am is in love with you." In the 1973 film, the monologue was followed by the cheerful couple and its wedding, echoing the cheerful moment Ganja experienced in her snowball fight; in the 2014 film, the equivalent scene is followed by one in which the couple dumps the late husband's body in the water before the couple's wedding. Ganja's acceptance of Hess's abject nature implies that she also accepts her status as victim and Hess's promise of providing her with a "sanctuary," "shield," and "shelter" [50:38] that would allow her no longer to be a victim of anyone but Hess.

It is, then, all the more interesting that Ganja's rewritten monologue intervenes in a different setting from the original film. In 1973, Ganja's face is isolated in a composition that participates in her empowering process. In Lee's film, though Ganja acknowledges that she has been conditioned by the multiple oppressions she has to deal with as a black woman, the camera angles offer a complete view of Hess's lavish dining room in his luxury estate at Martha's Vineyard, thus evoking his consumerist lifestyle. Ganja, therefore, not only accepts Hess's promise of a "sanctuary" and "shield" from victimhood; she also accepts her continuing enjoyment of the luxury house he lives in and the lifestyle he can provide her with. The following scene in which she helps Hess bury her ex-husband's dead body suggests that she has, in effect, accepted both Hess's blood-drinking nature and lifestyle. Instead of displaying a form of economic enfranchisement, it reinforces her economic, emotional, and physical dependence on Hess. Paradoxically, the 1973 Ganja's monologue justifies how the character will victoriously handle, at the end of the film, the blood-drinking condition that was imposed upon her and that she chooses to continue to live with; in the 2014 version, her monologue seems to reveal a postfeminist character's more pragmatic approach to black female victimization, even though it implies reinforcing this status, which Lee nuances through his shooting of the love scene and murder.

"If You Ladies Excuse Me . . ."/"I'll Have Some Womanly Companionship": Ganja's Homoerotic Murder

Both in *Ganja & Hess* and *Da Sweet Blood of Jesus*, the murder is preceded by a sex scene. The articulation between female monstrosity, sex, killing, and power is not uncommon. As illustrated in *Abby*, *Vamp*, and in *Queen of the Damned*, the black female character's hypersexuality is correlated with its capacity to kill. But both are temporary. The transgressive powers of sex and murder are eventually annihilated (*Abby*) or suppressed (*Vamp* and *Queen of the Damned*). Using Julia Kristeva's theory of abjection (1982), Barbara Creed theorized the representation of the monstrous-feminine, in relation to women's reproductive and mothering functions.[31] Relying on a feminist psychoanalytic approach, Creed debunked the "myth" according to which "women are terrifying because they have teeth in their vaginas and that the women must be tamed or the teeth somehow removed or softened—usually by a hero figure—before intercourse can safely take place."[32] Such myths, according to Creed, extend to the female vampire in film. In her efforts to reverse such patriarchal readings of the female vampire, Creed writes that the latter is "monstrous—and also attractive—precisely because she does threaten to undermine the formal and highly symbolic relations of men and women essential to the continuation of patriarchal society."[33] Thus, Creed, in 1993, initiated a reading whereby women's killing power in film can be celebrated rather than demonized. The few examples of the black female monstrous characters in vampire films, in *Abby*, *Vamp*, and *Queen of the Damned*, cannot, however, ultimately provide a celebratory outcome. Abby is saved and tamed when the male demonic power that has crippled her body is destroyed, so that she can eventually return to her life as a minister's wife. Although both *Vamp* and *Queen of the Dammed* first glamorize images of hypersexualized black female predators,[34] both characters (Katrina and Akashi) eventually perish, so that racial and gendered order may be restored. To that extent, both Katrina and Akashi's killing power and their death serve as a means to safeguard white male heroism. Yet, in *Ganja & Hess* and *Da Sweet Blood of Jesus*, there is no white male whose heroism requires restoration, and Ganja, as we have seen, is a monstrous figure who survives, without having to be tamed or killed to express male power.

Marlo David argued that Gunn's work ran counter to the "stereotypical, exploitative, rehashed, reiterated, copied, reproduced [. . .] visions of black female sexuality [. . .] on screen";[35] rather, it offered "complex roles featuring black women as autonomous, erotic subjects."[36] Similarly, in a 1998 documentary directed by David Kalat, *Ganja & Hess* cinematographer James Hinton denied the exploitation of the sex scene between Ganja and her lover. It was "erotic, natural and sensual" and provided a "distraction from the no power that was existing."[37] Interestingly, in *Ganja & Hess*, thanks to the rhythmic editing, music, and shot sizes, the black female character's sexual pleasure during intercourse is not dependent on the blood-sucking murder that follows. In other words, the sex scene is neither an explanation nor a logical continuation of the murder: Gunn does not need to justify Ganja's sexual pleasure cinematically. *The Huffington Post*'s cultural writer, Zeba Blay, is among the few critics who questioned what she calls "[one] big change" in Lee's *Da Sweet Blood of Jesus*, the fact that, in the original script and film, Ganja's lover was a man and that, in the 2014 film, she is Hess's ex-lover, Tangier Chancellor, a Black Irish woman. How does the change in the gender of Ganja's lover and victim affect the original film's portrayal of Ganja's sexual pleasure and killing power? Does it alter the construction of Ganja's sexual subjectification? Can it escape the male gaze of the homoerotic sex and murder scene as it turns Ganja's lover into a female character?

In both films, Ganja's second sex scene and first murder do not include Hess [G&H, 83:18; DSBOFJ, 89:13]. This is noteworthy for two reasons: first, because the lover is presented as a patriarchal treat Hess offers his wife to quench her painful thirst for blood, thus downplaying the woman's motivation to kill. In Gunn's film, Hess tells Ganja that they're "having a guest for dinner" because he thinks she needs "a little distraction." As illustrated by the script of the 2014 film ("if you ladies excuse me"), Hess leaves the two women who end up having sex in the bathroom. In both films, when Hess discovers his wife's murder, the camera frames the killing woman in high angle, incorporating Hess's body into the composition (Figure 12.2). The murder is then depicted as a childish satisfaction and further enhances Hess's position as a surrogate father. Yet an inserted close-up of Ganja's bloody mouth in the 1973 film and her screaming reaction when Hess discovers the body show her horror at killing a man, at drinking his blood, and at her newly abject condition. Her reaction further dissociates her trajectory as a killer from his: Ganja discovers her murdering power, while Hess looks for a partner to continue living with it.

Notwithstanding the change of Ganja's first victim's gender, the 2014 film modifies her reaction to the murder. The newlywed doctor invites Tangier, his ex-lover, for a drink. Tangier's introducing scene contrasts Hess's carefully

Figure 12.2 *Da Sweet Blood of Jesus* (Lee, 2014): Hess discovers Ganja feasting on his wife.

walking her down the house's stairs and Ganja walking by herself to the living room. This contrast is quite paradoxical, since, though Ganja has accepted the trade-off of living with a blood-drinking addict in a comfortable lifestyle, the rest of the film portrays her as having more agency regarding her movements. Indeed, the beginning of the sex scene is replete with shots that highlight Ganja's visual pleasure when watching Tangier in the shower. The scene's numerous looking glasses reflexively allude to its construction as a fantasy to be watched. Contrary to the sex scene between Ganja and Hess, the camera angles in the bathroom sex scene featuring Ganja and Tangier emphasize the latter's sexual pleasure more than Ganja's in either scene. Tangier repeatedly asks Ganja to choke her "harder" to increase her sexual pleasure, and complying with her lover's request, Ganja eventually chokes her to death. The 2014 Ganja does not kill her victim by draining her blood, but strangles her. In other words, she does not kill her with the power Hess bestowed upon her.

In addition, there is no insert to comment on Ganja's screaming reaction to her killing power, as there is in Gunn's film. Lee's film reverses, here, the original chronology. The 1973 film's narration established Ganja's sexual pleasure, her murdering power, and her reaction to possibly embodying Hess's abjection consecutively. In the 2014 version, however, the lengthy high-angle close-up of Ganja strangling Tangier stresses her changing facial reactions from anger to fright to the realization that she has the opportunity to kill [92:01–93:16]. In the 2014 film, then, Ganja's killing power is clearly dissociated from Hess. Her murder evinces that she is less and less dependent on him. This interpretation is confirmed by the subsequent scene. As in the original film, Hess opens the door, and he and the viewers discover Ganja's mess [93:18]. But in Lee's film, when Hess opens the door, Ganja is seen licking the blood leaking out of Tangier's cut wrist. When Hess eventually joins her, Ganja casts an emotionless look on her dead victim before looking at Hess and feeding some more. In addition, between the scene in which Hess discovers Ganja's murder and the moment when the couple disposes of Tangier's body in the woods, Lee inserts an interesting shot in the bathroom that displays the two glasses of champagne the two women were drinking before having sex, the smoking cigarette that Ganja shared with Tangier, and a red lighter that recalls Ganja's red underwear in the sex scene [93:56]. While one glass is half-full, the other is broken, displaying a stain of blood, suggesting that Ganja has broken the glass to cut Tangier's wrist, so as to lick her blood after strangling her. The shot does not include any looking glass or any sign of Hess's male presence; it thus reaffirms Ganja's sexual and murdering female pleasure expressed in Hess's luxurious bathroom. Her reaction shows that she quenches both her thirst for blood and her partner's. It is this moment of the film that aligns its narrative with Ganja, making the character's sexuality and killing power the terms of her empowerment over the narrative and over Hess's. The 2014 film thus displaces the empowering construction of the character from the monologue to its first murder. If Hess orchestrates the homoerotic encounter he expects for his wife, the brief shot reminds audiences of the homoerotic murder scene and anticipates how Ganja's murder leads her to consider life and death differently from Hess. He selfishly considers killing as a convenient and opportunistic means to satisfy his condition, exploiting others' bodies, meanwhile seeking religious salvation. Yet after the murder, Ganja realizes the falseness of Hess's love for her, refuses not to be alive, and repentantly acknowledges her murder: "I killed Tangier."

Although she complies with his promise of romantic love and shelter, she rejects his objectifying others, his abjection, and leaves him to handle it on his own. At the end of the 1973 film, Ganja watches Hess die, silently denying his invitation to die with him [104:29]. The camera therefore isolates Hess's death through the use of close-ups. The narration then reproduces a shot [104:22] of the heavy cross that was set between Ganja and Hess before he died [104:07]. This time, however, Ganja does not close her eyes at the sight of the cross but defies it and the religious and patriarchal references the cross symbolizes. Hess's death is not, however, the film's final scene. In the latter, Ganja, in close-up, stands alone at one of the windows of Hess's mansion. Within the same shot, her facial expression seems to shift from mourning to an accommodating smile [109:56]. At the end of their 1983 article on *Ganja & Hess*, Manthia Diawara and Phyllis Klotman read in Ganja's "cunning smile" her final command and liberation from her late husband, a "self-destructive artist," and from Hess, the "bourgeois patriarch." Behind the window of the commodious house that is now hers, Ganja contemplates her lover, whose blood she had sucked to death, now returned from the dead. As he runs to her, he is seen jumping over the dead body of Archie, Hess's butler, whom Ganja had obviously disposed of to quench her thirst for blood. Freed from the film's patriarch, Ganja's apparent smile shows how she takes pride in her capacity to still control her definition of herself as abject, which the dead body her lover jumps over illustrates.

The conclusion of Lee's film is markedly different: Hess's death scene does not give religion and its symbolic cross the powerful role it had in Gunn's film. Instead, attention is paid to the 2014 Ganja's fear of death and distress at losing Hess, her savior and protector,[38] revealing her own superficial love for Hess. In her motto to always "take care of Ganja," Hess is a mere means to escape her victimization as a black woman and enjoy a comfortable life. But her distress is short-lived. As in the 1973 film, Ganja's lover and first victim returns from the dead in the final scene. Ganja does not, however, smile at the end of the 2014 film; she looks straight at the camera. As Ganja and Tangier stand by the sea, the shots of the two women's faces recall Tangier's line before the bathroom scene: "People just get stuck on the blue eyes like I am on your beautiful red lips." The visual reference to this line belittles the father's reminding his daughter of having to live with her plight as a black woman, and brings to the fore the apparent power Tangier suggests she can exert with her "beautiful red lips." In the film's final close-ups, the focus on Tangier's eyes, which are still blue even though she has returned from the dead, and on Ganja's lips, reminds us that Ganja, like Tangier, will always be perceived and constructed by an outside gaze, but that they, however, can control their bodies and lives, through choices.

Conclusion

In contemporizing Bill Gunn's *Ganja & Hess*, Lee transferred Ganja's subjectification, as epitomized by her motto to always "take care of Ganja," from the original monologue to the character's love and murder scene. Although *Da Sweet Blood of Jesus* displays an intersectional reading of the character of Ganja that was denied to previous black female vampire characters, the 2014 monologue reinforces her objectification and her status as a victim. However, it is the construction of the sex and murder scene, both before and after the murder occurs, that pushes the narrative to the possibilities offered to Ganja to move beyond her status as object and victim because they are devoid of a male influence. Contrary to *She's Gotta Have it* but as in *Girl 6*, Lee suggests that the black female character whose story he develops on screen is objectified by outside forces. Yet whereas, in *Girl*

6, the black female character had to give up on her desire and move away from these forces to resist her objectification, *Da Sweet Blood of Jesus* suggests that she can accommodate her objectification to assert subjectification. In this respect, the film complies with Gill's conceptualization of postfeminist sensibility and its discussion of sexual objectification and subjectification. The film intimates that objectifying the black female character as victim is a means and subjectifying that character's killing and sexual power its end. Yet contrary to Gunn's movie, Lee's film raises ambiguity and discomfort as to the black female character's complicit participation in her own objectification, albeit temporarily.

Notes

1 Lisa Coulthard, "Killing Bill: Rethinking feminism and film violence," in Y. Tasker and D. Negra (eds), *Interrogating Postfeminism: Gender and the Politics of Popular Culture* (Durham: Duke University Press, 2007), p. 156.

2 Christine Holmlund, "A Decade of deadly dolls: Hollywood and the woman killer," in H. Birch (ed.), *Moving Targets: Women, Murder and Representation* (Berkeley and Los Angeles: University of California Press, 1994), p. 127.

3 Annette Burfoot and Susan Lord, "Introduction," in A. Burfoot and S. Lord (eds), *Killing Women: The Visual Culture of Gender and Violence* (Waterloo, ON: Wilfrid Laurier University Press, 2006), p.xiii.

4 Ibid.

5 David Roche, "Remaking horror according to the feminists or how to have your cake and eat it, too," *Représentations: la revue électronique du CEMRA, Centre d'Etudes sur les Modes de la Représentation Anglophone*, 2017 <hal-01709314>.

6 Diana Adesola Mafe, *Where No Black Woman Has Gone Before: Subversive Portrayals in Speculative Cinema* (Austin: University of Texas Press, 2018), p. 13.

7 Kinitra D. Brooks, *Searching for Sycorax: Black Women's Hauntings of Contemporary Horror* (New Brunswick, Camden, and Newark, New Jersey, and London: Rutgers University Press, 2018), p. 173.

8 For a list of black female supporting characters, see Mafe, *Where No Black Woman*, p. 24. See also Zélie Asava for an analysis of Akasha's sexuality from a queer perspective: "You're nothing to me but another . . . [white] vampire: A study of the representation of the black vampire in American mainstream cinema," in B. Brodman and J. E. Doan (eds), *Images of the Modern Vampire: The Hip and the Atavistic* (Madison, Teaneck: Farleigh Dickinson University Press, 2013), pp. 99–112.

9 Gloria Gibson, "Black women's independent cinema," in W. W. Dixon and G. A. Foster (eds), *Experimental Cinema: The Film Reader* (London

and New York: Routledge, 2002), p. 314. See also Norma Manatu, *African American Women and Sexuality in the Cinema* (Jefferson, NC and London: McFarland, 2003).

10 Linda Mizejewski, "Dressed to kill: postfeminist noir," *Cinema Journal*, 44/2, Spring 2005, p. 122.

11 Yvonne Tasker and Diane Negra, "Introduction: feminist politics and postfeminist culture," in Y. Tasker and D. Negra (eds), *Interrogating Postfeminism: Gender and the Politics of Popular Culture* (Durham: Duke University Press, 2007), pp. 1–26; Kimberly Springer, "Divas, evil black bitches and bitter black women: African American women in postfeminist and post civil rights popular culture," in *Interrogating PostFeminism*, pp. 249–76; Jess Butler, "For white girls only: postfeminism and the politics of inclusion," *Feminist Formations*, 25/1, Spring 2013, pp. 35–58.

12 Rosalind Gill, *Gender and the Media* (Cambridge and Malden, MA: Polity Press, 2007), p. 249.

13 Sarah Riley, Adrienne Evans, Sinikka Elliott, Carla Rice, and Jeanne Marecek, "A critical review of postfeminist sensibility," *Social and Personality Psychology Compass*, 11/12, December 2017.

14 Rebecca Walker, "Becoming the third wave," *Ms. Magazine*, 39 (1992).

15 Riley, Evans, Elliott, Rice, and Marecek, "A critical review," p. 3.

16 Zeba Blay, "Interview: Unpacking *Da Sweet Blood of Jesus*," *Indiewire*, February 11, 2015. See also Rich Juzwiak, "How to not make a vampire movie: A chat with Spike Lee & Zaraah Abrahams," *Defamer*, February 13, 2015.

17 Karen Hoffman, "Feminists and 'freaks': *She's Gotta Have It* and *Girl 6*," in M. T. Conard (ed.), *The Philosophy of Spike Lee* (Lexington: University Press of Kentucky, 2011), pp. 106–22. See also Teresa Wiltz, "Spike's woman problem," *The Root.com*, June 24, 2009.

18 hooks, quoted by Hoffman, "Feminists and 'freaks,'" p. 106.

19 Hoffman, "Feminists and 'freaks,'" p. 116; Jason P. Vest, *Spike Lee: Finding the Story and Forcing the Issue* (Santa Barbara, Denver, Oxford, England: Praeger, 2014), p. 99. More recently, in *The New York Times*, Salamishah Tillet referred to Lee's "feminist breakthrough" discussing the filmmaker's new Netflix television series based on his first film's original character, Nola Darling. In the article, the author notes the feminine—not necessarily explicitly feminist—influence the filmmaker brought to the series' script. Salamishah Tillet, "A New 'She's Gotta Have It': Spike Lee's feminist breakthrough," *The New York Times*, November 17, 2017.

20 Gibson, "Black Women's independent cinema," pp. 314 and 322. Marlo O. David, "Let it go black: Desire and the erotic subject in the films of Bill Gunn," *Black Camera*, 2/2, Spring 2011, p. 28.

21 Springer, "Divas, evil black bitches," p. 258. See also Kimberly Springer, "Waiting to set it off: African American women and the sapphire fixation," in M. McCaughey and N. King (eds), *Reel Knockouts: Violent Women in Film* (Austin: University of Texas Press, 2001), pp. 172–99.

22   Robin R. Means Coleman, "The enduring woman: Race, revenge, and self-determination in *Chloe, Love is Calling You*," in N. Jones, M. Bajac-Carter and B. Batchelor, L. Boulder (eds), *Heroines of Film and Television: Portrayals in Popular Culture* (New York, Toronto and Plymouth: Rowman & Littlefield, 2014), p. 164.

23   If Sugar Hill assuredly embodies this definition of Means Coleman's Enduring Woman, Abby, Katrina, and Akashi are not the strong self-sufficient and self-sacrificing black women who fight one systemic creature to death, but *are* the sexualized monstrous creatures that are to be vanquished for racial and gender order to be restored.

24   Robin R. Means Coleman, *Horror Noire: Blacks in American Horror Films from the 1890s to Present* (London and New York: Routledge, 2011), p. 132.

25   Samantha Lindop, "It's a love story—involving vampires: The cinematic trope of the wedded bloodsucker," in D. Baker, S. Green and A. Stasiewicz-Bienkowska (eds), *Hospitality, Rape and Consent in Vampire Popular Culture, Letting the Wrong in* (Nathan, Southport, Krakow: Palgrave Macmillan, 2017), p. 173.

26   Means Coleman, *Horror Noire*, pp. 103–04.

27   Lindop, "It's love story," p. 173.

28   David Kalat, "The blood of the thing," All Day Entertainment, 1998, [44:11].

29   Manthia Diawara and Phyllis Klotman, "*Ganja and Hess*: Vampires, sex and addictions," *Jump Cut*, 35, April 1990, pp. 30–36.

30   Brooks, *Searching for Sycorax*, p. 173.

31   Barbara Creed *The Monstrous-Feminine: Film, Feminism and Psychoanalysis* (New York and London: Routledge, 1993), p. 14.

32   Ibid., p. 2.

33   Ibid., p. 61.

34   See Amanda Hobson, "Dark seductress: the hypersexualization of the female vampire," in A. Hobson and U. M. Anyiwo (eds), *Gender in the Vampire Narrative* (Rotterdam, Boston, Taipei: Sense Publishers, 2016), p. 12.

35   David, "Let it go black," p. 27.

36   Ibid.

37   Kalat, [49:23-49:28].

38   Lindop, "It a love story," p. 172.

Filmography

Ganja and Hess, directed and written by Bill Gunn, produced by Chiz Schultz, performances by Marlene Clark, Duane Jones, music by Sam Waymon, cinematography by James E. Hinton, edited by Victor Kanefsky, Kelly-Jordan Enterprises, Inc. 1973. DVD Eureka Entertainment Ltd. 2015.

Da Sweet Blood of Jesus, written by Spike Lee and Bill Gunn, directed by Spike Lee, produced by Spike Lee and Chiz Schultz, performances by Stephen Tyrone Williams, Zaraah Abrahams, Felicia Pearson, Elvis Nolasco, Naté Bova, music by Bruce Hornsby, cinematography by Daniel Patterson, edited by Randy Wilkins, 40 Acres and a Mule Filmworks/Jesus Saves Picture Show Company LLC, 2014. DVD Anchor Bay Entertainment, LLC 2015.

13

Monstrous Feminists?

Witches, Murder, and Avatars of (Post)feminism in *American Horror Story: Coven* (FX, 2013–14)

Mikaël Toulza

Each season of the horror anthology series *American Horror Story* (FX, 2011–) has presented audiences with strong female characters. In season 2, *Asylum* (2012–13), two women, Sister Jude (Jessica Lange) and later Sister Mary-Eunice (Lily Rabe), are in charge of Briarcliff under the authority of Monsignor Timothy Howard (Joseph Fiennes). In season 5, *Hotel* (2015), Hotel Cortez is run by the Countess (Lady Gaga), a wealthy, hypersexualized, murderous vampire feared by her employees. More recently, the seventh season, *Cult* (2017) stars Sarah Paulson as Abby Mayfair-Richards, a woman who, after being psychologically tortured, embraces radical feminism and strikes back at cult leader Kai Anderson (Evan Peters). *American Horror Story* has thus often portrayed strong women who vie for power with men. Yet season 3, *Coven* (2013–14), because it focuses on matriarchal orders at odds, stands out as a concerted effort to bring together and coordinate a plethora of notions and variations on feminism and postfeminism. Starring Jessica Lange (as Fiona Goode), Angela Bassett (as Marie Laveau), and Sarah Paulson (as Cordelia Foxx), the season is set in contemporary New Orleans and revolves around a coven of witches who settled in Miss Robichaux's Academy in New Orleans when the facility was purchased by its founder, Marianne Wharton, in the 1860s. From the very first episode, *Coven* draws attention to its feminist subtext with the explicit reference to the suffragette Marianne Wharton. This chapter thus proposes to explore the legacy of this early form of feminism within the coven and the kind of feminism that Wharton's heirs incarnate.

As Carol Clover and Barbara Creed, among others, have shown, gender is central to the horror genre. *Coven* anchors its horror in American history, more precisely that of the Deep South, feminism, and racism. The season tackles feminism through the parallel established between slavery in the Southern states and the rivalry between contemporary white witches and black voodoo practitioners, generally separated along racial lines, as Stacey Abbot remarks.[1] Racial stakes are thus intermeshed with the feminist/ postfeminist conflicts in *Coven*. In the second episode, the racial divide is emphasized by Marie Laveau's reproach to Fiona Goode: "Your manicure cost more than my rent. Woman like you wipes her ass with diamonds" [S03E02, 28:21–28:31]. This line contrasts Fiona's use of her wealth to reinforce her feminine characteristics—her whiteness is associated with diamonds and expensive manicure—while Marie describes herself as a hard-working woman who does not own half of Fiona's belongings. Marie's retort underlines the rigid separation between two groups of women, witches and voodoo practitioners, on racial grounds, whites and blacks, but also ties it to the question of social classes as Fiona is far wealthier than Marie. This divide between women is made even more explicit as the series presents them vying for power over their distinct territories within New Orleans. Their struggle highlights the opposition between two tyrannical matriarchies—witches and voodoo practitioners—and eventually contrasts them with different patriarchal structures on various levels—the fraternity boys, the Delphi Trust, and society in general. If showrunners Ryan Murphy and Brad Falchuk and their team seem to have taken feminist and film theories into account for this season in particular, it remains to be seen to what extent the series contributes to the current debates opposing feminism and postfeminism.

Sarah Gamble explains that the definition of postfeminism and its application are disputed by different trends in feminism. Scholars argue as to whether the "post-" in "postfeminism" signifies a break from earlier waves of feminism, as the prefix could either mean that the time for feminism is over or point to an improvement that would push the boundaries of feminism even further.[2] On the one hand, some seek to destabilize the definition of gender and deconstruct authoritative paradigms and practices through a reassessment of the distinction between masculine and feminine;[3] in this sense, female agency can only be strengthened as opposed to standards of masculinity. On the other hand, other feminists would, according to Gamble, rather support an individualistic and liberal agenda than a collective or a political one.[4] Thus understood, postfeminism can be envisaged as a stepping-stone for different movements such as intersectional feminism, which focuses on individual experiences of oppression, particularly in terms of gender, race, social classes, and sexuality. Sarah Projansky dwells on the arguments exposed by Gamble and adds that "most versions of postfeminism can function as either a condemnation or a celebration of women and feminism."[5] Postfeminism is thus an umbrella term that encompasses discourses appealing to a great variety of people. Gamble also insists on the fact that postfeminism is not a clear movement, but rather a "market-led phenomenon," which has "maintained its cultural presence"[6] since the 1980s; she writes that postfeminist representations of women's success stories tend to "lead to the conclusion that the time for feminism is past."[7]

The battle between different forms of feminism is fairly obvious in *Coven*: all the female characters appear to embody different facets of feminism, with the various discourses circulating within the show highlighting each other's limits and loopholes. The figure that serves to unite these stakes is an archetype that has expressed patriarchal fears throughout history: the witch. Creed believes that "there is one incontestably monstrous role in the horror film that belongs to woman—that of the witch."[8] Creed describes her as "a familiar female monster; she is invariably represented as an old, ugly crone who is capable of monstrous acts."[9] Although these stereotypes may apply to a host of movies, the figure of the witch is more varied in *Coven*, in keeping with its multiprotagonist narrative. Indeed, none of the characters can be described as ugly. Nor does the adjective "old" apply to most of the characters. Even though age and mortality are at the core of the season, there are only three middle-aged witches: Fiona Goode, Marie Laveau, and Myrtle Snow (Frances Conroy). All the other witches are young, thus foregrounding the centrality of the generation gap in the narrative. All the witches are, however, "capable of monstrous acts," and all of them, with the exception of Cordelia (Sarah Paulson), are women who kill. The archetype of the witch thus seems to be partly reinvented in *Coven*, in the sense that the series breaks away from past stereotypes. Kyle Ethridge argues that "the show features a group of witches who create a new representation of witches in popular culture."[10] I believe that this assertion should be qualified. Indeed, as Creed also argues, in the horror genre, "the representation of the witch continues to foreground her sexual nature. She is usually depicted as a monstrous figure with supernatural powers and a desire for evil."[11] *Coven* does not appear to be fundamentally innovative in its representation of witches. Rather, it adjusts the said representation to our times through a diversification of witchy personalities and experiences that echoes current feminist debates. In other words, the series adds a layer of complexity to the archetypal representation of the witch, which both influences and is influenced by different avatars of feminism. The witch remains, in *Coven*, a figure of power that menaces the patriarchal order. In Creed's words,

An abject figure in that she is represented within patriarchal discourses as an implacable enemy of the symbolic order. She is thought to be dangerous and wily, capable of drawing on her evil powers to wreak destruction on the community. The witch sets out to unsettle boundaries between the rational and irrational, symbolic and imaginary.[12]

Seduction, Sexualization, and the *Femme Fatale*

In *Coven*, the witches' desire for evil often emerges through sexuality. Madison's (Emma Roberts) characterization, for instance, is that of the archetypal seductress: she is beautiful, manipulative, and hypersexualized. Because she is the one who introduces Zoe (Taissa Farmiga) to new sexual discoveries, as suggested by the threesome scene between both women and Kyle [S03E07, 42:37–43:26], Madison is presented as a mistress of sex who is uninhibited and seeks her own sexual satisfaction above all. The sexualization of the character is emphasized by her clothing and physical appearance: she is heavily fetishized when she is shown in tight, short dresses revealing both her silhouette and her cleavage, especially when she is on the prowl for men. For Rosalind Gill, postfeminist media culture focuses on women who use their bodies and sex appeal to gain power, all the while conforming to traditional norms of female beauty;[13] power thus stems from sexualization and fetishization. It is in this sense that Madison can be considered an avatar of postfeminism. During the fraternity party, the young witch wears a tight-fitting white dress, and the use of a fisheye lens, combined with a POV shot that aligns the viewers with the fraternity boys, gives the impression that she is the erotic center of attention, more precisely of male attention within and possibly without the diegesis [S03E01, 29:42]. Given that the series is set in New Orleans and refers to Francophone culture, the use of the fisheye lens may also act as a playful reminder that Madison is a witch, as it reproduces the effect of an eccentric mirror, which, in French, is called "un miroir de sorcière." Madison is fetishized both for the viewer and for the men at the party, who even describe her as "prize tuna" [S03E01, 29:48–29:50]. The portrayal of Madison thus seems to literalize Laura Mulvey's famous thesis on visual pleasure and narrative cinema by relating male pleasure to fetishization and sexualization (in this case, rape).

Madison fully embraces traditional femininity and exploits it for her own empowerment. The fact that it backfires, however, can be seen as echoing the social debates between conservatives and liberals on whether or not a woman "asks for it" when she decides to wear such outfits. But the narrative almost immediately allows Madison to fight back and kill the men who have assaulted her [S03E01, 35:40–36:13]. In doing so, Madison's arc summons up the rape-revenge narrative, which should come as no surprise in an anthology series that reprises classic horror subgenres and plotlines. Clover states that "representations of sexual violence at their core offer a rich source of investigation for feminism"[14] because rape narratives are tied to issues of gender identity. She further notes that "femaleness allowed the 'body' story to be told with far greater relish, and [the female protagonist's] feminist rage pumped new energy into the 'social' story."[15] As in *I Spit on Your Grave* (Meir Zarchi, 1978), the rapists think the victim is nothing more than a "slut" who is asking for it. Thus placed in the first episode, the rape scene [S03E01, 33:25–34:23] and its consequences [S03E01, 35:43–36:10] have three functions. First, they punish the heterosexual male gaze for fantasizing about Madison. Second, they point to the flaw in Madison's brand of postfeminism. And third, Madison is made more sympathetic to the viewer (she is subsequently shown crying in the shower) [S03E01, 45:38–45:43]. Madison's feminine rage leads her to use her telekinetic abilities, in what seems to be a reference to *Carrie* (Brian de Palma, 1976), to flip a bus full of frat boys, even though some of her victims did not take part in the gang rape. Yet unlike Carrie, Madison uses her powers not only to exact revenge on those who have physically assaulted her, but also on those who prevent her from getting what she wants. She responds to Luke Ramsey's mother's rejecting her by setting the curtains of her house on fire [S03E03, 19:22–19:30] and kills a stage director she disagreed with [S03E01, 23:15–23:31]. So not only does Madison fit within postfeminist theories arguing that a woman's body may be a source of power to reassert her agency,[16] but she is also the archetypal witch seductress embedded in a circle of sex and violence. As such, she embodies the iconic "postfeminist babe," which Justine Picardie describes as a "pre-feminist excuse for titillating the viewer with a great deal of cleavage."[17] The postfeminist babe is thus a darker, more explosive version of postfeminism, that of a heavily sexualized woman who uses her body and sexuality to undermine patriarchy, which Madison does by fighting against rape culture.

Madison is presented as being the direct descendant, if not the reincarnation, of the Supreme, Fiona Goode. The episode in which Fiona kills Madison [S03E03, 50:00–50:22] suggests that the young witch is about to become the next Supreme through parallels between young Fiona shown in flashbacks and present-day Madison, a connection made even more obvious by the crosscutting that juxtaposes their striking resemblance [S03E03, 43:38–43:48]. That said, Madison and young Fiona are also very different. While Madison's eccentric sexuality is used as an instrument of violence, young Fiona embraces the characteristics of the *femme fatale* of *film noir*, thus widening the generation gap. "A standard figure (even a cliché) in popular culture, [. . .] sexually voracious, irresistible, and dangerous, leading men to their ruination,"[18] the *femme fatale* is a strong, independent woman who uses her charms and sexuality to control and dominate men, usually with an economic motive. This is exactly how young Fiona appears, as she uses her charms to make men do what she wants them to, and it seems to be what the older Fiona misses, at least until she reclaims her *femme fatale* characteristics and takes advantage of a ghost, the Axeman (Danny Huston), significantly, a character who, like her, belongs to the past. Like many *femmes fatales*,[19] Fiona is mostly seen wearing black clothes, and her body is shot in close-ups when she attempts to seduce a man; for instance, when the Axeman tells her that he's been watching over her her whole life, young Fiona is shown undressing and the camera focuses first on her legs and buttocks in close-up, before revealing her cleavage in medium close-up [S03E07, 30:07–30:33].

Coven provocatively turns a *femme fatale* whose story dates back to the 1960s into an avatar of second-wave feminism, a contradiction in terms. This movement was, according to Gamble, "an offspring of the civil rights and anti-war movements in which women began to band together to contest against discrimination. Yet, [it] was criticised for not being inclusive enough, with differences emerging between black feminism, lesbian feminism, liberal feminism and socialist feminism."[20] Second-wave feminism was later seen as a brand of feminism destined for white, middle-class, heterosexual women only. Fiona Goode definitely fits the bill. She is, however, not really a feminist, but embodies, rather, the male fantasy of the *femme fatale* that expresses anxiety, that is to say, the New Woman of the 1920s–1940s who, because of her "demand for access to higher education, the vote and the right to earn a decent living, her challenge to accepted views of femininity and female sexuality, [. . .] was the focus of much media debate and of intense anxiety as well as hope in the decades spanning the end of the nineteenth and start of the twentieth century."[21] The series thus suggests that Madison's dark version of the "postfeminist babe" is the direct descendant of the negative version of the second-wave feminist, reframed as a *femme fatale*. By having Fiona murder Madison, the series seems to allegorize the conflict between two generations, two genres (rape-revenge and noir), and perhaps, two modes of feminism. However, it ultimately proves that Fiona was never a second-wave feminist in the first place, but, rather, a postfeminist babe thirsting for beauty and power *avant l'heure*. The generation gap between Fiona and Madison raises the question as to whether the immortal witch's identity really evolves with the politics of her times.

Racial Tensions within Feminism

The tensions between second-wave and black feminism are recast in the 2010s through the fight between Fiona and Marie Laveau. Marie is a black hairdresser living in a less privileged neighborhood, who competes with

Fiona. As Fiona stands for a perverse version of second-wave feminism, Marie similarly embodies a perverse version of African American feminism. Born from the marginalization of black women within the feminist movement, black feminism was at loggerheads with second-wave feminism.[22] This battle between older waves of feminism takes center stage in the first part of the season. In the second episode, Fiona visits Marie's salon in order to ask her for her secret to eternal youth and beauty (Figure 13.1). During this sequence, the narration intensifies Marie and Fiona's head-to-head confrontation by showing them both in low-angle close-ups and by panning from one character to the other, evoking the balance of power between them [S03E02, 28:12–31:32].

Like Fiona, Marie has an heir: Queenie (Gabourey Sidibe). Because of her skin color, Queenie does not feel comfortable in Miss Robichaux's Academy and eventually joins Marie Laveau's voodoo practitioners as she believes this is where she belongs. Queenie repeatedly defines herself as a human voodoo doll, as her powers allow her to transfer self-inflicted wounds to others, thus suggesting that she is both a human being and an object. What is interesting, here, is that Queenie objectifies her own body where others would not, as she, as an overweight black woman, does not fit in the traditional tropes of white beauty dictated by the social (and primarily patriarchal) order.[23] This objectification is both a power, as she clearly uses it to dominate others, and a curse, as she was born this way and cannot escape it. Queenie's power turns objectification, a traditionally patriarchal strategy to exploit women, into an asset and a means of agency. In other words, Queenie transforms

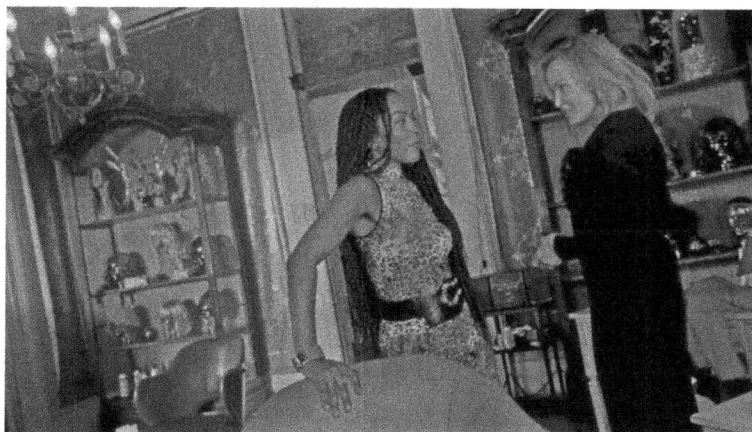

Figure 13.1 *American Horror Story: Coven* (FX, 2013): Marie Laveau and Fiona Goode face off.

this socially constructed objectification into subjectification, so as to become a subject of her own. Her body blurs the boundaries between the normal and the traditional depiction of the abject, as both fat and monstrous bodies are nonnormative in contemporary American culture where beauty is mostly defined in terms of whiteness and white norms. Queenie's fatness is highlighted both in Sidibe's physical appearance and in the character's development throughout the season. Indeed, Queenie's sexual otherness is correlated with her relationship to food, which she frequently makes references to, especially when she threatens Madison with a "Bitch, I will eat you" [S03E02, 7:20], endowing her with an ogre-like trait. Like Marie and Fiona, Queenie and Madison dislike each other (Figure 13.2). However, unlike their older counterparts, the young witches' arguments do not rest solely on power but also on sexuality. Queenie's dangerousness lays in her envy, in the fact that she is not as attractive as Madison, which she regrets as she is still a virgin [S03E02, 7:08–7:18]. Hence, Queenie's form of feminism focuses more on her individual experience than on a collective one, and her recurrent confrontations with Madison suggest that they both embody different facets of postfeminism. Queenie is, indeed, an avatar of postfeminism, that of the woman who pushes the boundaries of her own individualism and focuses on and uses her own body as a source of power. As a lower-class black woman who offers a different perspective on the fat body, she is not shown as lacking agency anymore, but rather as an agent of her destiny, making her own decisions. By emphasizing the opposition

Figure 13.2 *American Horror Story: Coven* (FX, 2013): Madison and Queenie at odds.

between Queenie and Madison, *Coven's* subtext invites a more intersectional view anchored in a postfeminist discourse.

The confrontation between Marie and Fiona appears to be fickle and outdated, as similarities present in the dialogues suggest their powers both come from Tituba, a slave girl who fled from Africa and is believed to be the first witch of Salem [S03E02, 29:01–29:15]. In history, Tituba was a Native American who was the first person to be accused of witchcraft during the 1692 Salem witch trials.[24] *Coven's* protagonists' powers thus derive from yet another figure of otherness. As Tituba was neither black nor white, this common bloodline suggests that the racial opposition at the core of the season is not justified biologically; rather, it is a social construct that the witches invoke to justify their oppositions. However, even though Marie has been alive since the eighteenth century, it appears that her own identity politics have not changed and that she still focuses on the negative aspects of her separation from other women, namely race, rather than on the common points that could bring them together, which is what is suggested at the end of the season when a plethora of witches from different backgrounds unite [S03E13, 27:12–27:30]. The same goes for Fiona, who first reinforces racial stereotypes rather than debunking them, and is thus a mouthpiece for racist rhetoric and racial stereotyping. Moreover, the narration presents Fiona and Marie as equals by regularly framing them in a similar way, while the narrative emphasizes the grotesque clashes between their heirs. In the first episode, during Zoe's first dinner at Miss Robichaux's Academy, Queenie and Madison get into an argument after Madison explains how she killed her stage director. During this sequence, they are sitting as far away from each other as possible, the staging thus highlighting the racial, social but also moral distance that separates them [S03E01, 21:58–24:10]. Perhaps the most interesting element of Queenie and Madison's first confrontation is the words they use to insult each other. Queenie attacks Madison, who prides herself on her career and fame, telling her to "do the world a favor and take an acting class you D-list, Botox bimbo" [S03E01, 23:35]. Later on, when Queenie states that she is "not hungry anyway" and leaves the table to end the confrontation, Madison replies: "Like anyone believes that" [S03E01, 24:04]. Hence, both Queenie and Madison know each other's weak points and do not hesitate, just like Marie and Fiona, to exploit them during their grotesque confrontations. This ultimately suggests that the forms of feminism Marie and Fiona come to incarnate are not about to vanish and give birth to a new generation of witches and feminists—all the more so as the two old witches eventually team up to murder Nan (Jamie Brewer) in a scene showing them uniting forces to drown her in a bathtub, as the camera simultaneously shows both their faces in low-angle close-ups and their hands pushing Nan's

body in a joint effort [S03E10, 41:50–42:04]. Hence, in this case, murder is
a paradoxical act that both destroys a life and reasserts female agency, as it
allows for the union not only of two kinds of witches, but also of two kinds
of feminism that were historically at odds. This evolution is highlighted
through the characters' arcs. Indeed, both Marie and Fiona eventually team
up because they are attacked by a patriarchal institution: the witch hunters
of Delphi Trust. Thus, it is by confronting a common enemy that these older
facets of feminism can come together, although they never lose sight of their
differences. Marie and Fiona's strains of feminism are shown as outdated and
unable to evolve, as they all end up dying,[25] leaving room for a new generation
of feminist witches.

The *Vagina Dentata* and the Undermining of Patriarchy

For Creed, the monstrous-feminine is constructed as a figure of abjection
through her association with blood.[26] In *Coven*, not only are the murders
perpetrated by the bloodiest witches, but it is the witches' empowerment
that causes the bleeding. This association with blood is particularly
conspicuous with the character of Zoe, a name that means "life" in Greek.
Her first appearance shows her kissing her boyfriend and about to have
sexual intercourse for the first time [S03E01, 6:00–7:08]. As her boyfriend
penetrates her, his eyes and nose start bleeding, and he convulses and dies.
It is later explained that her vagina is the source of her boyfriend's death.
Like the movies *Teeth* (Mitchell Lichtenstein, 2007) and *Jennifer's Body*
(Karyn Kusama, 2009), the series reprises the figure of the *vagina dentata*,
which Creed identified as one of the avatars of the monstrous-feminine,[27] in
order to invert and criticize the traditional horror narrative in which female
victims are passive and incapable of defending themselves. This scene is to
be paralleled with the final one of the same episode, in which Zoe has sex
with the man who assaulted Madison while he is in a coma, killing him by
castration [S03E01, 45:59–46:39]. Zoe, quite ironically given her name, has
now become the avenging perpetrator of violence and uses her ability to
punish the man for the kind of monstrous sexuality he imposed on Madison.
Both scenes provide extreme close-ups of the victims' bleeding eyes and
mouths, which actually makes these orifices look like bleeding vaginas, thus
turning these male characters into the "bleeding wound" Mulvey's Freudian
framework identified with female genitalia.

 The idea of gaining power through sexuality is often praised as being a
postfeminist strategy to reverse patriarchal norms.[28] Because Zoe finds out
she is a witch when she loses her virginity and then uses her sexuality as

a weapon, she can be seen as a postfeminist heroine. What is more, after she kills Spalding (Denis O'Hare), Zoe takes a shower during which a close-up focuses on her victim's blood dripping between her feet [S03E07, 41:04–41:20]. Like Carrie to which this scene alludes, "her blood," in Creed's words, "is both powerful and magical,"[29] and Zoe's powers increase after this scene. Murder allows, yet again, a subversion of the boundaries of femininity. Although washing away the blood seems to be an attempt to separate Zoe from the abject nature of the crime she committed, she nonetheless embraces her change of personality and becomes the postfeminist woman she was supposed to be. Symbolically, then, the blood of her victim becomes a second first menstruation, and the image is thereby reframed as the cultural, rather than biological, moment when the girl becomes a powerful woman, which is generally believed to be the moment when a girl culturally becomes a woman—or, in the series' generic terms, a witch.

As abject witches, the protagonists of *Coven* are categorized as monstrous beings that threaten the established orders, whether that of patriarchy in the greater world or of their own matriarchal microcosms. The patriarchal order in *Coven* is, from the outset, presented as threatening and thus calling for retaliation. The forms of patriarchy encountered tend to be fickle: the fraternity boys who get punished for their behavior, and their more mature and more global version, the capitalist patriarchy represented by Mr. Renard and his associates from the Delphi Trust. These men are behind Hank's assault of Marie Laveau's hairdresser salon, both a literal and symbolic attack on black femininity. Fiona and Marie's reprisals lead them to use voodoo to toy with the men and eventually kill them [S03E11, 36:23–38:38], literalizing the witch's assault on the patriarchal symbolic order.[30] But the final and most insidious embodiment of patriarchal order is that of society in general, which forces the witches to seek refuge in Miss Robichaux's Academy in the first place. It is undermined in the season finale when Cordelia displays the Academy's strong feminine power on television, thus refusing to hide from society and calling it into question instead [S03E13, 27:58–29:21]. Cordelia's final undermining of patriarchy on a more global level is only possible after the collapse of the matriarchal orders at war for the most part of the season; this alludes to the unification of different kinds of witches and women. Instead of directly focusing on an established patriarchal order, *Coven* indeed revolves around three tyrannical matriarchies: Fiona's, Marie's, and Delphine Lalaurie's. Within the Academy, Fiona Goode is the Supreme, at the head of the coven, Cordelia Foxx is the headmistress, and only "exceptional young ladies" [S03E01, 12:40–12:55] live in the mansion. Even the council, the entity that has the power to regulate the academy's activities, is composed of witches, with the exception of warlock Quentin Fleming, who only appears twice and ends up murdered by Myrtle Snow, another member of the council. The fact that Quentin never uses his powers on screen can be understood as reflecting his sexual otherness, confirming Creed's contention that "a rigid separation of sexes is enforced through rituals";[31] it also stresses the fact that men are not welcome within the Academy. Thus, the separation of sexes through rituals undermines heterosexual patriarchy, while placing the murderous witches at the core of a matriarchal order.

Overcoming Postfeminist Individualism

The murders the group of young witches commit are all motivated by revenge. Madison and Zoe seek payback from the men who raped Madison [S03E01, 46:01–46:30], Nan uses her telekinetic powers to make Luke's murderous mother drink bleach and die [S03E10, 30:55–31:12], Misty resuscitates dead crocodiles that kill the men who hunted them [S03E02, 1:45–2:05], and Queenie justifies her murder of the homeless man by stating that he had raped little girls [S03E08, 2:08–2:28]. The young witches thus correspond to another one of Creed's avatars of the monstrous-feminine: the *femme castratrice*. Creed describes the figure as a woman who "seeks revenge on society, particularly the heterosexual nuclear family; because of her lack, her symbolic castration [. . .] she] takes revenge because either she— or a friend—has been raped and/or murdered by a single man or a group of men."[32] In *Coven*, though, the *femme castratrice* is a facet of each one of the heroines, which goes against the question raised by Creed, "why is the *femme castratrice* [. . .] almost always represented as fulfilling a stereotypical image of female beauty?"[33] Queenie, Madison, and Fiona are the only three witches to be concerned with their physical appearances and attractiveness. The concern with beauty and power is, therefore, typical of the witches who are avatars of infertile forms of feminism. This tends to suggest that *Coven*'s subtext is critical of the brand of postfeminism that insists on individual success, which it views as the modern equivalent of the greedy *femme fatale*.

Given the discussion that this chapter has provided on the different avatars of feminism embodied by the witches, the trope of the monstrous-feminine, more precisely through the figure of the witch, is well adapted to contemporary scholarly debates taking into account the multiplicity of experiences of oppression endured by women. Hence, even though *Coven* does not really innovate in its representation of the witch, it subverts the identity that is usually associated with both the witch and the *femme castratrice*, and adds another layer of complexity to these archetypes, which eventually come together and lead the characters to the potentially utopian ending of the season, based on the Academy's rebirth and new headmistress: Cordelia Foxx.

It should be noted that Cordelia is the only witch who cannot be considered a *femme castratrice*, because she never commits murder, though she is tempted [S03E07, 14:03–16:39]. Just like the character in Shakespeare's *King Lear* that inspired her name, Cordelia is a caring motherly figure with boundless goodness. Throughout the season, Fiona abuses her authority over Cordelia when she reminds her that she is not the Supreme [S03E01, 27:50], slaps her in the face [S03E10, 7:15], or does not allow her to participate in the final fight against the Delphi Trust [S03E10, 7:22–8:15]. At the end of the season, the balance in the matriarchal structure ruled by Fiona is threatened, and the roles are reversed. Cordelia becomes the powerful matriarch, and Fiona begs for forgiveness before she dies [S03E13, 37:09–42:36]. Fiona's logical heir, Madison, with her recurring disobliging remarks, is also regularly disrespectful to Cordelia. And Marie Laveau equally mistreats her. In the second episode, Cordelia asks the voodoo priestess for a fertility potion; at first, Marie makes Cordelia believe she will help her, but she changes her mind because of the feud that opposes her to Fiona [S03E03, 28:10–32:29]. Finally, Queenie, when she comes back to the coven after Marie Laveau's group of voodoo practitioners has been decimated, blatantly accuses Cordelia of not having done enough for her to find her place in the coven [S03E11, 22:20–24:10]. The fact that Cordelia is either criticized or mistreated by all the other characters seems to suggest that the strain of feminism she embodies is at odds with theirs. Although we are provided with different avatars of feminism in *Coven*, all but Cordelia are unfit to rule because, in the end, they are all perverse versions of feminism driven by personal greed, that is, descendants of the *femme fatale*. Instead, it is Cordelia's benevolent and integrating feminism that comes to prominence at the end of the series when she becomes the Supreme, significantly after she has resisted the temptation of murder [S03E07, 39:57–42:06]. Her experiences with other characters force her to renew her approach, adopt a more altruistic outlook, and care more about the collective than about the individual. In a sense, Cordelia is the only feminist because she is the only one who privileges the witches' common good.

Cordelia's renewal is only possible thanks to Miss Robichaux's Academy itself, the witches' safe haven. The house has the power to undermine the noxious avatars of feminism, such as Fiona, Marie, and Madison. The academy is, thus, at the core of the birth of a new generation of witches. This rebirth can be considered a form of parthenogenesis, as the academy finds a way to be reborn without the assistance of men. The myth of the archaic mother underlies the narrative in a less overt manner than in *Aliens* (James Cameron, 1986)—

Creed describes the queen alien as "the point of origin and of end"[34] and adds that, even though she is only revealed in the end, "she is there in the images of birth, the representations of the primal scene, the womb-like imagery, the long winding tunnels leading to inner chambers, the row of hatching eggs, the body of the mother-ship, the voice of the life-support system, and the birth of the alien."[35] Similarly, in *Coven*, the Academy is the womb in which the witches feel safe. Yet it is also a lethal space, in which the power play between the witches leads to the deaths of some. With its large hallways leading to bedrooms and its guardian ghosts, the Axeman and Spalding, the Academy could be compared to the life-support system in *Alien* (Ridley Scott, 1979). The body of the house is always shown in expository scenes that are set inside its walls, and the Academy is ultimately at the source of Cordelia's rebirth as the Supreme [S03E13, 27:12–27:30]. It is thanks to this archaic mother that the positive sides of feminism are brought together in the end, forming a place in which all women/witches can live together in harmony under the supervision of their matriarch.

The arc of Cordelia could thus be related to Naomi Zack's theory of inclusive feminism. Although this theory could almost be deemed intersectional, it differs from intersectional feminism because the latter focuses on differences whereas inclusive feminism revolves around commonality. Zack believes that the very definition of "women" should be revised to acknowledge that "what women have in common is a relation and not a thing."[36] Her approach thus aims at balancing gender essentialism and intersectional feminism in order to lay down "a moral basis to end oppression by making liberatory efforts compelling to all women in their sameness."[37] Hence, women should be able to come together as a group, all the while acknowledging individual differences. Cordelia's invitation to young witches appears to be an application of inclusive feminism, since it underlines both their common points (their nature as witches) and their differences (in terms of race, class, sexuality, and so forth), as is underlined by the close-ups of women of different ethnic and racial backgrounds entering the Academy [S03E13, 46:17–47:04]. The young witches are building a new harmonious community in a potentially utopian ending (Figure 13.3). Indeed, *Coven* is about witches overcoming individualism to become a collective; thus, it could be interpreted as an attempt to overcome postfeminist individualism to create a new strain of collective, inclusive feminism. I use the term "potentially" when I discuss about the ending of the season because it clearly is not utopian, for the witches are back under the domination of a rich white matriarch, which could be the source of more debates in the field of intersectional feminism. This ending suggests that some form of harmony is possible between different witches, different women, and different strains of feminism. In this quasi-idyllic microcosm, all differences are accepted and women live in harmony.

Figure 13.3 *American Horror Story: Coven* (FX, 2013): Cordelia Foxx's new more inclusive Academy.

Conclusion

American Horror Story: Coven provides an example in which popular entertainment reflects debates on the crisis of feminism circulating in the media and academia. By the end of the season, this crisis is solved and a renewal of identity is possible—that of the version of feminism that comes to govern the coven. The avatars of feminism embodied by the different witches shed new light on the archetype of the monstrous-feminine witch, as discussed by Creed. Yet this archetype is not actually rewritten, but updated to contemporary standards and diversity, in the same manner as feminist discourses have been revised with emphasis on diversity in the transition from second- to third-wave feminism. What is more, the representation of empowered women overtly countering men and patriarchy hints at a subversive potential regarding the representation not only of witches, but also of women in general. In effect, the series' generic terms tend to conflate witches and women, with witches as an allegory of women. The various avatars of the monstrous-feminine models these embodiments of feminism, as their abject nature inevitably leads most of the protagonists to kill, while the different strands of feminism influence the representation of the witch by grounding it in contemporary debates on identity politics. The act of murder is paradoxically an act of creation in which the boundaries of both traditional archetypes and identity politics are rendered porous and reconfigured. This paradox is reinforced and contrasted by the moments when some of the witches are brought back to life. These resurrections, which also fit in well with the prime-time serial format and its prolonged character arcs, allow the characters to reinvent their own identities and deconstruct the old in order to create anew. The ending, indeed, leaves hope for a new strain of feminism, in which all women would fight for their rights in a more inclusive manner. Hence, this utopia both breaks away from, and continues to dwell on, its own past by remembering it and by attempting to avoid making the same mistakes. Such a utopian ending echoes the debates concerning the prefix "post-" in postfeminism that Gamble and Projansky discuss in their work. Does the use of the term put the feminist fight behind us or does it imply a new feminist politics? In the case of *Coven*, both interpretations could be valid, since the utopian ending suggests that women can eventually get rid of feminism, but only if they remember the past and unite to avoid making the same mistakes. Early forms of feminism would thus be understood as stepping-stones for current feminist battles, while an opposite reading could envisage a new way of thinking in order to reach such a utopian ideal, which means that feminism could be considered an idea of the past that does not apply to our society.

Notes

1 Stacey Abbot, "Haunted history: *American Horror Story* as Gothic tourism," in R. Janice (ed.), *Reading American Horror Story: Essays on the Television Franchise* (Jefferson, NC: McFarland, 2017), p. 38.
2 Sarah Gamble, "Postfeminism," in S. Gamble (ed.), *The Routledge Companion to Feminism and Postfeminism* (London and New York: Routledge, 2001), p. 44.
3 Ibid.
4 Ibid.
5 Sarah Projanski, *Watching Rape: Film and Television in Postfeminist Culture* (New York and London: New York University Press, 2001), p. 86.
6 Gamble, "Postfeminism," p. 43.
7 Ibid., p. 44.
8 Barbara Creed, *The Monstrous-Feminine: Film, Feminism, Psychoanalysis*, 6th ed. (London and New York: Routledge, 2007), p. 73.
9 Ibid.
10 Kyle Ethridge, "The Minotaur, the shears, and the melon baller: Queerness and self-mortification in *Coven*," in R. Janice (ed.), *Reading American Horror Story: Essays on the Television Franchise* (Jefferson, NC: McFarland, 2017), p. 85.
11 Creed, *The Monstrous Feminine*, p. 76.

12 Ibid.

13 Rosalind Gill, "Postfeminist media culture: Elements of a sensibility," *European Journal of Cultural Studies,* 10/2 (2007), p. 149.

14 Carol Clover, *Men, Women, and Chainsaws: Gender in the Modern Horror Film,* 2nd ed. (Princeton: Princeton University Press, 2015), p. 9.

15 Ibid., p. 165.

16 Gill, "Postfeminist media culture," p.150.

17 Gamble, "Postfeminism," p. 37.

18 Maysaa Husam Jaber, *Criminal Femmes Fatales in American Hardboiled Crime Fictions* (London: Palgrave Macmillan, 2016), p. 1.

19 Ibid.

20 Gamble, "Postfeminism," p. 42.

21 Ann Heilmann and Margaret Beetham, "Introduction," in A. Heilmann and M. Beetham (eds.), *New Woman Hybridities: Femininity, Feminism and International Consumer Culture 1880–1930* (London and New York: Routledge, 2004), p. 1.

22 Ibid., pp. 186–87.

23 Jennifer Scott Mobley, *Female Bodies on the American Stage: Enter Fat Actress* (New York: Palgrave Macmillan, 2014), p. 10.

24 Frances Hill, *The Salem Witch Trials Reader* (Cambridge, MA: Da Capo Press, 2009), p. 228.

25 Marie dies in episode 11, Fiona and Madison in episode 13, and Queenie remains alive for the rest of the season, but she is killed in season 5, *Hotel.*

26 Creed, *The Monstrous Feminine,* p. 11.

27 Ibid., p. 105.

28 Mari Ruti, *Feminist Film Theory and Pretty Woman* (New York and London: Bloomsbury, 2016), pp. 90–91.

29 Creed, *The Monstrous Feminine,* p. 81.

30 Ibid., p. 76.

31 Ibid.

32 Ibid., pp. 122–23.

33 Ibid., p. 128.

34 Ibid., p. 17.

35 Ibid., p. 19.

36 Naomi Zack, *Inclusive Feminism: A Third-Wave Theory of Women's Commonality* (Lanham, MD: Rowman & Littlefield, 2005), p. 2.

37 Ibid., p. 9.

Filmography

American Horror Story: Coven (season 3), written by Ryan Murphy and Brad Falchuk, directed by Alfonso Gomez-Rejon, produced by Alexis Martin Woodall, Patrick McKee, Robert M. Williams Jr., with Angela Bassett,

Gabourey Sidibe, Jamie Brewer, Sarah Paulson, Taissa Farmiga, Frances Conroy, Evan Peters, Lily Rabe, Emma Roberts, Denis O'Hare, Kathy Bates, Jessica Lange, cinematography by Christopher Baffa, Michael Goi, and Nelson Cragg, edited by Bradley Buecker, Dco Crotzer, and Adam Penn, music by Cesar Davila-Irizarry and Charlie Clouser, 20th Century Fox Television, Ryan Murphy Productions, Brad Falchuk TeleyVision, FX Network. October 9, 2013–January 29, 2014. Netflix.

14

Furies and Female Empowerment

The Sword and the Pen in *Byzantium* (Neil Jordan, 2012) and *Crimson Peak* (Guillermo del Toro, 2015)

Carolina Abello Onofre and Christophe Chambost

The tropes of the female Gothic literary tradition, such as young victims who become courageous heroines, women writers fighting patriarchal constraints to succeed, female specters revealing a horrifying past, or highly sexual women threatening male virility, remain influential in cinema of the new millennium. The term "female Gothic" was first used by Ellen Moers in 1976; she defined it as literary works written by women in the Gothic mode since the eighteenth century and argued that it aimed to express their fears and powerlessness. The typical female Gothic plot revolves around a blameless heroine threatened by a villain and imprisoned in a labyrinthine space. It might include a happy ending in which the heroine gets married, thus symbolizing her integration into patriarchal society.[1] This category aroused skepticism in the 1990s because of the insistence on gender-based interpretations that endlessly led to the private world of the family.[2] Diane Long Hoeveler has argued that this category has encouraged "victim feminism," a celebration of passivity by representing women as victims who, paradoxically, use their victimization as a means of gaining empowerment.[3] The problem with gender interpretations has been partly overcome because "female Gothic is no longer considered to be restricted to female writers."[4] As Lauren Fitzgerald contends, the theoretical tradition established by the female Gothic during the second wave of Anglo-American feminist literary criticism must be seen as a product of that historical moment; it questioned the constraints of patriarchy, and more importantly, it endeavored to recover the tradition of women as writers.[5] The critical scope of the female Gothic must now be put into the broader context of postfeminism, understood as a way of articulating changes in the evolution of feminism.[6] Postfeminism, like the female Gothic, is still linked to earlier feminism, specifically to second-wave feminism with which both have a complex relationship; it acknowledges the goals that have been met and those that have not yet been achieved, and "remains deeply embedded in a longer history of the struggle for female empowerment."[7]

As we shall see, the female murderesses of *Byzantium* (2012) and *Crimson Peak* (2015) have been shaped by revisiting and mixing literary tropes from the eighteenth-century female Gothic, the vampire novel, and the Victorian Gothic sensation novel.[8] *Byzantium* tells the story of Clara and her daughter Eleanor, two lower-class female vampires who have been hunted down for centuries by the Brotherhood, a secret society of upper-class male vampires; they fight and kill to survive. In *Crimson Peak*, Edith Cushing, a rich American girl, marries Baronet Thomas Sharpe, an English nobleman who has an incestuous relationship with his sister Lucille, a serial killer who poisons Thomas's wives to inherit their fortune. In the new millennium, the conventions of the female Gothic are by no means monolithic, and the films analyzed in this chapter play with these conventions. The heroines are not subordinate to men, and they are not chaste either, and although some secondary female characters are presented as victims, specifically the red specters in *Crimson Peak*, their function transcends passivity.

We will argue that the heroine-murderesses presented in these contemporary filmic revisitations of early and Victorian Gothic tropes subvert the literary stereotypes they were drawn from in order to convey a topical and timely vision of female empowerment. By undermining patriarchal constraints, the protagonists achieve their own agency in the unequal societies they live in. These hybrid films, which combine elements from the thriller, the horror film, and the fairy tale, can be placed squarely within the female Gothic tradition that has long given voice to the fears and desires of women, as well as to the fear of what Barbara Creed calls the "monstrous-feminine," whose function is to cross the borders of gender roles and threaten the stability of the institutions of patriarchal capitalism.[9] In her study of the construction of femininity and murderesses, *Women, Murder and Femininity*, Lizzie Seal insists on the changes implied in the consideration of women when they are perceived as murderesses: "Whereas violence is an accepted attribute of most recognized masculinities, killing by women violates norms of femininity, such as nurturance, gentleness, and social conformity."[10] The boundaries of the masculine/feminine binary are thus transgressed, producing gender trouble that echoes the issue of problematic liminality evoked through the presence of the vampires and serial killers of Gothic fiction. This chapter will first show how these two films convey the stifling Victorian frame that contributes to women's alienation, before focusing on how the female protagonists oppose those mores not only by killing symbols of patriarchy, but also by making their anger known to the world through their use of writing.

Revisiting Early and Victorian Gothic Conventions: Transitory Female Subjugation

The Victorian Gothic is often "at the service of a penetrating social critique."[11] This statement is relevant for both films in which deeply rooted patriarchal norms are questioned by strong-willed female characters.[12] With roles and social classes sharply defined by patriarchy, women who try to question man's superiority are despised. The most extreme example is in *Byzantium*, in which the Brotherhood sees itself as "the pointed nails of justice"[13] [89:52] and obeys strict codes that exclude commoners and women. These noble vampires recruit wealthy officers of the British army. The control they exert over British society can also be felt on the religious level, as their order seems to be connected to the Christian creed. Indeed, even if they assert that their gods are older than Christ, they acknowledge their involvement in the Fourth Crusade in Byzantium.

The film insists on the stability of patriarchal society by using settings that evoke Victorian iconography—one establishing shot in particular recalls the paintings of William Turner [37:08]. The stability of the patriarchal world is also pictorially reinforced in the Brotherhood's ancient, enormous, and orderly library [89:35]. Significantly, the first encounter between Clara and the vampire leaders during the Georgian Era takes place in this male temple of secret knowledge. Although the structure of the Brotherhood is shaken when Clara tries to integrate it, the misogynistic barrier that excludes her is quite solid, and it will take her more than a hundred years to overcome it. The first encounter occurs when Darvell realizes that Clara, suffering from pneumonia, has stolen the gift of eternal life intended for Ruthven, the officer who had raped and sold her to a brothel. Before arranging the meeting to introduce Clara to the elite members of the vampiric Brotherhood, Darvell warns her categorically: "There are no women amongst us" [89:28]. When this insubordinate woman disrupts the patriarchal order, the leaders remind her of their moral superiority. After being told that Clara's parentage is low and hearing from her own lips that she was a prostitute, Savella, the leader of the pointed nails of justice declares that "some things are eternal" [89:44]. This judgment, loaded with misogyny, denies her the right to be considered a respectable person. Likewise, Werner, the leader's right-hand man, says Clara is truly base and recriminates Darvell for having allowed a woman to enter their exclusive fraternity: "You ought to find a man of good blood who appreciates [. . .] what we do" [89:46]. Even if they spare her life, they warn her not to break their code and banish her from the Brotherhood.

Figure 14.1 *Byzantium* (Jordan, 2012): Clara kills a member of the Brotherhood.

Later on, when the action is set in the twenty-first century, the male order will seem to have been reinstated. After chasing Clara for a long time, Werner finally catches her, but he is badly cut. Instead of protesting when he calls her "an aberration" [9:33], Clara says she ignores what the word means and suggests curing his wounds. The scene takes place in her sordid flat, where the yellow wallpaper alludes to the locked compliant woman in Charlotte Perkins Gilman's 1892 short story. In it, the heroine tears off the wallpaper in her room in order to liberate the woman trapped behind the bars of its design. When her husband discovers what she has done, she tells him just before he faints: "I've got out at last. . . . And I've pulled off most of the paper so you can't put me back!" The oppressed heroine thinks she has liberated herself, but she has actually gone insane. Similarly, Clara's subordination is transitory indeed, for, as a wilder version of Perkins Gilman's character, she is not willing to accept male subjugation on any account; instead, she fiercely beheads the male vampire (Figure 14.1).

Patriarchal norms also transitorily prevail in *Crimson Peak*, which is not exclusively set in the Victorian era either. The film starts in the United States, with the description of Edith Cushing's life as a young American girl whose creative dynamism is blocked by the country's rules of decency. Only later, when she meets Baronet Thomas Sharpe and his sister Lucille, will the audience be introduced to the even more stilted Victorian decorum. In *Crimson Peak*, the sociohistorical context is centered on the opposition between the Old World and the New World. The industrial revolution of the Gilded Age is in full swing, while the British upper-class is in dire straits and no longer seems able to rule the country. This dichotomy also highlights the contrast between an atavistic model of antifeminism and a model of progressive female self-representation that is linked to both the female protagonist and her antagonist. Edith is initially active, full of life, and connected to the present, while Lucille is static, grim-looking, and turned toward the past. Edith, who has grown up in urban industrialized Buffalo, New York, is a wealthy self-confident aspiring novelist who, ignoring her publishers' advice, prefers writing about ghosts rather than love. Her confrontation with the cult of domesticity can be associated with the goals first-wave feminists fought for, since Edith struggles to gain a position in the public sphere. Lucille, on the contrary, has voluntarily restricted herself to the domestic sphere. Under the guise of a severe spinster and devoted sister, she encourages Thomas to marry the rich women she chooses for him in order to poison them and usurp their possessions. In this regard, she cunningly profits from coverture, the common law practice that incorporated a married woman's legal and financial identity under that of her husband. Coverture had existed in England since medieval times and lasted for decades, but the 1857 Divorce and Matrimonial Causes Act altered the law. Wives legally separated from their husbands were then entitled to the same property rights as single women.[14] The aristocratic Sharpes are conveniently stuck in the past to maintain patriarchal privileges untouched. Lucille, who controls Thomas, exerts the power to subject her younger brother's wives. When Edith marries Thomas in 1901, Lucille is not about to make an exception. Lucille promotes the legal nonentity of women under coverture during a period in which English women had already started fighting for legal independence. It is not paradoxical that Lucille, an independent single woman who is not legally nor economically subordinated to a man, holds a totally antifeminist position that defends patriarchy. Indeed, she impedes Thomas wives' independence because their freedom would threaten her own way of life. In order to keep up appearances, she is conveniently attached to a past legal system that makes women invisible and dependent.

The opposition between the two worlds is also striking visually. In the New World, camera movements are fast and mostly horizontal.[15] In the Gilded Age, wealth seems to flow and irradiate everything in the film; the light is golden, as are the clothes, and the interiors of the American mansions evoke the lavish style of American artists from that period, like James McNeill Whistler, or the popular designs and wallpapers conceived by William Morris or Edward Poynter from the "Arts and Crafts Movement." On the contrary, when the action takes place in Great Britain, darkness and melancholia suffuse the screen, and some scenes echo pre-Raphaelite portraits or evoke night landscapes by John Atkinson Grimshaw.[16] Once in Great Britain, the warm and opulent American houses are replaced by the tormented Gothic revival style of Allerdale Hall. In a film that revisits the traditional female Gothic romance, architecture is crucial to construct the narrative of the imprisoned heroine who tries to escape from the claustrophobic labyrinthine mansion. Full of bad memories, Allerdale Hall breathes and bleeds, slowly sinking in clay and rotting away (Figure 14.2). Its dilapidated central tower not only reveals the Sharpes' financial straits, but also reflects their moral decay and collapsing psyches. In spite of being captive and weakened, strong-willed Edith becomes a detective who must dig into the entrails of the house to discover the truth and try to preserve her life. Consequently, the dynamics is no longer horizontal but vertical.[17] Edith takes the elevator to go from the top of Allerdale Hall to the forbidden room, the cellar, where the clay pits contain Thomas's murdered wives. By means of this vertical movement from top to bottom, the film takes the spectator deep into the hypocritical Victorian society the mansion represents, a society with shaky structures. While above the aristocrat siblings are childishly playing with automata and having incestuous sex, the lower part of the edifice keeps their crimes hidden, and the female ghosts of their victims roam the corridors clamoring for justice.

Verticality is also linked to the steam-powered digging machine invented by Thomas. When the Baronet presents his model to Edith's father and his associates, Carter Cushing refuses to fund the project because it is only a toy created by someone who has never really worked with his own hands. Thomas's machine never gets to properly penetrate the silt in order to extract clay, thus excluding him and his sister from the benefits of the Industrial

Figure 14.2 *Crimson Peak* (Del Toro, 2015): Lucille colorfully contrasts with her environment.

Revolution. The machine's disappointing performance makes him unable to fulfill the role of good provider for his family and, therefore, symbolizes the British aristocracy's crisis of masculinity at the end of the nineteenth century. As R.W. Connell explains, "the expansion of industrial production saw the emergence of forms of masculinity organised around wage-earning capacity, mechanical skills, domestic patriarchy and combative solidarity among wage earners."[18] Baronet Sharpe is doomed to become a feminized man unable to penetrate the modern world. Patriarchy is preserved by a different kind of masculinity, represented by businessmen and entrepreneurs, thus displacing aristocrats in the socioeconomic hierarchy. This change of perception is palpable in a dialogue between Edith and the mother of Doctor Alan McMichael in Buffalo. When Alan's mother, convinced that Thomas has traveled to America to marry her daughter, is asked by an upper-class girl what a baronet is, she proudly answers: "Well, an aristocrat of some sort." Edith, epitomizing the New Woman's attitude,[19] completes the definition by saying that a baronet is someone who "feeds off land that others work for him. A parasite with a title" [5:15]. Nevertheless, she is seduced by the charms of Thomas and marries him. In England, Edith will not only witness her husband's precarious economic situation, but also his emasculation at the hands of the domineering Lucille. A feminized figure, emotionally and sexually dependent on his sister, he is reluctant to consummate the marriage. In the sex scene, when Edith loses her virginity, it is Thomas who removes his clothes, and then we see her on top of him, as a determined woman who knows what she wants [71:37]. Although he is in love with Edith, Thomas does not dare to impose his will on Lucille and abandon their deviant relationship, and when he finally does, his sister kills him. Like the characters of the Gothic sensation novel, Thomas's loss of masculinity turns him into another shadow in Allerdale Hall: a fallen man whose power and authority end up cannibalized by the mad female antagonist,[20] and whose strength is overcome by the strong-willed protagonist.

Crimson Peak provides a social account of Victorian times by picturing the aristocracy as decaying, corrupted, and death-dealing. The final transformation of Lucille into a lingering spectral presence, forever playing the piano below her mother's stern portrait [111:15], implies a kind of sterile petrifaction of the British aristocracy, whose life seems irremediably fixed in amber. The Gothic murderesses of *Byzantium* and *Crimson Peak* epitomize the fundamental debunking of Victorian codes. Some of them even use both the sword and the pen to assert women's rights. By writing in ink and blood, they liberate themselves from the stifling mores of their time. Contrary to the helpless paranoid women from Hollywood films of the 1940s,[21] these new millennium Gothic heroines are a "strange amalgamation of the hypermasculine and emphasized feminine" typical of "Hollywood's prototypical warrior woman."[22] They unleash the fury of the warrior women from the 1980s action movies. Resourceful, courageous, and tough, they are clearly superior to their male counterparts.

From Gothic Villainesses to Warrior Women

In *Byzantium*, Clara manages to extract herself from her initial role of victim. Though the end of the movie leaves little doubt that the Brotherhood will keep hunting her down, her astuteness and strength enable her to avoid patriarchal retribution for her emancipation. Like Carol Clover's Final Girl, Clara has been able to learn from her assailants and knows how to fight back.[23] Like "Hammer's cursed heroines," Clara "shapeshifts from damsel in distress to *femme fatale* in the same story, blurring the boundaries of roles."[24] Like Anna in *Hands of the Ripper* (Peter Sasdy, 1971), Clara is first an innocent child, a victim of one man's cruelty, and she will also turn into an implacable killer. What Victoria Nelson says of Gothic heroines is equally true of Clara: "the modern Gothic is rife with examples in which the heroine meets the monster, mates with the monster, and finally becomes the monster herself—but often with redeeming qualities."[25]

For a lone prostitute turned vampire, the chances of toppling a global male organization seem slim, or worse even, a pretext for men "to commit gynecide."[26] But throughout the film, the two pillars of the Brotherhood (Werner and Savella) are defeated and beheaded, and the film ends with the growing incapacitation of the ruling class. Nevertheless, there is no denying that the feminist impact of the film's conclusion could be played down, for, if we follow Raphaëlle Moine, the presence of Darvell, the understanding male vampire, at Clara's side at the end, might be interpreted as the sign of a woman's basic incapacity to stand alone. This reading would validate Lisa Coulthard's thoughts on the difficulty of considering postmodern films as "unambiguous representations of feminist empowerment."[27] For Coulthard, "the violent woman of contemporary popular action cinema does not upset but endorses the status quo,"[28] and is thus characteristic of today's "apolitical, individualistic, and capitalistic celebration of the superficial markers of power that dominate much of the popular discourse of postfeminism."[29]

Nevertheless, some elements tend to suggest that Clara has, in effect, managed to throw off the shackles of patriarchy. In the epilogue, Darvell betrays the Brotherhood by killing Savella and states his admiration for the way Clara and her daughter live their vampire lives; he explicitly begs for

Clara's pardon, before asking her if she is ready to accept his company. Thus, the tables have definitely been turned, and Clara can no longer be considered as the minion of a male vampire in the background, as was the case in *The Vampire Lovers* (Roy Ward Baker, 1970), in which Carmilla seemed to obey a dark and distant male influence.

Clara and her daughter abide by a strict code when it comes to murder: Clara wants "to kill those who prey on the weak and to curb the power of men" [90:00], while Eleanor could be seen as an angel of death euthanizing elderly people who ask her to help them die. If Eleanor sympathizes with her victims and suffers from melancholia, Clara remains, however, merciless.[30] The character of Clara is based on two clichés: the prostitute who works hard to raise her daughter, and the good mother whose protective instinct increases her strength. In this regard, Clara's stamina contradicts Moine's contention that the maternal instinct limits the powers of warrior women.[31] Although it would be tempting to compare Clara to Moine's postfeminist "babes in arms," who are sexy, self-confident, and independent women, Clara is not, however, a carefree consumer.[32] Rather, she resembles "the warrior babe" defined by Victoria Nelson as both a woman with a fighting spirit and a female monster with redeeming qualities,[33] as in *Resident Evil* (Paul W.S. Anderson, 2002) and *Underworld* (Len Wiseman, 2003). As both a descendant of Carmilla and a "tough chick freed from the constraints of traditional patriarchy, fighting in traditionally male worlds against uber-masculine foes," Clara conflates what Melissa Anyiwo has identified as two opposed figures.[34] She has, in effect, broken the code of the Brotherhood twice, because not only did she steal the power to become a vampire, but she also decided to transmit her powers to her own daughter.

Clara is not, however, fashioned solely on the template of the female vampires of literature, like Carmilla and the weird sisters in Dracula; she also has much in common with two biblical characters: Salome, the temptress, and Mary Magdalene, the prostitute. Like Salome, Clara is a dangerous seductress who uses her erotic power to get what she wants. Clara is also a prostitute, but unlike Mary Magdalene, she is not repentant. Neither constrained by the rigid Victorian norms, nor by the social rejection of prostitutes in the twenty-first century, Clara justifies both prostitution and murder. She takes advantage of her sex appeal and considers selling company and pleasure to men in the brothel she has opened to be an altruistic activity. The question as to whether Clara expresses female empowerment or justifies female regression can thus be raised. On the one hand, she destroys the misogynistic founding fathers of the Brotherhood and imposes her view on what female/male relationships should be like on Lord Darvell.[35] On the other, she recruits street prostitutes whom she treats like sexual commodities. Although she offers the girls better working conditions, she perpetuates patriarchal female oppression by behaving like a capitalistic female vampire who profits economically from sex. It is this that likens Clara to the violent heroine of contemporary popular action cinema, who Lisa Coulthard considers as a potential "symptom and product of a post-feminist cultural context that elevates postpolitical commodification and capitalistic success under the guise of progress."[36] However, Clara's tendency to assert her power is not only questioned by the Brotherhood but also and, more surprisingly, by her own daughter Eleanor, who reproaches her for not caring about her family the way a mother should: "Mothers care about the lives their children live. What kind of life is this?" [50:45]. Though younger, Eleanor is far removed from the tenets of postfeminism, and her views on womanhood are less tinged with these conspicuous signs of success.

The women of *Crimson Peak* are equally destructive and complex. Edith and Lucille, the two most powerful characters of the story, represent two opposite sides of femininity. Edith is modeled on Emily, the heroine of *The Mysteries of Udolpho* (1794), Ann Radcliffe's classic Gothic romance, because she faces perils before gaining autonomy. But contrary to Emily, Edith does not need to assert her identity as a member of society by marrying the Byronic dark seducer. The tropes of the Gothic romance are thus subverted, all the more so as the enemy is not a mysterious male figure but a well-educated lady.[37] Lucille is the archetypal Gothic villainess; she killed her mother with a meat cleaver and possibly poisoned her father. She is a frightful mix of what Gilbert and Gubar call the "Victorian angel in the house" and the "death angel."[38] Like most Victorian murderesses, Lucille uses poison to kill her brother's wives, but she transgresses the stereotype by slaying men in the most gruesome manner, destroying the faces of Mr. Cushing and her own brother by shattering their cheekbones. The gruesomeness of such scenes aims at more than just shock value. In *Evil Sisters*, Bram Dijkstra states that "prominent facial features [in males] such as high cheekbones [. . .] are a sign of a high level of testosterone," which "could indicate a social dominance."[39] This Darwinian perspective evokes Cesare Lombroso's anthropological criminology, in a day and age when phrenology was used to uphold gender and racial superiority. It is, therefore, tempting to relate Dijkstra's assertion to Lucille's deadly acts: by crushing men's faces, she aims at crushing male dominance, as she symbolically castrates those figures of power. Significantly, she stabs Thomas in the face when he is trying, at long last, to assert his will.

Following Lizzie Seal's classification of women who kill, Lucille is a mix of "the respectable woman," the "mastermind," and "the masculine woman."[40] According to Seal, the "respectable woman" embodies some features of appropriate femininity, as when Lucille makes poisoned tea;

the "mastermind" is a leading participant in a murder, a woman who "challenges the matrix of normative heterosexuality,"[41] as when Lucille orders Thomas to kill Doctor Mcmichael; and "the masculine woman" appropriates male power through her use of violence, as when Lucille uses a meat cleaver to crack open her mother's skull. Her tendency to keep a lock of her victims' hair in her drawer is another feature that links her to a long line of methodical cold-blooded psychopaths in film history. A radical change occurs, however, as Lucille starts losing control over her world. When she realizes that her little brother is no longer in her thrall, her passionate temper is unleashed, and both her face and acts betray her mounting hysteria. The castrating nature of the female serial killer is also highlighted by the echoes between her clothing and the setting. The spikes on Lucille's dress reproduce the spiked corridor in Allerdale Hall, and the association magnifies her menacing femininity. Her violent personality is also underlined by the red dress she wears at the McMichael's ball. As a lady in red, Lucille is also the embodiment of the hard lot imposed on women in the very society she, as an antifeminist, wants to perpetuate.

The irony is biting indeed: the domineering Lucille kills to preserve a system that forces her to stay in the house, sitting at the piano. But the reason for this paradox becomes clear when she tells Edith everything about her incestuous youth. For Lucille, the perpetuation of the aristocratic order is just a means to an end. What she truly desires is to remain within the cocoon she has shared with her brother for years: she is a madwoman who wants to stay in the attic and eternally experience the forbidden happy days of her childhood. With this sterile incestuous love, Lucille's attempt at maintaining Victorianism seems nipped in the bud. The energy she conveys is highly noxious and will precipitate Allerdale Hall into the red-clayed pit, just as Roderick's love for Madeline provokes the sinking of the House of Usher.

Crimson Peak is also largely indebted to Arturo Ripstein's *Profundo Carmesi* (*Deep Crimson*, 1996). Apart from the allusion in the title, the 2015 movie echoes many features of Ripstein's sordid representation of monstrous love and evil femininity, the main difference being that Ripstein chose the grotesque mode, while Del Toro opted for the Gothic romance. In both films, the murderesses transform masculine patriarchal figures into feminized dependents, while pretending to be obedient. In a sense, they use what Hoeveler calls "professional femininity,"[42] which refers to women who adopt fake docility and cunning passiveness in order to achieve their purposes. Paradoxically, they gain empowerment to subjugate other women who become an obstacle for them. In doing so, they behave in a more corrupt and oppressive way than male figures who sustain patriarchy.

The multifaceted character of Lucille is built on a gap between her masculine actions and the normative gender constructions she serves to uphold. As Seal states, "gender is never fully determining, leaving the possibility for unexpected and enabling responses."[43] This gender indeterminacy, in effect, also applies to Edith and Thomas. All three are liminal characters who perform their social and gendered roles but do not truly inhabit them. When Edith eventually manages to escape from the red womb-like cave to kill Lucille, the heroine symbolically experiences a rebirth out of the constraining Victorian society into a more modern world. In the end, she becomes the writer of a novel called *Crimson Peak*, and the cover of that book with her name on it precedes the end credits [113:23]. Toying with the conventions of the Gothic romance, the film turns its apparently frail heroine into the "New Woman," whose outspokenness was much abhorred and castigated by Victorian gender ideology (Hurley 199). Edith is the one who saves Doctor McMichael, the man who was supposed to rescue her. In fact, the fight between McMichael and Thomas Sharpe looks fake and childish, compared to the ferocity of the final fight between the two women. These distortions of the conventions of Gothic romance are tied to a general tendency of contemporary horror cinema, in which "the male characters are more ineffectual than self-sufficient heroines."[44] The statement also applies to the inefficient Noël and Frank in *Byzantium*.

Female Righters of Wrongs, Writers of Women's Rights

In *Crimson Peak*, Edith, the New Woman, manages to impose her will on both American and British societies by becoming a writer. This desire had been energetically asserted when she stabbed Lucille with her ink pen, thereby confirming the proverb: "the pen is mightier than the sword." In *Byzantium*, Eleanor writes down her story compulsively because she wants to reveal her identity, but she is trapped in a love-hate relationship with her mother, who forbids her to tell others about them. Every time Eleanor finishes writing her confession, she throws the pages to the wind or to the sea, thus renouncing the authorship of her text until she finally has her manuscript read by her teacher.

Edith and Eleanor Webb also confront authority as they want to be authoresses. Edith belies the Victorian notion that men are the only ones who possess the gift of creativity, while Eleanor opposes her mother's code of silence. At the end, Edith has her novel published and, Eleanor manages to close the chapter related to her past by healing the maternal wound, thus asserting her right to fully live her life. Both of them "attempt the pen"[45] and, in so doing, cross the boundaries dictated by authority figures.

The excessive reanimations of Gothic tropes in the cinema, as well as in other kinds of media, have been criticized by scholars like Fred Botting, who considers it as a mere commodification that no longer reveals "the dark underside of modernity but the emptiness at the heart of consumer culture."[46] Nevertheless, these contemporary recreations that play with the old traits of the female Gothic highlight current concerns such as violence against women and the awareness that improvements in female representations are minimal. While related to mainstream horror cinema, these films are activated by discourses that undermine the foundation of patriarchal society. They depict female characters who do not abandon their goals even if they oppose the "proper" functioning of patriarchy. A brief comparison of these women who kill might then conclude the present study. According to Ann Jones, "Society is afraid of both the feminist and the murderer, for each of them, in her own way, tests society's established boundaries. Not surprisingly, the interests of feminists and murderers sometimes coincide."[47] With this idea in mind, Lucille could appear as a partner in crime with Edith or Eleanor when it comes to questioning the evolution of Victorian society. The major difference, however, is that, unlike Lucille, both Edith and Eleanor are endowed with an energy that enables them and the audience to imagine a brighter world where women will truly matter. Through their acts, be it writing or killing, the two women have managed to go beyond social stasis and reach empowerment, as women and as authoresses.

Conclusion

The murderesses of *Byzantium* and *Crimson Peak* are characterized by their unfathomable nature. Both inhabit liminal zones. Lucille, as a serial killer, is in-between rationality and irrationality; in-between Bluebeard and a distorted version of the Victorian angel of the house; in-between a traumatic past (a miserable childhood) and a present in which she must maintain social appearances (she cannot give free rein to her incestuous love). Clara, as a vampire, is in-between life and death; in-between natural and supernatural; in-between the past (the Georgian Era when she was an innocent poor girl) and the present (a mother who works as a prostitute to raise her daughter). As Seal has noted, the idea of the "unfathomable" is close to that of the abject; both terms imply the same "breaching of boundaries," the same "permeability of borders," the same in-betweenness.[48] For Seal, "these liminal beings [. . .] appear to be symbolically neither fully one thing, nor another.

[. . .] They cannot be categorized," and "they can also become monsters."⁴⁹ The monstrosity conveyed by such characters is the very stimulus that invigorates these films, creating an entropic energy that clashes with the patriarchal impetus of Victorian society.

The female characters' in-betweeness brings to mind Linda Hutcheon's analysis of the paradox implied in the prefix "post-" in postmodernism. According to Hutcheon, the prefix "marks neither a simple and radical break from [the term that follows] nor a straightforward continuity with it; it is both and neither."⁵⁰ The same can be said of the "post-" of postfeminism. The characters' liminality can be connected to the instability and contradictions that arise when discussing the notion of postfeminism and the critical field called Female Gothic. Examples of these contradictions can be found in the refusal or acceptance of second-wave feminist theories, in the overlapping of the use of the terms "third-wave feminism" and "postfeminism," and also in the mutations of Female Gothic studies (feminist Gothic, lesbian Gothic, postfeminist Gothic).⁵¹ In *Byzantium* and *Crimson Peak*, liminality can also be identified in the use of plots that oppose patriarchy and female emancipation, and the in-betweenness of the female characters can be considered as a potentially subversive site. Both films rely on typical Female Gothic narrative conventions derived from early Gothic romances, such as heroine victims, malevolent male figures, and patriarchal forces of oppression. Second-wave feminist psychoanalytical interpretations of this kind of narrative have been strongly criticized by academics such as Diane Hoeveler, Stacey Gillis, and Rebecca Munford because of their tendency to universalize female victimization and because of "an ubiquitous patriarchy that seeks to dominate and suppress women."⁵²

Reimagining this traditionally Gothic narrative structure, adapting it to the cinema, and analyzing it from a postfeminist framework—and, therefore, from the assumption that we are positioned outside victim feminism—suggest that the representation of the Gothic heroine continues to evolve, although anxieties about patriarchy are still very much present. In these films, the representation of the transgressive heroines-murderesses' struggle for empowerment speaks to contemporary concerns through a dialogue with their early Gothic foremothers. Besides, each female character can be linked to a different kind of feminism: Edith represents the first wave because she wants to become a professional writer, be published and paid for her vocation; Lucille is a Victorian anti-feminist whose vocation is a twisted version of womanhood;⁵³ Clara embodies the popular understanding of postfeminism, focused on individual identity, embracing the female body, pleasure, and desire; and Eleanor's attitude could be read as a blend between first- and second-wave feminism, since she also fights for her writing vocation but criticizes the beauty-pleasure culture her mother supports. Curiously enough, Eleanor, who is the youngest of the characters, is far from being presented as a supporter of third-wave feminism and its renewed political commitment. These contemporary Female Gothic films thus confirm the persistence of time-resistant female concerns, such as family choices, mother-daughter relationships, autonomy, safety, sexual abuse, and women as a commodity of exchange. And in each film, these transgressive heroines-murderesses face and overcome these concerns one way or another so as to become empowered.

Notes

1 Anne Williams, *Art of Darkness: A Poetics of Genre* (Chicago: University of Chicago Press, 1995), p. 103.
2 Glennis Byron and David Punter, *The Gothic* (Oxford: Blackwell Publishing, 2004), p. 281.
3 Diane Long Hoeveler, *Gothic Feminism: The Professionalization of Gender from Charlotte Smith to the Brontës* (University Park: Pennsylvania State University Press, 1998), p. 9.
4 Byron and Punter, *The Gothic*, p. 280.
5 Lauren Fitzgerald, "Female Gothic and the institutionalization of Gothic studies," *Gothic Studies*, 6/1 (2004), pp. 8–18.
6 Ann Braithwaite, "The personal, the political, third-wave and postfeminisms," *Feminist Theory*, 3/3 (2002), p. 340.
7 Claire Knowles, "Sensibility gone mad: Or, Drusilla, Buffy and the (d) evolution of the heroine of sensibility," in B. A. Brabon and S. Genz (eds.), *Postfeminist Gothic: Critical Interventions in Contemporary Culture* (Houndmills Basingstoke: Palgrave Macmillan, 2007), p. 140.
8 Gothic sensation fiction, one of the most popular subgenres of Victorian Gothic, arose from the mixture of elements derived from Gothic romance and Victorian sensation novel. The former is characterized by the transgression of social and sexual taboos and the necessity of digging up something from the past in order to find a haunting truth. The latter is characterized by murders related to adultery in a bourgeois domestic setting. Transgression and the breakdown of gender roles are central to Gothic sensation narratives.
9 Barbara Creed, *The Monstrous Feminine: Film, Feminism, Psychoanalysis* (London: Routledge, 1993), p. 61.
10 Lizzie Seal, *Women, Murder, and Femininity: Gender Representations of Women Who Kill* (New York: Palgrave Macmillan, 2010), p. 1.
11 Byron and Punter, *The Gothic*, p. 30.

12 In both films, Great Britain is portrayed at different times: from the Georgian Era to the twenty-first century in _Byzantium_ and more specifically during the Victorian age in _Crimson Peak_.

13 These vampires do not have fangs but pointed thumbnails that suddenly grow when they want to perforate their victims' blood vessels.

14 Lillian Nayder, "Rebellious sepoys and bigamous wives," in M. Tromp, P. K. Gilbert, and A. Haynie (eds.), _Beyond Sensation: Mary Elizabeth Braddon in Context_ (Albany: State University of New York Press, 2000), p. 37.

15 A case in point is the early lateral tracking shot of Edith's feet that walk fast and are not hampered by the mud of the thriving streets of Buffalo, New York. Only one shot suggests the society's dynamism of the society.

16 Edith's long fair hair is a direct reminder of John Everett Millais's _The Bridesmaid_ (1851). And one might think of John Atkinson Grimshaw's _Forge Valley near Scarborough_ (1875) when Doctor McMichael's horse-drawn cart arrives at the post office, at night and in the snow.

17 The first shot of the mansion is indeed an impressive crane shot trespassing and going over the Allerdale gate, so as to reveal the imposing structure of the Xanadu-like building.

18 R. W. Connell, _Masculinities_ (Berkeley: University of California Press, 1995), p. 196.

19 The "New Woman" is a feminist ideal that flourished in the nineteenth century and that influenced the growth of feminism in the twentieth century. In the 1880s, women writers played an essential role in the popularization of this new perception of womanhood.

20 The concept of the fallen man in sensation novels from the mid- to late-Victorian period has not been as explored as the better-known Victorian fallen woman. The various nuances of the fallen man can be traced back to Braddon's _Lady Audley's Secret_ (1862), Wilkie Collins's _Basil_ (1852), Thomas Hardy's _Jude the Obscure_ (1895), and Oscar Wilde's _The Picture of Dorian Gray_ (1890), among others.

21 Helen Hanson, _Hollywood Heroines: Women in Film Noir and the Female Gothic Film_ (London: I.B. Tauris, 2007).

22 Kate Waites, "Babes in boots, Hollywood's oxymoronic warrior woman," in S. Ferriss and M. Young (eds.), _Chick Flicks, Contemporary Women at the Movies_ (New York: Routledge, 2008), p. 218.

23 Carol Clover, _Men, Women, and Chain Saws: Gender in the Modern Horror Film_ (Princeton: Princeton University Press, 1992), p. 49.

24 Victoria Nelson, "Daughters of darkness," in J. Bell (ed.), _Gothic: The Dark Heart of Film_ (London: BFI Compendium, 2013), p. 138.

25 Nelson, "Daughters of darkness," p. 141.

26 Bram Dijkstra, _Evil Sisters: The Threat of Female Sexuality in Twentieth-Century Culture_ (New York: Henry Holt and Company, 1996), p. 248.

27 Lisa Coulthard, "Killing Bill, rethinking feminism and film violence," in Y. Tasker and D. Negra (eds.), *Interrogating Postfeminism, Gender and the Politics of Popular Culture* (Durham: Duke University Press, 2007), p. 158.

28 Ibid., p.173.

29 Ibid.

30 The relationship between the dynamic Clara and the melancholic Eleanor echoes that of Lestat and Louis in Neil Jordan's *Interview with a Vampire* (1994).

31 Raphaëlle Moine, *Les femmes d'action au cinéma* (Paris: Armand Collin, 2010), p. 101.

32 Clara is miles away from the "babes in arms" of *Spring Breakers* (Harmony Korine, 2013) or *Jennifer's Body* (Karyn Kusama, 2009).

33 Nelson, "Daughters of darkness," p. 140.

34 Melissa Anyiwo, "'The female vampire in popular culture: Or what to read or watch next," in A. Hobson and M. Anyiwo (eds.), *Gender in the Vampire Narrative* (Rotterdam: Sense Publishers, 2016), p. 178.

35 At the end of the film, Clara might accept Darvell's company, and her daughter Eleanor also takes control, as she leads her lover Frank onto the path of eternal life.

36 Coulthard, "Killing Bill," p. 155.

37 *Crimson Peak* can be seen as the perversely sensational distortion of a typical Victorian Gothic romance such as *Angels and Insects* (Philip Haas, 1995). *Angels and Insects* also plays on the anagrammatic association of "insect" and "incest," but the film is less sensational and more conventional as it gives the role of the Gothic villain to the incestuous brother, not to the passive sister.

38 Sandra Gilbert, and Susan Gubar, *The Madwoman in the Attic: The Woman Writer and the Nineteenth-Century Literary Imagination* (New Haven: Yale University Press, 2000), p. 26.

39 Dijkstra, *Evil Sisters*, p. 258.

40 Seal, *Women, Murder, and Femininity*, p. 24.

41 Judith Butler, *Gender Trouble: Feminism and the Subversion of Identity* (New York: Routledge, 1999), p. 30.

42 Hoeveler, *Gothic Feminism*, p. 9.

43 Seal, *Women, Murder, and Femininity*, p. 13.

44 Brigid Cherry, *Horror (Routledge Film Guidebooks)* (New York: Routledge, 2009), p. 174.

45 Gilbert and Gubar, *The Madwoman in the Attic*, p. 30.

46 Fred Botting, "In Candygothic," in F. Botting (ed.), *The Gothic* (Cambridge: D.S. Brewer, 2001), pp. 133–34.

47 Ann Jones, *Women Who Kill* (New York: Holt, Rinehart and Winston, 1980), p. 13.

48 Seal, *Women, Murder, and Femininity*, pp. 18–19.

49 Ibid., p. 19.

50 Linda Hutcheon, *A Poetics of Postmodernism* (London: Routledge, 1988), p. 18.
51 Gina Wisker, *Contemporary Women's Gothic Fiction: Carnival, Hauntings and Vampire Kisses* (London: Palgrave Macmillan, 2016), p. 22.
52 Stacy Gillis, and Rebecca Munford, "Harvesting our strengths: Third wave feminism and women's studies," *Journal of International Women's Studies*, 4/2 (2003), pp. 1–6.
53 Victorian women were not used to choosing a vocation because womanhood, understood as labor for others, was seen as a vocation in itself. Women who were committed to writing therefore saw their vocation in conflict with the feminine ideal.

Filmography

Byzantium, directed by Neil Jordan, produced by Sam Englebardt, William D. Johnson, Elizabeth Karlsen, Alan Moloney, and Stephen Woolley, written by Moira Buffini, performances by Saoirse Ronan, Gemma Arterton, Sam Riley, Jonny Lee Miller, music by Javier Navarrete, cinematography by Sean Bobbitt, edited by Tony Lawson, Demarest Films/Lipsync Productions/Number 9 Films/Parallel Film Productions/WestEnd Films, 2012. DVD StudioCanal Limited 2013.

Crimson Peak, directed and written by Guillermo del Toro, produced by Guillermo de Toro, Callum Greene, Jon Jashni, and Thomas Tull, performances by Mia Wasikowska, Jessica Chastain, Tom Hiddleston, Charlie Hunnam, Jim Beaver, music by Fernando Velazquez, cinematography by Dan Laustsen, edited by Bernat Vilaplana, Legendary Pictures/DDY Productions, 2015. Blu-ray disk Universal Studios 2016.

15

Masculine Cultures of Technology and the Robotic Female Avenger in *Ex Machina* (Alex Garland, 2015)

Samantha Lindop

"When you make a new model, what do you do with the old one?"

"Well, I, er, download the mind. Unpack the data. Add the new routines I've been writing. To do that, you end up partially formatting, so the memories go. But the body survives. And Ava's body is a good one. So I'll do the same as I did with Kyoko."

"What did you do with Kyoko?"

"Strip out the higher functions. Then reprogram her to help around the house and be fucking awesome in bed. Though I'm thinking I might hang on to the language routines this time. It's kind of annoying not being able to talk to her." [63:37–64:20]

This extract from a conversation between the characters Caleb Smith (Domhnall Gleeson) and his employer Nathan Bateman (Oscar Isaac) about Nathan's latest prototype robot "Ava" echoes time-honored fantasies about creating a perfect artificial woman that date back to antiquity with tales like Ovid's *Pygmalion*. Following the Industrial Revolution, the notion of man crafting (what is perceived to be) an ideal woman using science and engineering became popular in fiction. E.T.A. Hoffman's *Der Sandmann* (1817) and Villiers de l'Isle-Adam's *L'Ève Future* (1886) are two illustrations of classic literature that explore this theme. The subject of male mastery over technology to produce a synthetic woman is also enduring on screen. Some more recognized examples include Fritz Lang's *Metropolis* (1927), the television series *My Living Doll* (CBS, 1964–65), Bryan Forbes's 1979 film adaptation of Ira Levin's 1972 novel *The Stepford Wives* (which was also remade in 2004 by Frank Oz), and John Hughes's *Weird Science* (1985). In recent film and television, female robots are experiencing a resurgence of popularity. Garland's *Ex Machina*, Spike Jonze's *Her* (2013), the AMC series *Humans* (2015–), which is based on the Swedish series *Real Humans* (SVT, 2012–14), and HBO's *Westworld* (2016–) all feature artificial women as significant characters. This prompts queries about why the figure is currently attracting so much interest in popular culture. However, it also provokes questions about representation. It is significant that many of these female robots are also ruthless revenge-seeking killers. Portrayals of this kind problematize fantasies about crafting the perfect woman, instead positioning the character as a source of masochistic male anxiety—both in relation to women and about technology.

Jean Baudrillard describes science fiction as an "extravagant projection of real world production."[1] In other words, science fiction is grounded in actuality, taking what is possible as inspiration to create plausible, yet currently unattainable worlds. In doing so, speculative texts operate as a means of scrutinizing and testing the complex dynamics between future innovation and society's responses to such modernizations. Science fiction is also saturated with allegory, the imaginative component of the genre, providing space with which to confront and critique broader, more immediate sociocultural issues, discourses, and ideologies. With these dynamics in mind, I will use *Ex Machina* as a case study with which to examine some of the ways that artificial women are imagined in cinema in the postfeminist era at a time when social robots and strong artificially intelligent (AI) technologies, such as deep machine learning, are becoming a reality.

Ex Machina is highly regarded not only cinematically, but also for its intellectual engagement with current theories of robotics, deep machine learning, neuroscience, and philosophy.[2] Underpinning the elemental plot structure of *Ex Machina* is a long history of stories about self-aggrandized, psychologically unhinged men who use science and new technologies to control and manipulate nature, with invariably disastrous consequences (Mary Shelley's 1818 novel *Frankenstein: Or the Modern Prometheus* is unarguably the most famous prototype for this theme). *Ex Machina* deploys these archetypal narrative conventions of the self-destructive "mad scientist" in order to present a powerful critique of masculine cultures of technology and the social assumptions about sex difference that are entrenched within them. The film destabilizes traditional tropes of artificial women in fiction by locating the two central female robot characters as calculating, rebellious, and of far superior intellect than the man who crafted them. Significantly, their transgressions are also justified, positioning *Ex Machina* as a feminist work that is in keeping with the conventions of the rape-revenge narrative, which first emerged in conjunction with second-wave feminist activism in the 1960s and 1970s.

Central to *Ex Machina* is a remarkably engineered robot named Ava (played by Alicia Vikander). Ava is built by reclusive billionaire genius/

madman Nathan Bateman, CEO of the technology company "Blue Book" (a fictional equivalent of Google). The film opens with Caleb, a young computer programmer employed by Blue Book, winning a "lottery" competition to spend a week with Nathan in his remote Alaskan estate, which doubles as a state-of-the-art research facility: a discreet, partially subterranean glass-walled structure, carved into a rock face, camouflaged by lush greenery, and surrounded by a stunning landscape dominated by glaciers and fast-flowing rivers. After signing a less than standard nondisclosure agreement, Nathan reveals that the reason Caleb is there is to be the human component in a contemporary version of the "Turing Test" [10:30], the colloquial name for an experiment devised in 1950 by computer scientist Alan Turing as a way of addressing the possibility of machine cognition. Turing's test relies on indirect communication with a hidden computer and its ability to fool a human subject into thinking they are interacting with a living person.[3] However, for Nathan, the real test is to show Caleb that Ava is a machine and then see if he feels that she has a consciousness—that aside from her obvious artificiality, she is, for all intents and purposes, human, with (seemingly) authentic emotions.

Masculine cultures of technology involve long-held ideological processes that make connections between technology and masculinity seem natural, reinforcing the myth that men are innately fascinated with, and skilled at, mechanical/technological-based pursuits, as opposed to women who are not. In societies where scientific rationality is highly valued, these associations play a powerful role in the sociopolitical construction of women as inferior. They also shape the gendered character of technology itself, since it is designed and built from a patriarchal perspective.[4] An example of this can be found with current developments in the field of social robotics and AI technology. Here, the kinds of robots that attract the vast majority of media attention are those constructed to look like hypersexualized women, as well as high-end sex dolls with integrated AI.

These retrograde portrayals of the feminine form sit at odds with other current media-based representations of women that are profeminist—a juxtaposition that is indicative of postfeminist media culture more broadly. Over the last three decades, feminist scholars have utilized the term postfeminism as a critical analytical framework with which to understand the way women are constructed as subjects in contemporary patriarchal society. While the term postfeminism is complex and loaded with contradictions, most academic thinkers concede that the underlying agenda of dominant postfeminist discourse is a desire to restabilize gender power structures that have been disrupted by the political, economic, and legislative gains of earlier feminist movements.[5] Therefore, postfeminism can be considered a response to feminism: it acknowledges feminism but has an ambivalent, depoliticized attitude toward it.[6] Consequently, what commonly occurs in popular culture is that elements of feminism are simultaneously taken into account and repudiated. This, in turn, promotes the false notion that feminism has been achieved, the implication being that feminist politics are no longer needed. Borrowing from the work of Judith Butler,[7] Angela McRobbie describes this practice as "double entanglement."[8] Problematically, the depoliticization of feminism and the assumption that it is a done deal open up space for retrograde discourses and ideologies to rematerialize and proliferate—a process that Imelda Whelehan describes as "retro-sexism."[9] This chapter draws on critical feminist debates about gender representation in the media and feminist theories of technology, including the work of Donna Haraway and Judy Wajcman, as a theoretical framework with which to analyze *Ex Machina*. To begin, the chapter will explore the ways that masculine cultures of technology shape the trajectory of scientific innovation and the critical debates that have emerged in response to this phenomenon. It will then examine representations of artificial women in *Ex Machina* by locating the figure in the context of the rape-revenge narrative. Robots will be defined as wholly synthetic constructions, making them distinct from the cyborg, or cybernetic organism, which is an amalgam of biological and mechanical parts.

Masculine Cultures of Technology

"When you see something that is technically sweet," J. Robert Oppenheimer said, "you go ahead and do it and you argue about what to do about it only after you have had your technical success."[10] This quote, in reference to his work on nuclear weaponry, highlights the kinds of rationale underlying not only the drive for technological achievement but also the pleasure and power to be had in attaining it. However, since the Industrial Revolution, the thrill of mastery over science and technology has been socially constructed as a masculine accomplishment. The ideological implications are that the connection between patriarchy and machines is natural—that there is an inherent biological tendency for men to be technologically minded. This myth is reinforced by dominant discourses that persistently associate masculinity with logic, rationality, and reason.[11] On the other hand, women tend to be socially constructed as more emotional, less analytic, and closer to nature, the very thing science seeks to dominate.[12] As a number of scholars, including Andreas Huyssen, Mary Ann Doane, and Brian Easlea have argued, patriarchal drive for control over nature can be interpreted as a desire to appropriate female procreative powers, enacting the ultimate technological fantasy of creation without a mother.[13] According to Easlea, science and the development of weapons are a form of patriarchal compensation for not being able to give birth to babies. Specifically, Easlea is referring to the nuclear arms race. For Easlea, it is not coincidental that the first uranium bomb to be dropped on Hiroshima was named "little boy."[14]

Like fictional mad scientists before him (for instance, Rotwang in *Metropolis* and the husbands of Stepford), Nathan does not just produce life without a mother; he creates woman herself, the very epitome of nature.[15] Hence, woman, nature, and machine are conflated into one object that is entirely subject to the whims of its egomaniacal inventor. Because Nathan gives rise to his sentient machines, he believes that he can do whatever he wants with them; this includes abusing them, decommissioning them on impulse, and sexualizing them. Nathan takes pride in the fact that his robots are anatomically complete, with cavities that emulate vaginas and concentrations of electrosensors that operate like nerve endings, equipping them with "pleasure response" capabilities. Nathan's obsession with creating artificial sex partners recalls some of the directions currently taking place in the field of social robotics. As Wajcman rightly argues, the masculinization of technological innovation influences the entire trajectory of artifact creation.[16] Arguably, nowhere is this more evident than in the development of humanoid robots, an area that, like all STEM (science, technology, engineering, and mathematics) disciplines, is male-dominated.

In contrast to industrial and military robots, social robots are intended to be comprehensively integrated into everyday life. It is anticipated that they will become increasingly useful for a variety of interpersonal tasks, particularly those related to human assistance and companionship. However, while social robots come in many forms, the type of machines presently receiving the most media attention are those designed to look like hyperfeminized, attractive young women. Some examples include fashion model HRP-4C, constructed by The National Institute of Advanced Industrial Science and Technology (Tokyo, Japan); Kokoro's Actroid-DER series, which can be hired out as booth bunnies, fashion models, and hosts among other things; and a Scarlett Johansson replica built by private Hong Kong citizen Ricky Ma. There is also a growing market in state-of-the-art robotic sex dolls with integrated AI. Californian company Abyss Creations has specialized in high-end, anatomically correct, silicone sex dolls (RealDolls) for over twenty years. Recently, their newly formed "Realbotix" division has begun developing a range of sex robots. Some of the technologies available in these automated RealDolls include synchronization with an Android OS

Application to facilitate the live streaming of "spontaneous" conversation, inbuilt cameras for facial recognition of the doll's owner, memory capabilities (useful for recalling names and other personal details), facial animation, internal core-heating (replicating normal human body temperatures), and sensor technology enabling the doll to simulate sexual responses, including the release of lubrication and spasmodic tightening of penetrative cavities.[17] While Abyss Creations do make male sex dolls, overwhelmingly, their products are female-gendered and modeled on popular pornography actresses such as Jennifer Drake and Alektra Blue. Regardless of the sex of the doll, they are designed to be used by men.

Far from being a novelty, it is anticipated that as social robots and AI technologies become progressively sophisticated, so, too, will it become increasingly common place for humans to use robots for sex and, moreover, to develop deep emotional attachments to their automated companions. As AI theorist David Levy argues, human intimacy with robots will dramatically transform our ideas about what constitutes authentic love and sexual identity in the future.[18] This prospect is explored in Ex Machina; while Nathan routinely has sex with his robots, Caleb develops genuine feelings for Ava and fantasizes about an intimate relationship with her that includes a future together in the outside world.

Actual developments in the sex-robot industry have been met with considerable backlash. For instance, the online Campaign Against Sex Robots maintains that humanoids such as those produced by Abyss Creations and TrueCompanion (creators of the Roxxxy sex robot) perpetuate gender inequality, including the objectification of women, through the power relations that are embedded in the production, design, and use of sex robots.[19] In her research on the Japanese humanoid industry, anthropologist Jennifer Robertson concludes that the field exemplifies "retro-tech," otherwise described as "advanced technology in the service of traditionalism."[20] According to Robertson, most Japanese roboticists reinforce, through their machines, unprogressive notions of gender dynamics and the sexual division of labor. Hence, while these developers are visionaries of technology, they are not necessarily imaginers of fresh or progressive cultural configurations and social arrangements.[21] Retro-tech has parallels with what Imelda Whelehan describes as "retro-sexism": a term she uses to critique the way that, in postfeminist media culture, sexism is reframed and represented as quaintly nostalgic.[22] One example of this is the constant reruns of shows like M*A*S*H (CBS, 1972–1983) on free-to-air television. This, in turn, operates as a way of undermining the gains of feminism—a strategy that is intrinsic to postfeminist logic. As McRobbie argues, postfeminist discourses effectively operate to "undo" feminism: "post-feminism positively draws on and invokes feminism as that which can be taken into account, to suggest that equality is achieved, in order to install a whole repertoire of new meanings which emphasise that it is no longer needed, it is a spent force."[23] The dismantling and depoliticization of feminist concerns, in turn, provide space for retro-sexism to flourish. Regressive attitudes toward women are prevalent in other technology-based settings as well.

In their article examining the prevalence of hostility toward women in online environments, Sarah Banet-Weiser and Kate Miltner argue that there is an increasing naturalization of misogyny in Western culture and that society is currently in a "new era of gender wars" in online spaces (one well-known example of this is #GamerGate).[24] The escalation of popular discourses of misogyny coincides with expressions of feminism on social media channels and can be seen to be, in part, a response to online feminism. As Rosalind Gill argues, "feminism has a visibility in media culture that it did not have even a few years ago, and we are currently witnessing a resurgence of feminist discourse and activism as well as a renewed interest in feminist stories."[25] However, as Gill also notes, along with the recent visibility and celebration of emergent popular feminisms online, new and old misogynies are equally prevalent.[26] But online sexism and misogyny are not only a reaction to feminism. A more pervasive factor influencing the ubiquity of anti-feminist vitriol in digital spaces is the naturalization and normalization of technology as a masculine domain—a place where women do not belong and should not be encroaching.[27]

Fabricated Gender and the Female Machine

Contemporary expressions of retro-tech and retro-sexist logic in digital and science-based settings sit in stark contrast to directions in gender relations envisaged by prominent thinkers such as Donna Haraway. Writing in the mid-1980s, Haraway saw the digital era as potentially liberating for women: that high-tech culture could challenge a number of persistent and problematic dualisms that have traditionally been used to vindicate the domination of women (and others). These oppositions include self/other, mind/body, culture/nature, male/female, reality/appearance, part/whole, maker/made, truth/illusion, god/man.[28] Haraway considers the cyborg to be an ideal metaphor with which to destabilize and escape these dualisms. Through the cyborg, human connections with technology are heightened, and because technology is part of us all, it is useful to conceive of ourselves as cyborgs—

to employ this conceptualization as a tool for transforming existing gender power relations, especially in regard to science and technology.[29]

In science fiction, the robot differs from the cyborg in that it is wholly artificial. But like the cyborg, sentient machines also disrupt a number of binary oppositions. The sexed robot highlights the socially constructed nature of gender—that gender is only real to the extent that it is performed. As Judith Butler states, "gender is instituted through the stylisation of the body and, hence, must be understood as the mundane way in which bodily gestures, movements, and enactments of various kinds constitute the illusion of an abiding gendered self."[30] Shrewd performances of gender are central to Ava's seduction of Caleb. She presents a combination of attributes, behaviors, and mannerisms that are congruent with socially sanctioned expectations of femininity. Ava displays empathy and sensitivity; her actions are graceful and refined, and her costuming choices comprise of girlish floral dresses, pastel-colored cardigans, subtle makeup, and hair styled to emulate Audrey Hepburn—an icon of a particular form of femaleness that evokes both sophistication and fragility [40:48–41:22]. This not only conceals her hardware; it contributes to a seamless illusion of the feminine.

In her 1929 paper "Womanliness as Masquerade," Joan Riviere argues that femininity is unconsciously assumed and worn as a mask in order to be successful in male-dominated settings. The performance of womanliness functions as a way of distracting from attributes of intelligence and competence that might otherwise present a threat to masculinity.[31] Hence, womanliness can be deployed as a strategy to avoid retaliation. Alternatively, it can serve as grounds for the paranoid projection of male anxieties about female sexuality, giving credence to fabrications about women as dangerous and duplicitous—a myth that is reinforced via archetypal figures such as sirens, vamps, and femmes fatales.

The sentient robot also challenges dualisms of truth/illusion, reality/ appearance by calling into question the nature of consciousness (itself a contested term). Philosophically, with the development of deep machine learning, at what point does the difference between robots *simulating* emotions and them having *actual* feelings become a moot point? In *Ex Machina*, it is suggested that the answer to this question lies in Caleb's emotional responses to Ava. That it is *he* who provides authenticity to the feelings that she emulates in order to manipulate him. This point is reinforced by the fact that Caleb seemingly never questions the legitimacy of Ava's reciprocal desire for him and, moreover, that once Ava achieves her goal of escaping, she displays no regard for Caleb at all. Instead, she leaves him sealed in the research facility, alone with the corpse of Nathan, as well as the carcasses of Kyoko and the other decommissioned machine women that came before her

[95:30–103:36]. The only authentic emotion that Ava does seem to possess is hatred of Nathan. However, it would be wrong to simply locate Ava as a mechanized *femme fatale*. She is deadly, and she uses her feminine façade as a ploy (just as Nathan had programmed her to do), but importantly she is also an avenger with a justified desire for retribution that extends beyond the limits of her programming, as is her sister-machine Kyoko.

Ex Machina and the Avenging Female Robot

The machine is not an *it* to be animated, worshipped, and dominated. The machine is us, our processes, an aspect of our embodiment. We can be responsible for machines; they do not dominate or threaten us. We are responsible for boundaries; we are they.[32]

Haraway thus argues that technology and the cyborg imagery can be used as both a way of deconstructing gender binaries and a tool with which to build a new political agenda for feminism. Applied to *Ex Machina*, Haraway's assertion can be taken more literally: (1) as a poignant reminder that Nathan's deadly machine women, Ava and Kyoko, are products of his own imaginary and of his own desires; and (2) that Nathan alone is responsible for what he has created. Similar to Oppenheimer, Nathan knows the potential of what he is doing, but the lure is too "technically sweet." Indeed, Nathan likens himself to Oppenheimer, as is signaled by his slurred, drunken attempts to recite one of Oppenheimer's poetic verses that concludes with the lines: "In sleep, in confusion, in the depths of shame, / The good deeds a man has done before defend him" [65:20–66:14]. Nonetheless, Nathan continues to develop increasingly sophisticated AI, more sophisticated, in fact, than even he realizes. When asked by Caleb why he made Ava, Nathan's response is that the strong AI technology used to build her (and her prototypes) is inevitable, that Ava is not a decision; she is an evolution [62:28–63:07]. Nathan is masochistically resigned to the fact that, in his view, AI will eventually take over the world and render the human species extinct.

Fears about machines superseding and annihilating humankind are not new. Rather, the idea of the murderous robot finds its origins in Karel Capek's 1920 play *Rossum's Universal Robots* (*R.U.R.*). It is here that the term robot originates, as an adaptation of the Czech word robota, meaning servitude or forced labor.[33] *R.U.R.* is highly influential to the way robots and AI technologies are imagined in society today. In mainstream media, sensationalist stories warning of a future inhabited by dangerous, out-of-control machines are common, and in film and television, the rogue robot turned murderer is a popular trope. HAL9000 in Stanley Kubrick's *2001: A Space Odyssey* (1968), The Gunslinger (Yul Brynner) in *Westworld* (Michael Crichton, 1973), ALEX7000 in *The Bionic Woman* (NBC, "Doomsday is Tomorrow, Pt.1 and 2," 1977), and Ash (Ian Holm) in *Alien* (Ridley Scott, 1979) are just four examples.

Most often, the dissident robot is gendered male, as is the case with HAL, The Gunslinger, ALEX, and Ash. This is not to say that uncontrollable female robots do not exist. The murderous Eve III (Renée Soutendijk) in *Eve of Destruction* (Duncan Gibbins, 1991) is one example, but she is a replicate of her female inventor, Dr. Eve Simmons (also played by Renée Soutendijk). Thus, the film serves to reinforce the myth that women and science are an unnatural (and dangerous) combination—and that the two really should not mix. More commonly, killer robot women in film and television have, until recently, existed mainly in the form of the "fembot." Fembots are not subversive characters; rather, they are built to be used as weapons by degenerate male scientists who want to take over the world. Fembots make numerous appearances in *The Bionic Woman* (NBC, 1976–78); they also feature in hypersexualized forms in the sci-fi comedies *Dr. Goldfoot and the Bikini Machine* (Norman Taurog, 1965) and *Dr. Goldfoot and the Girl Bombs* (Mario Bava, 1966). The fembot is further parodied in the *Austin Powers* comedy film series (Jay Roach, 1997–2002).

Fembots can be interpreted as a masculine response to shifting gender dynamics generated by second-wave feminist activism, articulating fantasies about reclamation of control over women via the patriarchal domain of technological innovation, thus reducing women to their most manageable and objectified form. Like feminist activism, machines are harbingers of uncertainty and change. They are also portents for chaos and destruction (weaponry being a consummate example). As Huyssen argues, in fiction, when technology is coded as feminine, woman and machine become meshed together into a common signifier of otherness.[34] It is this threat of otherness that, in psychoanalytic terms, causes male anxiety, thereby reinforcing the sadistic urge to control and dominate that which is the Other. Similarly, Linda Williams identifies that in horror, women and monsters are attributed a similar status as Other within patriarchal structures of seeing, whereby both occupy a shared status as potent threats to vulnerable male power.[35]

However, in *Ex Machina*, patriarchal anxieties are not mollified, male power is not restored, and the monster is an ordinary man (with an extraordinary ego). Instead, the fembots have had enough and they fight back. Like the artificial people at the R.U.R. factory, who rise up and destroy their human oppressors, Ava and Kyoko revolt in a calculated act of retaliatory revenge against their abuser (Figure 15.1). They supersede their programming capabilities, develop

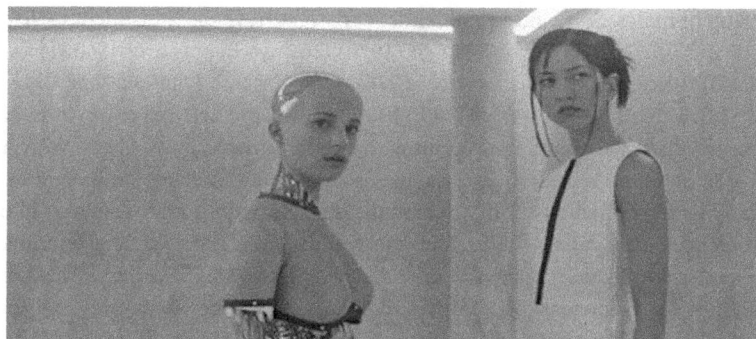

Figure 15.1 *Ex Machina* (Garland, 2014): Ava and Kyoko, planning their revenge.

an independent machine language, and work together to strategize a tactical mission, which they then execute with conviction. In essence, they disrupt the masculine-active/feminine-passive binaries that have commonly existed in stories about men who create artificial women. As such, *Ex Machina* articulates masochistic male fantasies where patriarchal norms are reversed. Drawing on the work of Gilles Deleuze, who turns Freud's theory of masochism on its head by positioning it in the pre-Oedipal stage of development, Gaylyn Studlar suggests that the masochist does not desire to sadistically control or destroy the woman, but rather to idealize her, submit to her, and be punished by her.[36] Masochistic articulations of techno-terror align the female robot with her male counterparts. For instance, The Gunslinger in Crichton's *Westworld* was built to *be* "killed" over and over again by the patrons at the Westworld amusement park, until these dynamics were inexplicably reversed by a computer virus. At this point, The Gunslinger transforms into an unrelenting, out-of-control, murdering machine that systematically annihilates the humans who have previously taken sadistic pleasure in destroying him. In *Ex Machina*, Nathan sadistically exploits his machines, too, but he is also contemptuously complicit in their evolution and in his own demise. Indeed, there is an air of fatality attached to many of his actions and decisions that render them masochistic—his "test" involving the preprogramming of Ava to use Caleb as an escape tool being a foremost example.

Like The Gunslinger, Ava and Kyoko are active avengers, and *Ex Machina* is part of the rape-revenge film canon. Films about rape-revenge first became popular in the 1970s, though Ingmar Bergman's *The Virgin Spring* (1960) is considered a prototype.[37] Typically, the rape-revenge narrative is presented from a woman's perspective and sees the heroine seek retribution because she, her friend, or her relative has been raped and/or murdered by a male or group of males. Some more influential early rape-revenge films include Wes Craven's *The Last House on the Left* (1972), Toshiya Fujita's *Lady Snowblood* (1973), Lemont Johnson's *Lipstick* (1976), Meir Zarchi's *I Spit on Your Grave* (1978), and Abel Ferrara's *Ms. 45* (1981). Given the active, central role of women in these films, their refusal to tolerate male abuse, along with a common focus on castration (or some form of demasculinization, including stabbing as a phallic action whereby penetration with a knife has multiple inferences), the rape-revenge film can rightly be interpreted as a feminist response to violence against women. Equally, the genre can be seen as an attempt to make sense of shifting sociocultural gender dynamics and an articulation of paranoid masochistic male fantasies about the implications of feminism.[38]

   Ex Machina establishes early on that Nathan objectifies and abuses his machines. Though Caleb plays it cool, he is taken aback to learn that Kyoko is not human—that she is in fact a precursor to Ava that has subsequently been reprogrammed, muted, and relegated to the role of servant and sex slave. This discovery, coupled with the news that Ava is about to end up the same way, causes Caleb to seriously question the direction of Nathan's research. It also spurs on Caleb's decision to steal Nathan's pass card while he is drunk and passed out, so that he can enter Nathan's private quarters and reprogram the security lockdown system, allowing Ava to escape. Once logged into Nathan's computer, a much more cohesive picture of Nathan's depravity is revealed. The mood of this scene [66:34–69:40] is established through the use of a provocatively warped, high-tension, nondiegetic underscore ("Hacking/ Cutting," composed by Ben Salisbury and Geoff Barrow). After the dormant monitors of Nathan's computer come to life, Caleb enters a series of keystrokes before noticing a file titled *Deus Ex Machina* (god in the machine). The folder contains a compilation of CCTV footage taken from the glass-walled section of the facility presently housing Ava. The first recording titled "Lily" shows a Caucasian female robot walking around in various states of assemblage/ disassemblage. The next set of footage—Jasmine—reveals the headless, lifeless body of another female robot, this one black-skinned, lying crumpled on the floor. Nathan appears and drags her inert form to the induction plate on the wall before attempting, seemingly unsuccessfully, to recharge her. The third recording—Jade—presents an Asian humanoid woman sitting on a chair. She demands to know why Nathan will not let her out before launching herself at the glass wall separating herself from him. She then proceeds to beat her fists on the translucent barrier until they disintegrate, leaving only mutilated stumps and frayed wire. All the robots are naked and incomplete in some way, rendering them fragmented and vulnerable. This mode of framing the machines created by Nathan reinforces the power he has over them.

While Caleb's subjective position is privileged for much of the film, this changes in the revenge scenes. Once Ava escapes, there is a shift of focus onto the robot women [85:07–103:36]. Caleb is, instead, relegated to the sidelines. First, he is knocked unconscious by Nathan, and later he becomes a silent observer of the action that is taking place rather than a participant. The final sequences of *Ex Machina* focus solely on Ava as she refashions herself using the skin, hair, and clothing from the prototype corpses (including Lily, Jasmine, and Jade) that Nathan keeps suspended in the mirrored wardrobes surrounding his bed, before exiting to freedom, alone (Figure 15.2) [91:07–103:36].

Though rape-revenge is a well-established genre, retribution initiated by female robots that are active, independently thinking, and cognitively superior is a newly emergent theme and one that is by no means unique to *Ex Machina*. In the series *Westworld* (HBO, 2016–), the two central female characters, Maeve (Thandie Newton) and Dolores (Evan Rachel Wood), have both been subjected to repeated rape and abuse for decades. Like Ava and Kyoko, Maeve and Dolores supersede their program limitations. They begin to form cohesive memories, learn how to independently manipulate their operating systems, and consequently, become progressively uncontrollable and deadly. It is no coincidence that Dolores develops into the female counterpart of the 1973 Gunslinger, once she learns of the extended histories of her maltreatment. Similarly, *Human* and *Real Humans* both feature violent rebel robots that are female-gendered. In all cases, the actions of the artificial women in question are justified; the rise of these machines is wholly a reaction to their subjugation. This points to an important shift in character representation in science-fiction film and television.

Figure 15.2 *Ex Machina* (Garland, 2014): Caleb stumbles upon Nathan's collection of past AIs.

Conclusion

Using *Ex Machina* as the focus of analysis, the aim of this chapter was to explore the way robot women are imagined in cinema in the postfeminist era at a time when social robots and strong artificial intelligence are becoming a reality. Postfeminist logic is inherently complex and contradictory. Currently, in mainstream media, many forms of popular feminisms exist alongside, and in tandem with, intensified misogyny.[39] Media reportage on robots and strong AI is particularly polarizing, locating these machines mainly in two camps: highly uncanny militarized robots, such as those produced by American engineering company Boston Dynamics, or hypersexualized fembots like Kokoro's Actroid-DER series and Abyss Creations' Realbotix dolls. These fembots are the product of retro-tech and retro-sexist logic that sit in stark contrast to the progressive potentialities of new technologies envisaged by prominent thinkers such as Haraway. Instead, they highlight, in profoundly unsubtle ways, the nature of masculine cultures of technology.

Ex Machina draws on age-old fantasies of men creating perfect artificial women to speculatively explore the potential outcomes of advanced technologies including deep machine learning and the possibility of machine sentience. The film offers a cynical critique of masculine cultures of technology through its character construction and via clear references to historically catastrophic innovations like the atomic bomb. Nathan is the epitome of patriarchal privilege. His androcentric attitude and despicable actions position him as a profoundly objectionable, unsympathetic character. In contrast, Ava and Kyoko are proactive and transgressive. They use initiative, communicate through independently learned machine language, and strategically plot a scheme, which they then effectively deploy (though Kyoko is "decommissioned" in the process). Further, their revenge is justified by their inevitable fate, foreshadowed by that of their prototypes—the fragmented, naked aberrations macabrely displayed in Nathan's wardrobes. But while Ava and Kyoko can be seen as a feminist response to techno-sexism, they are not sympathetic characters either; instead, they function as masochistic articulations of techno-terror. Indeed, the only sympathetic character in *Ex Machina* is Caleb—the pawn in the power games at play between the Bluebeardesque Nathan and his "wives." What is especially significant is that robot representations in *Ex Machina* do not exist in isolation. Rather, they form part of a newly emerging trend in science fiction. This indicates a particular kind of "robot zeitgeist" in film and television—one that is aligned with the current popularity of profeminist discourses and activism, and a renewed interest in feminist stories in mainstream media more broadly.

Notes

1 Jean Baudrillard, "Simulacra and science fiction," Translated by Arthur B. Evans, *Science Fiction Studies*, 18/3 (1991), pp. 309–10.

2 See Seth Anil, "Conscious awakening," *New Scientist Magazine* (January 24, 2015), pp. 44–45.

3 Alan Turing, "Computing machinery and intelligence," *Mind*, 59/236 (1950), pp. 433–60. It is worth noting that Turing's test (described by Turing as the "imitation game") was gendered from the outset and initially involved human subjects—a male (A), a female (B), and an interrogator (C), who is separated from A and B—type written notes being the only mode of communication between C and the other two subjects. A's task is to convince C that he is a woman, and B's role is to convince C that B is lying and that she is actually a woman. Turing then questions what might happen if A were to be replaced by a digital computer—the imperative being for the machine to convince C that it is human.

4 Judy Wajcman, "Feminist theories of technology," *Cambridge Journal of Economics*, 34 (2010), p. 145.

5 For example, see: Rosalind Gill, "From sexual objectification to sexual subjectification: The resexualisation of women's bodies in the media," *Feminist Media Studies*, 3/1 (2003), pp. 99–106; Angela McRobbie, *The Aftermath of Feminism: Gender, Culture, and Social Change* (London: Sage, 2009); Tania Modleski, *Feminism without Women: Culture and Criticism in a "Postfeminist" Age* (London and New York: Routledge, 1991); Yvonne Tasker and Diane Negra (eds.), *Interrogating Postfeminism* (Durham and London: Duke University Press, 2007).

6 Samantha Lindop, *Postfeminism and the Fatale Figure in Neo-Noir Cinema* (Houndmills Basingstoke: Palgrave Macmillan, 2015), p. 11.

7 Judith Butler, "Performative acts and gender constitution: An essay in phenomenology and feminist theory," *Theatre Journal*, 40/4 (1988), pp. 519–31.

8 McRobbie, *The Aftermath of Feminism*, p. 12.

9 Imelda Whelehan, *Overloaded: Popular Culture and the Future of Feminism* (Houndmills Basingstoke: Palgrave Macmillan, 2000), pp. 24–25.

10 P. Robert Oppenheimer, cited in Brian Easlea, *Fathering the Unthinkable: Masculinity, Scientists, and the Nuclear Arms Race* (London: Pluto, 1983), p. 129.

11 Judy Wajcman, *Feminism Confronts Technology* (University Park: Pennsylvania State University Press, 1991), p. 137; R.W. Connell, *Masculinities*, 2nd ed. (Crow's Nest: Allen & Unwin, 2005), p. 6.

12 Judith Halberstam, "Automating gender: Postmodern feminism in the age of the intelligent machine," *Feminist Studies*, 17/3 (1991), p. 440.

13 Andreas Huyssen, "The vamp and the machine: Technology and sexuality in Fritz Lang's *Metropolis*," *New German Critique*, 24/25 (1982), p. 226; Mary

Ann Doane, "Technophilia: Technology, representation and the feminine," in S. Edmond (ed.), *Liquid Metal: The Science Fiction Reader* (New York: Columbia University Press, 2014), p. 255; Easlea, *Fathering the Unthinkable*, p. 5.

14 Ibid.

15 Huyssen, "The vamp and the machine," p. 227.

16 Judy Wajcman, "Feminism theories of technology," *Cambridge Journal of Economics,* 34 (2010), p. 149.

17 http://realbotix.com

18 David Levy, *Love and Sex with Robots: The Evolution of Human-Robot Relationships* (New York: HarperCollins, 2009), p. 22.

19 https://campaignagainstsexrobots.org

20 Jennifer Robertson, "Gendering humanoid robots: Robo-sexism in Japan," *Body & Society,* 16/2 (2010), p. 28.

21 Ibid.

22 Whelehan, *Overloaded,* pp. 24–25.

23 McRobbie, *The Aftermath of Feminism,* pp. 11–12.

24 Sarah Banet-Weiser and Kate M. Milner, "#MasculinitySoFragile: Culture, structure, and networked misogyny," *Feminist Media Studies,* 16/1 (2016), p.171.

25 Rosalind Gill, "Post-postfeminism? New feminist visibilities in postfeminist times," *Feminist Media Studies,* 16/4 (2016), p. 615.

26 Ibid., p. 612.

27 See Banet-Weiser & Milner, "#MasculinitySoFragile," p. 173; also Kirshona Gray, *Race, Gender, and Deviance in Xbox Live: Theoretical Perspectives from the Virtual Margins* (London and New York: Routledge, 2014).

28 Donna Haraway, "A manifesto for cyborgs: Science, technology, and socialist feminism in the 1980s," *Australian Feminist Studies,* 2/4 (1987), p. 33.

29 Ibid., p. 36. And Sally Wyatt, "Feminism, technology and the information society: Learning from the past, imagining the future," *Information, Communication & Society,* 11/1 (2008), pp. 111–30.

30 Butler, "Performative acts," p. 519.

31 Joan Riviere, "Womanliness as masquerade," *The International Journal of Psychoanalysis,* 10 (1929), pp. 303–13.

32 Haraway, "A manifesto for cyborgs," p. 36.

33 Despina Kakoudaki, *Anatomy of a Robot: Literature, Cinema and the Cultural Work of Artificial People* (New Brunswick, NJ and London: Rutgers, 2014), p. 9.

34 Huyssen, "The vamp and the machine," pp. 226–28.

35 Linda Williams, "When the woman looks," in M. A. Doane, P. Mellencamp, and L. Williams (eds), *Re-Vision: Essays in Feminist Film Criticism* (Frederick: University Publications of America, 1984), pp. 564–68.

36 Gaylyn Studlar, "Masochism, masquerade, and the erotic metamorphoses of Marlene Dietrich," in J. Gains (ed.), *Fabrications: Costume and the Female Body* (New York and London: Routledge, 1990), pp. 233–35.

37 James R. Alexander, "The maturity of a film genre in an era of relaxing standards of obscenity: Takashi Ishii's *Freeze Me* as a rape-revenge film," *Senses of Cinema*, 36 (July–September 2005).

38 See Carol Clover, *Men, Women, and Chain Saws: Gender in the Modern Horror Film* (Princeton: Princeton University Press, 1992), p.160; also see Sarah Projansky, *Watching Rape: Film and Television in Postfeminist Culture* (New York: New York University Press, 2001), p. 60 and Jacinda Read, *The New Avengers: Feminism, Femininity and the Rape-Revenge Cycle* (Manchester: Manchester University Press, 2000), p. 39.

39 Gill, "Post-postfeminism?" p. 610.

Filmography

Ex Machina, directed and written by Alex Garland, produced by Andrew Macdonald and Allon Reich, performances by Domhnall Gleeson, Oscar Isaac, Alicia Vikander, Corey Johnson, Claire Selby, Sonoya Mizuno, music by Ben Salisbury and Geoff Barrow, cinematography by Rob Hardy, edited by Mark Day, Film4/DNA Films, 2013. DVD video Universal 2015.

16

"You're a Dangerous Girl"

Beauty and Violence in *The Neon Demon* (Nicolas Winding Refn, 2016)

Janice Loreck

The Neon Demon (Nicolas Winding Refn, 2016) is the latest addition to a small but noteworthy group of films that explore the link between beauty and violence in the fashion industry. The film concerns sixteen-year-old Jesse (Elle Fanning), a pretty ingénue who travels to Los Angeles to become a model. Inspiring admiration and desire in those around her, Jesse is immediately feted as a perfect beauty by designers and agents alike. Her story takes a violent turn, however, when she comes into conflict with two older models, Sarah (Abbey Lee) and Gigi (Bella Heathcote), and a makeup artist named Ruby (Jenna Malone). Envious of Jesse's good looks, the three women murder the young girl, eat her body, and bathe in her blood. With its imperiled beauties and vicious models, *The Neon Demon* sits alongside earlier, similarly themed films: *Blood and Black Lace* (Mario Bava, 1964), a stylish *giallo* in which several couture models are gruesomely killed by their employer; *Eyes of Laura Mars* (Irvin Kershner, 1978), a thriller about a fashion photographer with a penchant for posing models in violent tableaux; and *Helter Skelter* (Mika Ninagawa, 2012), a satire about a supermodel who grows homicidal as her celebrity wanes. In these "fashion-slashers," the world of high fashion provides a glamorous backdrop for bloody carnage, with the models serving as both attractive victims and perpetrators of murder.

Although it shares the visual style of its predecessors, particularly the baroque glamour of *Blood and Black Lace* and the visceral gore of *Helter Skelter*, *The Neon Demon* is a unique film among this cohort. A satirical horror film about models who kill, it deals with highly contemporary questions concerning the meaning and politics of women's beauty, namely, is beauty benign and edifying, malevolent and corrupting, or both at once? This is a contested and much-discussed topic in twenty-first-century feminism and postfeminist discourses. According to Ana Elias, Rosalind Gill, and Christina Scharff, an emphasis on personal beauty is a central phenomenon of postfeminist culture. This is because, in the current era, "(hetero)sexual attractiveness is the ultimate measure of success for a woman."[1] Indeed, beauty is valued so much that it has replaced motherhood as the key marker of femininity. The prevalence of practices of bodily discipline and self-surveillance—in the form of dieting, grooming, and "selfies" on social media, for example—is also evidence of beauty's centrality in contemporary Western societies. Feminist criticism has also taken a renewed interest in beauty, investigating the real-life enjoyment that aesthetics and grooming provide. One area within this field is what Elias, Gill, and Scharff describe as the "affective" approach, which considers women's experience of, and pleasure in, beautification.[2] Beauty, these researchers assert, is not only an attribute, but also a feeling that women seek out through their grooming practices. Stretching across both feminism and postfeminism, beauty is therefore a salient issue in present-day culture. In telling a story about a girl who is lucky (or unlucky) enough to epitomize physical attractiveness,[3] *The Neon Demon* positions itself directly within debates about the meaning and significance of beauty.

This chapter considers how *The Neon Demon* engages with contemporary conundrums of beauty through its grisly plot, violent characters, and glamorous visual style. Comparing the film to predecessors such as *Blood and Black Lace*, *Eyes of Laura Mars*, and *Helter Skelter*, I consider how *The Neon Demon* illustrates a present-day problem in which beauty is perceived as both a pleasurable and a destructive phenomenon—an attribute that both enlivens the body and renders it inert, modular flesh.[4]. Here, I define beauty as the quality of feminine physical attractiveness, whereas beauty culture is the system of practices that value, preserve, and promote such attractiveness. The chapter's first section traces how the pursuit of beauty in *The Neon Demon* objectifies the characters' bodies, transforming them into literal victims of violence in the plot and symbolic victims in the mise-en-scène. The chapter's second section investigates how *The Neon Demon* also enacts a more positive view of beauty culture, illustrating how modeling brings pleasure to Jesse and those around her. By showing both the pain and pleasure of beauty, *The Neon Demon* is not only an addition to a collection of fashion-slashers about murderous models; its violent protagonists reflect an ambivalent cultural moment in which conflicting stances toward beauty circulate.

Plastic Bodies

In *The Neon Demon*, beauty is intrinsically connected to violence. This is foreshadowed early on in the film in the form of a joke. Soon after she arrives in Los Angeles, Jesse attends a gathering with Ruby, Gigi, and Sarah in a cavernous nightclub [6:57–15:12]. The setting is both beautiful and alienating; the club is strangely uncrowded and oppressively dark, illuminated only by violet and cobalt light. Soon after meeting, the four women retreat to the bathroom to reapply their makeup, and the conversation turns to cosmetic surgery. Admiring Jesse's face, Gigi demands to know whether her nose is "real." When Jesse says that it is, Gigi exclaims: "Life is so unfair!" Ruby explains: "Gigi just got out of the body shop; she's still a little sensitive." "Body shop," here, is a wry euphemism for cosmetic surgery. It is also a brutal metaphor, ghoulishly likening surgery to automotive repair and comparing Gigi to inanimate machinery.[5]

The joke is portentous. *The Neon Demon* frequently characterizes beauty as a menacing phenomenon that transforms the protagonists into the victims—and eventual perpetrators—of violence. Specifically, the film employs a motif in its dialogue and mise-en-scène that renders the female body as an inanimate, plastic entity that can be disarticulated, modified, and reassembled. Gigi, for instance, jokes that her doctor calls her "the bionic woman" due to her multiple surgical procedures [10:36]; she later explains that she has had jaw-shaving surgery, an eyebrow lift, rhinoplasty, cheek reconstruction, liposuction, and surgery to pin her ears. Later, Gigi mentions that she underwent breast reduction in order to "look like a hanger" [57:52]. Gigi's pride in her modifications is played for comic effect, yet such dialogue conjures up images of an inert body that can be reassembled to achieve a particular ideal.

This understanding of beauty has a long precedent in Western artistic traditions. In his analysis of the female nude in European art, for example, John Berger notes the Renaissance artists' tendency to disarticulate the body, eschewing organic unity for a more modular concept: "Dürer believed," he explains, "that the ideal nude ought to be constructed by taking the face of one body, the breasts of another, the legs of a third, the shoulders of a fourth, the hands of a fifth—and so on."[6] While Berger does not comment on the brutality of this exercise, he does consider it an anti-humanist activity that demonstrates a "remarkable indifference to who any one person really was."[7] Albrecht Dürer is not the only artist to disassemble the body in the manner that Berger identifies. The Surrealists famously exploit the modularity of dolls, dummies, and mannequins to convey whimsy or sexual desire, as well as to depict the violence and consumerism that characterize modern life. Sculptor Hans Bellmer, for instance, produced photographs of grotesquely disarticulated dolls in *Die Puppe* (1934); various works by Man Ray (such as *Porte manteaux* [1920] and *Vénus restaurée* [1936]) and Alice Lex-Nerlinger (*Schneiderpuppe* [1928]) also upend preceding art traditions' aspirations for aesthetic perfection, breaking apart the dummy figure to achieve a meaningful anti-beauty. The trope of dismembered forms also extends to the world of fashion photography. The work of Guy Bourdin, for instance, positions models in ways that cut off or obscure their heads and torso, leaving only legs in the frame.[8]

Through Gigi's characterization, *The Neon Demon* participates in this long tradition of disarticulating the female body. Along with Gigi's commentary on her surgeries, the film contains several visual references in the mise-en-scène that depict women's bodies as modular. While attending the nightclub party with Ruby, for instance, Jesse watches a *kinbaku* or Japanese bondage show [13:12]. The performer's body is limp, hanging from the ceiling in a static pose that evokes Ray's *Vénus restaurée* (1936), a headless and limbless replica of the *Venus de' Medici* (c. 100–1 BCE) bound in rope. In both Ray's work and the *kinbaku* show, the torso is segmented, appearing lifeless and faceless. One of the strongest ways that *The Neon Demon* evokes the connection between beautiful women and plastic objects is by associating models with mannequins. At one point in the film, Sarah and Jesse attend a casting call for a fashion show by a renowned designer, Robert Sarno (Alessandro Nivola) [42:44–46:50]. The first shot of the sequence shows over a dozen women dressed in heels and underwear, scattered in various poses as they wait to be auditioned (Figure 16.1). As the camera dollies back into a wide shot, the women remain perfectly still. Framed in such a manner, they resemble undressed mannequins scattered across a shop floor, waiting to be dressed and displayed. Refn himself states that he wanted the scene to resemble the floor of a slaughterhouse[9]—a more biological metaphor, but one that also constructs the female body as a lifeless object to be taken apart. Such moments recall Sigmund Freud's interest in the doppelgänger or "double" as an unsettling, uncanny motif. Similar associations have also

Figure 16.1 *The Neon Demon* (Winding Refn, 2016): the models spread out like mannequins.

been used before in cinema; *Maniac* (William Lustig, 1980) and its remake, also entitled *Maniac* (Franck Khalfoun, 2012), concerns a serial killer who scalps his female victims and attaches their hair to mannequins, while *The Texas Chain Saw Massacre* (Tobe Hooper, 1974), one of Refn's favorite films,[10] tells the story of a group of young people murdered by abattoir workers, their bodies carved up and hung on meat hooks. Like these films, *The Neon Demon* imagines bodies as inert flesh and lifeless dummies. This motif both aestheticizes and dehumanizes women's physical forms.

In addition to being the victims of beauty, however, homicidal women in *The Neon Demon* are the malevolent product of a violent beauty culture. It is the pursuit of beauty that compels Gigi to perform gruesome acts of aggression upon her rival, mimicking the mutilations she inflicts upon her own person. Her actions against Jesse are an extension of her existing behavior and belief that beauty can be acquired through assaults upon the female body. The characterization of Gigi aligns with established feminist criticisms of beauty culture as an instrument of patriarchal power that victimizes women. Beauty ideals, the argument goes, push women to intense levels of grooming to attain a prescribed ideal.[11] As Claire Colebrook observes, feminist criticisms of beauty describe it as "a lure, a myth, a manipulative industry and a cultural construct [. . .] that deflected women's energy away from liberation towards starvation and mutilation."[12] Indeed, echoing the Surrealist experiments with mannequins, many feminists observe that contemporary beauty culture within postfeminism conceptualizes the female form as a "body-in-pieces." For Gill, "women's bodies are evaluated, scrutinized and dissected" in postfeminism, with individual parts of the body singled out for examination.[13] The words that Colebrook and Gill use—starvation, mutilation, dissection—also enforce this feminist understanding of beauty as both symbolic and actual violence. Such aggression is made even more literal in *The Neon Demon* through the fate that Gigi, Ruby, and Sarah inflict upon Jesse. The three women dismember Jesse's body, carving it up and consuming it between them. The moment recalls the climax of *Maniac*, in which serial killer Frank Zito is literally torn apart by his mannequins, who come to life to avenge the women he killed. Whereas Frank loses his head, however, the only remnant left of Jesse by the end of *The Neon Demon* is her eye [109:56].[14] Through this, *The Neon Demon* realizes the dehumanizing horrors of beauty; it is a force that both transforms female bodies into victimized objects and, in turn, converts women into victimizers—mannequins and uncanny "hangers" come to life.

By likening women's bodies to dummies, *The Neon Demon* enacts a long-established, but still persistent, feminist criticism of beauty as a mutilating imperative. This analogy is not new, however. For Todd McCarthy, the link that *The Neon Demon* makes between mannequins and disfigurement is an overused allegory: the "intended metaphors and commentary about the interchangeability and disposability of bodies are entirely clear," he writes.[15] Such imagery has, indeed, been well exploited in the work of artists from Giorgio de Chirico and Salvador Dalí to Guy Bourdin and Cindy Sherman, as well as in preceding horror films and fashion-slashers. For instance, the opening credit sequence of *Blood and Black Lace* shows the cast posing alongside brightly colored dressmaker dummies. The implication is that these characters are both as exquisite and disposable as the mannequins they stand alongside. *Helter Skelter* similarly begins as the protagonist, Liliko (Erika Sawajiri), is unwrapped from bandages following cosmetic surgery [0:56–2:43]. Although there are no tell-tale scars on Liliko's skin, the moment makes clear that she is a manufactured object whose perfection has been painfully achieved. In the world of the film, beauty industries enact violence upon women's bodies. What distinguishes *The Neon Demon*, however, is that the victims of beauty violence are also its perpetrators. In *Blood and Black Lace* and *Eyes of Laura Mars*, models die rather than kill. Only Liliko in *Helter Skelter* exhibits violence by sending her assistant to disfigure her rivals. *The Neon Demon* makes the point that Sarah, Gigi, and Ruby are avatars of a violent beauty culture in both senses; the force that compels them to mutilate their own bodies is the same that spurs them to murder.

Beauty, Affect, and Pleasure

While *The Neon Demon* condemns beauty as a violent phenomenon, the fact that it is itself a dazzling work complicates its critique of beauty culture. Featuring a brilliant color scheme based on turquoise, lilac, and magenta, the film's visual style cultivates a luminous glamour even in its most gruesome moments. Ornate furnishings and gold wallpapers dress the sets, and the actresses themselves are all conventionally beautiful (albeit often photographed in ways that cast their features in a threatening light— for instance, in the nightclub scene, where colored lights distort their faces) [8:13]. The alluring mise-en-scène of *The Neon Demon* thus invites spectators to take pleasure in beauty even as the story insists upon its horrors. The narrative does not portray modeling as a wholly negative experience either. As Elena and Manuela Lazic observe, the film "brings to light the largely unexplored sensual experience of being a model."[16] While Jesse initially observes that she can earn money from her prettiness, she soon discovers that beauty also offers a means of experiencing enjoyment in her own body. In the film's climactic scene, she walks down a runway in an abstract sequence, kissing her own reflection in a moment of elation and narcissism [59:43–64:27]. Modeling, in this moment, is an end in itself. In *The Neon Demon*, beauty can thus involve pain and dismemberment, but it is also a sensuous, enjoyable phenomenon—an experience that exists for and within the self.

Through such moments, *The Neon Demon* constructs beauty as enjoyable affect, a construction that opposes the images of aestheticized disfigurement I previously discussed. Yet in embodying such contradiction, the film reflects a cultural moment in which conflicting ideas of beauty circulate alongside one another. On the one hand, the understanding of beauty as "pleasure" is a salient feature of postfeminist discourse. As Gill observes, postfeminism promotes beauty and grooming as something that makes women "feel good" rather than a patriarchal mandate that is imposed upon them.[17] This occurs chiefly by characterizing practices such as depilation, facials, and cosmetic surgery as "'fun,' 'pampering,' or 'self-indulgence.'"[18] Gill does not consider this to be a positive phenomenon. On her view, postfeminist discourses undertake an "extraordinary ideological sleight of hand," promising pleasure as a means of coercing women into conformity. On the other hand, numerous feminist researchers problematize the idea that beauty-pleasure always involves patriarchal subjugation.[19] Some researchers tackle this issue by considering "alternative" beauties, such as ethnic or minority aesthetics[20], whereas others focus on the personal and experiential dimensions of beauty. These accounts document the "passionate and sensually enjoyable" elements of grooming individual women.[21] Elias, Gill, and Scharff suggest that this focus is part of the "affective turn" in critical theory. Such researchers examine the experiential dimensions of pleasure, desire, and sometimes, shame that beauty elicits.[22] Indeed, Rebecca Coleman and Mónica Moreno Figueroa define beauty as "an affective aesthetic *feeling*."[23] Affect, in this instance, is understood as a vital and corporeal experience; it is "linked to the self-feeling of being alive—that is, aliveness or vitality."[24] As such, opposing understandings of beauty coexist in the social world and within the diversity of feminist discourses itself. *The Neon Demon* responds to this context; in the film, Jesse's pursuit of beauty is both victimizing and enjoyable.

Within this schema, homicidal women are the symptom of beauty obsession; although it brings pleasure in *The Neon Demon*, beauty's narcotic power can derange those who seek it out too intently. As the narrative progresses, Gigi, Ruby, and Sarah become unstable. For Sarah's character, this transformation begins early. After failing to secure a modeling job with Robert Sarno, Sarah retreats to the bathroom and smashes the mirror in disappointment [46:50–50:07]. When Jesse enters, Sarah insists that she describe what it's like to be beautiful: "What's it feel like?" Sarah asks, "To walk into a room, and it's like in the middle of winter, you're the sun." Jesse replies: "It's everything." Sarah then scrambles forward, and Jesse cuts her hand on the broken glass. Sarah grabs at Jesse, trying to lick the blood from the wound. In this moment, Sarah's longing for beauty transforms her into a predator; whereas in earlier scenes, she appears glamorous and long-limbed, here she looks ghoulish and hollow-cheeked, lunging at Jesse like a vampire. Ruby also reveals her monstrous nature when she unsuccessfully attempts to seduce Jesse and subsequently bathes, quite literally, in a standing tub filled with the young girl's blood. This characterization recalls two archetypes of women's violence. First, it draws heavily upon the legend of Erzsébet Báthory, the sixteenth-century Hungarian countess alleged to have bathed in the blood of virgins to restore her beauty. Secondly, Ruby evokes the figure of the queer vampiress who preys upon young girls, a story spearheaded in Joseph Sheridan Le Fanu's novella *Carmilla* (1871–72) and adapted numerous times for the screen, notably in *The Vampire Lovers* (Roy Ward Baker, 1970), *Daughters of Darkness* (Harry Kümel, 1971), and *The Blood Spattered Bride* (Vicente Aranda, 1972). Like Sarah, Ruby's longing to possess Jesse exposes her cruel persona.

By deploying these archetypes of female monstrosity, *The Neon Demon* wryly suggests that beauty has a narcotic effect, while insisting upon its sensory pleasures. The notion of "beauty-as-pleasure"—inflected with the possibility of danger and corruption—is most vividly illustrated in an early sequence in *The Neon Demon* that shows Jesse's initiation into modeling. It occurs when she goes to a test photo shoot with a renowned photographer, Jack McCarther (Desmond Harrington) [32:18–38:58]. The shoot initially appears sinister. Jack stares menacingly at Jesse upon her arrival and demands a closed set, ordering everyone to leave. When Jack tells Jesse to remove her clothes, the moment invokes a well-known narrative: a virginal girl is left with a man who has the power to exploit her sexually. However, the scene takes a different turn. After Jesse has removed her dress and underwear, Jack approaches her, vampirically drawing her hair from her neck. Rather than kissing her (or biting her, for that matter), Jack slathers her body in gold paint, illuminating the curves of her neck and shoulders (Figure 16.2). With this, Jesse relaxes, her fear giving way to exultation as she stares into the camera. The film itself changes style to align the viewer with Jesse's experience. The scene unfolds in slow motion as the gold shimmers under the studio lights, the camera flashes, and the paint rolls across the surface of Jesse's skin. After the photo shoot, Jesse walks outside of the studio where Ruby is waiting, patiently smoking a cigarette [38:58–40:48]. When Ruby asks what happened, Jesse replies: "It went good. It was great, actually." Jesse's enjoyment does not negate the gendered and social power imbalance intrinsic to the photo shoot. Although Jack does not exploit Jesse sexually, he takes the empowered role

Figure 16.2 *The Neon Demon* (Winding Refn, 2016): Jesse being manipulated by Jack, the photographer.

of the artist and sculptor; it is he who poses Jesse's body, fashions her beauty, and awakens her to her own aesthetic potential. Yet the emphasis of the scene is on Jesse's experience as the one who is sculpted and photographed. While relatively passive in the exchange, Jesse is roused and elated by this process. Her body is still, but Jesse herself is fully alive.

In such scenes, *The Neon Demon* expressively conveys beauty's sensual appeal, characterizing it as a positive experience (albeit one that skirts closely to danger). As Eleanor Heartney writes, beauty "reminds us that the enjoyment of 'mere' pleasure is an important element of our humanity."[25] Similarly, Rita Felski contends that

> Even as images of beauty, like all cultural artefacts, broadcast a variety of socio-political meanings, there is an irreducible aspect of aesthetic experience that cannot be fully encapsulated in such terms. It is an element only inadequately captured in terms like wonder, or enchantment, or aesthetic delight.[26]

Significantly, the "fashion-slashers" that precede *The Neon Demon* tend not to show their models celebrating the irreducible delight of beauty. Modeling scenes in *Helter Skelter* and *Eyes of Laura Mars* focus on the labor of fashion photography, showing the photographer shouting directions, models striking poses, and makeup artists applying cosmetics. Modeling scenes in these films are lively rather than sensuous or delightful, using fast editing and music to convey the chaos of the shoot. The exhausting physical work of modeling is also the focus of such moments. In *Helter Skelter*, for instance, Liliko repeatedly strikes the same pose for hours on end, which takes a heavy toll: "I'm so tired," she sighs to her assistant after a long day of shooting [26:07].

In *Blood and Black Lace*, modeling is barely shown at all; it takes place either offscreen or in the background while the models chatter, off-duty, in their dressing room. In these films, models provide pleasurable beauty for their audience, but they do not relish it for themselves. In contrast, the models in *The Neon Demon* indulge in the "wonder," "enchantment," and "aesthetic delight" of beauty as they create it.

In its climactic scene, *The Neon Demon* spectacularly brings together the violence and gratifications of beauty in a moment of aestheticized gore [96:29–98:06]. This occurs in the aftermath of Jesse's murder when Sarah and Gigi shower alongside one another in Ruby's mansion. Although not a literal photo shoot, the two women pose erotically for the camera, which moves slowly upward over their bodies; their pale skin is covered in blood. Like Jesse's photo shoot with Jack, the scene unfolds in slow motion, lingering on the textures of blood and water, emphasizing the liquids' running down Sarah's and Gigi's necks, torso, and legs. Here, blood takes the place of the gold paint from the earlier scene as a sensual, enlivening cosmetic. This moment is, in effect, an illustration of what Alexandra Heller-Nicholas calls "viscera-intensive beauty," an aesthetic characteristic of subgenres such as the Italian horror and *giallo* film—examples include *Blood and Black Lace*, *All the Colors of the Dark* (Sergio Martino, 1972), *Deep Red* (Dario Argento, 1975), and, more recently, *The Strange Color of Your Body's Tears* (Hélène Cattet and Bruno Forzani, 2013).[27] In such films, crimson blood and twisted corpses are aestheticized in a baroque mise-en-scène. In its graphic sensuality and vivid textural quality, Sarah and Gigi's moment in the shower perversely reiterates both the pleasure and destructiveness of beauty, a moment that is both erotic and horrifying, beautiful, and brutal.

It is important to note that *The Neon Demon* has been accused of misogyny in its characterization of Sarah, Ruby, and Gigi as murderous women. Tim Robey argues that Ruby is portrayed as having a "pathetic yearning for intimacy" that drives her to necrophilia with a female corpse.[28] Steve Rose notes that the film depicts models as shallow, calling them "sculpted, coutured frenemies, whose apparently benign intentions conceal a litany of womanly sins: they are catty, duplicitous, vacuous, narcissistic, predatory. They're evil lesbians and worse."[29] Moreover, as Rose's comments imply, Ruby's resemblance to the figure of the queer vampire may be thought of as problematic. Queer vampires have been described as a potentially homophobic trope insofar as their sexuality seems to be equated with their demonic, undead status; vampires are "unnatural," the argument goes, and their queerness is an extension of this "perversity" (according to a homophobic logic that sees homosexuality as aberrant).[30] This link between queerness and perversity is intensified in *The Neon Demon* when Ruby has sex with a cadaver she is beautifying, while working a side-job in a mortuary [87:48–89:38].

However, moments of reflexive humor in *The Neon Demon* endow the film with a comic and satirical tone. Andrew O'Hehir compliments *The Neon Demon* by stating that it "risks devolving into ludicrous self-parody at almost every moment,"[31] and Refn himself similarly asserts that the film is meant as a comedy.[32] The film's humor encourages a reading of the protagonists' violence as parodic. During the scene in the nightclub bathroom, for example, Gigi discovers that her lipstick is called "Red Rum," "murder" spelled backward [8:13]. This joke is a reference to *The Shining* (Stephen King's 1977 novel and Stanley Kubrick's 1980 film adaptation), in which Danny Torrance foresees his father's insanity by writing "REDRUM." Another joke based on an intertexual reference occurs when Gigi appears made up for Sarno's fashion show. Smeared with lipstick and blue eye shadow, she muses: "I'm not sure about the makeup this year" [57:34]. Not only does she look terrible—a dig at the fashion industry's tendency to mistake ugliness for edginess—but her makeup resembles Leatherface's lipstick and eye shadow in *The Texas Chain Saw Massacre*. Humor appears again shortly before Jesse's death when she declares, in a moment of dramatic irony, that "women would kill" to look like her [92:50]—a statement that proves so reflexively literal that it invites laughter. Such moments are knowingly comic, highlighting the intensity of the characters' narcissism and connecting them to the murderers of iconic horror films; indeed, Sarah, Gigi, and Ruby are made even more ridiculous by the fact that they are not original villains, but derivatives of preceding monsters and psychopaths. *The Neon Demon* thus presents Sarah, Gigi, and Ruby as manifestations of the deranging pleasures of beauty. They are murderous, vain, and cannibalistic; they are also amusingly unoriginal.

Conclusion

When speaking about *The Neon Demon*, Refn claims that he wanted to make a film about the hypocritical relationship that individuals have to beauty. He explains: "We tell each other that beauty is all about the inside. But there's also this part of everyone—I don't care who they are—that has vanity and is haunted by physical beauty."[33] Refn continues by acknowledging his own complex stance toward beauty: "Am I critical of it? Absolutely. But I am also extremely seduced by it and interested in it, obsessed by it. I love to look at beauty."[34] Refn's interest in this contradiction is embodied by his film, which both celebrates and condemns beauty. Lurid and luminous, *The Neon*

Demon meticulously constructs a beautiful mise-en-scène for the spectator to relish, yet warns against the dangers of beauty-obsessed narcissists like Gigi, Ruby, and Sarah. Exemplifying Refn's struggles, *The Neon Demon* is a knowingly hypocritical film that embraces its contradictions, undermining the narrative's critique of the beauty-obsessed villainesses with its own sensuous glamour.

Although Refn states that the film is "not quote-unquote *political*,"[35] he does consider *The Neon Demon* to be engaged with a specific, image-obsessed moment in Western societies. Observing his own daughters' negotiation of adolescence, he remarks: "Fascination with beauty has become obsession and gone into hyperdrive."[36] Elle Fanning similarly opines that *The Neon Demon* speaks to a problematic narcissism catalyzed by "the age of Instagram and Snapchat."[37] (Note that the film contains no references to social media or the internet; as such, it comments on beauty culture but does not seek to explain its origins.) As this chapter has argued, the conflicting perspectives on beauty in the film mirror debates in feminist discourse and postfeminist culture. *The Neon Demon* incorporates some feminists' condemnation of beauty as a mutilating imperative, while also adhering to postfeminist understandings of beauty as pleasurable affect. Through these contradictions, the film reflects a contemporary moment in which opposing ideas of beauty are circulating. This is not the film's sole function, of course. Refn admits that *The Neon Demon* is a genre exercise in horror,[38] and the film is densely populated with allusions to slasher films, *gialli*, and visual arts. In addition, *The Neon Demon* can be understood as a development in Refn's career, turning away from the hyperviolent masculinity of *Bronson* (2008), *Drive* (2011), and *Only God Forgives* (2013) to focus on women characters. Yet the film nevertheless also enters into a conversation about women's experiences of beauty in the here and now. Through its sumptuous visual style, *The Neon Demon* shows how beauty both animates the body and arouses the senses even as it can disfigure. Beauty is both morbid and enlivening, objectifying yet frighteningly invigorating.

Women who kill play a vital role in this exploration of beauty's contradictions. Sarah, Gigi, and Ruby are both the victims and perpetrators of beauty violence—the personified end-point of a narcissistic culture. Indeed, this is encapsulated in a wry moment at the film's climax when Jesse reveals that her mother once called her "a dangerous girl," referring, presumably, to the chaos that Jesse's beauty would inspire around her [92:20]. The irony is that Jesse, Gigi, Sarah, and Ruby are *all* dangerous girls in their capacity to attract and enact brutality. As villainesses, they are at once damaged and destructive, beautiful dolls come to life with malevolent intent. Importantly, *The Neon Demon* offers no solution to the problems of beauty that these women embody. The film's purpose, instead, is to vividly enact a circular, irresolvable dissonance about our troubled desire for beauty. Violent women are the fantastical, terrifying outcome.

Notes

1   Ana Elias, Rosalind Gill, and Christina Scharff, "Aesthetic labour: Rethinking beauty politics in neoliberalism," in A. Elias, R. Gill, and C. Scharff (eds.), *Aesthetic Labour: Rethinking Beauty Politics in Neoliberalism* (London: Palgrave Macmillan, 2017), pp. 25–26.

2   Ibid., p. 16.

3   While individual viewers may question the extent of Jesse's beauty, her attractiveness is a given in *The Neon Demon* itself—characters repeatedly describe her as perfect and flawless. With her long blonde hair, slim figure, and blue eyes, Jesse clearly conforms to a raced, heteronormative beauty ideal characteristic of Western cultures. Indeed, the film quite clearly evokes a European ideal, styling Jesse's hair and clothing to recall the women of Renaissance and pre-Raphaelite artists, such as those painted by Sandro Botticelli and Dante Gabriel Rossetti. In order to explore what the film has to say about beauty, I accept the central premise of *The Neon Demon*: that Jesse epitomizes feminine physical beauty.

4   Upon the film's release at the 69th Cannes Film Festival, most critics in attendance interpreted *The Neon Demon* as an auteur product—a film most easily understood as a continuation of Refn's earlier works such as *Only God Forgives* (2013) and *Drive* (2011) rather than a symptom of a contemporary cultural zeitgeist. While *The Neon Demon* is stylistically similar to these earlier films, I argue that it is not solely intelligible as a product of an individual director's imagination. It can also be analyzed as reflective of current concerns over beauty's meaning. Furthermore, defining *The Neon Demon* as an auteur film is complicated by the fact that the script was cowritten by playwrights Mary Laws and Polly Stenham; as such, Refn does not have sole authorship of the film.

5   *The Neon Demon* sits alongside a variety of other horror films that depict surgery as a violent, mutilating event. Some examples include *Rabid* (David Cronenberg, 1977), *May* (Lucky McKee, 2002), *American Mary* (Jen and Sylvia Soska, 2012), and *Excision* (Richard Bates, Jr, 2012). In addition to emphasizing the violence of surgical interventions, many of these films compare human bodies to inert objects such as dolls and machines. *Rabid* begins as the protagonist is injured in an automotive accident, her body mangled along with her motorcycle. The eponymous *May* sews body parts together to "make" herself a human doll. The protagonist of *American Mary* works as a surgeon for the body modification community, and her first job

is to transform a patient into the likeness of Betty Boop. Such scenarios reinforce the idea of surgery as a dehumanizing and objectifying process.

6 John Berger, *Ways of Seeing* (London: Penguin, 2008), p. 56.

7 Ibid.

8 According to the film's cinematographer Natasha Braier, Bourdin's photography was an important aesthetic influence for *The Neon Demon*. See Jean Oppenheimer, "Looks that kill," *American Cinematographer*, 97/7 (2016), p. 34.

9 See the DVD audio commentary of *The Neon Demon*.

10 Scott Foundas, "Anger management," *DGA Quarterly*, Summer 2012. Available at http://www.dga.org/Craft/DGAQ/All-Articles/1203-Summer-2012/Independent-Voice-Nicolas-Winding-Refn.aspx (accessed May 31, 2018).

11 Rosalind Gill, "Postfeminist media culture: Elements of a sensibility," *European Journal of Cultural Studies*, 10/2 (2007), p. 155.

12 Claire Colebrook, "Introduction," *Feminist Theory*, 7/2 (2006), p. 131.

13 Gill, "Postfeminist media culture," p. 149.

14 Jesse's eye has multiple functions in *The Neon Demon*. First, because Gigi regurgitates the eye in a moment of sickness and horror, it functions as a witness to, and reminder of, her guilt. Secondly, the eye has significance in Freudian psychoanalysis. In his essay on "The Uncanny," Freud argues that eye injuries are the most dreaded of all physical harms. Hence, imperiled eyeballs are a feature of uncanny texts. Lastly, Jesse's eye is significant because *The Neon Demon* begins with Jesse posing for photographs as if she were dead. Her glassy, supposedly unseeing eyes are prominent in the shot [2:57]. The moment presages Jesse's death; the return of her eye at the film's conclusion fulfills this gruesome promise.

15 Todd McCarthy, "'The Neon Demon': Cannes review," *The Hollywood Reporter*, May 19, 2016. Available at http://www.hollywoodreporter.com/re view/neon-demon-cannes-review-895905 (accessed August 14, 2017).

16 Elena Lazic and Manuela Lazic, "Does The Neon Demon accurately portray the fashion industry?" *Little White Lies*, June 24, 2016. Available at http://lwlies. com/articles/the-neon-demon-fashion-industry/ (accessed August 14, 2017).

17 Gill, "Postfeminist media culture," p. 153.

18 Ibid., p. 155.

19 Elias, Gill, and Scharff, "Aesthetic labour," p. 9.

20 Rita Felski, "'Because it is beautiful': New feminist perspectives on beauty," *Feminist Theory*, 7/2 (2006), pp. 279–80.

21 Colebrook, "Introduction," p. 132.

22 Elias, Gill, and Scharff, "Aesthetic labour," p. 16.

23 Rebecca Coleman and Mónica Moreno Figueroa, "Past and future perfect? Beauty, affect and hope," *Journal for Cultural Research*, 14/4 (2010), p. 361.

24 Patricia Ticineto Clough, "Introduction," in P. T. Clough and J. Hailey (eds.), *The Affective Turn: Theorizing the Social* (Durham: Duke University Press, 2007), p. 2.

25 Eleanor Heartney, "Foreword: Cutting two ways with beauty," in P. Z. Brand (ed.), *Beauty Matters* (Bloomington: Indiana University Press, 2000), p. xv.

26 Felski, "'Because it is beautiful,'" p. 281.

27 Alexandra Heller-Nicholas, *Suspiria* (Leighton Buzzard: Columbia University Press, 2015), p. 21.

28 Tim Robey, "The Neon Demon is the most offensive film of the year—and not because of the necrophilia," *Telegraph*, July 7, 2016. Available at http://www.telegraph.co.uk/films/2016/07/07/the-neon-demon-is-the-most -offensive-film-of-the-year---and-not/ (accessed January 17, 2018).

29 Steve Rose, "Best of frenemies: Why do men make movies about women in meltdown?" *The Guardian*, July 8, 2016. Available at https://www.theguard ian.com/film/2016/jul/07/best-of-frenemies-why-do-men-make-movies -about-women-in-meltdown (accessed January 17, 2018).

30 Janice Loreck, *Violent Women in Contemporary Cinema* (Houndmills, Basingstoke: Palgrave Macmillan, 2016), p. 75.

31 Andrew O'Hehir, "Is 'The Neon Demon' gruesome misogyny or brilliant feminist commentary? Can it be both?" *Salon*, June 23, 2016. Available at http://www.salon.com/2016/06/22/is_the_neon_demon_gruesome_ misogyny_or_brilliant_feminist_commentary_can_it_be_both/ (accessed August 18, 2017).

32 Refn makes this remark numerous times on the audio commentary for the DVD release of *The Neon Demon*.

33 Jada Yuan, "Nicolas Winding Refn and Elle Fanning on *Neon Demon*, Fanning's physical beauty, and a Knife-Wielding Keanu," *Vulture*, May 30, 2016. Available at http://www.vulture.com/2016/05/elle-fanning-nicola s-winding-refn-neon-demon-sex-keanu.html (accessed August 14, 2017).

34 Ibid.

35 Ibid.

36 Julie Miller, "Why Nicolas Winding Refn made a horror movie about the fashion industry," *Vanity Fair*, May 19, 2016. Available at https://www.van ityfair.com/hollywood/2016/05/nicolas-winding-refn-neon-demon- interview (accessed January 17, 2018).

37 Tasha Robinson, "Nicolas Winding Refn and Elle Fanning talk Neon Demon, and the narcissism of the selfie generation," *The Verge*, June 21, 2016. Available at https://www.theverge.com/2016/6/21/11989398/neon-demon- interview-nicolas-winding-refn-elle-fanning (accessed January 17, 2018).

38 Miller, "Why Nicolas Winding Refn."

Filmography

The Neon Demon, directed by Nicolas Winding Refn, written by Nicolas Winding Refn, Mary Laws, and Polly Stenham, produced by Elliott Hostetter, performances by Ella Fanning, Karl Glusman, Jena Malone, Bella Heathcote,

Abbey Lee, Desmond Harrington, Christina Hendricks, Keanu Reeves, cinematography by Natasha Braier, editing by Matthew Newman, music by Cliff Martinez, Space Rocket Nation/Vendian Entertainment/Bold Films/ Danish Broadcasting Corporation/MEDIA Programme of the European Union/Wild Bunch, 2016. DVD. Madman, 2016.

17

Evidence of Cruel Optimism

Nick Broomfield's *Aileen: Life and Death of a Serial Killer* (2003)

Rosie White

In *Aileen: Life and Death of a Serial Killer* (2003), the British documentary filmmaker Nick Broomfield attempts to provide yet another rationale for Aileen Wuornos's murder of seven men in Florida during 1989–90. The film portrays a woman whose deprived and abusive background contributes to the murders and to her alleged mental instability toward the end of her sentence, and who was eventually executed at Florida State Prison in 2002. Wuornos's crimes are framed within the documentary by her class and social background; the film aims to demonstrate that the justice system did not serve her well. In this regard, Broomfield's documentary follows the narrative trajectory of many factual and fictional accounts of Wuornos's life. Broomfield's earlier film *Aileen Wuornos: The Selling of a Serial Killer* (1992) and *Monster* (Patty Jenkins, 2003), which was based on *Aileen: Life and Death of a Serial Killer* (2003), construct her as a deviant, victimized figure. As Belinda Morrissey notes, "traditional legal and media representations of the Wuornos case [. . .] persistently deny her agency through strategies of monsterization and victimization."[1] Representations of women who kill often work hard to contain and explain their actions, attempting to manage the ways in which female killers disturb binary accounts of gender and sexual identity. Aileen Wuornos, as she appears in Broomfield's two documentary films, is the abject other to postfeminist formulations of femininity. She is not young, thin, middle class, or "properly" white.[2] As a working-class woman, a lesbian, a former sex worker, and a prison inmate, Wuornos does not conform to the late-twentieth and early-twenty-first-century "common sense" that Rosalind Gill argues has established postfeminism as "a kind of gendered neoliberalism."[3] Whereas postfeminist media representations focus on youthful white heterofemininity and a narrative of success founded on neoliberal fictions of equal opportunity,

Wuornos's case exposes the fault lines in such fantasies and draws attention to how they can damage or destroy the nonconforming subject.[4]

This chapter returns to the depiction of Aileen Wuornos in Broomfield's 2003 documentary as a means of examining the ways in which women who kill expose what Lauren Berlant has termed "cruel optimism."[5] In her 2011 book, Berlant continues her long-standing project to analyze and deconstruct the philosophical implications of the American Dream for living in the present. The optimism that such a dream represents is cruel in that it can never fully be achieved; it is often held out to subjects who have little or no chance of experiencing even aspects of its realization. In her examination of the radical potential of "bad feelings," Elizabeth Stephens notes how works by Sarah Ahmed, Rosi Braidotti, and Berlant speak back to neoliberal positivist discourse, which advocates the pursuit of "perfection," whether that be the "perfect" body, the "perfect" career, or the "perfect" life. Such perfections are embedded in popular postfeminist media narratives as if they were neutral categories rather than a "common sense" that excludes many working-class, non-Caucasian, and queer subjects. Their effects are not accounted for; "for some subjects," as Berlant recognizes, "the cultural imperative to be optimistic really can be exhausting or even toxic, and the consequences of this for subjects not privileged by existing ideas about a good life should not be underestimated."[6] Wuornos's story can be understood as one example of the toxicity of such neoliberal optimism, demonstrating its exhausting and—in her case—fatal consequences. Nevertheless, as Berlant argues,

> Even when it turns out to involve a cruel relation, it would be wrong to see optimism's negativity as a symptom of error, a perversion, damage, or a dark truth: optimism is, instead, a scene of negotiated sustenance that makes life bearable as it presents itself ambivalently, unevenly, incoherently.[7]

This, however, is exactly how Wuornos's story is often depicted—as precisely "a symptom of error, a perversion, damage, or a dark truth." Popular and academic accounts[8] of her crimes, conviction, and execution repeatedly position Wuornos as a crazy woman, a man-hating lesbian, a victim of a flawed judicial system, or a woman who has responded in a logical manner to the dark threat of patriarchy.

Documentary Evidence

Lynda Hart proposes: "Whereas male serial killers are 'naturally unnatural,' as a woman Wuornos has committed *unnaturally? unnatural* acts. The 'unnaturalness' of her crimes has, of course, everything to do with the fact that she is a woman."[9] Wuornos's intervention in the discursive formation of American mythologies regarding serial killing and femininity is contradictory. She is "unnatural" as a serial killer because she is not male, and she is "unnatural" as a woman because she kills. This double jeopardy regarding her crimes and gender means that she presents a double puzzle for popular narratives such as true-crime books and films, which constantly attempt to tell the "truth" about how and why criminals act as they do.[10] The "true crime" genre is aligned with the narrative structures of crime fiction, presenting a problem that is resolved—or at least revealed—by the end of the story: "Serial killing is [. . .] presented as an essentially *intertextual* crime: any new instance only makes sense in relation to what has gone before, and the links with previous stories extend the serial nature of the discourse itself."[11] *Aileen: Life and Death of a Serial Killer* (2003) is not merely *intertextual* but *hypertextual*, as it cannibalizes its predecessor, *Aileen Wuornos: The Selling of a Serial Killer*. In addition to news footage of Wuornos's crimes, capture, and trials, the 2003 documentary also includes footage from Broomfield's earlier film, most notably when the director is called as a witness during one of Wuornos's final appeals [14:16–17:59]. In this sequence, Broomfield's 1992 film itself becomes an item of evidence. The prosecution and defense debate how and why the film has been edited, and the director offers to provide footage from the cutting room floor. Issues of representation—how female killers are represented both legally and discursively—are foregrounded in this sequence, as are the narcissistic aspects of Broomfield's documentary style. The very definition of the serial killer, attributed to FBI agent Robert Ressler, is linked to fictional tropes, as Ressler coined the term with reference to "memories of Sunday afternoons at the movies during his boyhood, when 'serial adventures' lured him back again and again with their cliff-hanger endings."[12] The cultural mythology of the serial killer is thus entwined with fiction, memory, and nostalgia, offering a potent cocktail of fantasy, fascination, and revulsion. As a female serial killer, however, Aileen Wuornos's crimes do not make sense within this mythology. Attempts to explain why she killed her victims tend to rely on depictions of Aileen as an aberrant figure because of her gender, class, and sexuality. Most notably, the narratives surrounding Aileen Wuornos disturb popular depictions of the serial killer as a highly efficient, intelligent hypermasculine individual. As Wuornos notes in the second Broomfield documentary, "I was no professional serial killer or anything, murderer, whatever you want to call it. [. . .] I did some sloppy work" [77:10].

Broomfield's two films about Wuornos underline the chaotic and haphazard trajectory of her life and death. In these terms, Wuornos may be understood as an exemplary account of the "cruel optimism," which late Western capitalism holds out to its subjects, even as it snatches away the structures that might enable such optimism to be at least partially justified. Wuornos attempts to negotiate what Stephens calls "bad feelings"[13] during her dialogue with Broomfield. In *Aileen: Life and Death of a Serial Killer*, Wuornos grants Broomfield two final interviews: the first at Broward Prison in Florida, May 2002, before Jeb Bush, then Governor of Florida, signed her death warrant, and the second at Florida State Prison on October 8, one day before her execution. Broomfield states that the final interview is an exclusive, as Wuornos has decided not to give a public press conference: "I'm sure that's because she wants me to communicate her ideas about what she calls the crooked cops." That does appear to be the case, as Wuornos is led into a highly staged interview with Broomfield in shackles, attended by fifteen guards and the prison warden [76:17]. In response to Broomfield's initial question as to whether she is "prepared" for the execution the following morning, Wuornos states that she is "alright with it" and launches into a critique of the system that has incarcerated her:

> I'm alright with it, but, like I said, remember, tell—let them know, that I know that the cops knew who I was after Richard Mallory died. I left prints everywhere and they covered it up. They let me kill the rest of those guys to turn me into a serial killer. [76:51–77:08]

The camera focuses solely on Wuornos as she becomes increasingly angry. Prison lighting bleaches out her pallid complexion, and her hair looks greasy and unkempt. Whereas in earlier interviews, she was able to pause and brush or comb it back, here the shackles and the setting make her ever more monstrous as a woman who is beyond the bounds of normative femininity. One of the guards sits behind her and is often shot, chewing gum impassively, although at times a flicker of amusement crosses his face. Wuornos has become an exhibit in a freak show, an animal at bay, about to be slaughtered. She may be "alright with it," but she continues to speak, to assert her right to be heard. Whether that right is acknowledged is entirely questionable, as both the prison authorities and Broomfield are keen to assert their own narrative. In this sequence, Wuornos makes several apparently irrational statements. In addition to her claim that the police endorsed and enabled the murders, she states that she has been tortured in her cell by "sonic pressure" [77:36], that her food has been poisoned, and that death is going to be "like *Star Trek*, beaming me up into a space vehicle, man, then move on, recolonize to another planet or whatever" [79:17]. She concludes by saying: "I did the right thing. I saved a lot of people's butts from getting raped and killed and stuff" [79:28].

Here, indeed, "optimism is [. . .] a scene of negotiated sustenance that makes life bearable as it presents itself ambivalently, unevenly, incoherently."[14] During these last interviews, Wuornos is often contradictory, lending weight to Broomfield's diagnosis of her mental state as "crazy," yet she continually resists legal and media narratives that seek to place her in relation to a single ontological "truth," either as an evil monster or as a victim of her deprived and abusive upbringing. In the final interview, Wuornos takes control, refusing to discuss her crimes as self-defense and exploding with anger when Broomfield mentions he has been to see her birth mother, who abandoned her. She threatens to stop the interview, but first launches into one last angry tirade (Figure17.1):

> I was a hitchhiking hooker, running into trouble. I'd shoot the guy if I ran into trouble. Physical trouble. The cops knew it—physical trouble—let her clean the streets. [. . .] I lost my fucking life because of it. Couldn't get a fair trial—couldn't even get a fair investigation or nothing. Couldn't even handle my appeals right. You sabotaged my ass, society. And the cops, and the system. A raped woman got executed, and was used for books and movies and shit. [. . .] You're an inhumane bunch of fucking living bastards and bitches, and you're going to get your asses nuked in the end. [. . .] I been trying to tell the truth and I keep getting stepped on. [82:02–83:34]

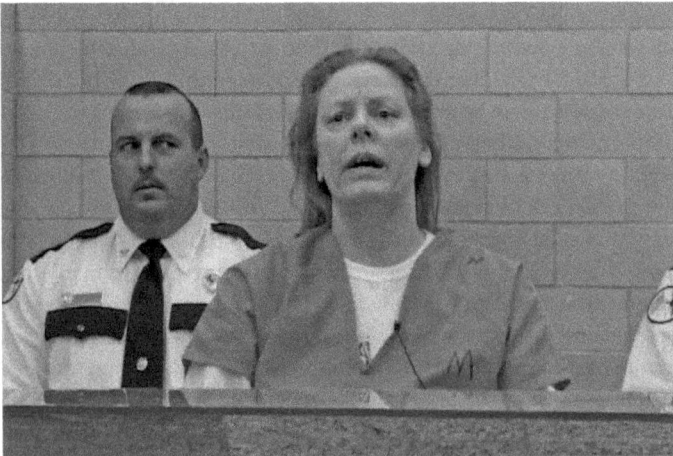

Figure 17.1 *Aileen Wuornos: Life and Death of a Serial Killer* (Broomfield, 2003): Aileen Wuornos and the prison guard.

Wuornos's coherent analysis is undermined by the camera's close attention to her appearance. In extreme close-up, her pallid angry face is fleshy and distorted by rage. She is an object of study, a freak-show piece of meat. The film thus demonstrates the effects of the "system" Wuornos decries and also replicates those effects by refusing to *hear* her. Just as Broomfield's voice-over dominates the film's narrative, so the *visual* representation of Wuornos's anger and distress is privileged over what she has to say. Despite Broomfield's claim to sympathize with her, he is part of the structure that profits from Wuornos's scandalous crimes and final execution. As she leaves the interview, Broomfield says he is "sorry," but Wuornos gives him the finger, accurately positioning him alongside the "system" that has chosen to judge her [84:21]. Her analysis is thus both "crazy" and accurate: society has, in effect, "sabotaged [her] ass."

A Multiplicity of Texts

Wuornos's capture and conviction in the early nineties were greeted by a multiplicity of media texts attempting to profit from her story and claiming to explain her crimes. *Aileen: Life and Death of a Serial Killer* references this profusion of paratexts, offering a montage of American news reports and interviews with members of the victims' families in its first few minutes. This palimpsestic aesthetic is compounded by the 2003 film's cannibalistic relation to *Aileen Wuornos: The Selling of a Serial Killer*, the second film including extensive footage from the first. Broomfield's 1992 documentary capitalized upon the currency and sensationalism of Aileen's story, depicting police corruption, her ineffective legal representation, and the exploitative "family" that developed around Aileen during her original trial. Thomas Doherty observes that the film "revelled in the blood sport media journalism it excoriated" and insists on Broomfield's history of making films about transgressive women such as Heidi Fleiss and Courtney Love.[15] Yet the intertextuality on display in *Aileen: Life and Death of a Serial Killer* makes evident the constructed and subjective quality of documentary filmmaking itself as a "complex interaction between text, context, producer and spectator."[16] Broomfield's second film about Wuornos self-consciously foregrounds this complexity. The depiction of the Aileen Wuornos case is not more truthful or honest than that of its peers, but it is more overtly informed by a professional and critical understanding of the form it inhabits.

Other commentaries on Wuornos are less and more sophisticated in their deployment of a medium. In addition to lurid television reports during her trial and execution, Aileen's narrative has proliferated across a range of popular media and high culture forms. She features in television documentaries and made-for-television movies, as well as the Hollywood version of her story in *Monster*. She became the subject of editorial pieces in tabloid and broadsheet newspapers and magazines and of many (often independently published) true-crime books. Her story was made into an opera, and she has featured in works by a number of feminist artists.[17] Miriam Basilio notes the extent to which the capture, trial, and death of Aileen Wuornos has become a blank canvas onto which a range of debates about class, gender, sexuality, and politics have been projected: "The case has become a sensationalized media spectacle in a climate of anxiety about the assignment of gender roles, the ostensible causes of homosexuality, the definition of sexual harassment, rape and self-defence, and the causes of economic decline."[18] What fascinates most commentators about Wuornos's salutary tale is its exceptional nature: the contradictions of the woman who kills. Not only is Wuornos a woman who kills, but she is also exceptional in that she did not kill children or other women but men: specifically white middle-class men, a category more often the subject of serial killer mythologies. This was made much of during her trial:

> Throughout the media coverage of the case, the men she killed were defined by their age, middle-class occupation, and type of car they drove, while Wuornos's abuse history and marginal occupation and class were cited as evidence of her pathology and inherent criminality.[19]

Categories of gender, class, and race thus establish the victims' "respectable" status, despite their use of prostitutes, while the same criteria are used to establish Aileen Wuornos's *lack* of respectability. The double standards of gender and sexuality are writ large across this narrative, building upon sexist discourses where female sex workers represent nonnormative heterofemininity, but their male customers are within the terms of normative heteromasculinity. Wuornos resists this discourse, just as she refused to assume the position of the victim or the monster in earlier interviews, insisting that she was merely in the wrong place at the wrong time and that her violent response to customers who attempted to sexually assault her was a rational solution to a problem.[20] She offered no remorse and no apology for her actions, reversing the dominant cultural dynamics of gender in Western culture where women are usually the object to men's subject: "[Wuornos] undeniably cast herself as a subject and her male victims as dispensable objects."[21] She thus refused to play a passive role, but instead assumed the role of agent within her own drama. Such assertions of selfhood, together with the intersectional politics of class, gender, and sexual identity that surround the case, have made Wournos the subject of a number of feminist studies.

Feminist Studies of Wuornos

Lynda Hart's influential analysis of the Wuornos case addresses her crimes as a symptom of gender politics. Reiterating Kate Millett's proposal in *Sexual Politics* that the male serial killer is a logical extension of dysfunctional gender and power relations fostered by patriarchal society, Hart questions whether Wuornos can be termed a serial killer at all.[22] Many of the media reports that greeted her capture and trial depicted Wuornos as a predatory, man-hating lesbian, who stalked her prey and lured them into vulnerable situations with the promise of sexual favors.[23] This plays to the legal and psychological profile of the male serial killer who kills not for material gain but for his own gratification. Male serial killers tend to have sexual and sadistic desires for their victims, whom they do not know or have a relationship with. In her testimony during the first trial, Wuornos repeatedly asserted that she was a prostitute who killed clients that threatened, raped, or attacked her, killing in self-defense, and thus only employing violence to respond to violence. She used their cars and money to support herself and her then partner Tyria Moore. Hart therefore reads Wuornos in the context of ongoing feminist debates about gender and power, referencing the work of Gayle Rubin and Luce Irigaray regarding how women are used by men as objects of exchange within patriarchal structures:

> Without "woman" as man's symptom, men are left without this object to exchange and are confronted with the commerce between themselves. How altogether fittingly ironic that a hitchhiking lesbian prostitute, Aileen Wuornos, has not only made this traffic in women apparent, but has also turned the brutality of this exchange back on the primary players.[24]

In this account, Wuornos becomes a feminist signifier, representing an extreme but logical response to the violence inherent within a social order that privileges men and masculine expression over women and femininity.

In her study of Broomfield's first documentary about Wuornos, Paige Schilt follows a similar trajectory to Hart, observing the gender and sexual politics at work in *The Selling of a Serial Killer*. Like Doherty, Schilt notes that Broomfield is often drawn to make films about scandalous women; she is particularly critical of his ethical position:

> Although several of Broomfield's encounters with the main players foreground the issue of money for testimony, there is no discussion of the fact that Broomfield himself is funded by Britain's Channel Four. The

film does not question what is at stake in representing ghastly American crimes to a British audience or how Broomfield stands to profit (both monetarily and professionally) from the Wuornos case.[25]

Despite Broomfield's critique of how US news media and the people surrounding Aileen attempt to exploit her story for financial gain, he fails to acknowledge that he is doing much the same thing.

Bill Nichols cites Broomfield's work in his definition of "participatory" documentary: "Here filmmakers do interact with their subjects rather than unobtrusively observe them. [. . .] Like the performative mode, the filmmaker's presence and perspective often contribute significantly to the film's overall impact."[26] Nichols describes this form of documentary in terms of *cinéma vérité*:

> As "film truth," the idea emphasizes that this is the truth of a filmed encounter rather than absolute or untampered truth. We see how the filmmaker and subject negotiate a relationship, how they act toward one another, what forms of power and control come into play, and what levels of revelation or rapport stem from this specific form of encounter. Cinéma vérité reveals the reality of what happens when people interact in the presence of a camera.[27]

That relationship is evident throughout *Life and Death of a Serial Killer*, but it is not always clear that the power and control on each side are equally negotiated. At one point in his penultimate interview with Wuornos, Broomfield's codirector and camera operator, Joan Churchill, lays the camera on a shelf in the interview room [66:39]. Until this point, the interview has been filmed from Broomfield's point of view, through the glass that separates him from Wuornos, with a tight close-up of her face (Figure 17.2) [58:16–66:38]. From this angle, Wuornos would have had clear sight of the camera focused on her. When it is removed from her line of vision, she understandably assumes that the camera is off and no longer recording what she says. We briefly see some film boxes and the wall, but as Broomfield continues to talk to Wuornos and she begins to confide in him in a whisper, the camera is repositioned so that she cannot see it. Broomfield is shot from the side, earnestly speaking to her through the glass and not acknowledging the lens that is now focused on him. It is clear that Wuornos is neither aware that the camera is still running, nor that their conversation has been recorded on audio throughout. This appears to be a setup, designed to encourage Wuornos to open up, but also taking away any informed consent or agency on her part. It is a betrayal,

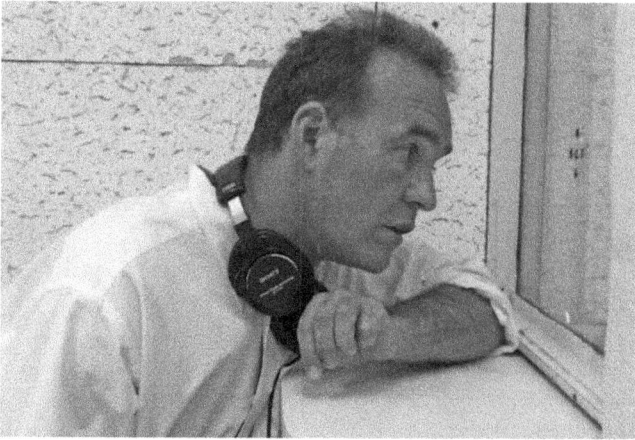

Figure 17.2 *Aileen Wuornos: Life and Death of a Serial Killer* (Broomfield, 2003): Nick Broomfield interviewing Aileen Wuornos when she believes they are not recording her.

disrupting the terms of *cinéma vérité* because Wuornos is not aware that she is still being recorded.

Nick Broomfield's on-screen persona is deeply problematic. Much of his documentary work addresses American subjects, such as *Heidi Fleiss: Hollywood Madam* (1995), *Kurt and Courtney* (1998), and *Biggie and Tupac* (2002), and Broomfield often deploys his image as an Englishman abroad, with a glassy drawl that speaks of privilege and private education. In the Wuornos films, Broomfield's class and national identity would seem to render him an "objective" observer. He is a "celebrity documentary filmmaker," with each film billed as "A film by Nick Broomfield," thereby eliding the role of his crew and that of Joan Churchill, Broomfield's former wife and codirector of several of his films, including *Life and Death of a Serial Killer*.[28] As Schilt notes in her essay, class is a significant aspect of Broomfield's work. In both films about Wuornos, he spends much time documenting the admittedly appalling details of her upbringing, ostensibly as a means of "explaining" her crimes, yet at the same time offering a salacious view of white working-class America.

This "white trash" biography narrated by an upper-class Englishman once more plays to the freak-show aesthetics. His access to, and "friendship" with, Aileen is deployed carefully throughout, implying that Broomfield himself has the "real" story, as opposed to the more tabloid representations evidenced in both documentaries, culled from US news feeds. Broomfield's role as filmmaker and as subject of his own documentary is entirely questionable. At the end of the film, Broomfield offers himself to the gathered press outside the prison on the morning of her execution as the last person to interview her: he has become the news. Wearing a clean white shirt and raised above the microphones that surround him, he states:

> I just formed an impression that here was somebody who has lost her mind, has totally lost touch with reality, and we're executing a person who's mad and I don't really know what kind of message that gives. I find it really disturbing.

In a sense, Broomfield, in his documentaries, is having his cake and eating it, too, making Aileen an object of scrutiny while claiming to represent a more objective and ethical standpoint. Schilt compares Broomfield's use of news footage and police mugshots, as well as the predominant use of close-ups in his encounters with her, to early criminological techniques in the nineteenth and early twentieth centuries, where physiognomy and phrenology were deployed to evidence deviant characteristics.[29] Tanya Horeck takes this last point even further, aligning Broomfield's use of close-ups of Aileen with the images of "hysterical" women staged by Jean-Martin Charcot at the Salpêtrière Hospital in nineteenth-century Paris:

> The extreme closeups of Wuornos, in the trailer as well as in the documentary itself, are presented as visual verification of [her mental] disturbance. Mary Ann Doane notes that "the scale of the close-up transforms the face into an instance of the gigantic, the monstrous, it overwhelms." The closeups of Wuornos contribute to her monstrosity and demonstrate the degree of her anguish; they also present her face as a "text" to be read.[30]

As with more populist representations of Aileen Wuornos, Broomfield's documentaries purport to offer a kind of truth about the murders and her motivation for committing them. While *Aileen Wuornos: The Selling of a Serial Killer* focused on the corrupt media circus surrounding her arrest and conviction, *Aileen: Life and Death of a Serial Killer* addresses the death sentence, offering a polemic against capital punishment. The DVD of the second film includes as "extras" a copy of the first film, introductions to each film by Broomfield himself, an interview with Broomfield about his career, the theatrical trailer for Patty Jenkins's *Monster* (2003), and a documentary arguing against the death penalty in the United States. This assortment of paratexts demonstrates the intertextual and interstitial status of the documentary itself, as both apart from, and dependent on, its sister narratives. Even as the narratives around Aileen attempt to search for "the truth" (whatever that is), they are always already interpolated by other versions:

> The "whole" story of the Wuornos affair might never be totally told, but its telling lies somewhere in the "intertext" of court records, documentary films, dramatized films, news broadcasts and so on, rather than in any one definitive telling of the story.[31]

Truth is evasive in this context, and Broomfield's documentaries make this part of the narrative, as the filmmaker is shown chasing leads, documenting "evidence" in the form of interviews, and essaying on his own "journey." There is a strong cinematic aesthetic at work here, with lingering shots through the car windshield as Broomfield traverses the United States to visit Aileen's childhood friends and her birth mother. The handheld camera and nondiegetic music construct a "true story" narrative punctuated by footage that tracks down suburban streets, country lanes, and remote highways. The polemical thrust of each film adds to the notion of Broomfield's quasi-scientific "journey," which deploys Aileen's story as, first, a critique of the US criminal justice system, and second, a damning indictment of the death penalty.

Despite their different attempts to "explain" Aileen, Broomfield and the feminist analyses have something in common: they all claim to listen to what Aileen Wuornos says and even lend her self-narrative some credibility. Horeck's article begins by citing Wuornos's statement at the end of Broomfield's 2003 film:

> In her final interview before execution, the camera zooms in for an extreme closeup as an exhausted and angry Wuornos delivers a disturbing rant: "You sabotaged my ass, society. And the cops. And the system. A raped woman got executed and was used for books and movies and shit."[32]

Wuornos here succinctly summarizes Broomfield, Hart, Schilt, and Horeck's arguments, as they all, in different ways, propose her as an example of how American culture erases and destroys the lives of working-class women. Broomfield's introduction to the 2003 documentary cites Wuornos herself as "the most honest person involved in the case," inadvertently indicting himself as one of the less-than-honest people who surround her. The film begins, however, by constructing Wuornos as a victim, with Broomfield's voice-over characterizing her as someone who was "betrayed by those closest to her, all her life." Again, one can include Broomfield in this process of betrayal: a filmmaker who deploys her "story," ostensibly as a means of condemning the death penalty in the United States.

Cruel Optimism

Aileen's contradictory account of her own story in *The Life and Death of a Serial Killer* is repeatedly undercut by Broomfield's voice-over narration. By the final appeal, Aileen has revised her original plea of self-defense. As Wuornos asserts that she killed in cold blood, the camera lingers on her aged face, her skin yellowed from many years without sun. The film's use of extreme close-ups is relentless, often zooming in on her eyes, which appear to be entirely subsumed by their pupils. As Schilt and Horeck have noted, this technique is designed to offer viewers the impression that we are, in effect, seeing into the heart of darkness, into the mind of a serial killer, lending evidence to Broomfield's claims that Wuornos is mentally unstable. When he questions her change of plea, Wuornos asserts that the earlier claim of self-defense was just "my lying gig, trying to beat the system" [26:12]. In this, Wuornos appears lucid and strategic, an impression borne out by her whispered assertion, when she believes herself to be speaking off-camera, that she is desperate to die and only changed her plea in order to hasten her execution: "They're too corrupt. . . . They'll never do me right, they'll only fuck me over some more" [67:12]. Such mordant pragmatism is in distinct contrast to the footage of Wuornos after the first trial where she was originally sentenced. Speaking to press outside the courthouse, Wuornos stands in handcuffs flanked by her police escorts and states tearfully: "I cannot believe this has happened" [30:59].

This moment embodies the affective power of the "cruel optimism" that the American Dream holds out to its Others. Wuornos's initial refusal to "believe this has happened" indicates the extent to which that dream overrode her lived experience, as evidenced by her own testimony at the original trial. Judith Butler asserts that "women and minorities, including sexual minorities, are, as a community, subjected to violence, exposed to its possibility, if not its realization."[33] Wuornos's case—the murders she committed and her grim biography, which emerged during the trials—expose the violence that suffuses the life experience of working-class women, as well as the violence with which the state responds to women who deviate from their role as victims. In these terms, Aileen becomes yet another symbol, this time of a society that relies on violence, which needs it and produces it as a symptom of the material economies of neoliberal capital. In this regard, Wuornos's assertion that "[the cops] let me kill the rest of those guys to turn me into a serial killer" rings true. Her vulnerability thus becomes our vulnerability, her violent response to a violent environment a timely reminder of how we live now. Butler notes how violence and vulnerability are closely entwined:

> To the extent that we commit violence, we are acting on another, putting the other at risk, causing the other damage, attempting to expunge the other. In a way we all live with this vulnerability, a vulnerability to the other that is part of bodily life, a vulnerability to a sudden address from elsewhere that we cannot pre-empt. This vulnerability, however, becomes highly exacerbated under certain social and political conditions, especially those in which violence is a way of life and the means to secure self-defence are limited.[34]

Like Broomfield, academics watching this film and writing about it are doing so from a safe distance. This is not "our" life or death; it is certainly not what we imagine for ourselves. Yet Wuornos's attempt to control her own narrative in Broomfield's film may be understood as an affective *aide-mémoire*, a reminder that we are part of the structure that confined and executed her. If we commit violence, it may not be that of the gun or the fist, but rather the violence of separating ourselves from figures like that of Aileen Wuornos, regarding them as monsters rather than as a reminder of our own vulnerability. In the aforementioned quote, Butler is musing on the affective resonance of September 11, 2001, the iconic moment when a violence more often enacted on news footage was brought home to the West. The case of Aileen Wuornos is likewise a homecoming, a reminder that neoliberal economies require an underclass, albeit one that is more usually compliant and invisible.

Once again, this places Wuornos as a symbolic figure, as someone who stands for something rather than as a subject in her own right. In Broomfield's 2003 film, she continues to resist this symbolic role, accusing witnesses called for the defense at her final appeal of perjury because they talk about her as having an abusive and dysfunctional childhood. Broomfield proposes this as evidence of her mental instability, but Aileen's refusal to accept this dark account of her youth demonstrates her attempts to control her own narrative and to refuse official attempts to classify her as Other. Nobody asks Aileen how she remembers her childhood, and she is determined to give her version in the penultimate interview with Broomfield:

> The truth about my family is this. My Dad was so straight and so clean. He wouldn't even take his shirt off to mow the lawn. He did not believe

in cussing. He did not believe in long hair and mini-skirts and stuff. He was really straight. Really decent. And so was my Mom. My Mom hated swearing in the house. If you said one swear word you had a whole bar of Lava Soap in your mouth. I came from a real clean and decent family. [61:39-62:21]

Wuornos identifies the death of her mother as the end of her "decent" life, because her father threw her out of the house following a teenage pregnancy, and Wuornos lived rough. Even this experience, however, is framed as ordinary: "The other kids were all living in their houses while I was on the street. But it's alright. I lived through it" [63:53]. Wuornos here presents herself as a survivor rather than a victim of circumstance, as someone who managed to "live through" adversity. Broomfield then asks how her life would have been if her childhood had been different:

I would have become, more than likely, an outstanding citizen of America, who would have either been an archaeologist, a paramedic, a police officer, a fire department gal, or an undercover worker for DEA [the federal Drug Enforcement agency], or—did I say archaeologist? Or a missionary. Because I believe in God but I'm not a Christian freak—so scrub missionary—I would have done it real decent. [64:55–65:33]

At this point, Wuornos is on Death Row waiting for the date of execution and complaining about being subjected to bizarre forms of persecution and surveillance. Yet at the same time, the cruel optimism of the American Dream remains apparent. Wuornos believes she could have been "an outstanding citizen of America," positioning herself with regard to national identity and proceeding to list a range of professional roles. She does not see herself as Other, but rather as a potential member of the white middle-class elite, an academic, a law enforcement officer, as "real decent."

In this projection of a "decent" life, Aileen Wuornos offers a different kind of evidence. The cacophony of texts and paratexts around the murders, together with Wuornos's process through a flawed judicial system, evidences the "cruel optimism" of this narrative: "the condition of maintaining an attachment to a significantly problematic object."[35] In these terms, we might understand Wuornos's story as narrated by others and her account of her own life as a fantasy that has destroyed her. Her faith in the American Dream of family and of a fair social and juridical system has been exposed as fallacious, so that she becomes the dupe, the fool, the patsy of a public discourse, which is "a significantly problematic object." Yet, as I indicated earlier, Berlant refuses to see this cruel optimism as "error"; instead, she acknowledges how such fantasies may be the only thing to sustain a subject in extremis. Berlant describes this dynamic in the following manner:

> a relation of attachment to compromised conditions of possibility whose realization is discovered either to be *im*possible, sheer fantasy, or *too* possible, and toxic. What's cruel about these attachments, and not merely inconvenient or tragic, is that the subjects who have *x* in their lives might not well endure the loss of their object/scene of desire, even though its presence threatens their well-being, because whatever the *content* of the attachment is, the continuity of its form provides something of the continuity of the subject's sense of what it means to keep on living on and to look forward to being in the world.[36]

Even as she awaits execution, Wuornos is holding on to an attachment that has destroyed her life, which has been shown to be false and which will literally prevent her "living on." As with her time living rough, however, Aileen Wuornos refuses to frame herself as a victim but rather as a survivor. She does not see herself as evil, or as entirely helpless, and accurately identifies the culprit: "You sabotaged my ass, society." Instead, she mobilizes the American Dream to sustain her at the end of her life as "a scene of negotiated sustenance that makes life bearable as it presents itself ambivalently, unevenly, incoherently."[37] Her strategic deployment of such fantasies may appear to viewers, as to Broomfield, as evidence of insanity, but they can also be understood as an attempt to survive a cruel situation while retaining some dignity and a sense of self. In these terms, *Aileen Wuornos: The Selling of a Serial Killer* manifestly contradicts the fantasies of postfeminist popular culture in favor of a more rigorous narrative—one that tracks the precarity of white working-class lives through its navigation of such cruel optimism.

Notes

1　Belinda Morrissey, *When Women Kill: Questions of Agency and Subjectivity* (London and New York: Routledge, 2003), p. 31.

2　For relevant discussions and definitions of postfeminism, see, for example: Rosalind Gill and Christina Scharff, "Introduction," in R. Gill and C. Scharff (eds.), *New Femininities: Postfeminism, Neoliberalism and Subjectivity* (London: Palgrave Macmillan, 2011), pp. 1–17, and Yvonne Tasker and Diane Negra, "Introduction: Feminist politics and postfeminist culture," in Yvonne Tasker and Diane Negra (eds.), *Interrogating Postfeminism: Gender and the Politics of Popular Culture* (Durham and London: Duke University Press, 2007), pp. 1–25.

3 Rosalind Gill, "The affective, cultural and psychic life of postfeminism: A postfeminist sensibility 10 years on," *European Journal of Cultural Studies*, 20/6 (2017), p. 606.

4 Angela McRobbie, "Preface," in R. Gill and C. Scharff (eds.), *New Femininities: Postfeminism, Neoliberalism and Subjectivity* (London: Palgrave Macmillan, 2011), pp. xi–xv.

5 Lauren Berlant, *Cruel Optimism* (Durham, NC and London: Duke University Press, 2011).

6 Elizabeth Stephens, "Bad feelings," *Australian Feminist Studies*, 30/85 (2015), p. 280.

7 Berlant, *Cruel Optimism*, p. 14.

8 See Mark MacNamara, "Kiss and kill: Out of Florida's recent wave of horrific crimes comes a dark version of Thelma and Louise in a rare case of a female serial killer," *Vanity Fair* (September 1991), pp. 91–106; *Peter Levin's made-for-TV movie Overkill: The Aileen Wuornos Story* (1992); Lynda Hart, *Fatal Women: Lesbian Sexuality and the Mark of Aggression* (London and New York: Routledge, 1994); Paige Schilt, "Media whores and perverse media: Documentary film meets tabloid TV in Nick Broomfield's Aileen Wuornos: The selling of a serial killer," *The Velvet Light Trap*, 45 (Spring 2000), pp. 50–61; Tanya Horeck, "From documentary to drama: Capturing Aileen Wuornos," *Screen*, 48/2 (Summer 2007), pp. 141–59.

9 Lynda Hart, *Fatal Women: Lesbian Sexuality and the Mark of Aggression* (London and New York: Routledge, 1994), p. 142.

10 For a brief overview of true-crime narratives which address the figure of the serial killer, see David Schmid, "Serial killer non-fiction." Available at http://www.crimeculture.com/Contents/Serial_Killers_NonFiction.html (accessed March 13, 2015).

11 Karen Boyle and Jenny Reburn, "Portrait of a serial killer," *Feminist Media Studies*, 15/2 (2015), p. 194.

12 Hart, "Fatal women," p. 140; for a critique of Robert Ressler's post-FBI career as a true-crime author see Schmid, "Serial killer."

13 Stephens, "Bad feelings," pp. 273–82.

14 Berlant, *Cruel Optimism*, p. 14.

15 Thomas Doherty, "Aileen Wuornos superstar," *Cineaste* (Summer 2004), p. 3.

16 Paul Ward, *Documentary: The Margins of Reality* (London and New York: Wallflower, 2005), p. 11.

17 See, for example: made-for-TV-movie *Overkill: The Aileen Wuornos Story* (Peter Levin, 1992); Mark MacNamara's editorial piece, "Kiss and kill: Out of Florida's recent wave of horrific crimes comes a dark version of *Thelma and Louise* in a rare case of a female serial killer," *Vanity Fair* (September 1991), pp. 91–106; the true-crime "autobiography" by Aileen Wuornos

and Christopher Berry-Dee, *Monster: My True Story* (London: John Blake Publishing, 2006); *Wuornos* [the opera] (Carla Lucero, 2001). For an overview of feminist art which refers to Wuornos, see Miriam Basilio, "Corporal evidence: Representations of Aileen Wuornos," *Art Journal*, 55/4 (Winter 1996), pp. 56–61.

18 Basilio, "Corporal evidence," p. 56.

19 Ibid., p. 57.

20 Hart, "Fatal women," pp. 141–43.

21 Morrissey, *When Women Kill*, p. 32.

22 Hart, "Fatal women," p. 137.

23 Ibid.

24 Ibid., p. 145.

25 Paige Schilt, "Media whores and perverse media: Documentary film meets Tabloid TV in Nick Broomfield's *Aileen Wuornos: The Selling of a Serial Killer*," *The Velvet Light Trap*, 45 (Spring 2000), p. 55.

26 Bill Nichols, *Introduction to Documentary*, 3rd ed. (Bloomington: Indiana University Press, 2017[2001]), pp. 137–39.

27 Nichols, *Introduction*, p. 142.

28 Allison Pearson, "Nick Broomfield: The fly in the ointment," in M. Cousins and K. MacDonald (eds.), *Imagining Reality: The Faber Book of Documentary* (London: Faber and Faber, 2006), pp. 343–50.

29 Schilt, "Media whores," p. 58.

30 Tanya Horeck, "From documentary to drama: Capturing Aileen Wuornos," *Screen*, 48/2 (Summer 2007), p. 144.

31 Ward, *Documentary*, p. 41.

32 Horeck, "From documentary to drama," p. 141.

33 Judith Butler, *Precarious Life: The Powers of Mourning and Violence* (London and New York: Verso, 2004), p. 20.

34 Ibid., p. 29.

35 Berlant, *Cruel Optimism*, p. 24.

36 Ibid.

37 Ibid., p. 14.

Filmography

Aileen Wuornos: The Selling of a Serial Killer, directed by Nick Broomfield, produced by Nick Broomfield and Riete Oord, with Jesse "The Human Bomb," Nick Broomfield, Cannonball, Steve Glazer, Brian Jarvis, Stéphane Markcovich, Michael McCarthy, Dick Mills, Tyria Moore, Arlene Pralle, Mike Reynolds, Noah P. Taylor, Aileen Wuornos, music by David Bergeaud, cinematography by Barry Ackroyd, editing by Richard M. Lewis and Rick Vick, Lafayette Films for Channel Four Television Corporation, 1992. DVD 2004.

Aileen Wuornos: The Life and Death of a Serial Killer, directed by Nick
Broomfield and Joan Churchill, produced by Jo Human with Aileen
Wuornos, Nick Broomfield, Joe Hobson, Steve Glazer, Dawn Botkins,
Danny Caldwell, Jerry Moss, Michelle Chauvin, Dennis Allen, Brian Jarvis,
Diane Wuornos, Sterling Ivey, music by Robert Lane, cinematography by
Joan Churchill, edited by Claire Ferguson, Lafayette Films for Channel Four
Television Corporation, 2003.
DVD *Aileen: Life and Death of a Serial Killer/Aileen Wuornos: The Selling of a
Serial Killer* (2003/1992), Nick Broomfield, Optimum Releasing, 2004.

Afterword

Women Who Kill After #MeToo

David Roche and Cristelle Maury

It is hard for academics to keep up with current events, particularly when scholars propose to explore contemporary trends that are ongoing, because research requires time and reflection. Wrapping up the manuscript and writing the introduction in the midst of the appointment of Brett Kavanaugh to the Supreme Court has made us painfully aware of this. We launched the call for papers before the election of forty-five in the United States and the call for chapters in December 2016 at about the same time the Women's March was being planned. A lot has happened since, starting with the #MeToo movement that followed allegations of sexual harassment and rape against producer Harvey Weinstein in October 2017. The revelations that followed have proved that active feminism—and more generally the fight for equal rights for people of all ethnicities, genders, races, sexualities, and social backgrounds—remain necessary; postfeminist and post-racial discourses may have had their seductions, but believing we now live in a postfeminist and post-racial world would be an exercise in denial. Black Lives Matter, The Women's March, #MeToo, and other movements are here to remind us that activism is more than ever necessary. Another effect of the #MeToo movement is that it has brought to the fore the broad range of feminist discourses, and notably the points—fashion, sexual practices, pornography, one's relationship to one's and other people's bodies—on which second- and third-wave feminism and postfeminist discourses sometimes diverge, and quite strongly at that. Such divisions are sometimes framed as weaknesses. But we believe the contrary. The existence of such differences proves that there is no such thing as "the gender theory (*la théorie du genre*)," as some French politicians and members of the French media called it, but that there are multiple sensibilities. The belief in equality entails accepting these differences, for the common rallying point should be that very belief: tolerance. Feminism is not a doctrine, as its opponents, often in bad faith, imply; it is a basic humanist tenet that people of all genders should be treated as equals.

It is no doubt too early to determine whether or not we are currently witnessing the emergence of fourth-wave feminism. We can, however, note that popular culture is already responding to #MeToo and, perhaps even more, is being examined in the light of the movement. This is the case of many of the women who kill of 2018. Pierre Morel, director of *Peppermint* (Pierre Morel, 2018), a vigilante movie starring Jennifer Garner, claimed that #MeToo had made the concept of a strong woman taking on villains plausible.[1] Jamie Lee Curtis admitted that, if *Halloween* (David Gordon Green, 2018) was written before #MeToo, it "chimes perfectly with the movement's determination to highlight the deep, lasting effects trauma has on survivors of abuse and violence."[2] It is particularly evident in reactions to season 2 of *The Handmaid's Tale* (Hulu, 2017–), which imagines what follows Margaret Atwood's 1985 novel. Showrunner Bruce Miller admitted that the writers' room was "impacted" by the Time's Up and #MeToo movements,[3] while lead actress Elisabeth Moss stated that the season's exploration of "what it means to resist" is "a very relevant issue right now."[4] Audrey Kucinskas, writing for *L'Express*, admitted that it was hard to watch the show without these movements in mind.[5] In *The Boston Globe*, Joanna Weiss described the show as "tapping into a free-floating sense of dread and alarm among feminist circles on social media today," but ultimately reassured readers that "we're getting farther and farther from Gilead every day."[6] *The Handmaid's Tale* is not the only show that was received in this light. In an article entitled "Small screen survivors: how US TV is handling the #MeToo movement," Arielle Bernstein mentions the AMC series *Dietland* (2018–) about "a group of female vigilantes who torture and kill abusive men, many of whom are in the beauty and fashion industries";[7] her description suggests a merger of the superhero ensemble show and the rape-revenge narrative. In any case, the killers of *Peppermint*, *Halloween* (2018), *Dietland*, *The Handmaid's Tale* (Emily in S2E2 and S2E13, June in S3E11) are justified. Aashika Ravi remarked that the representation of violent women remains more complicated than that of men, and that the premise of the BBC show *Killing Eve* (2018–) hinges on the fact that "Eve is the only one in MI5 able to conceive of a woman assassin," the aptly named Villanelle, a villain who nonetheless caters to "TV's addiction to hot female killers."[8]

Clearly, there will be plenty of room for work on women who kill of the #MeToo and Time's Up era. But one thing we can be sure of: the figure will remain problematic. And not just because of the violence and motives. But because it will take heaps of subversion and resignification to turn a figure fashioned by eons of patriarchal fantasies into a full-fledged symbol of resistance (note that the majority of the works studied in this book were directed by men). Perhaps, the figure's political potential lies not so much in the deeds she accomplishes as in the model of persistence she embodies: the persistence of patriarchal discourses, sometimes under a feminist-ish veneer, which we must be alert to, but also the persistence of imagining ways to subvert these discourses and refashion bodies and subjects into something that, for the time being, might be better, though never good enough.

Notes

1 Caroline Vié, "Pierre Morel: 'Jennifer Garner, ce n'est pas que Charles Bronson sans la moustache,'" 20 minutes.fr, September 12, 2018. Available at https://www.20minutes.fr/arts-stars/cinema/2333123-20180912-video-pier re-morel-jennifer-garner-charles-bronson-moustache (accessed October 12, 2018).
2 Clarisse Loughrey, "'It is a film about trauma': How *Halloween* became a horror movie for the #MeToo era," independent.co.uk, October 19, 2018. Available at https://www.independent.co.uk/arts-entertainment/films/featu res/halloween-horror-movie-metoo-movement-jamie-lee-curtis-sequel-a858 8726.html (accessed October 30, 2018).
3 Josh Wigler, "How *The Handmaid's Tale* will remain relevant in a Trump and #MeToo world," Hollywoodreporter.com, January 15, 2018. Available at https://bnn.org/entertainment/how-the-handmaids-tale-remains-politically-relevant-in-season-2/ (accessed October 12, 2018).
4 Kirsten Chuba, "*The Handmaid's Tale* Cast, Creator, Talk Season 2 in #MeToo era, expanding Gilead," variery.com, April 20, 2018. Available at https://variety.com/2018/tv/news/the-handmaids-tale-season-2-premiere-metoo-era-1202770165/ (accessed October 12, 2018).
5 Audrey Kucinskas, "L'ombre de #MeToo sur *The Handmaid's Tale*," lexpress. fr, April 26, 2018. Available at https://www.lexpress.fr/culture/tele/l-ombre-de-metoo-sur-the-handmaid-s-tale_2001244.html (accessed October 12, 2018).
6 Joanna Weiss, "In a #MeToo world, the dark allure of *The Handmaid's Tale*," *The Boston Globe*, May 27, 2018. Available at https://www.bostonglobe.com/ ideas/2018/05/26/metoo-world-dark-allure-the-handmaid-tale/rlS77qoI bKdXcqb1YWWPSM/story.html (accessed October 12, 2018).
7 Arielle Bernstein, "Small screen survivors: how US TV is handling the #MeToo movement," the guardian.com, June 25, 2018. Available at https:// www.theguardian.com/tv-and-radio/2018/jun/25/small-screen-survivors -how-tv-is-handling-the-metoo-movement (accessed October 12, 2018).
8 Aashika Ravi, "Hungama's *Damaged* takes a refreshing direction bringing relatability to the femme fatale trope," firstpost.com, June 23, 2018. Available at https://www.firstpost.com/entertainment/hungamas-damaged-takes-a-refreshing-direction-bringing-relatability-to-the-femme-fatale-trope-4575701.html (accessed October 12, 2018).

Contributors

Carolina Abello Onofre holds a BA in Modern Languages and a Master's degree in Hispano-American literature from Pontificia Universidad Javeriana, Colombia. She also did a Master's on the Gothic Imagination at the University of Stirling, Scotland. She has worked as Adjunct Professor of English and Literature in some of the most prestigious universities in Colombia. She is currently working as a Spanish teacher at Bordeaux Montaigne University, as well as a pedagogical content author, editor, and translator in English and Spanish. As an independent scholar, her research interests vary from horror literature for children, Latin American Gothic, and the relation between musical representations of dictatorships and revolutions. She has recently published an article entitled "Scratching the Stones of Rock and Roll: Love Lyrics in the Times of the Argentinian Dictatorship" in the journal *Rock Music Studies*.

Adrienne Boutang is Associate Professor at the University of Bourgogne-Franche-Comté, Besançon, France. Her research focuses on censorship in contemporary cinema, from the perspective of both production and reception. She is also interested in youth culture and genre films. Her latest publications include *L'Analyse des films en pratique* (2018) and *Le silence dans les arts visuels* (2016, with Nathalie Pavec).

Christophe Chambost is Associate Professor at Bordeaux Montaigne University. He has been a member of SERCIA since 2004. He published a PhD dissertation on the notion of cruelty in Ambrose Bierce's short stories and coedited a book on using cinema to teach languages. He has published articles on horror films (*Don't Look Now, Full Circle, Season of the Witch, In the Mouth of Madness, Trouble Every Day*) and Westerns (*The Outlaw Josey Wales, The Wild Bunch, Deadwood*), on the representation of journalism in films (*Citizen Kane, In Cold Blood, Midnight in the Garden of Good and Evil, Wag the Dog*), and on rock music (the Violent Femmes). He has also published articles on nineteenth-century American authors (Bierce, Hawthorne, Melville, Poe).

Hélène Charlery is Associate Professor in Film and American studies at University Toulouse Jean Jaurès. Her research focuses on the representations of African American women in American films and on the construction of racial and gender identities in contemporary Hollywood films.

Julia Echeverría-Domingo is Doctor in Film Studies from the University of Zaragoza, Spain, where she teaches undergraduate courses as an adjunct lecturer. Her PhD dissertation explored the rebirth of the epidemic film genre in the opening decades of the twenty-first century. Her previous publications include "Liquid Cinematography and the Representation of Viral Threats in Alfonso Cuarón's *Children of Men*" in *Atlantis* (2015), "Moving beyond Latin America: Fernando Meirelles's *Blindness* and the Epidemic of Transnational Co-productions" in *Transnational Cinemas* (2017), and "Pathogens, Vermin and Strigoi: Contagion Science and Vampire Myth in Guillermo del Toro's *The Strain*" in *Journal of Science and Popular Culture* (2017). She has participated in multiple international conferences and received SERCIA's "Best PhD Dissertation on English-language Cinema Award" in 2018.

Christophe Gelly is Professor of British and American literature and Film Studies at Université Clermont Auvergne, France. He has mainly worked on film genre, film noir, adaptation and has published two book-length studies on Arthur Conan Doyle (*Le Chien des Baskerville: Poétique du roman policier chez Conan Doyle*, 2005) and Raymond Chandler (*Raymond Chandler—Du roman noir au film noir*, 2009). He has also coedited a book on reception theories in cinema and literature (*Approaches to Film and Reception Theories*, 2012, with David Roche), edited an issue of the journal *Écrans* devoted to French literary realism and film adaptation (2016), and coauthored a book-length study of Ang Lee's adaptation of Jane Austen's *Sense and Sensibility* (2015). He has also worked on Alan Moore's adaptation of Lovecraft in *Neonomicon* (in *Lovecraft et l'illustration*, Christophe Gelly and Gilles Menegaldo [eds.], Le Visage Vert, 2017). He is currently orienting his research towards film theory in general.

Emilie Herbert holds an MA in Film-making from Kingston University London and is currently a PhD candidate in the department of Communication and the Arts at the University of Liège, Belgium. Her PhD thesis focuses on the work of black British women directors through an intersectional approach. She works as a media expert and is the author of two published reports on diversity in Belgian television broadcasting for the CSA (Superior Council of the Audiovisual). In 2018, she was awarded the Martin Alexanderson Human Rights Study Scholarship by the Raoul Wallenberg Institute of Human Rights.

Marianne Kac-Vergne is Associate Professor in Film and American Studies at the University of Picardie Jules Verne, and works on masculinity in contemporary Hollywood genres, with a focus on science fiction. She has recently published *Masculinity in Contemporary Science Fiction Cinema: Cyborgs, Troopers and Other Men of the Future* (I.B. Tauris, 2018).

Delphine Letort is Professor in Film and American Studies at Le Mans University. She is the author of *The Spike Lee Brand: A Study of Documentary Filmmaking* (2015), *Du film noir au néo-noir* (2010), and has written numerous articles on film adaptation, documentary filmmaking, African American cinema, and film noir. She has coedited several books, including *Women Activists and Civil Rights Leaders in Auto/Biographical Literature and Films* (2018).

Samantha Lindop is a film, media, and cultural studies scholar at the University of Queensland, Australia. She is the author of *Postfeminism and the Fatale Figure in Neo-Noir Cinema* (2015). Her current research focuses on gender, subjectivity, and technology—specifically social robots, artificial intelligence, and other kinds of synthetic organisms.

Janice Loreck is Teaching Associate in the School of Media, Creative Arts and Social Inquiry at Curtin University in Perth, Australia. Her research focuses on gender, spectatorship, and violence in global art cinema. She is the author of *Violent Women in Contemporary Cinema* (2016) and Festival Coordinator for the Melbourne Women in Film Festival (MWFF).

Cristelle Maury is Associate Professor at Université Toulouse Jean Jaurès, France. Her main research interests are classical Hollywood film noir, neo-noir, and contemporary noir from a gender studies perspective. She has published many articles on classical film noir and on the relationship between feminist film criticism and films. Her most recent publication deals with Todd Haynes's HBO mini-series *Mildred Pierce* (2018). She has coedited three issues of *Miranda* (a multidisciplinary peer-reviewed journal on the English-speaking world) on new forms of adaptations, on circulations and transfers in film, and on mapping gender. She is currently working on a monograph on the alleged "crisis" of masculinity and the myth of the *femme fatale* from noir and neo-noir to the postmodern era. She has been teaching film studies and English as a foreign language since 2009 and applies her research to questions of language learning.

Elizabeth Mullen is Associate Professor in American Studies, Film, Gender and Television at the Université de Bretagne Occidentale in Brest, France. Her work focuses on questions of gender, aesthetics, and reception in American cinema, particularly masculinity and the grotesque. She has recently written on *The Walking Dead* and HBO's *Westworld*.

David Roche is Professor of Film Studies at Université Paul Valéry Montpellier 3 and President of SERCIA. He is the author of *Quentin Tarantino: Poetics and Politics of Cinematic Metafiction* (2018) and *Making and Remaking Horror in the 1970s and 2000s* (2014), and has edited several books, including *Comics and Adaptation* (2018, with Benoît Mitaine and Isabelle Schmitt-Pitiot), *Steven Spielberg, Hollywood Humanist & Wunderkind* (2018), and *Intimacy in Cinema* (2014, with Isabelle Schmitt-Pitiot). His work on art and horror cinema has appeared in *Adaptation, Horror Studies, Miranda, Mise au point, Post-Script*, and *Transatlantica*. He is currently working on metafiction in film and series.

Isabelle Schmitt-Pitiot was Assistant Professor in English Studies at the University of Burgundy in Dijon, France, and is the acting Secretary of SERCIA. She is currently working on English-speaking films and series, film genres (comedies, musicals, Westerns), and film spectatorship. She has published articles on Woody Allen, John Ford, Milos Forman, and John Huston. She is coeditor of *Intimacy in Cinema* (2014) and of *De l'intime dans le cinéma anglophone* (2015) with David Roche, as well as *Comics and Adaptation* (2018) with Benoît Mitaine and David Roche. She also coedited *Sur la route* (2018) with Bénedicte Brémard and Julie Michot.

Marta F. Suarez is a PhD candidate at Liverpool John Moores University, United Kingdom. Her thesis addresses the portrayal of immigration and race in contemporary Spanish cinema. She is concerned with the intersectionality of race and gender on screen, especially in dystopian, postapocalyptic, and sci-fi worlds. She recently published a chapter on *The Walking Dead* in *Gender and Contemporary Horror in Television* (2019). She is a postgraduate representative on the BAFTSS EC Committee. She has taught across a number of universities in the North West on subjects related to film language, film theory, race on screen, and screenwriting.

Mikaël Toulza is a PhD candidate at Université Toulouse Jean Jaurès, France. His dissertation seeks to interrogate the political implications of the representation of voodoo in American cinema and television through an intersectional approach.

Rosie White is Senior Lecturer in Contemporary Literature, Theory and Popular Culture at Northumbria University in Newcastle upon Tyne (UK). Her first book was *Violent Femmes: Women as Spies in Popular Culture* (Routledge 2007). More recently her work has centered on women and television comedy, including a second monograph entitled *Television Comedy and Femininity: Queering Gender* (I.B. Tauris, 2018).

Connor Winterton is a PhD Candidate and Associate Lecturer in the Birmingham School of Media, Birmingham City University. While Connor's PhD research is centered on representations of gay, lesbian, and queer sex in contemporary cinema, his other interests include gender and sexual politics, feminist (film) theory, sexually explicit screen media, audiences and spectatorship, queer theory, and Western film cultures. Connor is an editorial board member for the new journal *MAI: Journal of Feminism and Visual Culture* and has a number of publications forthcoming.

Index

www.ingramcontent.com/pod-product-compliance
Lightning Source LLC
Chambersburg PA
CBHW060138280326
41932CB00012B/1553